ROMANTICS, REFORMERS, REACTIONARIES

ALEXANDER M. MARTIN

ROMANTICS, REFORMERS, REACTIONARIES

Russian Conservative Thought and Politics
in the Reign of Alexander I

NORTHERN ILLINOIS UNIVERSITY PRESS

DEKALB 1997

Library of Congress Cataloging-in-Publication Data

Martin, Alexander M.

Romantics, reformers, reactionaries : Russian conservative thought and politics in the reign of Alexander I / Alexander M. Martin.

p.   cm.

Includes bibliographical references (p.   ) and index.

ISBN 0-87580-226-5 (alk. paper)

1. Russia—History—Alexander I, 1801–1825. 2. Conservatism—Russia—History. I. Title.

DK194.M3   1997

947'.072-dc21   96-53558

CIP

to Laurie

Contents

Acknowledgments

This study could not have been written without the generous support I received from many institutions and individuals.

The University of Pennsylvania History Department and Center for Soviet and East European Studies, as well as the U.S. Department of Education, provided vital financial support during my years as a graduate student. The International Research & Exchanges Board made possible my research in the USSR in 1990–1991, and funding from the American Council of Teachers of Russian permitted me to return to Russia in 1994 and 1996.

My greatest debt of gratitude is to Alfred J. Rieber, my adviser, who encouraged me to undertake this study and kept me focused on the "big picture" whenever I became too distracted by the fascinating minutiae of my subject. The other members of my committee, Moshe Lewin and Thomas Childers, were always supportive, as was Alexander V. Riasanovsky. Marc Raeff and David McDonald were immensely helpful by giving their encouragement and reading the manuscript and offering their insights. In Russia, I benefited from the gracious assistance of Aleksei N. Tsamutali, Mikhail M. Safonov, and Mikhail Sh. Fainshtein, among other historians. I also thank Francis Ley, who let me use his private archive of writings by his ancestor, Baroness von Krüdener, and my father, Dr. Donald W. Martin, for reading the manuscript and offering valuable suggestions for its improvement.

In both the United States and Russia I received much help from librarians and archivists. I thank the staff of the interlibrary loan office at Penn's Van Pelt Library for their patience with the obscure titles I requested, as well as the staffs of the Leningrad and Moscow archives in which I worked (especially Eleonora N. Filippova of ARAN and Galina A. Ippolitova of RGIA). A particular word of thanks to the photocopying department at the Russian National Library for routinely letting me order copies well in excess of the official daily limit. Without their indulgence, I would not have been able to use many of the rare printed sources cited in this study.

I might never have become interested in Russia had not my parents awakened my interest in European history and culture, and without the Russian studies community during my college years at Cornell University, particularly Walter Pintner, Slava Paperno, Alexander Kraft, and Richard Leed. Graduate study at Penn had both exciting and frustrating moments, and I was fortunate to have friends to share them with, including John Ahtes, Sue Brotherton, Jim Heinzen, Dave Kerans, Peter Martin, and Lesley Rimmel. In Leningrad, Laura Phillips and Loyal Cowles helped me keep my sanity, as did Samvel Avetissian and Tonia Slavinskaia, who were always generous with ideas and hospitality. I also want to thank Jed Greer and the late Aron I. Paperno, whose names I will forever associate with the beautiful city on the Neva.

My colleagues and students at Oglethorpe University have given me unfailing moral and intellectual support in my historical studies; my gratitude goes to them as well.

Finally, none of this would have been researched or written without the assistance and encouragement of Laurie, my wife and editor, and the cheerful patience of Jeffrey and Nicole.

ROMANTICS, REFORMERS, REACTIONARIES

Introduction

Yes, we were opponents, but very odd ones. We all shared *one* love, but *not an identical one*.

From an early age, they and we were shaped by the same powerful, unreasoning, physiological, passionate feeling, which they took for a memory, and we, for a prophesy: the feeling of boundless, all-encompassing love for the Russian people, the Russian form of life, the Russian way of thinking. Like Janus or the double-headed eagle, we gazed in different directions, even while *a single heart beat in us.*

—Aleksandr Herzen, on the difference between Russia's Westernizers and Slavophiles

Modern conservatism in Russia and Europe arose out of a rejection of the Enlightenment rationalism and materialism that culminated in the French Revolution,[1] and it was a multifaceted phenomenon full of contradictions. Certain conservatives pursued the narrow aim of defending the old regime's sociopolitical interests and ideological values. Others, however, regarded the revolutionary upheaval they hated as a consequence of the same Enlightenment culture that also undergirded the old regime, and concluded that the old regime could not be revitalized until it fully repudiated Enlightenment culture and values. Finally, a few conservatives actually shared the revolutionaries' criticisms of the old regime's immorality and oppressiveness, but they believed that the solution to these evils lay in a return to ancestral traditions, not a leap forward into *liberté, égalité, fraternité*. Wracked by these internal tensions, conservatism was intellectually coherent and politically effective usually only when its adherents built a convincing antirevolutionary, traditionalist ideology and wielded it to defend the concrete interests of its natural constituency, the upper classes.

In its effort to achieve this coherence, Russian conservatism was crippled at birth by the revolutionary dynamic of the state that it set out to defend. Indeed, the Romanovs had worked for generations to uproot tradition and Westernize their country along Enlightenment lines. As Pushkin had put it, in Russia's development the reforming despot Peter the Great had played the role of both Robespierre and Napoleon.[2] He had demolished the old Muscovite order and replaced it with an explicitly new conception of the state, involving a docile service nobility, a tamed church, and a rigid caste structure for peasants and townspeople, a system his successors further refined and to which I refer as Russia's old regime.[3] When the French Revolution finally revealed the explosive implications of Enlightenment ideas, it was too late to turn back from them without weakening the ideological foundations of the Russian monarchy itself. In addition, as a consequence of the Petrine reforms, the social base of a conservative movement—an assertive nobility, a traditionalist church, and organized interest groups like France's *parlements* and Germany's guilds—was either nonexistent in Russia or intimately linked to the reforming, Westernizing state.[4]

Russian conservatives therefore faced a painful dilemma. Cultural traditionalists were forced to criticize the nobility and the crown for their openness to Westernization, whereas defenders of concrete old regime interests had to sidestep thorny cultural and religious concerns. A synthesis of cultural traditionalism and sociopolitical interests, however, eluded them. Did conservatives believe in the Orthodox Church? Then they must reject its subjugation by the autocracy. Did they believe in hereditary aristocracy? Then the principle of a service nobility was unacceptable. Did they long for ancestral morals and customs? Then a century of Westernization needed to be reconsidered. Aleksandr Herzen argued in the passage quoted above, referring to the 1840s, that contemporary Westernizing "progressives" and Slavophile "conservatives" were united in their antipathy toward Russia's old regime; his observation would have been equally valid for the years 1801–1825, the period examined in this study.

The Russian conservative response to the ideas of the French Revolution did not really take shape until after 1801. Catherine II had enjoyed immense authority among the upper class, and her repressive measures after 1789 both allayed their fears that revolution might spread to Russia and prevented an open political debate. Paul I carried his fear of revolution almost to the point of lunacy: under his rule censorship and police spying reached extraordinary levels, and his arbitrariness aroused widespread hostility among the nobles; but there was little grounds for concern (and certainly no public debate) about domestic revolution. This changed after Paul's assassination, when some discussion became possible. Russian society had by then had time to draw conclusions about the events in France. Inevitably, these were not uniform. Among Russians hostile to the French Revolution, Napoleon attracted both admiration (for restoring "order") and hatred (for "usurping" the Bourbon crown). French culture remained the epitome of civilization for some, while others saw it as inextricably tied to the revolution. *"Liberté, égalité, fraternité"* both attracted and repelled. When, at the outset of his reign, Alexander I liberalized censorship rules and abandoned the arbitrary repression of dissent, he made possible a dramatic expansion of the periodical press and book printing, and the long-simmering debate on the implications of France's experience for Russia burst into the public arena. Furthermore, Alexander's commitment to political and social reform gave the debate between conservatives and progressives a new urgency. It was also under Alexander that Russia first experienced a direct French military threat. Liberalized censorship, the government's reform plans, and the Napoleonic menace together created the conditions under which a conservative ideology could develop and spread.

Conservatism was divided—along ideological, social, and generational fault lines—rather than united in pursuit of practical goals. Three principal conservative currents crystallized to influence both contemporary state policy and future intellectual developments: romantic nationalism, gentry conservatism, and religious conservatism. Romantic nationalism (articulated by Aleksandr Shishkov and Sergei Glinka) sought in the uncorrupted culture of the common people an antidote to the moral and political dangers associated with Westernization. Gentry conservatism (whose main spokesmen were Nikolai Karamzin and Fedor Rostopchin) represented the defense of noble caste interests, with little concern for cultural matters. Finally, religious conservatism (whose leading figures included Aleksandr Golitsyn and Roksandra and Aleksandr Sturdza), inspired by British and German Protestant models, hoped that Christian spirituality and state-supported social activism might reconcile the elite as well as the masses in Russia with their old regime and grant its institutions a new lease on life. These three currents—the romantic nationalists, the reform-oriented religious conservatives, and the often purely reactionary gentry conservatives—form the core of this study.

Alexander I toyed with parts of these ideas but never fully accepted any of them, because any formulation of a conservative ideology in Russia was bound to be both subversive and fraught with contradiction. The romantic nationalists denounced Westernization yet glorified Westernizing monarchs, praised the peasantry's Russianness yet defended its bondage. The gentry conservatives emulated the assertiveness of the British and French nobility but advocated absolutism, because they required a strong monarch to protect their privileges and because Russian history provided no precedent or discourse for noble assertions of corporate rights. The religious conservatives, finally, held that the spiritual cleansing of Europe could proceed only if nobles and kings everywhere repented of their wicked ways, and they never resolved the problem of their own highly ambivalent attitude toward that pillar of Russian religious tradition, the Orthodox Church.

None of these ideas could form a stable basis for governing society, defending the status quo or confirming the crown's mission of authoritarian modernization. Ultimately, just as the French Revolution had ended in partial failure in the dictatorship of Napoleon, Alexandrine conservatism would peter out in the second quarter of the nineteenth century under Nicholas I's bureaucratic-absolutist regime. In both cases, and across Europe, the ideas of the revolutionary era were both institutionalized and suffocated by a raw state power that was now stripped of old regime restraints and disguised by only a thin ideological veneer.

Although conservatism, in Russia and elsewhere, was the enemy of revolution, the two movements, conservative and revolutionary, had grown out of the same eighteenth-century European culture and inhabited the same intellectual universe. Often conservatives and radicals were literally siblings: Aleksandr Turgenev and Sergei Glinka became defenders of autocracy while their brothers Nikolai and Fedor were linked with the Decembrists.[5] More broadly, the Francophone Enlightenment that shaped the French revolutionaries decisively molded the thinking of the Russian nobility, too. As Herzen put it, even during the Napoleonic Wars, Russian nationalists "rearranged [Russian history] to fit European sensibilities" and "translated Greco-Roman patriotism from French into Russian."[6]

In addition to these direct French influences, there were parallel developments in Russia and Europe. The late eighteenth century, Lynn Hunt argues, witnessed the erosion of the patriarchal idea of the monarchy that had buttressed the legitimacy of French absolutism. Furthermore, the same period, as Stephen L. Baehr points out, saw the breakdown in Russia of the "paradise myth": the notion that the tsar was God's "icon" on earth and that the Russian people, under the tsar's leadership, could restore the earthly paradise. In particular, the literary elite ceased to celebrate the tsar-as-"icon" and adopted for themselves the opposing role of "iconoclast—the breaker (rather than the maker) of the sacred political icon." The politically neutral (or prepolitical) nature of this cultural shift is apparent from Baehr's examples, which range from Aleksandr Radishchev, the critic of absolutism and serfdom, to Gavriil Derzhavin, the social conservative and defender of autocracy.[7] The Russian elite also joined masonic lodges that promoted social progress through moral self-improvement. The lodges were a crucible in which were formed the critical attitudes toward the ancien régime that Russian conservatives shared with Western radicals. As Jean Starobinski notes, eighteenth-century European freemasonry thought of its program as "purely moral, not political," and yet it "developed a radical critique of the institution of the state, so that the scope of its activity was all the more political for claiming to be unpolitical."[8]

Like the French revolutionary leaders, Russia's aristocrats had received a classical education shaped by sentimentalism and the philosophy of Rousseau. The real and fictional characters they idealized were loyal, righteous, eloquent, "natural," rural, stoic, prepared to give all for *la patrie,* devoted to the universal good of humanity, prone to intense passion, easy tears, and deep emotion. These heroes were not generally noteworthy for their individualism, practicality, sober calculation, or their love of things contrived, urban, or artificial, let alone for ironic detachment. These images in turn shaped the Russian readers' reality: their pathos intensified loves and hatreds and militated against compromise; they responded to issues more according to emotional than pragmatic considerations; and contemporaries' view of their era and its protagonists (especially Napoleon and Alexander I) teetered between apocalyptic terror and millenarian hope.

The culture of the late eighteenth century also encouraged a new concern for the lower classes, since a person raised on an intellectual diet of Enlightenment moralism could hardly regard as the sum of society's priorities the corporate interests of dynasty, bureaucracy, nobility, and church.[9] Even peasants had feelings—the culture of *sensibilité* and "return to nature" had taught—and it was an honorable calling to see to their well-being and to that of the entire *patrie* in the abstract. Furthermore, the French Revolution had forcefully demonstrated the destructive potential of an aroused populace. Accordingly, Russian conservative publicists (like their British and German counterparts of the 1790s)[10] reached out to the lower classes. In 1812, Fedor Rostopchin addressed his broadsheets to the common people of Moscow, for example, and among the subscribers to Sergei Glinka's *Russian Messenger* were both a grand duke in St. Petersburg and a poor townsman in far northeastern Siberia. In addition to these sporadic efforts at direct communication, conservatives made the character and needs of the common people central themes of debate. Had the peasantry preserved some elusive, primal quality of "Russianness" that the elite had squandered? Was the preservation of serfdom in the peasantry's best interest? Was it loyal to the state? What were its religious sentiments?

Conservatism and radicalism, in Russia as elsewhere, were thus the outcome of deep, a priori nonpolitical movements along the tectonic fault lines of European culture and sensibilities, and both Jacobins and conservatives turned the new ideas to their advantage. Social critics such as Radishchev used the cliché of the virtuous peasant to condemn serfdom, for example, while Glinka resorted to similar imagery in idealizing the bond between master and serf. Whereas in Paris mass gatherings had helped topple the Bourbons, the outpouring of the populace of Moscow during Alexander I's visit became (in Glinka's description) a kind of apotheosis of the Romanov monarchy. The notion that the common people possessed a brutal, honest sort of wisdom influenced both the *sans-culotte* propaganda of Marat and Hébert and also Rostopchin's efforts to rally Muscovites against Napoleon. Public oratory was a tool of revolutionary politics; Shishkov put it to conservative uses. Robespierre and Saint-Just hoped to çonvert the people to republican "virtue"; Aleksandr Sturdza and Prince Aleksandr Golitsyn sought to create through their own program of censorship and education a utopian "Christian state." The Girondins saw foreign policy as an arena for ideological struggle; the Holy Alliance was created for identical reasons. The similarities between the radical and the conservative camps were so great that, as Massimo Boffa points out, nineteenth-century radicals would find counter-revolutionary theory a useful source of ideas for their own programs.[11]

Russian conservatism under Alexander I benefited from, contributed to, and was decisively shaped by the slow emergence of a civil society. "Civil society," however, did not mean in Russia what it meant elsewhere. According to François Furet, by the end of the old regime in France, "public opinion" meant a nationwide community of literate people, free from domination by state or caste, sitting in judgment and reaching consensus on public affairs, and ultimately disputing the king's very sovereignty. Essential to this conception of public opinion was the existence of an educated stratum—the bourgeoisie and the *noblesse de robe*—whose culture and vital interests at times challenged the system of hereditary "orders." Nothing of the sort existed in Russia. In Germany on the other hand, as Klaus Epstein tells us, the bourgeoisie was very small, and the German Enlightenment differed from its British and French counterparts in being largely the work of university scholars pursuing learned interests, not of a politicized middle class.[12] This comes closer to the Russian model. But the Russians went farther still in shifting the focus of the Enlightenment, and of intellectual life in general, away from politics and toward the esthetic and philosophical, and this tended to give their conservatism a peculiarly academic flavor. After all, educated Russians were usually serf owners or officials, neither group independent of the state or especially interested in social change; as a result, the great sociopolitical issues that divided the French and the Germans—the future of the guilds and the nobility, the status of Jews and women, the power of the established church, the rights of religious minorities, the struggle between absolutism and aristocratic constitutionalism, the fate of provincial liberties—aroused less discussion in Russia, where (aside from serfdom and certain noble rights) more metaphysical issues such as the national soul, the meaning of history, and the nature of God took precedence. Also, until 1825, the state and the nobility were the engines of modernization in Russia, so that "enlightened" Russians had less cause for the visceral hatred toward the nobility that many German *Aufklärer* felt for the rulers of their petty principalities.[13] The intelligentsia, which would provide a politically concerned "public opinion," was still in an embryonic state—and it too, of course, would internalize the scholarly, intellectualized understanding of politics that its predecessors had evolved.

The Romanovs did not govern in a vacuum. The "public" helped to shape their behavior, and it is important to understand how this functioned. The "public" consisted primarily of the nobility or gentry *(dvorianstvo)* and, to a much lesser degree, the most educated segments of the clergy and merchantry. The peasantry and lower urban strata *(narod)* rarely interacted culturally with the "public," although the wars of 1805–1807 and 1812–1814 provided important opportunities for contact across caste lines. Mostly, however, "public opinion" was the opinion of the upper classes. The difficulty with using the term *public opinion* is that it evokes an image of a cohesive, informed collectivity responding quickly and regularly to all notable events. This image does not represent reality anywhere at the time, least of all Russia, with its ethnic diversity, illiteracy, huge distances, and censorship. Even among the *dvorianstvo,* a poor provincial gentry family was considered in an altogether different league from a magnate family owning vast lands and thousands of "souls." Yet certain shared experiences also gave nobles of different strata a sense of community: state service, ownership of serfs, literacy, Westernized cultural aspirations, and the geographic mobility that permitted them, to a limited degree, to mingle with each other.

The Russian "public," though small numerically, was of extraordinary political import. Disproportionately concentrated in the two capitals, St. Petersburg and Moscow, it effectively *was* the state. The vast majority of the monarch's civilian officials and military officers were drawn from the nobility, as were almost all his advisers. What information he received about his empire was provided by a noble-staffed bureaucracy, and the orders he issued were likewise to be carried out by noble officials. Beyond the capital cities, the true government of much of Russia was constituted of tens of thousands of noble landlords. The emperor himself was surrounded by nobles and shared their perspective on life. Finally, the nobles were in a position to overthrow and kill a monarch who attacked their interests, a fate they visited on Alexander I's father (Paul I) and grandfather (Peter III). The nobility's political support was therefore indispensable to any Russian monarch.

This "public" was small, especially the select circles of the most influential families and individuals who had distinguished themselves at court, in the imperial service, or in the arts. This coterie formed an important channel for disseminating political news and ideas among the broader "public"; it also reported the broader "public's" views back to the government. As one studies this group through the letters, diaries, and memoirs of its members, one cannot avoid the impression that everyone seemed to know, or be related to, almost everyone else.[14] As a result of this interconnectedness, ideology was only one criterion among many that influenced relations between members of the elite. "Conservatives" and "progressives" might be friends or even close relatives, individuals who influenced one another and shared the same formative experiences. This social proximity contributed to the relative shapelessness of the political landscape, where, prior to the Decembrist revolt of 1825, ideological divisions had not yet fully crystallized.

Nonetheless, in the late eighteenth century, members of the upper class had made considerable strides toward forming a public opinion based on factors other than personal loyalties, kinship networks, neighborship, the Orthodox Church, and state service. Instrumental in this process was the steady expansion of printed communication and of private associations, both of which brought nobles into contacts outside of traditional settings. The nobility's emancipation from compulsory state service in 1762 had left many nobles without a satisfying purpose in life, and some now focused their moral energies on notions of individual honor, corporate liberty, and service to the nation rather than on unquestioning loyalty to the crown.[15] Furthermore, the influence of Western thought undermined the role of Orthodoxy as a spiritual and moral guide, while at the same time increasing numbers of landed nobles settled in the capitals and were thus removed somewhat from the traditionalist influences of family ties and regional particularism.

Opinions spread among the nobility through a variety of formal and informal channels. Schools, universities, and the government service itself provided institutional settings where noblemen mingled and exchanged ideas, although these were also the easiest for authorities to control. Another formal channel of communication was the medium of print. Books and periodicals were printed and circulated in ever greater numbers.[16] The audience reached by any one publication was usually small, but cumulatively the press had a considerable impact. Although there was little tradition of political journalism and the censors remained vigilant, writers could address issues of social importance under such guises as literary criticism, travel accounts, and moralizing fiction. Aesopian language became a popular means of evading censorship. In addition to the press, there was a tradition of circulating writings informally, in manuscript form, copied over and over by different readers. This had obvious advantages in a society where books and journals were few and difficult to obtain and where it was easier to copy something (even though it caused popular works to be circulated in differing versions) than to buy it (if it even existed in print) or find a publisher for it. A further advantage was in skirting the censors; and pamphlets, poems, and epigrams that were politically risqué were often distributed surreptitiously in this *samizdat* form. The authorities occasionally tried to monitor the flow of these writings and apprehend the authors of particularly subversive works, but they were never able to assert effective control over the medium. Playwrights likewise addressed current events in their works, and audiences cheered actors who appeared to comment on contemporary issues.

Social gatherings were important in the development of public opinion. Some of these were relatively structured. This era witnessed the creation of

Russia's first clubs: associations that provided members with facilities for dining, socializing, and playing cards and that typically had reading rooms where they could keep abreast of the latest periodicals. The "English clubs" of Moscow and St. Petersburg, which had hundreds of members, were the most significant but by no means the only such groups. Masonic lodges, too, provided settings for social interaction among men of the nobility. Freemasonry in Russia had flourished in the 1770s and 1780s, was largely suppressed after Catherine suspected the freemasons of subversive activities, and then revived with great vigor under Alexander I. Its secretiveness, the oddness of its rituals, and the rumored links between some masonic lodges (particularly the more mystical, so-called Martinist ones) and the French Revolution gave freemasonry a reputation as being dangerous and seditious, but among its followers, the spirituality of the masons was comforting to people whom Western rationalism had shaken in their Orthodox faith but not in their religious longings; however, that spirituality also earned freemasonry the stigma of being insufficiently loyal to the established church.

Aside from such organized gatherings, there were many informal ones, especially the salons, which played a major role in the social life of the larger cities. Prominent Russians as well as foreign diplomats hosted these on a regular basis, often inviting the same groups of people as guests, and different salons enjoyed varying degrees of social prestige. Some (such as that of Grand Duchess Ekaterina Pavlovna in Tver' in 1809–1812) had an unmistakably political character: thus when Napoleon's ambassador was refused invitations to virtually all St. Petersburg salons in 1807, the snub was an unambiguous expression of public opinion's hostility to the Peace of Tilsit.

Salons, freemasonry, and the bureaucracy provided the models for the "political" organizations that developed at this time. Out of the salon tradition, for example, developed the Symposium of the Lovers of the Russian Word, which was founded in 1810 and became the first formal public association dedicated to promoting conservative ideas. The conspiratorial groupings of the Decembrists after 1815 were rooted in the more secretive tradition of masonic lodges. The third type of public gathering, also especially significant after 1815, was derived from the habits and structures of the state bureaucracy; exemplifying this was the Russian Bible Society (in which membership became almost obligatory for the prominent and ambitious), a theoretically private organization that was in fact semigovernmental and whose hierarchy was closely linked to that of the state.

Since the government was made up of the same population who joined the lodges and attended the salons, it was usually well informed about the state of public opinion. The government also made extensive use of police informers, and the nonconfidentiality of the mail was so obvious that letter writers almost never criticized the monarch. Public opinion and the state shared a modus vivendi under which the public expressed itself surreptitiously and often obliquely so as not to provoke repressive action by the authorities, but the state, attuned to these subtleties, saw through the euphemisms. Despite its intimidating façade of autocracy, the government listened to public opinion and occasionally buckled under its pressure. The gossip of the salons, the *samizdat* pamphlets, and the gatherings of the masonic lodges, far from being incidental by-products of an authoritarian polity, in fact formed an active component of the political process by which Russia governed itself.[17]

The ideological currents of the time did not appear entirely clear-cut to contemporaries, in part because of the nature of Russian politics in the early nineteenth century. To earn high office one depended on favors and patronage from those in power, not primarily on support from organized public opinion. What developed, therefore, were networks that exchanged patron support for client loyalty.[18] Among figures important to the history of conservatism, the ties between Grand Duchess Ekaterina and Rostopchin illustrate this pattern: they shared common political views but were also linked by their bond with Paul I and their friendship with Nikolai Karamzin. Effective power depended on access to the ruler and the ruler's confidants, not on formal titles or offices. Thus Aleksandr Shishkov in 1812 inherited the reformer Mikhail Speranskii's position as state secretary but not his influence, because he did not enjoy Alexander I's confidence to the same degree. Aleksei Arakcheev, on the other hand, became a virtual dictator in domestic policy after 1821 because the tsar trusted him, not because of a formal office he held. Personal loyalties were fundamental to the system, and they worked against the formation of organized, ideologically cohesive blocs.

The personal nature of politics and its interaction with public opinion determine the structure of this study. In the absence of real parties or articulate ideologies, the history of political thought and action of the early nineteenth century traces a dialectical relationship between individuals and their social milieu. Individuals' personal experiences were shaped by societal attitudes, which they then refined and systematized into ideologies, which in turn gave focus to the thinking of society at large. Thus the story of conservatism from 1800 to the 1820s is that of different generations and sociocultural milieux that are best studied through representative figures who both typified and shaped their collective outlook. The individuals who dominate this study—Shishkov, Glinka, Karamzin, Rostopchin, the Sturdzas, Dmitrii Runich, Golitsyn—left behind copious writings and figure prominently in the letters and reminiscences of their contemporaries, so their life and thought can be reconstructed with some confidence. Generalizations about their effect on public opinion are necessarily more tentative, but I believe that the mass of available primary sources gives us at least a useful, if unscientific, glimpse of "society's" responses and attitudes toward the conservatives' ideas and policies.

Finally, a word about the historiography on Alexandrine conservatism. Much of the extant scholarship predates the 1917 Revolution, particularly the pioneering work of A. Pypin, S. Mel'gunov, N. Bulich, and A. Kizevetter and the more specialized monographs of N. Dubrovin, I. Chistovich, A. Kochubinskii, M.

Sukhomlinov, V. Stoiunin, and others. This material remains valuable, but it has become methodologically dated. That their works seethe with the passion of pre-revolutionary politics makes some of these writers, such as Mel'gunov and Kizevetter, fascinating to read but suspect in their interpretive approaches: their dim view of earlier conservatives is colored by experiences under Alexander III and Nicholas II, and they do not hide their desire to study the past in order to comment on the present. (For details on these and all other works cited, please consult the bibliography at the end of this volume.)

After 1917, the early nineteenth century came to be viewed in Russian historiography in the context of revolutionary ancestor worship. Soviet historians insisted on a sharp and often artificial dichotomy between progressives and reactionaries. They labored hard to document the laudable history of the Decembrists but treated their conservative contemporaries as incapable of creative thought. Furthermore, they generally emphasized the dominant role of purely external factors (fiscal pressures, peasant rebelliousness, the growth of "bourgeois" economic relations) in motivating the actions of the elite and so underestimated cultural and ideological factors. We find this slant even in the work of such talented scholars as Anatolii Predtechenskii and Semen Okun'. The latter argues, for example, that the Holy Alliance was nothing more than "an alliance of rulers for the struggle against progressive ideas, an alliance of absolute monarchs for the struggle against the revolutionary movement."[19] Exceptions to this one-sided interpretation come from some Soviet scholars of Russian literary and intellectual history, such as Iurii Lotman and Mikhail Fainshtein, as well as Mark Al'tshuller. Finally, both the valuable new edition of Rostopchin's works by G. D. Ovchinnikov and the crudely chauvinistic biography of Shishkov by Vladimir Karpets suggest that some Russians have discovered in the early conservatives food for thought about their country's present-day concerns.

Outside of Russia the Alexandrine conservatives attracted little scholarly interest until the late 1950s (with a few exceptions, such as Ernst Benz, Wolfgang Mitter and Alexandre Koyré). When Russian conservatives were studied at all, as by Nicholas Riasanovsky and Andrzej Walicki, the focus was on the second quarter of the nineteenth century, the era of Nicholas I. Western historians of tsarist Russia, for obvious reasons related to 1917 and the Cold War, have tended disproportionately to study the revolutionary movement. Indeed, as Arno Mayer—himself no admirer of nineteenth-century conservatives—has pointed out, historians of Europe between 1789 and 1914 have in general been "far more preoccupied with [the] forces of innovation and the making of the new society than with the forces of inertia and resistance that slowed the waning of the old order."[20]

In recent decades, however, a new interest in Alexandrine conservatism has emerged, in the works of J. Laurence Black, Anthony Glenn Cross, James Flynn, Richard Pipes, Judith Cohen Zacek, Cynthia Whittaker, Franklin Walker, and others. This is part of a broader reevaluation of Europe's old regimes and

Restoration governments that has questioned the thesis of "progressive" social forces challenging "reactionary" rulers.[21] These historians have shifted their focus away from what Eric Hobsbawm called the "dual" (liberal and industrial) revolution[22] and placed cultural change and the growth of state power at the center of their analysis. The present study is indebted to their work and broadly shares their conclusions.

Admiral Shishkov and Romantic Nationalism

The figure of A. S. Shishkov is a key to understanding post-1800 Russian conservatism because of his generational identity and his romantic nationalist ideas. He was a veteran of Catherine II's Westernizing service nobility; however, under the impact of the traumatic experiences of 1789–1805, he reinterpreted the traditions of that class in light of more modern intellectual notions, developing an original doctrine of cultural nativism and hostility to sociopolitical reform and thereby becoming one of the founders of Russian romantic nationalism. Yet to conservatives who had come of age after 1789 he already seemed something of a dinosaur, so profound was the sociocultural divide separating him from his juniors. His life and thought therefore illumine, as do few others, the degree to which nineteenth-century Russian conservatism was both rooted in and estranged from the world of the eighteenth-century nobility. Shishkov also helped to popularize two notions fundamental to right-wing thought: that the Enlightenment and intellectual cosmopolitanism were the causes of revolutionary upheaval and that cultural progress should strengthen a society's sense of unity and spiritual harmony, not promote individualistic, critical thinking. Russia, he contended, ought to turn its back on the nefarious tradition of Westernization (with its legacy of divisive freethinking and cultural alienation) and instead return to an identity rooted in pre-Petrine Muscovy.

Aleksandr S. Shishkov

While Shishkov's intellectual odyssey thus illustrates
the native origins of modern
Russian conservatism, he and
other romantic nationalists
also were part of a Europe-
wide movement that repudiated the values of the old order and sought alternatives to
them. Some of the alternatives they articulated were
conservative, others revolutionary, but they grew from
the same cultural soil. Thus
the French Revolution had in part been a revolt, in the name of an austere "virtue"
modeled by Rousseau and Benjamin Franklin, against the effete culture of the
aristocracy. The newly fashionable revolutionary earthiness was inspired by several sources, including the medieval past, the moral purity of the common people,
and the heroes of antiquity. It was argued that the nation, manly and virtuous, was
reclaiming its birthright from effeminate, degenerate foreigners who had usurped
it.[1] These themes were appropriated by romantic nationalists, of whom perhaps
the most influential was Johann Gottfried Herder in Germany. The romantic nationalists believed that a nation, understood in an ethnic (not political) sense, derived its identity and significance from its shared cultural heritage. Against the
Enlightenment's rationalist, French-tinged universalism, they asserted that a nation's evolution was governed by mysterious inner laws immune to conscious
manipulation. Participation in the national soul gave meaning to the life of the individual. To be capable of dynamic development, a culture must first understand
the wellsprings of its own identity, particularly the emotional forces lurking in the
darkest recesses of the national soul. This meant exploring past eras such as the
Middle Ages, when that soul had manifested itself with uncorrupted vigor; it also
meant studying the nation's language (which codified its unique thought process)
and purging it of alien accretions, as well as learning from the lower classes, who
had preserved tradition in its purest form. Romantic nationalists in areas that were
culturally dominated by outsiders (Slavs, Norwegians, Greeks, Germans, Celts)
built on the previous century's interest in history by standardizing their national
languages, compiling dictionaries, and collecting folktales and medieval epics. In
Eric Hobsbawm's excellent phrase, they were "inventing traditions" on which to
base their conception of national identity.[2]

Certain sensibilities of romantic nationalism were shared by all the major Alexandrine conservative currents—one finds them in Karamzin's *History of the Russian State* as well as in Aleksandr Sturdza's faith in the messianic destiny of the Russian people—but the key figure in introducing them into the Russian cultural debate was Admiral Shishkov. His long career spanned four reigns and seven decades, from the 1770s to the 1840s; he was a transitional figure who linked two very different centuries. He believed in autocracy and serfdom, yet he implicitly subverted both. He regarded Russia as a part of Europe politically but demanded that they part ways culturally. He was both a state official and an intellectual, at a time when men combining these roles were increasingly rare in Russia owing to the widening split between "state" and "society."[3] His patriotism, his wish for a better society, and his hatred for revolution together led him to beliefs—expressed also by the eighteenth-century critic of Westernization Mikhail Shcherbatov in his *On the Corruption of Morals in Russia* (1786–1787)—that were nationalistic, backward-looking, and utopian. Unlike Shcherbatov, Shishkov was a romantic nationalist who held that Russia's conservative virtues were best preserved among the peasants. However, his admiration for both Peter I (which Shcherbatov had not shared) and Catherine II suggests that he was too near his roots in the eighteenth-century service nobility, and too much the product of a generation untrained in systematic philosophical thinking, to be counted among the Slavophiles whose spiritual ancestor he was.[4]

By his own account, Aleksandr Semenovich Shishkov was born in Moscow on March 8, 1754.[5] His paternal ancestors had come from Poland in the fifteenth century, and according to his 1780 navy personnel file, he was "of Russian nationality, member of the nobility, owner of fifteen male peasant souls in the Kashin *uezd* [district]."[6] Whether this was his family's entire fortune or merely his own share is unclear, as is much else about his first thirty-five years.[7] Still, Shishkov's personal and intellectual development offers a glimpse of how an apparently unpolitical, and probably typical, eighteenth-century Russian nobleman could develop into a nineteenth-century conservative.

Semen Nikiforovich Shishkov (Aleksandr's father), his wife, Praskov'ia Nikolaevna, and their five sons[8] probably spent summers in the country near Kashin, one hundred miles due north of Moscow. This was the heartland of old Muscovy, far from its western border or eastern settlement frontier. Here, everyone was Orthodox and Russian, and most peasants had long been serfs of the nobility. The Shishkovs, if indeed fifteen "souls" were their entire holding, were typical provincial gentry: poor but of proud and ancient lineage, and situated in the middle tier of their class in terms of the number of serfs owned.[9] Little Aleksandr thus grew up in a modest rural setting and, like many young nobles, may have played with serf children and been entrusted to a peasant nanny, which would have introduced him to folk culture and village lore.[10]

Shishkov's parents raised able, ambitious sons. Ardalion was accepted by the upper crust of Moscow, if membership in the exclusive English Club is any indication.[11]

Dmitrii served in the prestigious Preobrazhenskii Guards regiment, became a provincial governor, and married into the aristocratic Tolstoi clan.[12] Yet he had only a limited grasp of Russian spelling and punctuation.[13] Indeed, like many modest nobles, the Shishkovs lacked polish, and even Aleksandr later exhibited the eclectic (if broad) knowledge and idiosyncratic reasoning habits of an autodidact. It is telling that he never wrote in French, the true sign of aristocratic breeding. The brothers were thus self-made men who remained marked by their relatively humble origins. Nothing is known of the remaining brothers, Nikolai and Gerasim, except that, according to some sources, the latter's son married the daughter of the writer Andrei Bolotov.[14]

Most likely the family, like much of the area's gentry, spent winters in Moscow, for Aleksandr was born there and at least one of his brothers spent much of his life there. Upper-class Moscow bustled with intellectual and cultural activity, yet the old capital was also a stronghold of national and religious conservatism—in contrast to the Westernized metropolis founded by Peter the Great on the shores of the Baltic. Moscow may have both awakened Shishkov's literary interests and reinforced the patriotic traditionalism that he had internalized at home, including the reverence for Peter I and the great Russian scholar and poet Mikhail Lomonosov that he already harbored as a youth.[15] His upbringing probably accounts for his intellectual seriousness, his attachment to Russian folkways, and his knowledge of the literature, rituals, and language of the Orthodox Church. On the other hand, that he was only thirteen years old when he moved to St. Petersburg, where he spent most of his life thereafter, may explain why he later knew little of the peasantry. He idealized rural life on the basis of his literary pursuits and, most likely, fond childhood memories, but he had little personal exposure to it from adolescence on. If such was indeed his background, it was entirely typical of many contemporary noblemen who had limited means but a lively intellect, and an ambition to rise in the monarch's service that made them intensely loyal to the monarch herself and also distrustful of the aristocracy (i.e., the elite families that dominated the nobility), with its unearned wealth and privileges and its Westernized ways.

Although it has been argued that Shishkov's cultural conservatism grew out of this distinctly Russian environment,[16] it was also—like all Russian conservatism—shaped by Western influences. His lifelong fondness for Germany illustrates the profound impact of German culture and historical-philological scholarship in eighteenth-century Russia.[17] For example, Shishkov's own family enjoyed the personal and intellectual friendship of the celebrated scholar August Ludwig von Schlözer.[18] The issues Schlözer studied—medieval Russia, Church Slavonic, other Slavic cultures—were the same ones that later fascinated Shishkov,[19] and he is credited with having influenced Shishkov's linguistic theories. Yet it is telling that Shishkov's considerable library contained only one volume by him,[20] for there is little evidence that his views were influenced directly by individual Western thinkers; rather, he felt their influence through the intellectual atmosphere that their work helped to create.

Aleksandr Shishkov's long career began on September 17, 1767, when he entered the Naval Cadet Corps in St. Petersburg. There he received a largely European education in technical disciplines, mathematics, and languages, after which he entered service as a naval officer.[21] An intelligent, ambitious, and uncritically loyal servant of enlightened absolutism, he (unlike the more sophisticated and restless conservatives who came of age after 1789) was fully at ease with his old regime universe: he was grateful for the chance to discover the wider world during missions abroad,[22] pious but no zealot, patriotic but open to other cultures, unpolitical but firmly rooted in the values of gentry and bureaucracy. In the 1780s he taught at the Naval Cadet Corps and joined the staff of the vice president of the Admiralty College. In 1790 he served in the war against Sweden, and he was about to enter the staff of Prince Zubov, the commander of the Black Sea fleet, when Catherine II died in 1796.[23]

During the 1780s and 1790s, alongside his official activities, Shishkov also began to try his hand at writing. He wrote a play commissioned by Catherine II's theater director,[24] a translation of German children's stories and verses that was widely used well into the next century to teach children to read,[25] and books on naval affairs.[26] He received encouragement from Admiral Greig, the commander of the Baltic fleet, as well as from Catherine, who had some of his writings published at her cabinet's expense. Still, his letters to high dignitaries, seeking help in getting his books published, indicate the limits of the patronage he enjoyed.[27]

One of his literary mentors was Admiral Ivan Golenishchev-Kutuzov, the director of the Naval Cadet Corps and himself a writer, whose salon was a gathering place for literati and high dignitaries.[28] Kutuzov encouraged Shishkov to write and helped shape his nationalistic views for, as Shishkov later recalled, he "enjoyed reading foreign writers, but enjoyed [Russian ones] even more. Feofan, Kantemir, Lomonosov, and especially the reading of spiritual books consolidated his knowledge of the national language."[29] Shishkov had ample opportunity to associate with him over a period of almost thirty-five years. They were both linked to freemasonry, and Kutuzov may have introduced him to other writers, as well as to the Russian Academy, which Shishkov joined in 1796. Shishkov also befriended other members of the Kutuzov family, including Mikhail Ilarionovich, the hero of 1812 and also a freemason.[30]

In the late 1780s, Shishkov was associated with the Society of Friends of the Literary Sciences,[31] a group founded by the freemason M. I. Antonovskii and believed to have had dozens if not hundreds of members. Those linked with it included the mystic Aleksandr Labzin, two future heads of the Russian Academy (Shishkov and A. A. Nartov), and the writers Derzhavin, Dmitriev, Krylov, and Radishchev. It also included a large contingent of navy officers, who were often men of cosmopolitan sophistication and themselves full-fledged freemasons (such as Admiral Greig). Shishkov's literary activity thus developed in a milieu where naval service, literature, and freemasonry intersected.

The society encouraged social conservatism, humane treatment of serfs, and a religious moralism that was critical of the Orthodox Church: in other words, a politically ecumenical program of moral edification. Shishkov's ties to the society seem to have lasted until at least about 1790, although he later became a critic of freemasonry and a supporter of the church hierarchy. The freemasons' opposition to foreign linguistic influences prefigured his own later campaigns; and his future literary adversary, Nikolai M. Karamzin, was already a target of masonic criticism in the late 1780s and early 1790s. Earlier, Karamzin had (like Antonovskii) been a disciple of Nikolai I. Novikov, one of Russia's great masonic leaders, but they had since parted ways ideologically. The attacks on Karamzin shaped the atmosphere in which Shishkov formed his literary views, and some of Shishkov's later arguments grew out of those of the freemasons.[32]

Freemasonry played an important role in Russian aristocratic culture. It was vaguely egalitarian and free from direct state control, and hence inherently a challenge to the bureaucratic-absolutist regime's rigid chain of command. Its importance for the growth of a (still prepolitical) public opinion is apparent from the fact that leaders of the major currents of post-1801 conservatism (the romantic nationalist Shishkov, the gentry conservative Karamzin, and the religious conservative Labzin) could all mingle with each other and with the radical social critic Radishchev in this milieu. What they all had in common was the eighteenth-century belief that "virtue" was the key to social progress; they parted ways politically only once it became clear that "virtue" could mean various things in reality. Catherine II herself generally distrusted the freemasons. She despised their esoteric rituals as charlatanism and suspected them of links with Grand Duke Paul (her estranged son) and with the Prussian court (her adversary in European affairs). As a result, her officials particularly harassed the Moscow Rosicrucians throughout the late 1780s. However, like the latent conflicts within the lodges themselves, her disapproval acquired a sharp edge only during the European crisis that accompanied the French Revolution, when, out of fear of political subversion, she ordered leading freemasons arrested and imprisoned.[33]

In the early 1780s Shishkov wrote a poem, "The Old Time and the New," that shows his evolution from Enlightenment moralist to romantic nationalist. This work, his earliest surviving statement on history and society, anticipates his later idealization of the pre-Petrine era as an age when life had been better and morals purer—a theme found in, among other sources, the moral teachings of the freemasons.[34] In the poem, however, the idyllic "past" that Shishkov constructs is still a timeless Russia free from European influence; in contrast to the deliberate historicism of his later works, he does not yet attempt to situate the utopia at a particular historical moment.[35] Though he subsequently idealized Catherine's reign in similar terms, he yearned for a past golden age even while she was alive. His ethical sensibility had been honed by the Enlightenment, and as a child he had learned to equate rustic ways with good morals, which were shockingly absent from the official St. Petersburg where he spent most of his life. Hence his concern for Russian "tradition," which he constructed from his childhood memories, literary pursuits, patriotism, and anti-aristocratic indignation. Yet he was not a xeno-phobe, for the Russian capital whose vices he deplored was hardly "the West," and his love for Sweden, Germany, Italy, and classical culture, like his marriage to a Lutheran, indicate that he did not hate Europe. He believed in the inherent value of "tradition," which each nation should derive from its own sources; for-eign cultures were a threat only when they corroded basic Russian values. In these views he was typical of many romantic nationalists who followed Herder in believing that Europe would be a peaceful community if each nation remained loyal to its own unique destiny.[36]

By the early 1790s, Shishkov occupied a recognized, if minor, place in the of-ficial world. He had reached level seven on the Table of Ranks (the naval equiva-lent of a lieutenant colonel), and his service with Admiral Chichagov in the war with Sweden in 1790 had even drawn the attention of the empress. Chichagov and Kutuzov provided valuable patronage, as did Shishkov's friend Admiral Mordvi-nov.[37] Kutuzov and the freemasons, meanwhile, had introduced him to the liter-ary world, to which he had made his first, modest contributions.

Yet Shishkov's stable universe was crumbling. Even while the revolutionary soldiers of the French Republic were defeating the royal armies of Europe, Catherine's death brought to power the distasteful Paul I, whose assassination led in turn to the accession of his alarmingly reformist son. Shishkov felt like an old man who no longer understood the world. He reacted first with angry bewilder-ment, then with the determination to force this upside-down world back onto its feet. In the process, however, he formulated an ideology that inadvertently under-mined the very ancien régime he had set out to defend.

Both the moralist and the monarchist in him recoiled at the regicide in France. "Peace there cannot be," he thundered,

> Where God's law is broken,
> Where the royal scepter and throne are trampled,
> Where by evil hearts the monarch himself,
> Like a martyr of old,
> With all his kin
> Lies foully murdered.

Russia, fortunately, lived blissfully under Catherine's wise rule:

> Rejoicing in your love for tsar and God,
> What nation, so many years,
> Living years of peace,
> Blossoms in such happiness?
> . . . .
> Most fortunate of all peoples,
> You know not ruinous change.[38]

In light of the French Revolution, Catherine's Russia appeared an island of sanity and decency, and so her sudden death stunned Shishkov. "Russia's sun had been extinguished!" he recalled later. "Catherine's mild and glorious reign, which had lasted thirty-five years, had so lulled everyone that it seemed as though it had been entrusted to some good and immortal divinity and would never end." He was appalled by the demoralized officials and armed troops he saw at the Winter Palace the next day: "This transformation was so great that it appeared to me like an enemy invasion." Catherine's grandees were soon replaced with "people of lowly rank, to whom, a day earlier, no one had given any thought, whom almost nobody had known." Shishkov observed the beginning of the new reign with unease, for he had earlier attracted the disfavor of the new emperor. He was concerned about his own career, and the "oppressiveness that was growing daily, the orders, arrests, and similar hitherto unheard-of innovations" left him worried about his future.[39]

Paul's accession to the throne was an emotional watershed in Shishkov's life. Catherine had come to power when he was only eight years old, and life without her was difficult to imagine. He fondly recalled her respect for her servitors, her deference toward meritorious elder dignitaries, her willingness to overlook mistakes made in good faith, and her refusal to penalize honest officials who lacked refinement or book learning. Shishkov admired her commitment to Russia's national identity and regarded her as the very embodiment of imperial grace, majesty, and virtue. This view was shared by an entire noble generation. As her biographer tells us: "Those who remembered Catherine's rule looked back on it [later] as a time when autocracy had been 'cleansed from the stains of tyranny,' when a despotism had been turned into a monarchy, when men obeyed through honor, not through fear."[40]

Paul did not measure up to that standard. His mother's bizarre funeral, orchestrated by the vengeful son to include a reinterment of her murdered husband's remains, deeply disturbed Shishkov, as did Paul's love of things Prussian (another throwback to his father's reign). Having trampled both Catherine's memory and Russian pride, the new emperor humiliated his officers by capriciously advancing and demoting them and publicly insulting them, and he tormented his troops with ill-fitting uniforms and mindless drills, all imported from Prussia. Senior officials were arbitrarily purged, and their places taken by such upstarts as Aleksei Arakcheev, Fedor Rostopchin, and Ivan Kutaisov.[41]

Shishkov's personal worries proved unfounded. Perhaps because of his connections at court, he was promoted, and he rose into the upper stratum of serf owners through an imperial grant of 250 peasant "souls" in his home district of Kashin.[42] In 1797, Paul even made him aide-de-camp, but Shishkov soon wearied of carrying out the irascible monarch's petty errands and enduring his military formalism. He gradually lost imperial favor, which suited him: "I actually desired to distance myself from [Paul], so that I would not, owing to the severity of his temper, fall into a sudden disgrace accompanied by persecution, which had already befallen many others."[43]

He disliked his sovereign, hated the French Revolution, and loved Russian literature, but these sentiments, though they clouded his earlier, cheerfully unpolitical monarchism, had not yet crystallized into the bitterly Francophobic passion for Russia's Slavic identity that he was to develop later on. This is apparent from the letters he sent home from his first extended trip to Central Europe, where he was on a mission for Paul I.[44] It was his first visit to other Slavic lands, yet their cultures elicited almost no commentary from him,[45] nor was he above sprinkling his letters with the very Gallicisms that he soon came to regard as the symbol of all that was wrong with Russia. On the other hand, he took a liking to the Germans. They seemed steeped in tradition and morality and immune to political upheaval, which appealed to both the romantic and the conservative in him. His Germanophilia and deep aversion to the French[46] were related to Russia's Westernization, and both intensified in the wake of the events of the 1790s: the ideology and institutions of enlightened absolutism linked Russia with the German states, as did the cultural influence of Schlözer and other Germans, whereas the aristocracy's elegance and skepticism (which he despised)—and, of course, the Jacobin threat—were French in origin.

He had risen quickly under Paul (reaching the rank of vice-admiral, level three on the Table of Ranks) because he served at court, where the mercurial emperor made and unmade careers with dizzying swiftness, but also because he was capable and determined, good-natured and honest, and skillful in avoiding the submerged rocks of court politics. Yet Shishkov was no obsequious flatterer, and his natural caution was tempered by the conviction, acquired under Catherine's rule, that one could be a loyal subject and nonetheless stand up for one's principles.[47] He now belonged to what John LeDonne defines as Russia's "ruling elite." Thanks to the importance of service rank in determining one's social status, he not only was eligible for top state positions; his views in cultural matters also carried greater weight.[48] His service career and his intellectual influence were thus mutually reinforcing, and he was convinced that the principles of rank and hierarchy should prevail in the intellectual world as they did at court and in the navy.

In March 1801, someone knocked on his door in the middle of the night. When his servant announced a *Feldjäger*, Shishkov was convinced that Paul had ordered his arrest. He later recalled having told his wife: "Farewell! Perhaps I shall not return." Instead, the visitor turned out to be a naval officer, there to inform him of the emperor's death and to take him to the Admiralty to swear loyalty to Alexander I. Shishkov was stunned: "I confess," this loyal monarchist recalled, "[that, while] my gratitude for [Paul's] good deeds toward me aroused grief and regret in my heart, . . . [still] the liberation from the incessant fear, in which I and almost everyone had lived, mixed this grief with a certain involuntary joy." He sympathetically likened the plot against Paul to the one that had overthrown Peter III, and noted that no one wept at Paul's funeral. He seems to have shed no tears himself, and his verses to the new emperor were heartfelt:

> With him, justice will mount the throne;
> Loving the fatherland, keeping its peace,
> With the great soul of Catherine,
> He will be a new Peter in law and in battle.[49]

Shishkov hoped that Alexander I would live up to his promise to govern in Catherine's spirit,[50] and he was satisfied with the new monarch's early steps to make government less brutal and arbitrary. Statesmen of Catherine's time reappeared who, he later wrote, had the duty to guide Paul's young and impressionable successor by encouraging him to emulate his grandmother. But "Catherine's old men" passed up their opportunity, he recalled: as they spent those decisive first days feasting and celebrating the downfall of the tyrant, Alexander gathered a group of young advisers, the "Unofficial Committee," whose influence would neutralize that of the older statesmen.

Shishkov had, of course, resented Arakcheev, Kutaisov, and the other *arrivistes* who had followed Paul from Gatchina to the Winter Palace. Still, his distaste for Paul's cronies paled next to his outrage at Adam Czartoryski, Pavel Stroganov, Nikolai Novosil'tsev, and others who appeared to enjoy Alexander's confidence. Because "public opinion" lacked any real knowledge of the inner workings of the autocracy, Shishkov was not alone in mistakenly fearing that the "Unofficial Committee" intended to remake Russia in the image of 1789 France.[51] The advisers' class and generation had, he believed, been corrupted by their foreign education, to the point where humility, patriotism, God, common sense, and respect for one's elders and ancestors—the cement of Russian society—meant nothing to them. Older men, he noted bitterly, had been "forced to fall silent and yield to the new way of thinking, the new ideas, that had arisen from the chaos of the monstrous French Revolution." The emperor's friends, "pompous with pride and having neither experience nor knowledge," decided to "attack all of Russia's prior decrees, laws and rites, and to call them obsolete and ignorant. The words 'liberty' and 'equality,' understood in a wrong and distorted sense, began to be repeated before the young tsar, who unfortunately had had for a tutor the Frenchman La Harpe, who had instilled the same ideas in him." To make matters even worse, the new leaders also imitated the disrespect for rank and seniority shown by Paul's cronies in 1796. Alexander I's policies soon left Shishkov bitter and disappointed: "Paul's reign continued, admittedly with less severity, but with the same imitation of foreigners and the same innovations."[52]

His relations with Alexander, which earlier had been good, deteriorated. He continued to report to him on naval affairs, but by late summer 1801, Alexander had noticeably cooled toward him.[53] Shishkov disapproved of the transformation in 1802 of the government's colleges into ministries as a needless departure from the wise course charted by Peter I and Catherine II; by now, the century before 1796 had firmly established itself in his mind as the locus of the political tradition that needed to be defended against the forces of change. His own access to the court was cut off through what he regarded as the intrigues of the emperor's pro-tégé, Admiral Pavel Chichagov (the son of Shishkov's erstwhile commander). The two admirals were eventually reconciled, and in 1805 Shishkov was ap-pointed to head the marine ministry's Academic Committee. Yet the emperor's personal dislike for him remained.[54]

Two aspects of Shishkov's position at this juncture were significant in deter-mining his subsequent activities. First, he was disappointed in Alexander I, who carried on aspects of his father's reign and took after foreign *vol' nodumtsy* (free-thinkers). To Shishkov's dismay, Paul had followed in his own father's footsteps in imitating the militarism of Prussia. Paul, although Shishkov did not address this point directly, had basically sought to combat the French Revolution by in-fusing Russia with the spirit of a medieval crusading order. From his ties to the (Catholic) Order of Malta to the design of his Mikhailovskii castle, the tsar had enveloped himself in an atmosphere that was decidedly un-Russian. Alexander abandoned his father's medievalism but retained his love for Prussia, surrounded himself with Anglophile advisers, and plotted domestic reforms modeled on Western practices of which Shishkov was deeply suspicious. Shishkov admired Peter I and Catherine II for having reached their goal of helping Russia learn from Europe without sacrificing its national identity, but neither Paul nor Alexander had been able to meet the challenge. This led Shishkov to reconsider the wisdom of using Europe as a model for Russian society in the first place.[55]

Second, the turn taken by his naval career may have influenced his mood. He was approaching fifty (an age then regarded as quite advanced) and may have felt the need to reassess his priorities. His age and poor health made it unlikely that he would serve again at sea. Although he retained a strong interest in maritime af-fairs,[56] it was not an exclusive passion. His position as aide-de-camp, the apex of his service career, had caused him such frustration that he had gladly relinquished it. Yet his assignment to the Academic Committee, although an escape from the court, was a move downward in the hierarchy, and his difficult relationship with the young and forceful monarch bode ill for his future advancement.

These two circumstances redirected his thoughts toward his other great inter-est, literature. The upheavals in the world around him interacted with his career frustrations, and perhaps a sense of his own mortality, to arouse in him a deep sense of disaffection. He articulated this anxiety in writings that linked literary is-sues that had long interested him with the traditional sociopolitical and moral or-der that he now believed in danger. Viewed in isolation, the literary component of his arguments seems crude and ignorant and the political side simplistic. To-gether, however, they represent an awkward effort by a man of a passing era to use modern intellectual tools to criticize a changing society. By promoting his ideas in a manner that was at once blunt and persuasive, Shishkov established his place in Russian history.

The amateurish yet stubborn nature of his theories was shaped by life in the state service, which had taught him that unfamiliar problems could be solved with common sense, that rank would add weight to his ideas, and that abstract philosophical reflection was useless since the answers to life's larger questions were provided by religion and tradition. This mindset, while admirably suited to the needs of governing the empire, appeared quaint and archaic to the increasingly professionalized literary elite on whose terrain the amateur Shishkov was intruding. Indeed, the younger writers who provide much of our information on him regarded him as a cranky old-timer who embodied a crude, innocent, bygone era. These aspects of his persona also emerge from his writings and contrast with the *mise-en-scène* found in conservatives of a younger generation: Sergei Glinka's melodramatic introspection, Roksandra Sturdza's elegantly discreet self-censorship, her brother Aleksandr's relentless grinding of ideological axes or Rostopchin's arrogance and self-promotion. Shishkov, by contrast, exhibited an uncomplicated self-confidence, utter humorlessness in "doctrinal" matters, and a striking candor.[57] His home life likewise reflected both the simplicity and cosmopolitan aspirations of the traditional service milieu, on one hand, and the eccentric obsessiveness of an aging man who had belatedly discovered a "cause," on the other. Church Slavonic texts now absorbed all Shishkov's thoughts, and his absent-mindedness made him the butt of countless jokes.[58] He had married the widow Dar'ia Alekseevna Shel'ting,[59] granddaughter of a Dutch admiral who had served Peter the Great, and she and Aleksandr had a happy marriage: while she ran the household, the admiral (who lived "as a most undemanding guest in his own house") devoted himself to what she affectionately dismissed as "patriotic fantasies" that found no application in their own home. She remained a Lutheran, hired a French tutor for the nephews they raised, and spoke French with the boys and with visitors, even in her husband's presence.[60]

He defended his opinions with a stubbornness that bordered on the irrational. In this, too, he reflected an eighteenth-century culture of simple morality and blunt, uninhibited self-assertion, not the awkward combination of sophisticated, critical thinking and fearful conformism that became common under Paul I and his sons. Shishkov commanded the grudging respect of even his critics, such as Petr Viazemskii, who (in the completely different atmosphere of the 1840s) would remember him as "neither a wise man nor a gifted author, but a man of unchanging will, with an idea, an *idée fixe*," who "had a personality of his own, and therefore carved out a place for himself in our literary and even our governmental world." Such people, Viazemskii believed, "are rare in Russia, and therefore Shishkov is, among us, a historical figure."[61]

Shishkov's specifically philological views may be summarized as follows. His love of Russian letters, knowledge of foreign literatures, and work on naval dictionaries had kindled in him a deep interest in linguistics. This preoccupation reflected a typically romantic belief that the distinctive genius of a people could be discovered in the lexical peculiarities of its language. In particular, Shishkov believed that every language developed unique ways of modifying existing words to convey new meanings; in the primary words and the vocabulary subsequently derived from them was stored, he thought, the historical memory of each people's unique spirit and consciousness. Consequently, he sought to fathom the Russian soul by elaborating a system of etymological "trees," in which a single "root" word produced a "stem" that sprouted many "branch" words. As prerevolutionary scholar M. I. Sukhomlinov condescendingly put it, Shishkov "roamed freely in the philological forest of his imagination, extracted from it the roots and branches of words, and broke and transplanted them as he pleased, in the naïve certainty that his labor would bear abundant and highly useful fruit."[62] Unfortunately, like other linguists of his time (and he lacked all formal training in the subject), he made no allowance for historical or cultural context, disregarded the profound changes Russian had undergone over the preceding nine hundred years, and treated it as an essentially static, timeless idiom.[63] Instead of studying its historical evolution, he created an etymology based on the notion that words that sounded alike and had similar meanings must be related; for instance, in one widely ridiculed example, he argued that the words *shiroko* (broad), *vysoko* (high) and *daleko* (far) were derived from *shir'* (expanse) + *oko* (eye), *vys'* (height) + *oko,* and *dal'* (distance) + *oko.*[64] He likewise believed that Church Slavonic was the ancestor of all modern languages;[65] that its use by the Orthodox Church was essentially of divine origin;[66] and that Russian was merely its spoken form. On this point he brooked no contradiction. "He became fanatical," a friend wrote, "only when someone refused to recognize the church language as identical to modern Russian."[67]

By promoting these theories, Shishkov entered a raging dispute over basic aspects of Russian history and culture, a conflict whose outcome shaped the Russian literary vernacular that crystallized in the 1820s and 1830s. The dispute also anticipated the debate between Westernizers and Slavophiles in the 1840s, raising similar issues regarding Russia's institutions, traditions, and spiritual identity. Like the Westernizers and Slavophiles, the champions of the New and Old Style (as the two sides of the linquistic debate were called) had in common a Westernized education and a hope of bridging the cultural divide between Russia's social classes.[68] Both debates reveal the intellectuals' desire to create a synthesis of the Westernized elite and native Russian tradition and to shake off the cultural tutelage of the autocracy.

Russian linguistic thinking had undergone a fundamental transformation during the eighteenth century. The earlier relationship between Russian and Church Slavonic had been a diglossia, a situation in which two separate languages, one used only for oral and one only for written expression, were conceptualized as constituting a single, unified language system.[69] Muscovite culture had regarded Church Slavonic as the written, "higher" form, while Russian was the spoken, "lower" language. Since Peter I, however, Russian had increasingly become a written language in its own right. This changed the diglossia into outright bilingualism: once Russian had transcended the role of a purely oral language with a relatively unsystematized grammar and limited vocabulary, Russian and Church Slavonic became functional equivalents, and Church Slavonic accordingly lost its function as the sole vehicle for formal, eloquent, written speech. Church Slavonic, therefore, became obsolete as a living secular language.

Yet the mindset engendered by the diglossia lived on. Since a Russian secular literature was being created expressly as a replica of Western models (initially through translations), foreign influences took over the traditional function of Church Slavonic in the overall linguistic scheme. As before, the language linked with refined expression was the "foreign" one (whether Church Slavonic or French), not the "native" tongue (colloquial Russian). Europeanisms lent an air of sophistication to oral speech, just as Slavonicisms rendered written texts weightier and more formal. The need to translate foreign writings, with their unfamiliar vocabulary, into a Russian that was distinct from the common spoken language led writers back to Church Slavonic for the building blocks of their new vocabulary. As a result, literary Russian used a growing number of Slavonicisms, including newly invented ones, because "processes such as borrowing, loan translation and so on, in principle promote the activization of Church Slavonic elements in Russian . . . and ultimately the Slavonicization of the literary language."[70] Slavonicisms and Russian archaisms, used originally to convey the "gravity" associated with foreign literature, also began to shape the language of original productions by Russian writers. The deliberately archaic literary style that evolved in the eighteenth century was therefore a product of European literary influences, not a continuation of traditional Russian cultural patterns.

Because Church Slavonic itself was not affected by borrowings from Western languages, it came to be identified with the national Russian tradition, and even with an ethnic and folk heritage that Russians shared with other Slavs. Therefore, those struggling to defend Russia's linguistic sovereignty against foreign encroachment fought their literary battle with the aid of an artificially archaic, Slavonicized style. In a complete reversal of the original diglossia, this Church Slavonic vocabulary was deemed by the late eighteenth century to be quintessentially "Russian." The widespread (though mistaken) belief that Church Slavonic was the linguistic ancestor of Russian encouraged its use for restoring, or even creating artificially, an "unadulterated" Russian language. In this context, the actual history of Church Slavonic as the language of the Orthodox Church was deemed less significant than its ethnic identification with Slavdom, a tie that in turn permitted its use for the creation of a genuine "Russian" language free of "foreign" influences.

Russian thinking about language was linked to traditional eschatology. Medieval Russians had anticipated that God would one day transform the world and eradicate all evil. Owing to the subsequent secularization of Russian culture under Ivan IV and especially Peter I, such far-reaching hopes now attached themselves to state reform policies, whose goal was "not the partial improvement of the concrete sphere of state activity, but the ultimate transformation of the entire system of life." To Peter and others, according to Iu. Lotman and B. Uspenskii, the "psychology of reform" involved "the utter rejection of existing tradition and of the continuity linking them to their immediate political predecessors," so that "reform in Russia was always associated with the *beginning,* and never with the *continuation,* of a particular political course."[71] The attitude that the existing order must be overthrown was shared by Ivan IV, Peter I, Paul I, and Alexander I (although not Catherine II), and they viewed the state as the agent for this transformation. One aspect of the ritual destruction of the old order was the practice of government-sponsored language change in the eighteenth century: new terms such as *Rossiiskaia Imperiia* (Russian Empire) and *imperator* (emperor) symbolized this process, as did the wholesale renaming of state titles and offices.

This view of language was deeply rooted in the past, for language itself had an eschatological role. Medieval Russia had expected the destruction of the temporal world to entail the destruction of its language as well; linguistic change could be one aspect of deeper changes in the world. It was no accident that Peter I himself took part in redesigning the alphabet, that Catherine II cared about the purity of the Russian language, and that Paul tried to ban much foreign political terminology as a means to blunt the influence of the French Revolution. One of the achievements of Mikhail Speranskii was to model a sober, precise style for the Westernized bureaucracy that consciously departed from traditional official prose. In order to arouse atavistic nationalist emotions in 1812, on the other hand, state proclamations (drafted by Shishkov) adopted a style that was deliberately grand and archaic. Government's use of, and attitude toward, language was closely linked to efforts to promote particular policies or shape the national culture.

The relationship of Russian, Church Slavonic, and foreign linguistic elements was therefore of profound significance to late-eighteenth-century Russian culture as a whole and was one dimension of the linguistic debate in which Shishkov became embroiled. Because of language's eschatological associations, contemporaries considered its condition an important indicator of the state of society. The French-influenced Russian of the upper classes and the German and French terminology of government suggested that Russia's destiny lay with Europe. The archaization of eighteenth-century literary Russian, on the other hand, testified to a desire to protect the national culture from foreign domination. Ironically, however, this Slavonicized, "old" literary style—like Russian secular literature itself, and like the educated, cosmopolitan nobility that had created it—was a hybrid product of Russia's encounter with Western Europe. Consequently, this was not a genuine movement back to the ways of the past, but rather an effort to graft certain Old Russian elements onto the Europeanized high culture of post-Petrine Russia.

The second dimension of the debate Shishkov entered was literary. Alexander I's reign was, to quote Jean Bonamour, "an epoch in search of itself," whose individualistic writers (Krylov, A. S. Pushkin, Griboedov) did not really fit into identifiable literary currents. Several trends coexisted, including sentimentalism, archaism, romanticism, and classicism. Among the most influential was sentimentalism, practiced most prominently by Karamzin in the 1790s.[72] In contrast to the emphasis of Lomonosov, Sumarokov, and other earlier writers whom

Shishkov admired on grand themes and genres, sentimentalism encouraged the examination of private emotions through poems and short stories that were deliberately unpretentious in both length and style. Prominent sentimentalists included V. A. Zhukovskii, P. I. Shalikov, V. L. Pushkin, and I. I. Dmitriev. As avant-garde art, it had passed its peak by 1800, when younger writers were already experimenting with romanticism, but the output of sentimentalist writers continued unabated. Karamzin himself had by this time virtually retired from the literary scene to work on his *History of the Russian State,* but the prestige of his earlier works ensured him his continuing place as the movement's patron saint.[73]

The contrast between sentimentalism and its predecessors was accentuated by the efforts of the *karamzinisty* to develop, in a conscious adaptation of European patterns, a literary language modeled on the French-influenced Russian spoken by the educated classes. This New Style used French words that were given a Russian form or were translated literally into Russian. Writers who preferred the Old Style, on the other hand, relied more on borrowings from Church Slavonic to give their writings the "gravity" *(vazhnost')* as against the "delicacy" *(nezhnost')* and "pleasantness" *(priiatnost')* to which sentimentalism aspired.

This dichotomy of "gravity" and "delicacy" leads us to the third dimension of the debate: the place of Russian culture in the broader European context. Generally speaking, the sentimentalists took their cues from Europe, especially old regime France. In their eyes, the refined elegance of French aristocratic society and manners was a civilizing antidote to Russian illiteracy and backwater oppressiveness; Russia's future was to lie in the urbane, cosmopolitan, deliberately feminized culture of the aristocracy. They believed neither that Russia and the West were inherent opposites nor that Russia should slavishly ape Europe, but rather that Russia was an integral part of Europe and should build on that element of its identity.[74]

The sentimentalists' critics, on the other hand, constructed Russia's identity from national Russian sources, with less reference to Europe. Russian history and folk culture, and the Orthodox Church, loomed large in their thinking. They favored a pious, stern, "masculine" culture, rooted in the country's past glories and the traditions of the folk, over what they saw as a godless, self-indulgent, immoral, rootless aristocratic culture that imitated the worst in foreign societies and cut itself off from the real sources of Russian identity.

The hostility between "traditionalists" and "innovators" was intense. Among the traditionalists were A. S. Khvostov, N. M. Shatrov, D. P. Gorchakov, and especially P. I. Golenishchev-Kutuzov, who denounced Karamzin to the authorities as a Jacobin. For the older writers, according to one historian, "Karamzin, a younger man with fresher ideas, seemed to be the progeny of eighteenth-century French philosophy and the representative in literature of immorality, materialism and godlessness."[75] Reflecting later on these controversies, Shishkov remained convinced that fundamental values had been at stake. "Disdain for the faith began to manifest itself in disdain for the Slavonic language," he wrote. "The healthy understanding of literature and eloquence turned into a frivolous and false one," and "the propriety of words, the purity of morals, the soundness and maturity of reason—all of this was sacrificed to some *lightness of style* that required neither intellect nor knowledge."[76]

The debate had a political side as well. Especially during the early years of Alexander's reign, there was much discussion about two types of reforms: the first, to mitigate social inequalities, especially through a reform or even abolition of serfdom; and the second, to secure guaranteed civil rights and a formal structure for participation in government, at least for the nobles. In practice these two types of reform were often mutually exclusive, since a politically empowered nobility was unlikely to relinquish its social prerogatives; but both reflected a belief that Western societies were a model that Russia should emulate. By and large, the proponents of the Karamzinian style in literature and of the aristocratic-Europeanized conception of language and culture were attracted to these kinds of reforms (although Karamzin himself was not). Their opponents usually opposed such reform plans.

In 1803, Shishkov noisily entered the fray with the publication of his *Treatise on the Old and New Styles of the Russian Language*. The concerns he voiced had been raised by others (such as Shakhovskoi, Krylov, Turgenev, Bobrov), but his aggressive polemic attracted unprecedented attention.[77] The accuracy of his terms was relative, of course, since the Old Style was no older than a few decades. Yet there was a different sort of truth in this dichotomy, for the Old Style looked to supposed ancestral ways for inspiration and legitimacy while the New Style advertised itself as a forward-looking departure from tradition. The past as actual, historical reality was secondary. Instead, what counted was the emotional and ideological identification with it, or rejection of it, as an idea defined by contemporary cultural values.[78]

Shishkov opened with a pointed restatement of the Old Style's basic thesis: "The ancient Slavonic language, father of many dialects, is the root and the source of the Russian language, which in itself was always abundant and rich, but which flourished and enriched itself even more by borrowing from the beauty of its kin, the Hellenic language." Therefore, he asked, why "construct our idiom anew on the meager foundation of the French language? Who would have the idea to move his comfortable house from fertile ground to barren marshy ground?" This cultural kinship with Orthodox Greece was not a major element in his thinking, but it underscored his contention that a deep cultural divide separated Russia from Latin Europe. It was also important that he also thought Church Slavonic to be not merely the equal of French but even richer and more fertile. In his view, like that of the Slavophiles forty years later, the foundations of Western culture were sterile and unimpressive. He and his successors also believed Russia had seen a past glory that would eventually revive. The implication, made explicit by the Slavophiles, was that the West had already reached—and perhaps passed—the zenith of its development.

The duty of Russian writers was to develop the national culture, but a misguided enthusiasm for French literature was hampering this effort, for the

"Voltaires, Jean-Jacques, Corneilles, Racines, and Molières" could not be models for writing in Russian. "If we do not know our own language, we will be imitating them exactly as parrots imitate man." Shishkov was careful not to disparage French literature as such, but he vigorously dissented from the central argument of the Karamzinists, that foreign influences enriched Russia's literature. He was also irritated by the claim, which he turned against the "innovators," that Russians needed to imitate the French because they lacked their own native models of good style. "Indeed, whose fault is it that, among the multitude of books we have written and translated, we have but a very small number that are good and worthy of imitation? Our attachment to French, and our aversion to reading ecclesiastical books."

Russians, unwilling to explore the literary and lexical treasures of the Church Slavonic tradition, filled the gaps in their vocabulary with neologisms: Russified Gallicisms (such as *epokha, stsena*), newly concocted words *(nastoiashchnost')*, and direct translations of French concepts into Russian *(sosredotochit'* for *concentrer* and *razvitie* for *développement)*. As a result, Shishkov charged, no one could now read Russian who did not understand French; but then, everyone knew French now, so that was of no consequence. In fact, he complained, now writers knew only French, and when confronted with an author using Church Slavonic (that is, *truly* Russian) words "that they have not heard in all their lives, . . . they say of such a writer, with proud disdain: 'He is a pedant who stinks of Slavism [*Slavianshchinoiu*] and does not have an elegant style in French.'" However, Shishkov was reluctant to explore fully the anti-Petrine implications of his theories: if the New Style's words *stsena* and *razvitie* were un-Russian and subversive, what did that mean for him as an *admiral,* for *ministr* and *imperator,* and the myriad borrowed phrases that described the vital concepts imperial Russian society had imported from Europe?

Shishkov argued that all languages conceptualized concrete objects identically (for example, all had a word for "tree" or "moon") but derived different abstract concepts from these concrete meanings. The choice of the concrete object on which to base a word describing an abstraction influenced the connotations and flavor of that word and revealed a nation's thinking about the abstraction being described. Consequently, the vocabularies of different languages were not interchangeable. It was precisely the diversity of these abstract and derived meanings, and the ability of a language to create new ones from its existing stock of concrete concepts, that made each language unique, and the way each nation built and shaped its vocabulary revealed its own distinctive personality: "Every people has its own complement of styles and its own combination of ideas, and therefore it should express them in its own words, not foreign words or words borrowed from foreigners." Reproducing in Russian an alien pattern of meanings specific to French actually damaged the expressive power of Russian, which needed to build a vocabulary that grew organically out of the Russian linguistic soil. French had become a great literary medium by developing its own resources, not by cannibalizing other languages, so to transplant French words into Russian was to learn exactly the wrong lesson. Russian therefore faced a choice: it could doom itself to sterile, imitative artificiality by aping another language, or it could thrive by drawing on the earthy vitality and poetic range of its own (Church Slavonic) heritage, a heritage that recent writers had incomprehensibly neglected.[79]

The Karamzinian idea of basing the written language on the spoken tongue held little appeal for Shishkov. Colloquial Russian and the speech of delicate aristocratic ladies (invoked by Karamzin as arbiters of refinement)[80] were filled with Gallicisms and hence unsuitable as models of good taste, he wrote. Instead, writers should pay more attention to church literature. As early as the twelfth century, he argued, its language had attained a level of sophistication and beauty that French would reach only in the seventeenth, and medieval texts proved "how learned and thoughtful the Slavic people already were." He thus deftly redefined Church Slavonic as the national language of the "Slavic people," rather than as a foreign idiom brought to Russia by missionaries, and the accomplishments of Kievan Rus', supposedly untainted by the West, as a source of inspiration for modern Russians. Instead of building on this past, however, Russia idolized the French and refused to distinguish between the useful and the frivolous in their culture.

The agents of this subversion were the French tutors who were a fixture in aristocratic households. These foreigners, Shishkov argued, "have taught us to marvel at all that they do, to despise the pious morals of our forefathers and to ridicule all their opinions and actions." The self-hatred they induced was not only offensive to Russia's culture and a menace to its morals; indeed, the French "have harnessed us to their chariot, triumphantly seated themselves in it, and are directing us—and we are proudly pulling them, and mock those among us who do not rush to distinguish themselves by the honor of pulling them!" Russia had defeated France in battle, yet the French "defeat their conquerors with comedies, novels, powder and combs."[81] This accusation was particularly damning in light of France's military expansionism and recent revolutionary past. His charges against the New Style are reminiscent of his theory that the tsar's advisers were spreading revolutionary teachings. Unlike the advocates of the New Style, Shishkov did not distinguish between the "good" culture of the French aristocracy and the "bad" ideas of the revolutionaries. They were two sides of the same coin, and the Old Style was a necessary corollary of the traditional order of Russian society.[82]

It is significant that Shishkov concentrated his fire on the educated upper classes but spared the common people, the *narod*. This was to become a central idea in Russian culture: the people and the nobility lived culturally and spiritually separate lives, and the people were the locus of moral virtue and genuine Russianness. The peasants, Shishkov believed, had preserved the language and values that had once been common to all of Russian society. In his faith that Russia's spiritual division could be overcome by reshaping aristocratic speech and culture along pre-Petrine lines, he was, in the words of one scholar, "the precursor, the first ideologist of Russian Slavophilism."[83] This impression of him is confirmed by an anecdote recounted by Sergei Aksakov. A delegation of Shishkov's serfs, whom apparently he had previously charged no quitrent, had arrived at his house to offer to pay him anyway. He was not interested in the money, but he "experienced indescribable delight, or, more accurately, deep emotion, not so much at the honest, conscientious action of his peasants, but at the fact that their speeches, which he immediately wrote down, were very similar to the language of ancient documents." He promptly "showed his peasants to [his friends] and made them repeat the same speeches."[84] This episode also, of course, illustrates the remoteness of rural realities from his mental world.

Reactions to the *Treatise* were impassioned. With his biting style and instinct for the jugular, Shishkov had set off, in the words of Jean Bonamour, "a literary revolution whose violent tone is comparable only to that of the futurists." He received a sympathetic hearing from his colleagues at the Russian Academy, but the academy itself was not the literary force that Catherine II, its founder, had hoped it would become. By the time Shishkov had joined, in 1796, it was becoming a stronghold of mediocrity, estranged from the innovative young writers who were the future of Russian letters (Karamzin, for example, was not a member). By 1803, its pronouncements carried little weight and its endorsement was insufficient to armor Shishkov against his critics.[85] Privately, one academician wrote that he wished "today's writers would read [Shishkov's] treatise with an open mind" but that stopping the senseless craze for neologisms seemed as hopeless as stopping "a river that is overflowing its banks." Journals sometimes echoed Shishkov's attacks on clumsy neologisms, and his friends were quick to express their support, but no figure of any significance would join his crusade in print. On the other hand, the minister of education (Count Zavadovskii, a veteran of Catherine's reign) submitted a copy of the *Treatise* to Alexander I, who sent Shishkov a ring as a token of imperial approval for his efforts.[86]

The failure of the *Treatise* to evoke a more favorable response (Shishkov thought it had been "but a small drop of water to extinguish a conflagration") may have deepened Shishkov's pessimism. He feared that the evils he decried had struck deep roots in Russia and lamented how few people were as willing as he to voice unpopular opinions,[87] especially if they held ideas like his own that were neither unambiguous nor easy to implement. The difference he perceived between Russia and the West, and between the peasants and the nobles, was fundamentally a moral one. Reason, as embodied in the philosophy of the French Enlightenment, had ruined mankind in a way that stupidity or simpleheartedness never could have. Yet he grasped the dilemma that, while people who were as peaceful and kind as doves would also be as stupid, those who attained the wisdom of a snake took on its crooked personality as well. The solution he proposed bespeaks his helplessness before this problem: "Man should arrange his life in such a manner" that "after spending only an hour in the school of the snake, he would at once run for the remainder of the day to the doves' school, and rush there especially fast so that Messrs. Pride, Cupidity, Ambition and their other fellows do not succeed in making themselves his very close acquaintances."[88]

Few observers were as kind about the *Treatise* as Shishkov's friends of the Russian Academy. Younger writers in particular often reacted scathingly. Petr Viazemskii later commented on "Shishkov's prose? As though that were prose, as though he had a style?" Filip Vigel', another supporter of Karamzin, dismissed Shishkov as a "bad writer" whose influential connections came from playing cards with important people who, out of sheer ignorance, accepted his linguistic views. Konstantin Batiushkov thought the most effective parody of Shishkov's writing was in fact "his own verse, which is beneath mediocrity." Sergei Aksakov's fellow students at Kazan' University stayed up all night to read the treatise, which "drove youth to insanity," and then vented their wrath on young Aksakov, whom they suspected (correctly) of sympathizing with the admiral's views. Shishkov himself, meanwhile, took a kind of perverse pride in the hostility of a public whose views he despised.[89]

There was also, however, the occasional favorable response from younger readers. Aksakov was enthusiastic about Shishkov, who articulated nationalist, anti-Karamzinian views that Aksakov had dimly sensed in himself but had not felt able to define. Nikolai Turgenev was another example. From an unfavorable review[90] he had concluded in 1808 that the *Treatise* seemed to contain "*very* much that is *very* foolish," but he thought that a letter by Shishkov (in *The Messenger of Europe*) denouncing Francophilia was "outstanding in its own way." A year later, having apparently read Shishkov's book while studying in Germany, Turgenev found it "very good." By late 1810 he was evidently reading it again and found himself in agreement with its basic point, the relationship between French and Church Slavonic, although he disapproved of its harsh (if indirect) criticisms of Karamzin. The intensity of the attacks on Shishkov was incomprehensible to Turgenev, who, in faraway Göttingen at the nadir of Russia's humiliation by Napoleon, savored the admiral's defiant patriotism. "What a pleasure it is to lie down with my pipe and Shishkov!"[91]

One of the earliest and most combative public responses to Shishkov came from P. I. Makarov, editor of *The Moscow Mercury*. (Karamzin himself refused to get involved in the debate.) Makarov habitually defended all that was European in Russia and deliberately put down the national past and traditions; he even went out of his way to report on the latest trends in European fashion, a gesture intended to provoke, because subservience to fashion was widely perceived as one of the moral evils attendant to Russia's Europeanization. The fundamental belief reflected in his editorial policy was that progress was good, and change (exemplified by evolving fashions) desirable.

Makarov's faith in progress informed his merciless review of the *Treatise*. He denounced the thesis that literary traditions provided a timeless standard for excellence, arguing instead that "language always follows the sciences, the arts, enlightenment, morals and customs." This was the basic tenet of the New Style:

language reflected the evolution of society. It was Shishkov turned on his head; he had argued that the language's living essence needed to be protected from the gangrene of thoughtless innovation, but here his ideas were presented as an effort to kill that very vitality by freezing Russian at an arbitrarily chosen stage of its development and arresting its growth. Shishkov's defense of Church Slavonic was motivated by the wish to preserve Russia's identity. If Russians only spoke like their ancestors, he implied, they would also think as they had. It was at this very continuity (and its desirability) that Makarov took aim when he asserted: "We today are by no means the same nation that our ancestors were; consequently we want to write sentences and create words in accordance with our own present views, *thinking like the French, like the Germans, like all of today's enlightened peoples.*" Shishkov acknowledged a kinship with Orthodox Greece, whose modern culture had little significance for Russia, and he even liked the Germans; however, the French were the alien culture whose influence he feared. For the same reason, of course, Makarov looked to them as models for Russia's future: "We don't want to return to our ancestral ways, because we find that, notwithstanding the unfounded complaints of strict people, morals are daily becoming better!" The warm welcome this review received among Karamzin's followers was indicative of the passions that Shishkov had stirred.[92]

Shishkov took offense at Makarov's sarcasm and found his criticisms unfair. In his response, he scoffed at the idea that Russians could improve their literary skills by studying French. After all, "what Frenchman has learned from a German how to write in French?" The notion that Russia's earlier lack of a secular literary tradition was to be regretted, and that morals had improved in recent times, met with his scathing disapproval. What had occurred in the past fifty years, he asserted, was a moral decline that far outweighed any conceivable advance in the purely literary domain.

> Until the times of Lomonosov and his contemporaries, we stayed with our earlier spiritual songs, our sacred books, reflections on God's greatness, and thoughts about Christian duties and about the faith that teaches man to live gently and in peace; but [that faith does not teach] the depraved morals that modern philosophers have taught to mankind, and whose pernicious fruits, after such bloodshed, continue even now to have their seat in France.[93]

This was his most powerful accusation: the link between the Enlightenment, the French Revolution, and Russian writers. Shishkov reiterated the importance of the distinction between written and spoken language, a distinction he also discerned in English, Italian, and German, and he even found arguments against the New Style in Voltaire. He countered the implicit charge that he was a narrow-minded xenophobe by presenting himself as one who respected foreign cultures but understood that Russia needed to be itself, not degenerate into a mediocre imitation of France.

Russians' forefathers, he continued, had possessed virtues—piety, loyalty, patriotism, hospitality, kindness—at which their descendants, including Makarov, had no cause to sneer. It hardly became the "enlightened" to despise their ancestors: "Enlightenment does not mean that the son who powders himself should ridicule his father who does not." (This particular example, in fact, illustrates his commonalities with late-eighteenth-century French culture, for the powdered wig, associated in Russia with the foreigners who introduced European ways, also symbolized aristocratic decadence to the Jacobins. Of course, Shishkov associated it with new ways, and they with the old.) He also made more explicit the propeasant bias of his ideas; the dangerous implications for the old regime appear to have escaped his attention, which was absorbed by the scholarly, literary, moral dimension of the issue:

> We did not shave off our beards in order to despise those who formerly wore them or continue even now to wear them; we did not don the short German dress in order to abhor those who wear long homespun coats. We learned to dance the minuet; but why should we ridicule the country dance of the cheerful and merry lads who feed us with their labor? The way they dance is exactly how our grandfathers and grandmothers used to dance. . . . Enlightenment commands us to avoid vices, both old and new; but enlightenment does not command one who is riding in a coach to despise a cart. On the contrary, in accordance with nature, it gives rise in our souls to a feeling of love even for the inanimate things of those places where our ancestors and we ourselves were born.[94]

Shishkov was expressing his anger at the apparent arrogance of people who presumed to overthrow ancient traditions and moral values that so many held dear, when the critics themselves had done nothing to justify the authority to which they brashly laid claim. They did not bother to familiarize themselves with Russia's literary tradition before declaring it obsolete. Without even knowing Russian they deemed it inferior to French. Without taking so much as a second look at the country's native culture, they coolly dismissed it as passé. And, to add insult to injury, they did not even realize how ridiculous were their pathetic efforts to imitate the very Frenchmen who were so cynically using them. "Enlightenment," in Shishkov's thinking, meant moral, rather than cultural, refinement. Nobody who despised his forebears could in any genuine sense be considered "enlightened."[95]

This argument had political ramifications. Alexander I and his "young friends" were guilty of the same sins as the Karamzinists, whereas Catherine II, for example, had shown genuine respect for Russian national tradition. The tsar's distrust of the admiral was thus both well founded and reciprocal. The dispute over the New Style entailed a paradox. Its advocates (Karamzin himself being a notable exception) tended to favor individual liberty, popular education, and representative government for the Russian people, yet their inspiration was foreign and their implication was that Russia should become even more Europeanized than it already was. Shishkov, on the other hand, was a devoted defender of Russia's right to be "Russian," but that "Russianness" also included opposition to peasant freedom and literacy.[96]

Because the state was the main force promoting change, and the elite of the ruling class was the bearer of the alien influences that Shishkov opposed, his defense of the cultural traditions of the nation could not mean unconditionally supporting the status quo, or even the recent past. For all his fond memories of Catherine and his efforts to dissociate her and Peter from the damage caused by Westernization, it must have been clear even to Shishkov that the current state of affairs was the logical product of Russia's entire eighteenth-century history.[97] Yet the golden age for which he yearned contained elements that were clearly derived from the present.[98] Thus he praised the Church Slavonic literary tradition but did not advocate reviving it. Instead, he proposed merging it with the modern, secular, Russian-language literature exemplified by Lomonosov and Derzhavin. This compromise, however, seems difficult to reconcile with his notion of a nobility united spiritually with the peasantry. What he had in mind was inherently impossible, just as it was impossible to be both meek as a dove and clever as a snake: the monarchy and nobility should combine the sophistication of Catherinian St. Petersburg with the spiritual humility of Muscovy.

Despite its inadequacies and contradictions, Shishkov's theory of language, literature, history, and morality drew on ideas that were "in the air" but had not, until then, been convincingly systematized. He helped turn these vague ideas into a coherent challenge to Westernization. As rumors spread about Alexander I's reform plans and Russia headed into the era of Austerlitz, Tilsit, and Borodino, Shishkov's message became ever more appealing to an angry and frightened nobility.

Government Policy and Public Opinion 1801–1811

During the first decade of his reign, Alexander I was unpopular with many nobles who shared Shishkov's antipathy to his actual or anticipated reforms: limiting the autocracy, weakening serfdom, tightening educational requirements for those entering state service. During the years 1801–1805 and again in 1807–1812, the conservative opposition was defined by its hostility to encroachments on absolutism and privilege. After 1805, the conservative camp also took on a nationalistic coloring, supporting the War of the Third Coalition and then opposing Russia's alliance with France. Conservative discontent crossed generational lines; it manifested itself in St. Petersburg, Moscow, and the provinces alike; and it was found among grandees and junior officials, petty landowners and retired dignitaries.

I will begin by considering, by way of example, several individual malcontents. The remainder of the chapter is then devoted to the interaction between public opinion and the domestic policies of Alexander's government. My survey of public opinion is highly impressionistic, for the sources on which it is based are limited in number and unverifiable in their accuracy. However, they broadly agree with each other on the general public mood, and it was on sources such as these that contemporaries based their own impressions. Despite their many inadequacies, they do, I believe, offer helpful insight into the mental world of the Russian educated classes.

Gavriil Romanovich Derzhavin, poet and crusader against official corruption as well as Alexander's first minister of justice, was typical of many officials who had grown up and risen to prominence under Catherine II. He distrusted the two basic political reform currents of the day: aristocratic constitutionalism, which would limit the monarch's power, and the centralization of bureaucratic authority in the hands of powerful ministers (instituted by Alexander I to replace the committees or "colleges" that had previously guided Russia's administration). The very novelty and foreignness of the regime's ideas and statesmen disturbed him, and his goal was the retention of what he believed to be the traditional Russian form of government: a system in which a benign and omnipotent monarch acted as an honest broker between his subjects. He proposed to safeguard the emperor's powers but weaken his ministers by subordinating them to the Senate. Alexander's advisers (in whom Derzhavin detected "a French and Polish constitutional spirit") and the prospect of ministerial despotism equally appalled Derzhavin, who regarded the emperor's "Unofficial Committee" of advisers (Czartoryski, Kochubei, Novosil'tsev, and Stroganov) as a "Jacobin gang," "people who lacked in-depth knowledge of the state and civil affairs." On the other hand, the attempt by Senator Seweryn Potocki, a Pole, to invoke the Senate's newly granted prerogatives in defense of the nobility's right to avoid military service, appeared to Derzhavin to be a conspiracy by "the Poles" to subvert Russian military preparedness.[1] Alexander I's Edict on the Free Farmers, which allowed nobles to emancipate their serfs, also inflamed him. This law, he argued, was dangerous in dangling before the simple, uneducated peasants the chimera of "imaginary freedom." Wrangling over the proper financial cost of peasant freedom would lead to endless litigation, which the nobles would usually win in the gentry-controlled courts; and the peasants, "out of their willfulness and sloth," would do all they could to avoid military recruitment and taxes, for such was the peasant conception of freedom. Derzhavin's stubbornness and blunt tone finally antagonized all his fellow ministers and senators and Alexander himself, and on October 7, 1803, he was dismissed from his ministerial post.[2]

Derzhavin and Shishkov shared a similar personal biography, and indeed they were representative of the mentality and way of life of many rural nobles. However, whereas Shishkov attended the elite Naval Cadet Corps, Derzhavin, owing to his hardscrabble background, could not afford such an education and entered the imperial guards as an enlisted man. They were born around mid-century (Derzhavin was eleven years older than Shishkov) in modest provincial gentry families. Although bright and intellectually curious, they received little systematic humanistic education and were largely self-taught in philosophy, literature, and political theory. Both rose gradually through the ranks of the state service under Catherine II. They were religious and had a deep emotional commitment to justice and decency, but the rationalist European intellectual world of the *Encyclopédistes,* which exerted such a powerful influence on Alexander I and the "Unofficial Committee," remained alien to them. Their social ideal resembled their ancestors': a timeless patriarchal hierarchy, linking God, the wise tsar, the loyal gentry, and the contented serfs. Such a vision of life left little room for legal formalism or bureaucratic government, let alone a constitutionally limited monarchy.[3]

There was murmuring among privileged aristocratic clans, such as the Vorontsovs, as well. Critics of the emperor's policies included Foreign Minister Aleksandr Romanovich Vorontsov and his brother, Semen, who was the ambassador in London and an admirer of Great Britain's aristocratic political system. They, like Derzhavin, were linked to the unsuccessful 1801 effort to obtain greater powers for the Senate, not in order to limit the monarch's authority but to ensure that he not be insulated from noble opinion by a screen of favorites or "despotic" ministers. As Olga Narkiewicz points out, however, because of the Senate's appointed, aristocratic composition, it was unlikely to become a bridge to representative forms of government, while the senators' lack of administrative and judicial professionalism and their "leisurely amateur methods" of work limited their effectiveness as an advisory and administrative body and as a supreme court of appeals. In a new era when European politics would gradually come to be dominated by elected politicians and bureaucratic professionals, this "Senatorial party," whose views Shishkov shared, was a stubborn throwback to a bygone age.[4]

Among young, Europeanized aristocrats from the "best" families, one sometimes heard similar concerns. Filip Filippovich Vigel', for example, was an aspiring writer and a follower of the New Style whose gossipy memoirs are a valuable source for Russian aristocratic culture and attitudes after 1800. Alexander I, he complained, had been educated to love all things foreign and to despise Russia, and his "Unofficial Committee" of nullities, Anglomaniacs, and traitors reflected these leanings. Like the senators, Derzhavin, and Shishkov, Vigel' worried that ministerial rule would lead to bureaucratic tyranny. Regarding the general prospects for freedom in Russia, he wrote in retrospect that the ostensibly liberal Alexander had been "entirely Russian" in his love for power, while "our ignorant masses and our unenlightened nobility even now see freedom only as the right to act willfully."[5] Like almost all Russian conservatives, he viewed serfdom and autocracy as essential features of Russia's national identity.

Aside from these domestic Russian issues, what held the conservative opposition together was its hostility to France as the embodiment of modern ideas. Educated Russian opinion had long been ambivalent on relations with France. The initial reaction of many Russians to the French Revolution had been favorable. After 1792, however, this attitude changed completely, under the impact of the execution of Louis XVI and Marie-Antoinette, the news of revolutionary atrocities spread by French émigrés and the anti-French stance of Catherine II's government, which continued for several years under Paul I. Magnifying the revulsion against the revolution was a fashionable Francophobia that drew on a widespread, if superficial, admiration for Great Britain and on the sort of Russian cultural nationalism propagated by Shishkov.

Yet the influence of French culture remained immense. Spread by books and journals, by tutors and émigrés, it permeated all spheres of aristocratic life. French literature was an integral part of aristocratic culture, which is why Shishkov thought it such a threat. Of the conservatives whom I discuss elsewhere in this study, Rostopchin and the Sturdzas wrote most of their personal correspondence in French, and Dmitrii P. Runich did the same with his memoirs. It is telling that most of the French émigrés who came to Russia after 1789 never felt the need to learn Russian, since they could easily get by in their native language, and Catherine Wilmot (a young British friend of Princess Ekaterina Dashkova) found Russian aristocrats "childishly Silly in their reprobating Buonaparte when they can't eat their dinners without a french Cook to dress it, when they can't educate their Children without unprincipled adventurers from Paris to act as Tutors and Governesses."[6]

The Russian nobility's opinion of Napoleon himself evolved considerably. Many first became aware of him at the time of his campaigns in Italy and Egypt, in 1796–1798; these captured the imagination of young romantics such as Sergei N. Glinka, who later wrote that "the pinnacle of our desires was to march under his banners among the simple enlisted men. . . . Anyone who had been studying the heroes of Greece and Rome since youth was a Bonapartist then."[7] When Paul switched alliances and joined France against Britain, hagiographic brochures began to appear in Russia about the French leader, and Russian liberals were initially drawn to him. Whatever credit Napoleon enjoyed in Russia, however, was wiped out by the outrage over the death of the Duke d'Enghien[8] and by his coronation as emperor. From then on, the Russian gentry generally perceived Napoleon as a despot and usurper, their often very personal hostility being exemplified by the nobleman who displayed his contempt by naming his dogs "Napoleoshka" and "Josephinka." Indeed, Napoleon embodied the darkest fears of many nobles, who understood the connection between "legitimate" monarchy and noble privileges, especially the right to own serfs. In some quarters, however, especially in the bureaucracy, there remained a certain admiration for Napoleon the self-made man, and Russian officers in the War of the Third Coalition would continue to respect his extraordinary generalship.[9]

Napoleon's growing power and Alexander I's reform ideas both appeared profoundly threatening to the gentry. Yet the prospect of war with France unsettled them as well. The Sardinian ambassador Joseph de Maistre had the impression, in the fall of 1804, that anger at Napoleon did not translate into a widespread desire for war,[10] but contemporary opinion was painfully ambivalent. As one witness later recalled: "Anyone who did not live in Napoleon's time cannot imagine the magnitude of the moral sway he held over the minds of his contemporaries. . . . His name was familiar to everyone and conveyed an inexplicable notion of a power without any limits."[11] These intense emotions must be kept in mind in assessing Russian views of the possibility of a conflict. Hatred of the French Revolution, fear that Russia's own social order was being threatened from without and within (by Alexander's "Jacobin gang" of advisers), and decades of uninterrupted Russian military success—all spoke in favor of war. Further contributing to this mood were the French threat to Russian-British commercial ties, British anti-Napoleonic propaganda, the Anglophile party at court, and the fear that the victories of Napoleon might cause peasant unrest in Russia.[12] Still, the stakes were higher than in any war in living memory: Napoleon was formidable, and he might choose to infect the Russian serfs with the revolutionary virus.

Hostility to Napoleonic France was thus linked to opposition to Alexander's reform plans, and both were rooted in the profound social and political conservatism of the upper class. There had been minimal public support for the Senate reform, since, in a society where power relationships were mainly personal, not institutional, and where upper-class corporate life was undeveloped in comparison with Western countries, imperial favor seemed a far sturdier foundation for gentry interests than oligarchic rule by an aristocratic elite. There was no social base in Russia's autocratic service state for a movement analogous to the defense of noble "rights" by the provincial *parlements* in the last decades of the French old regime. Similar instincts governed gentry views of serfdom. Since serfdom was fundamental to the gentry's privileged status, its demise could not be countenanced. Neither could serious reform, because, like autocracy, serfdom was a social system based on personal relationships unhampered by legal constraints. Any reform was likely to give the serf a more complex legal status and thereby erode the gentry's position as the exclusive intermediary between the people and the state. That unique function made the nobles indispensable to the state and helped motivate the crown to side with that tiny social minority against the rest of the population. Besides, granting the serfs legal rights might whet their appetite, and the entire serf system might collapse if the peasantry ever ceased to regard its enserfment as part of the natural order of things. It was essential that the villages remain quiet. Anything that might disrupt that tranquillity—imperial reform edicts, serfs who asserted legal rights, appeals by Napoleon to the Russian peasantry, or even rumors of such appeals—was absolutely unacceptable to the nobility.

Because of their support for serfdom and autocracy, it seemed unlikely that Russian nobles could ever truly make their peace with Napoleon, who was perceived, after all, as the heir of Robespierre. As they discovered under Speranskii, the example of Napoleon's regime (an authoritarian *Rechtsstaat* governed by a meritocratic bureaucracy) was eating away at their privileged position from above even while peasant unrest threatened it from below. One response to this predicament was a conservative nationalism that stressed the nobility's role as bearer of national traditions and military defender of the regime. In this sense, xenophobic chauvinism was a mechanism of social defense.

Several factors lured Russian nobles into believing themselves destined, even entitled, to effortless battlefield victory over Napoleon: Russia's record of military success, and the gentry's traditional self-identification as a warrior class and arrogant contempt for the "rabble" that had governed France since 1789. Expectations were heightened by a prickly sense of personal and national dignity that clouded noblemen's judgment and inhibited a sober analysis of the enemy's capabilities, and by the intellectual insularity of many Russians, who had little conception of France's awesome military might. These pernicious mental habits fed on each other, as prudence was equated with cowardice, contempt for the French was deemed a patriotic duty and irrational belligerence a matter of "honor." The government, with its characteristically secretive and authoritarian ways, encouraged this attitude by obstructing any cogent discussion of military affairs. Denied the information required to form thoughtful opinions (in both foreign and domestic policy), the public indulged in delusions of national superiority and in unreal conspiracy theories about treason by Russia's leaders and allies.[13]

When the War of the Third Coalition finally began in 1805, the public mood in Russia was generally belligerent. Stepan Petrovich Zhikharev, a seventeen-year-old Muscovite, kept a detailed diary in letters to his cousin of what he saw and heard that autumn. The monarch's September 1 decree on military recruitment touched off patriotic enthusiasm in Moscow, he wrote, and the nobility's anti-Napoleonic fervor sometimes reached a striking level of blindness and hubris. For example, Zhikharev witnessed an irate *pomeshchik* (noble landowner) exclaiming at the English Club: "Give me that scoundrel Bonaparte! I'll bring him to the club in fetters." This prompted an innocent visitor to ask whether the man was a famous general, whereupon another club member extemporized in verse:

> One month in the guards he served
> And forty years in retirement lived,
> Smoked his tobacco,
> Fed his dogs,
> Whipped his peasants—
> And that is how he's spent his life!

Young Zhikharev worried that "society" took the war too lightly. Jingoistic fantasies, he observed, alternated with parents' fears for their sons' safety. The nobility craved information, but many hindrances conspired to keep the city in the dark: official secretiveness, the primitive state of journalism, the effects of censorship and police surveillance of the mail, and the vast distances separating Moscow from the war zone. In the absence of reliable news, the city was rife with the wildest rumors, and its social scene consequently allowed those to shine who had access to news. One prominent Muscovite, Prince Odoevskii, even rented an apartment across from the post office so he could be the first to hear and spread the news; and the fashionable English Club resembled a "veritable Sunday bazaar," always abuzz with rumors. This situation lasted through September, October and November of 1805.[14]

Then, on November 20 (December 2, according to the European calendar),

Alexander I and his Austrian allies were decisively defeated at Austerlitz. Shishkov later recalled, with angry sarcasm, that the war had "fired all the young people with a sense of arrogance," so "everyone, even the sovereign, galloped to the battlefield; they were afraid the French might not wait for them." However, "unfortunately, [the French] had not left, and showed [the Russians] that, in such circumstances, patient experience is better than inexperienced haste."[15]

Weeks passed before details of the battle became known; the influential *Messenger of Europe* was still wondering in January 1806 just what the outcome had been. Yet the psychological impact was devastating. De Maistre (in St. Petersburg) and Zhikharev (in Moscow) both noted that Russians were not accustomed to defeat. Vigel', returning in early 1806 from a long diplomatic mission to China, was astonished at the loss of confidence in Russia's power and in the emperor, who appeared to be especially unpopular in Moscow; St. Petersburg seemed more inclined to stand behind him in this time of national crisis. Alexander's old friend Novosil'tsev recalled that the emperor was initially welcomed with patriotic enthusiasm on his return to St. Petersburg, but his standing soon deteriorated as the public learned more about his conduct of the battle. The Swedish ambassador, Count Curt von Stedingk, reported to his king in April that Alexander's unpopularity was only aggravated by his hasty departure from the war zone after Austerlitz. The army "is murmuring loudly," he continued, but the grumbling was especially audible in Moscow. Thus, he wrote, the city had recently given General Bagration a hero's welcome for his role in the campaign, but "there was not one word of praise for the emperor." While this contradicts Zhikharev's eyewitness account of the gala dinner thrown for Bagration at the English Club on March 3, 1806, when two hundred fifty club members and fifty guests brought a rousing toast to the emperor, Stedingk reflects the conventional wisdom regarding Alexander's popularity, and routine public displays of loyalty were not necessarily expressions of genuine sentiment.

However, as Bagration's reception also suggests, the mood could swing abruptly from dejection to defiance. Many, from the empress downward, blamed Austrian perfidy for the disaster. In Moscow, Zhikharev reported, people reasoned that one could hardly expect every battle to end in victory, and Russia still had plenty of men to carry on the struggle. As one French historian has argued, Russians were animated by "the spirit of 1792": defeat by France was bad enough, but what really stung was humiliation at the hands of "yesterday's *sans-culottes*. Reconciliation with them, especially following a defeat, meant losing caste, degrading oneself in the eyes of the entire universe and particularly in those of the ladies of Petersburg."[16]

After failed peace negotiations during the summer of 1806, war again appeared likely, and Prince Odoevskii moved back into his apartment by the post office to keep abreast of the news. When Alexander's war manifesto of August 30 reached Moscow, the public greeted it, Zhikharev noted, with a grim determination to do anything necessary for victory.[17] As before Austerlitz, opinion was very confident, and Stedingk reported to Stockholm that rumors of a decisive French defeat (rumors he attributed to French agents) had only magnified the shock produced by Napoleon's stunning victory over the Prussian armies at Jena and Auerstedt on October 2/14. Despite Prussia's speedy collapse, the Russians did not lose heart and soon engaged the French forces in Poland. They brought the same resolve to the war as a year earlier. One young Russian-German officer, describing his departure for the army that fall, wrote that "a war against Napoleon was regarded as something sacred [and] he himself was personally hated in Russia and viewed as an enemy of mankind."[18]

Nonetheless, the regime took no risks on the home front. Rather than mobilize the patriotism of the upper classes (or the peasantry) to back the war effort, the state attempted to quash any public discussion that might turn critical. Thus, before departing for the army in 1805, Alexander had created a secret committee to deal with questions of internal security, in effect restoring the secret police he had abolished in 1801. This committee was charged with, among other duties, conducting surveillance of suspicious individuals, gatherings, and correspondence, investigating panic-mongering, and generally selecting "the most suitable ways to avoid any hostile and alarming thoughts from arising among the citizens." Though mainly concerned with the capital, the committee was also to keep in touch with provincial governors and monitor dangerous rumors there, especially regarding war-related tax increases. Its members were urged, however, to use proper judgment in distinguishing between subversive and harmless rumors.[19]

The secret committee was evidently superseded by the Committee for General Safety *(Komitet obshchei bezopasnosti),* a body with an oddly Jacobin-sounding name that was officially established on January 13, 1807. This committee inherited its predecessor's functions and was instructed specifically to investigate the "remnants of the [mystical, masonic] secret societies known as *Illuminati, Martinists* and the like," believed to be made up of Napoleon's agents, as well as instances of sabotage, treason, and espionage and rumors about freedom for the serfs.[20] The committee's mission is revealing of what the government, and much of the nobility, viewed as the twin threats to the existing order: secretive upper-class organizations (which Catherine II had already suspected of subversive intentions and links to hostile powers) and the belief among the peasants that Napoleon would free them.

These peasant rumors particularly disturbed the authorities. For instance, it apparently was whispered that Napoleon had demanded the abolition of Russian serfdom as a precondition for peace, prompting one serf to express the hope that the war would end injustice in Russia. It was also said that Napoleon saw only Russian nobles as his enemies and would bring the Russian peasants freedom. These rumors were encouraged by French agents, who in Russia's western borderlands in 1807 distributed leaflets extolling Napoleon's abolition of serfdom in the Grand Duchy of Warsaw. In addition to intensifying police surveillance, the Russian government responded with its own campaign aimed at discrediting Napoleon through books and brochures.[21]

The Committee for General Safety owed its existence to the domestic troubles facing the regime: grumbling among the gentry and, especially, restlessness among the peasantry. Fear of serf revolts was, of course, a normal part of Russian life, but in 1806–1807 the problem was aggravated by widespread discontent over the militia. The formation of a vast peasant militia was announced in an imperial manifesto of November 30, 1806. The nobility may have been generally pleased with the idea,[22] but not all peasants were. Senator Ivan Vladimirovich Lopukhin reported on the mood in the provinces just south and east of Moscow at the beginning of 1807, for example. The peasants did not trust the government's promise that militia service would be temporary (given that the term of regular military service was twenty-five years), he warned, and the haste with which the militia had been set up convinced many peasants that the enemy must already be deep in Russian territory. Financial contributions to the war effort, he found, were being made with enthusiasm by some segments of the urban population but reluctantly by others, and there was a widespread feeling that the sacrifices needed for the war were being imposed disproportionately on certain provinces.[23]

Preventing the enserfed masses from rising up against their masters was a challenge in the best of times, but the nature of the enemy made it seem still more daunting during this war. In December 1806, imperial guidelines to local officials explained that, "after bursting into the territory of powers that are at war with him," Napoleon "always seeks first to end all obedience to the local authorities, arouse the peasants against their lawful masters, annihilate the powers of the landlords, destroy the nobility and . . . steal the lawful property and possessions of the previous owners."[24] To counteract the possible attraction that Napoleon might hold for Russian serfs, Alexander called on the moral authority of the Orthodox Church. The Holy Synod dutifully issued its appeal. First it explained the cosmological significance of the current struggle. Napoleon, it claimed, had forsworn Christianity and taken part in the idolatrous festivities of the godless French Revolution. During his Egyptian campaign he had preached Islam, then restored the Jewish Great Sanhedrin (the body that had condemned Jesus), and was now devising the diabolical plan of uniting all Jews to destroy Christianity and proclaim him the new messiah. The Orthodox faithful were therefore urged to be brave in battle and obedient to the established authorities and to resist the enemy's fiendish temptations. In a separate appeal, the Synod described the nightmare that had befallen "the French people, blinded by the dream of freedom," for whom "the horrors of anarchy were followed by the horrors of oppression." These appeals apparently were highly effective in mobilizing popular sentiment against Napoleon, but the Russian government soon regretted having issued them, because, ironically, they made it all the more difficult to justify to the masses its subsequent alliance with the "Antichrist."[25]

By the spring of 1807, the Russian military was bogged down in Poland and East Prussia, and Alexander's personal popularity in the capital continued to drop, as de Maistre reported to his superiors. Zhikharev (now in St. Petersburg) watched the mood shift uncertainly between aggressiveness, fear, frustration, and overpowering curiosity. On April 7, 1807, he described a conversation he had witnessed among members of the aristocracy: "One of them condemned the actions of the supreme commander of the army, another appointed his own generals, and the third asserted that, to end the war, he 'would simply take Paris and hang Bonaparte like a robber,' etc., etc." On April 25, he recorded that "at public gatherings one notices a kind of uneasiness" and that (as after Austerlitz) people were busily blaming Russia's German and British allies for the absence of good news from the battlefield. By May 16, he was writing: "God grant that we hear good news! Meanwhile, news from the army has somehow ceased: the guardsmen write little, there is no official information at all, and the public's curiosity is growing by the hour." Even after the disastrous battle at Friedland on June 2/14, 1807, and the opening of peace negotiations at Tilsit, the government remained reluctant to provide the home front with accurate information. Diplomats in the capital were reduced to gathering rumors. On June 18, for instance, Stedingk reported that details about Friedland remained unavailable and there were conflicting accounts about the terms of the armistice said to have been concluded. By July 26, he was still unable to supply any details on the peace agreement the two emperors had reached on June 25.[26] On July 4, the emperor returned to his capital, but only on August 9 did he issue an official manifesto to his subjects informing them of the end of the war. In the meantime, however, his government had already made the first awkward concession to the changed realities: as of July 18, the Synod's proclamation condemning Napoleon, as well as sermons based on it, were banned from Russian churches. Yesterday's false messiah was today's valued ally.[27]

The initial response to "Tilsit" was not unfavorable. The cannon salvoes announcing the event in the capital on July 3, the monarch's arrival the next day, and the service at the Kazan' cathedral on July 5, followed by an illumination, were welcomed by a population anxious for peace and ignorant of the treaty's details. Before long, however, the mood changed. On July 15, Catherine Wilmot wrote from St. Petersburg that "'tis the general observation here that the Illumination last Night for the Peace was demonstrative of the public *sensation,* & if so no great approbation can be augur'd for it was as shabby as possible. . . . Everyone rails against the English for being such dilatory Allies." Her sister observed the same in Moscow.[28]

Indeed, public support for the treaty of Tilsit quickly soured. Shishkov later remarked that Russia and other continental powers were now forced to recognize Napoleon "as being, in a way, the master and lord over everyone."[29] The suspicion was widespread, as the Wilmots noticed, that, in fighting Napoleon, Russia had been pulling foreign (especially British) chestnuts out of the fire and had been betrayed by its German allies and its own ethnically German generals.[30] Alexander's old friends of the "Unofficial Committee" were dismayed over his pro-French foreign policy, and a vengeful mood swept through the officer corps after the defeats of 1805 and 1807. Even among the peasants, memories of the

Synod's condemnation of Napoleon spawned rumors that "evil, unnatural forces had been involved in concluding the peace."[31] After all, Viazemskii later wrote, Napoleon was "the personification and the *elevation to monarchical status* of the *revolutionary* principle," who "equally terrified both kings and peoples. . . . All lived as though in fear of an earthquake or a volcanic eruption. No one could act or breathe freely."[32] This tense atmosphere extended well beyond the aristocracy of the capitals. As Alexander was warned, Petersburg was generating rumors that soon found their way to Moscow, and Moscow, in turn, played host every winter to nobles and their servants from the entire country. As a result, "the disastrous fashion of blaming the government passes into the provinces . . . and shakes everywhere to its foundations that beneficent confidence in the government that is so valuable in [the government's] important moments."[33]

Alexander sought to shore up his government's credibility by changing his foreign ministers. In 1806 the deeply unpopular Czartoryski had been replaced as foreign minister by Andrei Budberg, a Livonian general with no distinctive profile in foreign policy. In 1808, Budberg was in turn replaced by Count Nikolai Petrovich Rumiantsev, a sincere advocate of the French alliance who had opposed the war. Henceforth the spokesman for the Tilsit alliance, Rumiantsev was valued by Napoleon and unpopular in Russia. His role in shaping policy was limited, however, because apparently Alexander was making preparations for the next war with France behind Rumiantsev's back.[34]

When Alexander met with Napoleon at Erfurt in the fall of 1808, the alliance was already beginning to fray (the public display of harmony notwithstanding); yet Russian wits sarcastically spoke of his traveling to the "Erfurt Horde," like medieval Russian princes who abjectly paid homage to their Tatar overlords of the Golden Horde. This event and the reaction it produced were symptomatic of his predicament between 1807 and 1812, as he maneuvered between his menacing French partner and a public opinion whose antagonism toward France he shared more than he could afford to admit. He conducted two strategies at once: the publicly acknowledged alliance policy, and a behind-the-scenes policy of confrontation and preparation for war with France. Politically, this was the worst of both worlds: Paris was not fooled by verbal assurances of friendship contradicted by actual policies (such as his lackadaisical support for France's 1809 campaign against Austria and for the Continental System from 1810 on), and revanchist public opinion excoriated him for associating with Napoleon at all.[35]

Napoleon's envoy Savary discovered the irritable mood when he first arrived in St. Petersburg in July 1807 and could find no accommodations except in a French-owned hotel, and no one but the emperor invited him to any social functions during the next six weeks. He was shocked at young nobles' bitterness toward the emperor and noted with concern the influence on public opinion of British representatives, especially in light of Russian trade relations with Britain; merchants seemed particularly angry about the severing of these ties. Alexander was gracious toward the ambassador of his fearsome ally, but public opinion was virtually unanimous. As a German diplomat told U.S. Minister John Quincy Adams, "There is the Emperor and [Foreign Minister Rumiantsev] on one side, and the whole people on the other."[36] The first winter after Tilsit witnessed exceptionally many balls in St. Petersburg, since the emperor hoped to raise the public's spirits and persuade it to accept the French ambassador, but to no avail. Savary's successor, Caulaincourt, was treated with more distinction by Alexander than was any other diplomat, but he faced the same social boycott. When the Prussian royal couple (Russia's hapless allies of 1806–1807) visited St. Petersburg at the beginning of 1809, their festive welcome by local society was a deliberate insult to Caulaincourt. At the same time, Russians were conspicuously sympathetic to the Spanish guerrillas fighting the French, and many saw the "people's war" in Spain as a model Russia might follow in the future.[37]

Discontent was indeed rife. Negotiations regarding a marriage of Napoleon with Alexander's sister Anna were unpopular because of public hostility toward the prospective bridegroom. When it became known that Napoleon would marry the Austrian princess Marie Louise instead, however, and that he had been negotiating with the Romanovs and the Habsburgs at the same time, the Russians were again offended.[38] Also feeding discontent were the peasant unrest and economic troubles associated with the 1806–1807 militia mobilization, the trade disruptions caused by the Continental System, and the inflation stemming from the government's deficit.[39] Among the lower classes, hatred for Napoleon (the "Antichrist") was not to be dispelled as easily as it had been created. At one postal station in the remote interior of the Russian Empire, for example, where the French emperor's likeness graced the walls of the postmaster's room, the man explained that this would help him to identify and arrest the villain should he ever pass through the area under an alias or with false papers.[40]

The tendency to grumble even reached the imperial family. Of particular significance were the three women who played a role in Alexander I's life: his mother Mariia Fedorovna (Paul I's widow); his wife, Elisaveta Alekseevna; and his sister, Ekaterina Pavlovna. Their roles should come as no surprise: the state-service milieu of Shishkov and Derzhavin may have been exclusively masculine, but cultivated, aristocratic women had an important place in the unofficial world of the salon, and the imperial court was the ultimate salon. As we shall see later in this study, women also participated influentially in aristocratic religious life, with significant political consequences.

Mariia Fedorovna was conservative, strong-willed, and meddlesome. Ambassador Savary noted that, while the monarch's own court was modest, around her "one finds all the pomp of the Russian court. It is here that one sees ceremony extending into the most minute details of private life." Cultured, sincere, and above reproach in her personal life, she was also narrow-minded and intellectually shallow. After Paul's murder in 1801, she had briefly tried to succeed him before ceding the crown to her son. Her German background and clumsy Russian made her an unlikely leader for conservative Russian "patriots," but she apparently opposed Czartoryski's appointment as foreign minister and then advocated his dismissal, and she disapproved of her son's going to Erfurt in 1808, as did his brother, Konstantin.[41] Mariia cultivated her ties to the aristocracy; her friends were drawn from the highest levels of the state and included prominent critics of the French alliance. As Savary reported to Paris, "the grandees of St. Petersburg would never let two weeks pass without making an appearance at the empress-mother's court, and even though she resides twelve leagues from the city, they go to attend her company until midnight and return home." He added that the emperor dined with her twice a week and often spent the night at her residence.[42]

Alexander's estranged German wife, Elisaveta Alekseevna, had become deeply attached to Russia in the decade and a half she had lived there and (unlike her mother-in-law) was well versed in its language and culture. Savary considered her "very sharp and of sound judgment," but reported that "around her there is absolutely no pomp or ceremony and little gaiety"; "she is almost continually on bad terms with the empress-mother and has not lived with her husband in a long time." Despite the virtual seclusion in which Elisaveta lived, she had prominent friends and confidants, including the Senator Seweryn Potocki, Aleksandr Golitsyn (Alexander I's childhood friend and overprocurator of the Holy Synod) and "Unofficial Committee" members Czartoryski and Stroganov.[43] Almost alone in the imperial family, she loyally supported her husband's pro-French policies, although she privately found them distasteful.[44] Judging from her numerous letters to her mother, the sensitive and lonely empress could not restrain her bitter contempt for Mariia Fedorovna, who, with "that excessive pride that leads her into any opportunity to flatter public opinion and attract base fawning," had "managed to resemble the leader of a *fronde:* all the malcontents, of whom there are many, rally around her." As for her crude and irascible brother-in-law, "it is said that, behind his brother's back, Grand Duke Konstantin howls like the others about what has happened and is still happening. . . . I believe him capable of it, knowing all the falseness of his character." Another in-law given to politicking was Grand Duchess Ekaterina Pavlovna, Alexander's younger sister (she was nineteen years old in 1807). "She is on the wrong path," Elisaveta wrote, "because she has modeled her opinions, her conduct and even her manners on her dear brother, Konstantin. She has a tone that would not be suitable for a woman of forty years, much less a girl of nineteen."[45]

Ekaterina was bright, charming, passionate, and even spoke and wrote good Russian, which was unusual for someone of her social status. She was close to her brother, Konstantin, whose views she shared (although she treated him somewhat condescendingly because of his erratic personality); she was the confidante of Alexander; Mariia Fedorovna, who oppressed the rest of the family, doted on her; and she was on good terms with Alexander's mistress. All of this, presumably, soured her personal relationship with Elisaveta Alekseevna and aggravated their disagreement over the alliance with Napoleon.[46] Her friendship with Bagration and other generals and statesmen, her well-known Francophobia, and her grand visions of Russia's future all appealed to grumblers who disliked her mother and found Konstantin politically shallow and personally disagreeable. Her urging Alexander to stand up to Napoleon at Tilsit could only boost her standing among these disgruntled elements.[47]

Stubborn rumors of a possible coup named Ekaterina as a likely replacement for her brother. French diplomats appear to have been particularly suspicious of her, but Adams similarly reported hearing from the Dutch ambassador that she was "the most ambitious woman in the world. . . . Grand Duchess Catherine is her grandmother [Catherine II, who had overthrown her husband, Peter III] over again. If anything should ever happen here, it will be in her favor. The idea has never yet occurred to her, but it is impossible that it should not occur."[48] These rumors persisted at least from 1807 until 1810 and are indicative of Ekaterina's hawkish opinions and presumed influence—and also, of course, of Alexander I's alarming lack of popularity after Tilsit.

In 1807–1808, intensive efforts were under way to find a husband for her. Candidates included Austria's Emperor Francis I and an assortment of German princes. There was even talk of marrying her to Napoleon, but that plan was not carried out, partly as a consequence of her own political distaste for the French ruler. In April 1809 she married Prince Georg of Oldenburg, a staid, decent, colorless man whom Alexander appointed governor-general of Novgorod, Iaroslavl', and Tver', where the young couple took up residence in August 1809.[49] From Tver', Ekaterina Pavlovna could play a larger political role than if she had married a prominent foreign prince and moved abroad. Even her usually indulgent mother was irritated by the restless politicking in Tver': "I don't know what Ekaterina wants," Mariia Fedorovna complained. "She has the most beautiful provinces in Russia, and she is not happy!"[50] Alexander, who enjoyed her company and valued her opinions, discussed issues of state with her, and their close relationship did not pass unnoticed. Stedingk reported to Stockholm about "these frequent trips to see a sister whom the emperor loves very much and who is very outspoken against Napoleon." She was "said to be highly influential with the rest of the imperial family," especially Konstantin; "all that does not meet the wishes of the French government is commonly attributed to her," and she was thought to "make her brother the emperor vacillate occasionally in his political opinions on France."[51]

From this broad (if hardly "scientific") sampling of the public mood, we may conclude that Russians between Tilsit and 1812 were unhappy, afraid, and confused. In addition, nobles remembered Alexander's earlier tinkering with their caste privileges; some peasants still hoped Napoleon might bring them freedom; village life had been disrupted by service in the militia; the Continental System hurt nobles and merchants; and all seemed angry or perplexed about the government's conciliatory policy toward France. Under these trying circumstances, Alexander I adopted a typically Janus-faced domestic policy: repression of dissent combined with a resumption of the reform policies that he had pursued before the War of the Third Coalition.

Epitomizing the deepening authoritarianism of Alexander's domestic policy was the rise of Arakcheev. A career artillery officer of obscure provincial lineage, Count Aleksei Andreevich Arakcheev took pride in his own crudeness and lack of sophistication. He had been a faithful crony to Paul I and had befriended then–Grand Duke Alexander as well; father and son were equally impressed with his unflinching energy, dependability, and obedience. Other contemporaries, however, detested him for his pitiless brutality in executing any imperial order, his relentless and sadistic devotion to military formalism, and the seeming delight with which he trampled underfoot the sensibilities of respectable society. But his own utter lack of popularity in no way disturbed Arakcheev so long as he enjoyed the confidence of the emperor, and this situation had much to recommend it in his master's opinion.[52] His personal loyalty made him an invaluable lieutenant in times of political uncertainty.

After falling from grace toward the end of Paul's erratic reign, Arakcheev began his climb back to power in 1803. Initially he had to content himself with the relatively low-profile post of inspector of artillery (an appointment the artillery itself sought strenuously to prevent), but his star began to rise more markedly after Tilsit. On June 27, 1807, two days after the peace treaty was signed, he was promoted to general of the artillery in recognition of the artillery's strong performance during the campaign. In December, he was granted the highly unusual authority to issue orders with the force of imperial decrees. Finally, on January 13, 1808, he was named minister of war, evidently in response to the public complaints about the French alliance.[53] The emperor was concerned about rumors of a coup; with Arakcheev in control of the army—whose loyalty represented the decisive factor in any effort to overthrow the regime—he could sleep a little easier.

Arakcheev's power did not add to his master's already waning popularity. Vigel' spoke for many when he complained that, already under Paul I, "Arakcheev had been considered our Russian Marat"; for example, he wrote, as commander of the Preobrazhenskii Guards regiment, the irascible Arakcheev had once bitten off the nose of one of his grenadiers and torn out the moustache of another. That Paul's supposedly gentle and "enlightened" son would favor this violent boor was baffling.[54] De Maistre quickly grasped the significance of Arakcheev's promotion to minister of war and, within a week of the appointment, reported: "It is more than likely that, at this time, order can be established only by a man of this sort." Indeed Arakcheev was hated by *all who matter here and all who are linked with all who matter.* To stay in office, "he must be holding on tightly and His Imperial Majesty must be very determined. Meanwhile he is crushing everything. He has made the most noteworthy influences disappear like a fog."[55]

In 1810, internal security was further tightened with the creation of the Ministry of Police, headed by Aleksandr D. Balashov. Count Viktor Kochubei, Alexander's former adviser, subsequently accused Balashov of using his agency as a "ministry of espionage." St. Petersburg, he charged, was "filled with spies of all descriptions . . . almost always police officers in disguise, and it is said that even the minister himself took part in the disguise." These plainclothesmen, Kochubei observed, not only monitored public opinion and fought actual subversion but lured unsuspecting citizens into making hostile statements about the government. This extensive network of police informers was also used to gather information on leading officials, which Balashov then used for his own political intrigues.[56] The secret police, and the Ministry of the Interior's habit of opening and reading people's mail, became so intrusive that the emperor himself avoided discussing sensitive matters in his own private correspondence unless it was delivered by special couriers.[57]

Alexander placed Arakcheev and Balashov in positions of authority after Tilsit to ensure he not suffer the tragic fate of his father and grandfather, and the government leaned heavily on the press to see to it that its policies were not publicly criticized.[58] At the same time, however, Alexander was also pursuing the policies of reform that he had initiated in 1801–1803 and then temporarily abandoned. This second era of reform is associated primarily with Mikhail Mikhailovich Speranskii.

Though the son of a lowly country priest, by the time of Tilsit, Speranskii had received an excellent clerical education, impressed influential people, and risen to a senior position in the Ministry of the Interior. His erudition, industry, intelligence, and unrivaled skill at presenting complex issues in clear Russian prose were uncommon qualifications. After all, few aspiring bureaucrats had much to offer beyond a pedigree, friends in high places, and passable French, and many were marginally educated, corrupt, and more concerned with leisure than efficiency. In this environment, men like Speranskii were rare.[59] In one significant way, he resembled Arakcheev, with whom he shared imperial favor between 1808 and 1812: with his humble background and aloof, slick (according to some, arrogant or insecure) personality, he kept his distance from St. Petersburg "society." The aristocrats who feared Arakcheev's whip also resented being snubbed by this clever upstart. In Alexander's eyes, of course, his chief assistants' social isolation made them all the more reliable. Their careers were entirely of his making, so he could count on their loyalty even in the face of widespread public resentment of his policies.

While Arakcheev was entrusted with the regime's security, Speranskii was to be the architect of its creative transformation. His activities after 1808 were widely regarded as the continuation of the "Unofficial Committee's" work, and he met with the same distrust among conservatives. In light of the shortage of well-trained officials, the ex-seminarian Speranskii regarded seminarians as a valuable talent pool for the government. This aroused the ire of Derzhavin, who alleged that in 1802–1803 Speranskii had placed seminary alumni in key positions and used their "inside" information against officials of whose views the "Unofficial Committee" disapproved. These intrigues, Derzhavin suspected, had helped bring about his own fall from favor in 1803. Vigel' particularly hated

Speranskii: he believed him to have been pulling the strings in Alexander's early reforms (especially the ministerial reform) and saw him as a "secret enemy of Orthodoxy, autocracy and Russia, and in it especially one class," the nobles. Vigel' apparently had frequent contact with Speranskii, and "I always thought that I could smell a sulfuric odor and that in his blue eyes I could see the greenish flame of the underworld."[60]

The venom behind such attacks was due mainly to two 1809 decrees that clearly bore Speranskii's imprint. The first, of April 3, required that courtiers who held the honorific title of "gentleman of the chamber" either perform the duties that the position officially entailed or else transfer to civilian or military service if they wished to retain their service rank. Court officials who had come to feel entitled to their service rank were appalled. On August 6, a further decree mandated that no one be promoted to ranks eight (equivalent to the lowest rank for an army staff officer) and five (the lowest rank for a general officer) who had not passed a series of examinations in various academic subjects. This order complemented Alexander's earlier efforts to expand the educational system, efforts that had been hampered by the nobility's reluctance to send its sons to the newly established universities.

The decree of August 6 devastated officials who had hoped that advancement by seniority would assure them of eventual retirement at an honorable rank and with an adequate pension. Many had never even heard of the subjects they were now expected to master. The brainchild of the uppity son of a priest, this legislation seemed a direct assault on the privileges of the nobility. As one contemporary later wrote indignantly: "What means have poor nobles . . . to study languages, Roman law, philosophy, physics and so forth?" Clearly, "with these examinations all positions ought to be filled with seminarians like Speranskii."[61] Patronage and guaranteed careers were regarded as sacred noble prerogatives, and Speranskii's meritocratic ideal was perceived, not unreasonably, as incompatible with class rule by the nobility.

As Speranskii himself observed in his report on the year 1810, he was regarded as "a Martinist, a champion of freemasonry, an advocate for freedom, a persecutor of servitude . . . an inveterate Illuminatus."[62] This suggests a generalized opposition to him as an agent of social change, rather than specific criticism of individual policies, and it was typical of the mood of the time that freemasonry was associated with conspiratorial revolutionary activity. Speranskii was seen as an enemy of two essential noble privileges: the right to own serfs (he was a "persecutor of servitude") and the monopoly on positions in government service. As the emperor acknowledged: "Here in Petersburg, one might almost say in the entire state, Speranskii is the object of universal hatred."[63]

The 1809 decrees were a part of a broader package of reforms that Speranskii proposed to Alexander I between 1808 and 1811. Among these was a reform of the central administration, carried out in 1810, designed to clarify and rationalize the jurisdiction and internal structure of the individual ministries. However, plans for a broader restructuring of the imperial government—to permit greater citizen involvement and create an assembly with legislative functions—were not implemented. Speranskii also drafted a civil law code patterned extensively after the Napoleonic Code, but the draft's French pedigree merely provided grist for the mills of his enemies, and it was never given force of law. Lastly, he drew up an ambitious plan in 1810–1811 to reorder the government's chaotic finances. This proposal involved an unpopular tax increase for the peasants and, most painful politically, a "temporary" levy (which was, in fact, repeatedly extended in the following years) on noble landowners.[64]

The gentry had solid reasons to be distrustful. After more than a decade of upheaval—the tumultuous reign of Paul I, the coup of 1801, the early reforms under Alexander, and the disastrous wars of 1805–1807—they desired the return to "normal" conditions that had been implicit in Alexander's 1801 promise to govern in the spirit of Catherine II. Instead, he had brought military and diplomatic defeat, Russia's foreign trade was in ruins, the peasants were restless, and now he had apparently given control of the state to this devious priest's son. Speranskii's deliberations with Alexander I were kept secret, so outsiders could only guess at the scope of the reform plans, and given the monarch's record and Speranskii's reputation, the nobility saw little reason for optimism. Furthermore, the secretiveness of the government had ensured, for example, that Russia's fiscal woes remained unknown to the public, which therefore was unable to appreciate the urgent need for new state revenue.[65]

The adoring crowds that greeted Alexander in Moscow on December 6, 1809, provided welcome reassurance about his people's continued loyalty. The unofficial purpose of the visit was to soothe his subjects' irritation over the recent Austro-French and Russo-Swedish wars. Remarkably, this brief trip (he spent only a week in Moscow) was his first to the old capital since his coronation in September 1801.[66] It is revealing that Alexander had taken so little interest in the city, since its grumpy, traditionalist elite was unlikely to back any of his reform plans. Traveling to Moscow in 1809 was a belated sign of recognition that Russia extended beyond the court and the bureaucracy, and that he faced an uphill battle to rally public opinion behind his policies.

In the first two chapters I have argued that the conservative reaction against Alexander I was fed from two sources: the passionate yet mainly theoretical cultural-moral concerns voiced by Admiral Shishkov and other romantic nationalist literati, and the concrete social and political worries of a nobility fearful for its status and privileges. As foreign armies and domestic reformers cast their lengthening shadow over Russia's old regime in 1805–1812, this backlash intensified. Among its most forceful proponents was a highly influential group of Moscow writers and aristocrats, of whom some espoused romantic nationalism while others advocated a defiantly nationalistic gentry conservatism. These Moscow conservatives form the subject of the next chapter.

CHAPTER THREE

The
Moscow
Conservatives

Much of the opposition to Alexander I's policies originated in Moscow, re-flecting Moscow's long-standing rivalry with St. Petersburg. The two cities' contrasting personalities were apparent in their social composition, cultural out-look, and even architectural styles. Petersburg was home to the court and the central bureaucracy, so its inhabitants included many officials, soldiers, and courtiers. Out of a nontransient population of almost 270,000, low-ranking mili-tary personnel and their dependents numbered about 37,000, while another al-most 20,000 were "commissioned officers below the rank of general and nobles and their families," and fully 2,200 were "holders of the top five ranks and their families," that is, the elite of the Russian state. Two of every nine residents were thus noble or in the military (or both). This testifies to St. Petersburg's character as a bureaucratic and garrison city, as does the fact that the 20,000 nobles—mostly officials receiving modest salaries—had only about 35,000 "house serfs and their families."

The northern capital was an insular world, teeming with ambition, where poli-tics, culture, and social life were inseparable, and a careless remark could make or break a career. Its residents lived in the overpowering shadow of the court, where the dreams of a lifetime often hung on an introduction or a good word. Careerism,

Balashov's agents, and the unnerving proximity of Arakcheev all helped dampen any political rebelliousness, while the leading figures in the city were the people who themselves shaped official policy. The city was also, as Peter I had intended, Russia's "window to Europe." Caulaincourt, Adams, Stedingk, de Maistre, and many other diplomats and émigrés played important roles in local society. Ethnic non-Russians filled the upper reaches of government; there were also European tutors and governesses, foreign-language newspapers, Catholic and Protestant churches, and foreign scholars in the Imperial Academy of Sciences; finally, many foreign merchants (2,552 as of 1808) and well-traveled Russian naval officers lived in the empire's largest port city, where countless foreign vessels called. Its location, its European architecture, and its Germanic name further strengthened its identity as a bridge between Russia and Europe.[1]

Moscow was very different. Set in the continental heart of the empire, its name, buildings, and history evoked the heritage of pre-Petrine "Holy Russia." It was also the most dynamic center of Russia's modern culture: it had the oldest (and, prior to Alexander I, the only) university in Russia, the largest botanical garden, the most extensive private libraries, and some of the most significant publishing companies. While Catherine II's enthusiasm for French culture had permeated the court and through it the entire upper class of St. Petersburg, foreign intellectual influence in Moscow was more often German and English. Catherine's Voltaire-anism had given St. Petersburg society a rationalist and skeptical bent that was at odds with the sentimentalism and mysticism common in Moscow.[2] Thus, Moscow was the residence of the older freemasons (men such as Novikov and Lopukhin, pioneers of Russian intellectual life) and of the country's most promising younger writers (Karamzin, I. I. Dmitriev, Zhukovskii, and other champions of the New Style), while in St. Petersburg Shishkov's Old Style held sway.

Moscow thus retained many traits of a capital, yet it lacked the most important: the government. This peculiar situation determined the division of roles between Russia's "two capitals." Prince Petr Andreevich Viazemskii, a young poet and scion of a prominent Moscow family, observed that "in Petersburg is the stage, in Moscow the spectators; the former performs, the latter judges."[3] As Karamzin put it, in Moscow "there is more freedom, though not of thought, but of life," and more "discussions about public affairs" than in Petersburg, where "the minds are entertained by the Court, the obligations of service, the search [for advancement] and personalities."[4] As befitted a former capital, much of Moscow's wealthy, sophisticated, and hospitable elite was made up of former grandees. Catherine Wilmot felt as though she had "flitted amongst the Ghosts of the Court of Catherine"; Moscow, she found, was "the Imperial terrestrial political Elysium of Russia," and retired or digraced dignitaries of past reigns "hold an *ideal* Consequence awarded by Courtesy alone in this lazy idle magnificent & Asiatic town." This was an extremely hierarchical society, reflecting both ancestral patriarchal tradition and the post-Petrine concern with service rank. Here, Wilmot observed, "Alexander is esteem'd a driveller, a frenchified innovator, a Schoolboy & a

Tyrant in embryo"; the "Ghosts" believed that "since they themselves have quit-
ted the Helm of Public affairs the Vessel has been they think, toss'd in a hurricane
of Error & impending misfortune."[5] A focal point of this elite was the exclusive
English Club, whose six hundred members gathered to read Russian and foreign
newspapers, to play cards, chess, or billiards, to have dinner and to exchange society gossip and political opinions. Its membership, Zhikharev wrote with awe,
included "the entire aristocracy, all the best people in the city," among them
Shishkov's brother Ardalion and Karamzin.[6]

The political influence of the Moscow elite extended in two directions. First,
they had contacts in St. Petersburg, where their friends and relatives served in the
bureaucracy and the military and at court. Second, Moscow was a gathering place
for the provincial gentry. The large presence of wealthy nobles gave Moscow a
different atmosphere than St. Petersburg. Of a permanent pre-1812 population of
around 250,000, nobles constituted barely more than 14,000, but they had almost
85,000 servants, a third of the city's entire population. While fewer nobles
resided permanently in Moscow than in Petersburg, there were more than twice as
many house serfs. During the winter, moreover, the city's population reportedly
doubled as a result of the mass seasonal influx of nobles and their retinue, with
some *pomeshchiki* bringing over a thousand servants.[7]

While the city's upper crust had the European air of the Petersburg aristocracy,
the rural nobles brought to Moscow the traditional attitudes of the countryside.
They typically came with their families around Christmas, bringing their own
provisions, and they settled into their modest wooden townhouses, socialized
with acquaintances from home, and attended the weekly gatherings at the Noble
Assembly.[8] The assembly often drew five thousand and more people: "That was a
true congress of Russia," Viazemskii recalled, "from the grandee all the way to
the petty landowner . . . from the lady-in-waiting to the modest marriageable girl
from the country, whom her parents had brought to this assembly so she could
look at people and, especially, show herself off, and, as a result, get married."[9]
These gatherings made a deep impression on the provincial nobles. After they
went home in the first week of Lent, they had "stories to tell in their district for
nine whole months," until they returned to Moscow the following winter.[10]
Hence, Viazemskii wrote, Moscow "set the tone for Russia. Governmental measures emanated from Petersburg, but the way to understand and evaluate them,
and to judge them, and also their moral power," was determined in Moscow.[11] In
the winter, the city gathered opinions from all over Russia; in the summer, the
provincials returned to their nests and disgorged news and rumors from Petersburg throughout the empire. Much more than Petersburg, Moscow remained the
center of the country's spiritual life, and it approached politics with a defiant
spirit of nationalism and *fronde*.[12]

The most prominent of Moscow's aristocratic conservatives was Count Fedor
Vasil'evich Rostopchin.[13] He was born in 1763, in the province of Orel; his
father, a retired major, traced his ancestry to Genghis Khan. Rostopchin's early

career was in many regards typical of his time and social status. He spent his first fifteen years on his father's estate, educated by both foreign tutors and the local Russian priest. He then joined the Preobrazhenskii Guards regiment, and in 1786 took a long leave to travel to Germany, France, and Great Britain, where he began a lifelong friendship with S. R. Vorontsov, Russia's ambassador in London. After his return to Russia in 1788, he served in the wars against Sweden and the Ottoman Empire, wishing to distinguish himself and further his career. Those hopes were disappointed and he considered abandoning the army and retiring in disgust to the country. Before he could act on these plans, however, in 1791 Vorontsov arranged for him to participate in the Russo-Turkish peace talks underway at Iassy. After the treaty was signed, he reported to Catherine II on the conduct of the negotiations and was rewarded for his role with a position at court.

Fedor V. Rostopchin.

Viazemskii, in his retrospective effort to understand the dynamics of the vanished world of pre-Decembrist, pre-Nikolaevan Russia, remembered Rostopchin as "a true Muscovite, but also an authentic Parisian." He meant that the count had the wit, polish, and *savoir-vivre* of a French aristocrat, but that underneath the smooth surface there lurked a hard Russian serf owner. Even more than Shishkov or Derzhavin (for he was more refined in culture and lifestyle than they), Rostopchin embodied the eighteenth-century Russian aristocrat-as-amateur: landowner, bon vivant, man of letters, soldier, administrator, courtier, and (briefly) imperial favorite. These roles spilled over into one another and shaped each other; hence that peculiar blend of easy, blasé elegance and ruthless pragmatism observed by Viazemskii. Rostopchin was an accomplished speaker and writer of French, but his rural childhood had also taught him a colorful, folksy Russian style that he later used to considerable political effect. He fancied himself as blending the sophistication of Versailles with the earthy vitality of the Russian countryside, and took pride in harboring no illusions about either. In Viazemskii's recollection, he was a "monarchist in the full sense of the word, an enemy of popular assemblies and of the people's power, in general an enemy of so-called liberal ideas," and "it was with bitterness, with a kind of monomania, an idée fixe, that he everywhere sought out and persecuted Jacobins and Martinists, who in his eyes were likewise Jacobins."[14]

Rostopchin was politically ambitious but had only contempt for the people one met in politics and for human foibles in general, although he was an entertaining conversationalist who could not live without an audience to appreciate his wit. Empress Elisaveta Alekseevna found that "he is likable when he is of good humor, and when he was younger, his originality often delighted me." The German writer Varnhagen von Ense was struck, as Viazemskii had been, by the complexity of his deceptively genial personality: Rostopchin left his audience "spellbound with his easy, free conversation, whose charm was further heightened when one quickly came to understand . . . [his] iron willpower and ruthless self-determination, which were almost inseparable from . . . half-savage passion and raw violence." Varnhagen concluded that "his being would have been merely repulsive without his oratorical talent, which was irresistibly attractive."[15]

Rostopchin's service at court disappointed him, for Catherine found him amusing but refused to advance his career. In 1792, however, he was assigned to service with Grand Duke Paul—the starting point for his subsequent meteoric rise. He realized only too well that being linked with Paul, whom the court treated with unconcealed contempt, left his own career in limbo; also, he was appalled at the grand duke's paranoid fear of revolution and his knack for offending people, and "even the most honest" members of his entourage (which included Arakcheev) seemed to be scoundrels who deserved to be "broken upon the wheel without a trial." Gradually, though, a bond seems to have formed between them, and he found that "this prince, who is forgotten, humiliated and despised, makes me wink at his shortcomings, which arise perhaps from an embittered character." Paul, in turn, was grateful to men such as Rostopchin and Arakcheev who remained loyal to him despite the hostility of the court. Rostopchin disliked the "paradomania" (as contemporary Russians described their monarch's love for the minutiae of military life) of Paul and Arakcheev, and Paul's austere, imitation-Prussian court at Gatchina could hardly have satisfied his predilection for the life of a *grand seigneur*. Yet Gatchina's utter hostility to the progressive ideas of the Enlightenment may have appealed to him, and Paul's irascible personality and sense of personal frustration and alienation from the court recalled his own. Besides, there were no inviting alternatives. The court refused to help his career and was generally distasteful to this caustic misanthrope: "Here at court," he had written in 1792, he found "each day one person more to despise." Also, serving Paul was an investment in the future, since Catherine's courtiers would become irrelevant the instant she died; so he was a bit disingenuous to claim that "I am not ambitious enough to think about the chimeras of the future" and "have several times surprised myself dreaming of a quiet and retired life rather than of all these brilliant illusions that cost one's sleep, one's happiness and most often one's honor."[16]

Rostopchin's loyalty was rewarded upon Catherine's death, for he was at once appointed aide-de-camp and given extensive powers over the army, and he was one of the few people capable of restraining Paul in his more impulsive and irrational moments. As Paul's premier foreign policy adviser, he helped bring about the sharp reversal of Russia's European alliances that Paul executed in 1800. Rostopchin was leery of Great Britain's quest for naval supremacy. France appeared to him a lesser threat to Russian interests,[17] and he believed that a strong, albeit republican, France was a more effective check on Austrian and Prussian ambitions than a France weakened by the internal strife that might ensue if the Bourbons were forcibly restored to power. In a memorandum that Paul endorsed in October 1800, Rostopchin proposed joining forces with Austria, Prussia, and France to partition the Ottoman Empire (Russia and Austria were to share the Balkans, France would receive Egypt, and Prussia would be compensated by an extension of its territories in Germany). Rostopchin's pragmatism gained the support of the emperor, whose thinking on foreign policy was confused by notions of chivalry, unrealistic ideas of Russian power, and a touchy sense of honor. In the words of one of Rostopchin's biographers, "Machiavelli advised Don Quixote."[18] In the same spirit, he proposed seizing the Prussian lands east of the Vistula and compensating Berlin with territories in Germany. Reversing this policy of dividing Europe into French and Russian spheres was one of the first steps Alexander I undertook after Paul was overthrown five months later.[19]

Paul was aware of the public's muttering against his capricious regime, but his unbalanced nature made it difficult for him to distinguish friends from enemies. In the fall of 1799, a court intrigue led him to dismiss Arakcheev, and on February 20, 1801, Rostopchin suffered the same fate. Without his trustworthy lieutenants, Paul was at the mercy of the courtiers who were plotting his death. In March, sensing the precariousness of his position, he apparently commanded Rostopchin and Arakcheev to return to Petersburg, but he was assassinated before they could act on his instructions. Rostopchin despised the conspirators and had no sympathy for the reform policies of the new monarch. His relations with Alexander had deteriorated even before 1801, and after Paul's murder Rostopchin had no place in the new government.[20]

He therefore stayed put at his estate at Voronovo, southwest of Moscow, in disgruntled withdrawal from the world. In some respects, this was an emotionally satisfying position. He shifted from his identity as courtier to his alternative identity as independent aristocrat, and could reflect righteously on his years as Paul's assistant, when "I was continually forced to fight against the envy, the jealousy and the lack of honor of my colleagues, and when I also had to overcome the hatred everyone felt toward the deceased monarch." His view of the current government's reform policies, and specifically of the new monarch, was equally jaundiced. Alexander I, he observed contemptuously, was "a Croesus in his good intentions but a Lazarus in their execution." For his own part, however, he proudly announced his determination to wash his hands of politics: his life was now "that of a farmer who loves God, his family, does good, goes to sleep and rises without regret," and he was content to live "far from the world, which I leave to its agitation and to the folly that governs it."[21]

Yet life away from the court was not all he had hoped it would be. The cane with which Peter the Great had enforced his authority was still needed, he wrote to his friend Tsitsianov, but had prematurely been consigned to a museum. He was exasperated by both the idle, tedious existence of the landed gentry and the vacuous and immodest ways of the Moscow aristocracy.[22] In the summer of 1803, he wrote to Vorontsov about the state of Russian society, describing for the first time the connection he saw between national identity and political stability. "Who will be able to contain the selfishness, rapacity and foolishness of most of the people in office?" he asked. "We have many bad minds, bad hearts and not one Russian soul, thanks to our education and to the way of thinking of the public. I don't know how this happens, but, except for young rascals and a few so-called philosophers, one meets only malcontents." Then came a list of his current and future villains: "The Germans have once again united themselves. The Martinists . . . have reappeared and are making many converts. Our youth are worse than in France: they obey and fear no one." Last, he complained that, "although we are dressed like Europeans, we are still quite far from being civilized. The worst is that we have ceased to be Russians and we have bought the knowledge of foreign languages at the price of the morals of our ancestors."[23]

These arguments bear a superficial resemblance to Shishkov's in his *Treatise on the Old and New Styles of the Russian Language,* especially the notion that Russia's cultural Europeanization had inflicted unacceptable damage on Russia's own identity. Yet the divergences between the two men's views were extensive. It is telling that Shishkov's book was written in Russian, while Rostopchin's letter, like most of his correspondence, was in French. Speaking about life at Voronovo in 1801, he described his entourage there (other than his family): a German doctor, a German equerry, a French tutor for his son, his wife's former English governess, and a Russian noblewoman. When he first settled in Voronovo, he intended to stay for a decade, then go abroad to allow his children to complete their education. His complaints about the inertia and narrow horizons of the rural gentry do not suggest an idealized view of traditional country life, and unlike the rustics he lampooned, Rostopchin was an agricultural entrepreneur open to foreign techniques and ideas.[24]

To Rostopchin, the function of national identity was to reinforce social cohesion. Its cultural content was immaterial to its practical purpose, and it was entirely compatible with a Europeanized way of life so long as one remained loyal to the social order. He was, in this regard, a child of the eighteenth century and the age of "enlightened absolutism"—like Napoleon, whose dictum on the Catholic Church ("I don't see in religion the mystery of the incarnation, but the mystery of the social order")[25] sums up Rostopchin's view of nationalism as well.

He had never admired the French; as early as 1794, commenting on French émigrés in Russia, he had accused them of lacking depth and seriousness of character.[26] Yet he accepted the language and lifestyle of the French aristocracy as a universally relevant model, which he considered not to be the property of the French alone, and he saw no contradiction in being a "real" Russian who nonetheless patterned his life after foreigners.

His views on foreign policy had remained largely unchanged since Paul's reign. He mistrusted Britain, advised against conflict with France, and believed that Russia should stay out of European wars, an opinion that reflected the isolationist nationalism common among nobles in the countryside and in Moscow. He perceptively argued that Napoleon was the key to French power and that Britain, in its ruthless bid for world domination, would "triumph over [France] through the same perseverance that made a band of its merchants sovereign in India and made [Britain] itself the arbiter of the seas. French power is terrifying, but it rests in a single individual. When he will be no more, anarchy will succeed him."[27] On another occasion Rostopchin exclaimed, "I know nothing more disgusting than English policy" and fretted that Pitt, "with his intelligence, his financial means and his thirst for ruining France . . . will drag behind him the land powers and make them into milksops." This outcome seemed inevitable: Napoleon's coronation, the death of the Duke d'Enghien, and the Francophobia of the Vorontsov brothers (Aleksandr, the foreign minister, and Semen, the ambassador to Great Britain)—"all of that will inevitably draw us into a war that can only hurt us," he wrote presciently in June 1804.[28]

Rostopchin himself had advocated grandiose foreign policy schemes, was devoted to state power, admired talent and ambition, despised both radical windbags and lethargic country squires, and made no fetish of ideology. It was natural, therefore, that he should respect Napoleon, whom he regarded as "a great general" and "the benefactor of France when he enchained the Revolution" (although he was dismayed at the human cost of his ambitions).[29] In 1803 he declared that he would be "quite sorry, were [Napoleon] to cease to exist, for I see him as a great man, and, knowing the human race as I do, I even excuse his upstart's weaknesses." Not even Napoleon's monarchical pretensions offended the legitimist in Rostopchin, for they appeared to him a reasonable tool for consolidating the ruler's authority in France.[30]

As war drew closer, Rostopchin became gloomy and apprehensive. In March 1805, he wrote to Tsitsianov, "It is impossible that all governments are so blind that they do not notice Bonaparte's adventurous designs," adding that, "as it is more than certain that the Prussians will not want to meddle with the French, Russia again will become an instrument of pillage for English policy and will fight a useless war." He faulted Russia for not recognizing Napoleon as French emperor even as it accepted the Habsburg decision to transform the elective Holy Roman emperorship into a hereditary Austrian crown. He expected "a general conflagration in Europe" and anticipated that Napoleon, "letting the English continue their brigandage at sea," would seize the rest of Italy; Prussia would expand in Germany; and Austria would make a bid for Moldavia and Wallachia. "Would it not be better to partition Turkey without a war, while giving Egypt to France?" he asked wistfully. "But it seems decided by God's wisdom that Napoleon shall be the scourge of sovereigns"; his old idea of a Franco- Russian partnership seemed moot. In his view, Russia's aim should be to "prevent the other states from expanding too much or take itself what is convenient for it." After all, "if France, which is inhabited only by madmen, has nonetheless succeeded, half by force, half through public opinion, in conquering a large part of Europe, what could Russia not do?"[31]

He analyzed affairs pragmatically. Napoleon was a tough-minded statesman who had subdued a revolution, not a "usurper," and Rostopchin understood the French Revolution itself as a breakdown not of "legitimacy" but of order. Though unsympathetic to the revolution's aims or to the progressive features of the Napoleonic regime, he respected the Corsican as another ambitious, jaded politician. Russia's interests as a great power, not legitimist scruples, informed his view of France's rivalry with Britain, and he may have found the authoritarian regime of the French emperor—however dubious its constitutional credentials—more attractive than British parliamentarism. As one historian has pointed out, Russia's eighteenth-century history of government by coup d'état worked against belief in the divine-right rule of particular dynasties (as did, one might add, the principles of meritocracy and social mobility introduced by Peter the Great), and Rostopchin made "no fetish of legitimacy in the Latin sense. . . . If order [was] restored in France, it mattered little how and by whom."[32] His commitment was to the essence of the social order, not the specific structures that upheld it.

Even from his retreat at Voronovo, Rostopchin kept his finger on the pulse of Russian society, and he continued to do so when, in 1805, he began to spend winters in Moscow at his house on the Lubianka. One of his closest friends was the famous Princess Dashkova (sister of the Vorontsov brothers), who declared that he, Frederick the Great, and Diderot were the only people she had ever met who did honor to humanity. Another close friend was Karamzin, who was a relative of Rostopchin's wife. Rostopchin had defended him in front of Paul I when Karamzin had been falsely denounced by a literary rival as an enemy of the state. He frequently visited Karamzin in Moscow, and they typically stayed up until the early morning hours, animatedly discussing current events. Although Rostopchin's ambitious and outgoing personality differed considerably from Karamzin's contemplative and solitary character, the two men were good friends and ideological soulmates.[33]

Rostopchin also frequented the interconnected milieus of the mystical "Martinist" (a term that was used very loosely) lodges—his outbursts against them notwithstanding—and of the freemasons, who focused less on religious contemplation and more on spiritual and moral self-improvement. Thus he often corresponded with Aleksandr F. Labzin, the most prominent mystic of the Alexandrine era. They had probably met at Paul's court and were further linked by a shared interest in art, since Labzin was associated with the Academy of Arts and Rostopchin was an enthusiastic collector. Friends of Labzin's in Moscow included Semen I. Gamaleia and Nikolai Novikov, who was considered the patriarch of Russian freemasons and lived in modest retirement.

Novikov and other freemasons had been persecuted by Catherine II, but Paul had rehabilitated them, partly out of spite against his mother and partly because their teachings appealed to him.[34] Their mysticism and quest for metaphysical perfection may have struck Rostopchin as bizarre and perhaps seemed a threat to his own influence. Furthermore, the Russian masonic world had strong ties to Britain and Prussia, while he sought an alliance with France. Like many suspicious contemporaries, he lumped the highly dissimilar lodges together as "Martinists," a term that evoked secretive groups with esoteric rituals. He denounced them to Paul as subversives and later recalled with evident satisfaction, though with some exaggeration, that his denunciation had "struck a fatal blow" against them. He was even more pleased that, as a result of this conversation, Lopukhin (another of Novikov's friends) was dismissed from court and sent to Moscow and Novikov himself was expelled from Petersburg and placed under police surveillance.[35]

Rostopchin's attitude toward the "Martinists" was either puzzlingly complex or highly deceitful. Apparently he viewed them as dangerous radicals, as his 1803 letter to Vorontsov suggests. Yet he was friendly with Labzin, a disciple of Novikov's who tried to introduce Rostopchin and Novikov to each other. Labzin's first attempt failed, since the perceptive Novikov worried "whether he is not a philosopher? i.e., is he not a freethinker? (these are now synonymous) and does he not regard [freemasonry] either as foolishness and feeblemindedness, or as a fraud only for fools?"[36] The two became acquainted anyway, albeit only by letter. In 1804, Novikov asked Labzin to write to Rostopchin, to recommend a friend of Novikov's for an apprenticeship in English-style agronomy that Rostopchin had established. In his response, Rostopchin praised Novikov's "zeal to promote enlightenment and morality," deploring that "you have suffered the usual persecution that befalls superior minds and souls," but consoling him that Providence "has rewarded you with spiritual peace and the memory of a virtuous life." What motivated such hypocrisy remains a mystery, since Novikov had no resources or influence that could have served Rostopchin. Novikov, baffled by this letter, wrote to Labzin that he was delighted at Rostopchin's "gracious remarks, his magnanimous disposition toward me, his character, the lofty goodness of his heart, his intellect and his intention to travel" (Novikov may have hoped to make contact with foreign masonic lodges through Rostopchin). Rostopchin professed the same sentiments. He wrote Labzin that he had long admired Novikov and had successfully defended him before Paul, adding that "I honor your friendship and am not surprised by it. Why, when Orestes had Pylades, might not Nikolai [Novikov] have Aleksandr

[Labzin] and Aleksandr have Fedor [Rostopchin]?" Before long, however, he rediscovered the usefulness of "masonic conspiracies" for promoting his own career, and Novikov and his fellow freemasons would suffer at Rostopchin's hands in 1812.[37]

When war broke out in 1805, Rostopchin publicly displayed confidence in Russia's victory. Privately, however, his mood was not upbeat. The defeat at Austerlitz, he was certain, had been caused by treason: the Russian battle plan had been betrayed to the French, and the Austrians had deserted their Russian allies and made common cause with the enemy.[38] He also blamed Arakcheev, who had been responsible for the artillery. Two months later, he saw nothing but ruin. "My God," he wrote: wherever one looked—the army, the navy, the state's budget deficit, peasant unrest, governmental corruption, the overreliance on German officials—"everything is falling in ruins and in collapsing will crush poor Russia."[39] Not even the emperor escaped his bitter criticism, and he wrote, with reference to Alexander's role in Paul's assassination, that "God cannot protect the armies of a bad son." That remark became known to the monarch and fueled his suspicions and unfriendliness toward Rostopchin.[40]

The year 1806, when Napoleon overran Prussia, brought a decisive shift in Rostopchin's thinking. He had once welcomed French power as a counterweight to Austria and Prussia. Now he discovered (not unlike Stalin in 1940–1941) that the other European powers, whom he had hoped to see merely kept off balance, had been crushed, and Russia was left alone to face a formidable enemy on its own borders. The sociopolitical nature of the Napoleonic empire now became a far greater concern to him than it had been when it was separated from Russia by a solid barrier of German states. Henceforth he regarded Napoleon as Russia's most dangerous enemy, and declared all French influence in Russia (political, cultural, or otherwise) to be by definition subversive.[41]

The first step he took to propagate these views was a letter to the emperor in December. He asserted, "At last even you yourself, Sire, have justly recognized [the nobility] as the sole pillar of the throne," and warned that the militia and other defensive measures would be "reduced to naught in the twinkling of an eye, once the rumor of an imaginary freedom arouses the people to [become free] through the destruction of the nobility," a goal to which "the rabble now aspires with even greater urgency, following the example of France and having already been prepared for this by the unfortunate enlightenment whose inevitable consequence is the destruction of laws and kings." The remedy was the mass expulsion of foreigners from Russia. Foreigners, he argued, were spreading subversive ideas "in the servant class, which already awaits Bonaparte in order to be free," and their "pernicious influence is ruining the minds and souls of your unreasoning subjects." He urged the emperor to think carefully "about the disposition of minds, about the philosophers, about the Martinists," and he painted a grim picture of public opinion in Moscow. "Come to this city for a few days," he urged the emperor, "and kindle once more in the hearts the love that has almost been extinguished."[42]

Alexander acted perplexed at Rostopchin's claim that the emperor had only recently come to appreciate the nobility's importance and that his subjects were so dissatisfied; his own information supposedly indicated (this was perhaps a warning to Rostopchin) that all classes of society, especially the nobility, were loyal to crown and country. This seems disingenuous, though, given the government's nervous efforts to "manage" public opinion during the war. Alexander denied any link between peasant rumors and "true enlightenment" (rumors of serf emancipation in fact represented "nothing other than ignorance"), and he assured Rostopchin that the authorities had planned for the eventuality of such rumors and were keeping matters well under control. As for subversive activities by foreigners and his own unpopularity in Moscow, he challenged Rostopchin to provide evidence.[43] His tone, defensive but not discourteous, suggests that he saw no reason to antagonize unnecessarily Rostopchin and the other influential Muscovites who, it may be surmised, were aware of this exchange of letters.

Rostopchin spoke for many nobles who feared peasant unrest.[44] The well-known humanitarian Lopukhin, for example, harbored the same concerns. Like many freemasons and mystics, he saw no connection between the moral self-improvement he advocated and any changes in the country's social structure. In January 1807, in his letter to Alexander I on the militia's unpopularity among the peasants, Lopukhin impressed upon the emperor that "in Russia a weakening of the ties of subordination of the peasants to the landlords is more dangerous than an actual enemy invasion." Two weeks after answering Rostopchin's letter, and in similar language, Alexander responded to Lopukhin, who summarized the monarch's blunt message thus: "He was astonished to find, in my report, considerations utterly extraneous to the task entrusted to me."[45]

Rostopchin became the chief representative of this Francophobia with the publication, early in 1807, of *Thoughts Aloud on the Staircase of Honor*. Political pamphlets, a genre with a long and venerable history, had recently surged to great popularity in connection with the French Revolution. This one was a short brochure, disguised as the reflections of one Sila Andreevich Bogatyrev (*sila* means "strength," and a *bogatyr'* is a knightly hero from Russian folklore). A retired officer and decorated veteran, the narrator had come to Moscow to find out whether his relatives had survived the battle with Napoleon at Preußisch-Eylau. First, as a good Orthodox Russian, he prayed for the emperor in the Kremlin's Cathedral of the Assumption, the epicenter of the Muscovite monarchic-ecclesiastical tradition. Then this archetypal nobleman sat down on the Staircase of Honor and mused: "Lord have mercy! When is this going to end? Are we to keep aping them much longer? Isn't it time to come to our senses . . . and tell the Frenchman: Begone, you devilish apparition, go to hell, or home, it doesn't matter, just don't stay in Russia."

Bogatyrev complained that the dregs of French society were lionized by ignorant, self-hating Russians. French tutors, he charged, had undermined the tradition of piety toward God, tsar, and country and taught the young to despise their own language, elders, religion, and heritage. For young aristocrats, "their fatherland is the Kuznetskii Most, but Heaven for them is Paris." (The Kuznetskii Most was a fashionable Moscow street lined with the shops of French merchants,[46] whom, together with the tutors, he considered the agents of Russia's national decay.) It was an offense to Russia's national dignity as well as to the nobility's caste pride that the immigrants were automatically granted such high status in Russia; would it not seem ridiculous "if Klimka the huntsman, Abrashka the cook, Vavilka the serf, Grushka the laundress and Lushka the tart began to educate well-born children [abroad] and teach them what is right"? Anyway, "we have everything, or could have it. A merciful SOVEREIGN, a magnanimous nobility, a rich merchantry, an industrious people." He recited a list of illustrious Russians, whose valor in battle he praised, and contrasted them with the French: "They make up lies, have neither shame nor conscience. They fool you with their tongue while their hands clean you out." In the same tone he described the French Revolution ("chopping heads like cabbages") and the rise of Napoleon, ending with an appeal to the Russian army: Napoleon "came like a ferocious lion," but "now he is fleeing like a hungry wolf. . . . Show no mercy toward the wicked beast."[47]

Like many of Rostopchin's writings, this pamphlet initially circulated, apparently anonymously, in manuscript form. One copy found its way to St. Petersburg, where it fell into the hands of Admiral Shishkov. He was pleased to have found a kindred spirit, and in March he had *Thoughts Aloud* printed, with a few changes to soften its Francophobic edge. These alterations irritated Rostopchin, who then had the original version printed in Moscow in May 1807.[48] And rapidly "this little book spread across Russia," as one contemporary recalled; "people read it with rapture! . . . In this little book Rostopchin was the voice of the people; no wonder that all Russians understood him."[49] Rostopchin's friend Golovin reported from the capital that the members of the St. Petersburg English Club (like its Moscow counterpart a gathering place for the elite, in this case including high officials and foreign diplomats) found *Thoughts Aloud* both entertaining and satisfying but that the authorities were not amused by this unsolicited advice.[50]

Thoughts Aloud quickly sold an impressive seven thousand copies. (By comparison, in revolutionary France, where literacy was much higher and the press far more active, the largest dailies had a press run of ten to fifteen thousand.)[51] Since each copy was usually shared by several people, Rostopchin may have reached much of the reading public. *Thoughts Aloud* was popular among merchants as well, indicating that the appeal of its folksy prose and simple themes transcended class boundaries.[52] It constructed a Russian identity based on a crude cultural and even social populism: Bogatyrev was a kind of Russian upper-class counterpart to the notorious Père Duchesne (the coarse, violent *sans-culotte* archetype popularized during the Terror by the Parisian journalist René Hébert), and its tone resembled even more Père Duchesne's spiritual legacy—

the swaggering, populistic militarism of the Napoleonic empire.[53] Rostopchin's choice of the rhetorical low road to mobilize the humbler strata of society (a strategy that would reach new depths in 1812) showed his opportunistic pragmatism and distinguished him from other conservatives who had greater ideological scruples.

Given Rostopchin's willingness to use the propaganda weapons of the enemy, Shishkov was mistaken in thinking he had discovered a soulmate. It was characteristic of their differences that Shishkov saw the peasantry as a locus of "true" Russianness, a view that implicitly challenged the nobility's claim that serfdom was justified by the peasants' brutish and uncivilized nature. The more politically circumspect Rostopchin, on the other hand, carefully made his character Bogatyrev a nobleman, so that his cultural criticism would not suggest a challenge to the social hierarchy. The admiral was devoted to the traditions of Russian culture and critical of foreigners only insofar as their influence threatened Russia's own national tradition. Rostopchin, unlike Shishkov, regarded Francophobic, nationalist demagogy as a political weapon; he was also less inhibited about attacking the French nation *en bloc*. In a later (French-language) brochure, Rostopchin almost apologized for what he termed "the small writing that I published in 1807," which, he explained, had been intended to warn Russian townspeople about French residents who were spreading defeatist propaganda. "I said nothing good about them; but we were at war and Russians were allowed not to like them at that time." He even went so far as to praise Russia for its allegedly tolerant attitude toward its French residents in 1812, although he personally had done all he could, in *Thoughts Aloud* and subsequently, to undermine that tolerance.[54]

Shishkov and Rostopchin both were firm believers in autocracy and serfdom, but for different reasons. Shishkov assumed that all Russian social classes—once freed from the cancer of alien culture—could and should form a single, harmonious, organic whole in the framework of the traditional sociopolitical order. In Rostopchin's view, on the other hand, society was naturally riven with conflict, and only an overwhelmingly powerful state could protect the privileges of the nobility. Hence, as Kizevetter has argued, the paradox at the core of his thinking: he was taken with the "fantastical ideal of the independent citizen who professes an ideology of political servitude and wholeheartedly espouses that ideology, not out of fear, but as an expression of his conscience." Indeed, he sought to square a political circle. The social order could be preserved only through the strictest adherence to autocracy and serfdom, he believed, yet the autocrat could not be permitted to tamper with the social order.[55] Again we are faced with the contradictions and ironies of Russian conservatism. The romantic nationalist Shishkov glorified both Muscovite tradition and Peter I; the gentry conservative Rostopchin wanted "society" to ensure that the monarch granted it no rights. The difference between them is apparent in the literary styles and genres they cultivated. Shishkov wrote bluntly, without humor, in what he considered a model of elevated literary Russian; the authorial voice was Shishkov as he viewed himself. On the other hand, in Bogatyrev, Rostopchin created a persona utterly unlike himself, almost a caricature of a conservative landowner. This sarcasm and desire to both entertain and manipulate the reader were absent in the work of Shishkov.

The following winter, encouraged by the success of *Thoughts Aloud,* Rostopchin published a comedy, *News, or The Dead Man Lives.* The plot, set in Moscow, is simple. The now-familiar Bogatyrev learns from a visitor that his prospective son-in-law has been wounded in battle. Two other acquaintances drop by his house, each eager to give him the same general news, but each having heard completely different details. A fourth visitor then arrives to announce that the young man has been killed. At that very moment the allegedly dead man makes his appearance, safe and sound, and Bogatyrev gives the rumormongers the tongue-lashing that they deserve. Here Bogatyrev is the embodiment of Russian country virtue, while the gossiping visitors represent the spineless, cowardly, Westernized urban nobility. There are proud patriotic diatribes by the protagonist: "I love all that is Russian, and were I not a Russian, I should wish to be a Russian; because I know of nothing better or more glorious. It is a diamond among stones, a lion among beasts, an eagle among birds." At one point, two of the visitors, Pustiakov ("Mr. Nonsense") and the German doctor Mohrenkopf ("Moor's head"—possibly an ironic expression referring to Baltic Germans),[56] discuss the latest battle, of which the news so far is sketchy. Pustiakov points out that even the identity of the Russian commander is still unknown.

> *Mohrenkopf:* Zere vaz sree Cherman chenerals. . . .
> *Pustiakov:* But the troops at least were Russian.
> *Mohrenkopf:* Vell, you can say zat, but veezout ze chenerals being zere, sings vould hef turnt out bat.

Here Rostopchin develops one of his favorite themes: that Russia is being taken over by foreigners. The German's heavy accent is typical of the author's reliance on easy comic effects. At last Bogatyrev interrupts this shameful glorification of foreign generals (presumably including Bennigsen, the Russians' 1807 commander, whom Rostopchin particularly disliked, perhaps because of his prominent role in Paul I's assassination)[57] with a patriotic reference to that great *Russian* hero, *"the invincible Suvorov."* He also tells us that news "has its own factories and offices"; it "is bartered and people rush to resell it for a handsome little profit. . . . Often the stories of these public orderlies even govern, for a time, the opinion of the public itself, which is estimable but a bit gullible." This reflects Rostopchin's view of his own audience, but it also describes a genuine phenomenon of Moscow social life. Prince Odoevskii's renting an apartment by the post office so as to be the first to hear and disseminate news is evidence of the mentality Rostopchin was lampooning in his comedy.[58]

News was performed at the Arbat Theater only three times in early 1808 (and twice in the summer of 1812), but Muscovites discussed it "from the bazaar to the writer's study, from the antechamber and the maidservants' workroom all the way to the Noble Assembly," as one contemporary recalled.[59] The theater, it should be remembered, was almost the only place—together with the church— where Russians of different social classes actually mingled. At St. Petersburg's Bolshoi Theater, for instance, the galleries were occupied by "merchants, shop assistants, servants—a most undemanding and grateful audience." The boxes, on the other hand, were an elegant see-and-be-seen forum for the aristocracy, while the front seats of the pit were reserved for important dignitaries, and the standing room behind them was filled with the young noble devotees of the stage who lived only for the theater.[60]

Rostopchin's play was not a success, because the satire was evidently too heavy-handed. Sergei Glinka observed that the comedy "targeted in their most vulnerable spot various people who were well known in the Moscow high society of the time." Rostopchin was understandably dismayed at the failure of his play, and he vented his feelings in a letter to Bogatyrev from a fictional friend: "Although Messrs. Actors did their best and the jury members in the gallery clapped their hands plenty, yet, to tell the truth, the audience in the boxes and stalls did not receive you particularly favorably and concluded that . . . you put on too much salt." Or as Glinka put it, "The fateful echoes of the [spectators' jeering] whistles whizzed no worse than bullets." Rostopchin's sarcastic advice to his character was therefore: "Leave the old times in the Kremlin and in the pictures on Spasskii Most." He chose to see the public reaction as a rejection of Bogatyrev's patriotic philosophy, not of an insulting satire.[61]

As this "letter to Bogatyrev" suggests, only the common people ("the jury members in the gallery"), not the elite, were true Russian patriots in Rostopchin's opinion. He made the same point in *Oh, the French!*, a novel of sorts written around this time but, like most of his writings, intended to be read to his friends only.[62] It dealt with the same subjects as *Thoughts Aloud* and *News,* focusing on a virtuous rural nobleman and showing the decadence induced in Russia when France's influence replaced that of old Muscovy. After *News*'s annoying Dr. Mohrenkopf, Rostopchin now created another shady German character, the soothsayer and charlatan Mina Schnapgeld ("Grabmoney"). His negative ideas about Germans were not new: years earlier he had complained that the Germans "always have the idea that they should be the schoolmasters of us Russians,"[63] and their conspicuous presence in Russia made them inviting targets for xenophobic propaganda.

Rostopchin's Francophobic tracts were popular and helped start a trend. One Levshin followed Rostopchin's example by publishing *A Message from a Russian to the Francophiles.* Another example of this genre was the comedy *The Expulsion of the French.* Supplementing this literature were a large number of anti-Napoleonic and Francophobic writings imported from Germany and published in translation. Ivan Krylov, the popular playwright, also joined the anti-French campaign with his comedies *The Fashionable Shop* and *A Lesson for Daughters,* which echoed the ideas of Shishkov's *Treatise.*[64]

On a Thursday evening late in 1807, Rostopchin attended the salon of A. S. Nebol'sina, one of Moscow's most celebrated hostesses. After entertaining the other guests with his anecdotes and *bons mots,* he struck up a conversation with Sergei Glinka, a struggling young playwright who the previous week, in a notice in the *Moscow News,* had announced the founding of the *Russian Messenger,* a journal dedicated to Russian patriotism. Rostopchin had seen the advertisement and was interested in working with him. Flattered by the attention of so great a personage, Glinka assured him that he was merely seeking to perpetuate the spirit of *Thoughts Aloud by the Staircase of Honor.* (On hearing this, the count commented sourly that he was still unhappy with Admiral Shishkov not only for publishing the booklet without permission but also for adding the name of General Bennigsen to Bogatyrev's list of great Russian warriors, from which Rostopchin had specifically excluded it.) When Glinka meekly pointed out the vast distance in status separating them, Rostopchin graciously yet emphatically cut him off: "Enough, enough; where the common good is involved, there is no distance, and there men are not measured by their rank."[65]

A partnership was born that would reach its climax in the terrifying summer months of 1812. Rostopchin and Glinka were an odd pair: the grandee and the writer, the hard pragmatist and the naïve idealist. Yet they made common cause, and together with Shishkov and Karamzin they became the figures most strikingly associated with Russian conservatism and nationalism between Tilsit and 1812. That their biographies were profoundly different, yet their views on current issues remarkably similar, reflects the complexity of Russian conservatism at that time.

Sensitive, generous, trusting, and religious, Sergei Nikolaevich Glinka willingly endured privations for causes in which he believed. He was an intelligent and cultivated man, though disorganized, as is apparent from the countless digressions that clutter his otherwise engaging memoirs. In a Russia where few nobles saw any need to reconcile their Enlightenment-inspired theoretical views with their daily conduct as serf owners and state officials, Glinka was determined that his practical life reflect his ideological convictions; in this, as in so many ways, he resembled the future Decembrists.[66] Whereas Shishkov became a conservative nationalist out of childhood habit and intellectual interest and Rostopchin turned to nationalism out of political convenience, Glinka's nationalism responded to an emotional need to harmonize his ideals with reality. More than any leading Russian conservative, the impressionable Glinka resembled the more exuberantly idealistic of the French revolutionaries, in background as well as temperament. He was a nobleman, highly educated, a lachrymose sentimentalist if there ever was one, his mind full of images of ancient heroes, a passionate orator with a penchant for theatrical poses, and self-consciously a dreamer and moralist who longed for the national moral redemption that a great collective catharsis would bring.

Sergei N. Glinka

Glinka was born on July 5, 1776, to a noble family in Smolensk province. His idyllic recollections of his rustic childhood have a Rousseauesque quality, with God-fearing, modest, hospitable parents who took seriously their duty to care for their serfs. These traits, idealized by the late Enlightenment, he would come to see as quintessentially Russian and as the foundation of the social order. In 1781, Catherine II passed through the area, met the family, and promised to arrange for him and his brother to be educated in St. Petersburg.[67] A year later, on his sixth birthday, little Sergei bade his family a tearful farewell and set off for the distant capital. He would remain there without interruption for thirteen formative years. Young Glinka was enrolled in the Infantry Noble Cadet Corps, one of Russia's most prestigious schools. Life in the cadet corps soon displaced memories of his rural home. Its gentle and affectionate directors, I. I. Betskoi and Count F. E. Anhalt, induced a strong emotional bond between Glinka and the corps. They taught a curriculum distilled from the late Enlightenment and inspired by Rousseau's *Emile,* emphasizing moral introspection, the power of reason, and ideals of justice, love, and equality (though Betskoi believed in both serfdom and monarchy). Betskoi's goal was to improve Russia by creating a class of people insulated by their schooling from the vices of the world.[68]

More than anywhere else, we see here the common cultural ground from which both Russian conservatism and the French Revolution arose. Like Robespierre and Camille Desmoulins at their *lycée* a decade earlier,[69] Glinka was raised on heroic Greek and Roman history, and on the sentimental moralism and vague egalitarianism of Rousseau and his disciples. However, although the curricula may have been similar at the Lycée Louis-le-Grand and the Infantry Noble Cadet Corps, the world their students entered upon graduation was not. In prerevolutionary France, thanks to the increase in social mobility, growing prosperity of commerce, vigorous publishing industry, and assertiveness of bourgeois and aristocratic corporate institutions, ambitious ex-*lycéens* had the opportunity, as lawyers, journalists, and eventually politicians, to live what they had been taught. The cadet corps, on the other hand, prepared soldiers for a caste society of rigid hierarchy and arbitrary power, to which the education it gave Glinka seemed to have little relevance. Since in Russia (unlike France) the prospects for radical change were nil, he tried instead to overcome his extreme sense of alienation by reconstructing reality through his imagination, until his envisioned world matched the ideals of freedom, social harmony, and civic virtue that he, like his French contemporaries, had been taught to cherish. Other cadet corps graduates a decade later, who also experienced this disturbing contrast between the expectations instilled by the corps and Russian reality, repudiated the old regime altogether and ultimately joined the Decembrists.[70]

The cadet corps so emphasized the classics, Glinka recalled, that he "did not know under what kind of government I lived, but I knew that liberty had been the soul of the Romans." He likewise "did not understand the difference between Russian social classes, but I knew that the name of Roman citizen had been almost as lofty as the demigods. The gigantic phantom of ancient Rome hid our native country from us, and in Russia it seems that all we saw and knew was Catherine," who indeed took a strong interest in the cadets' education. Despite Count Anhalt's efforts to encourage Russian studies, "Russia still remained hidden from us in some distant haze." Instead, the cadets' cultural homeland was France, and Glinka became extremely well versed in French literature. He later remembered, without bitterness, that "having fallen passionately in love with the French language . . . I strove to convince [others] that I had been born in France and not in Russia." Classics, like everything at the cadet corps, stressed moral values (admiration for Spartan bravery, for example, but also condemnation of their tyrannical social structure), not empirical knowledge. Ethical principles of noblesse oblige and the universal brotherhood of man were reinforced by the teaching of respect for the common peasant who feeds society, and the teachers inculcated moral principles in their students with the help of Russian folk sayings, in an effort to bring the cadets closer to their national heritage.[71]

Glinka denied that this training left graduates unprepared for life in society and government service. He believed it had strengthened his best character traits: his refusal to grovel before the mighty and a deep respect for the dignity of all humans. Yet he could not overcome the feeling that this beautiful education had not readied him for life's hard realities. Among his fellows he noted three future successful officers and diplomats. Only six cadets were distinguished with a star in 1794: these three were not among them, but Glinka was. "However, they later obtained stars in service, while I did not seek to earn them; my star shone and faded within the walls of the corps."[72] This is an important theme in Glinka's life. At a time when a Russian nobleman typically could choose between only two paths in life—landowner and government servant—Glinka followed neither. Instead, he eventually chose the still unusual role of professional man of letters. Had he lived in old regime France, this choice might not have been too painful; in Russia, it was. Also, it was not an existence for which he had deliberately prepared himself. Rather, the circumstances of his life led him in that direction, and forever trusting in the benevolence of divine providence, he followed. For the decade after his graduation in 1795, his life seemed aimless, as he tried to live up to the cadet corps's ethical teachings and come to terms with his own failure to parlay an elite education into a successful career.

On January 1, 1795, Glinka graduated from the corps and was commissioned as a lieutenant.[73] Soon afterward, he traveled home to Smolensk province for the first time (he had hardly ever left St. Petersburg as a cadet) and came face-to-face with "Russia." Like Radishchev, whose banned *Journey from St. Petersburg to Moscow* he read on the trip (he also read his teacher Kniazhnin's historical play *Vadim of Novgorod*—banned, like Radishchev's book, for its criticisms of absolutism),[74] Glinka waxed sentimental about the spiritual nobility of the common people; yet the theme of omnipresent misery and oppression is much less prominent in his "journey" than in Radishchev's. The cadet corps had given him only vague notions of Russian history, but it had encouraged an active and romantic imagination, to which this voyage gave a new direction: it was "the main impression of my youth" that on this trip "I learned about the soul of the Russian people, not from books, but under the open sky and by listening to the soul of the Russian word. That is what subsequently became the foundation for [the periodical] the *Russian Messenger*." Yet the nationalist in him remained dormant. His mind was dominated by Europe, and a visit to Moscow (his first) in March made no impression on him because it was not Rome or Athens.[75]

Here a brief digression is in order about Glinka's memoirs, which constitute our main source about his life. In contrast to Shishkov's memoirs, whose tone is opinionated but also candid and matter-of-fact, Glinka's are a kind of sentimentalist *Bildungsroman:* the young protagonist, after an innocent, rustic childhood, embarks first on his spiritual self-discovery (at the cadet corps) and then on the literal and figurative voyage of exploration that leads him to his destiny as the journalistic prophet of Russia's national revival. His several volumes of reminiscences are carefully constructed literary works, intended to show the unfolding both of his own fate and of the larger designs of divine providence in 1812, and must be approached with caution. However, they are nonetheless useful biographical sources, for two reasons. First, he was an honest man. While his memoirs express much wishful thinking, it would seem out of character for him to have invented episodes entirely. Second, the ideas articulated in his reminiscences from the 1830s broadly resemble what he had written in the *Russian Messenger* between 1808 and 1812, so we may assume that, regardless of their factual accuracy, his memoirs reflect his state of mind during the period we are discussing.

In the summer of 1795, Glinka went to Moscow to become aide-de-camp to Prince Iurii Dolgorukov. "Things Russian were far from my thoughts," he later recalled ruefully, "and for the time being I lost myself in the realm of so-called high society, which was equally removed from ancient Moscow and from traditional Russia." His new friends in the theatrical and literary world encouraged him in his first poetic efforts. He also discovered ugly realities about which the cadet corps had remained silent, such as the aristocracy's moral dissoluteness and its arrogance toward the lower orders of society.[76] Foreign affairs did not particularly interest him and his friends, but at any rate he did not favor war with France.

Napoleon had captured his romantic imagination with his Egyptian campaign, Dolgorukov opposed helping the British fight Napoleon, and while Glinka admired Suvorov, he also believed that his campaign in Italy had resulted from Britain and Austria's using Russia to defend their interests.[77] In 1799 his battalion was sent to support Suvorov, but the campaign was called off and the troops returned to Moscow.

To supplement his salary, Glinka began translating foreign operas. When the army left him too little time for this activity, he resigned, on October 30, 1800, with the rank of major.[78] Military service had not satisfied his desire to be financially independent and contribute positively to society. Neither did owning serfs. When a wealthy friend offered him the handsome gift of sixty peasant "souls," Glinka tore up the certificate of ownership and declared: "I won't accept it; I will never have a man as property, and besides, I don't understand rural life."[79] He thus repudiated the two traditional roles of a Russian nobleman—state servitor and serf owner—and instead attempted, like the intelligentsia of later decades, to support himself by his own labor.

For the next years he drifted. He worked for the theater, even writing an opera, but this was not enough to support him. He returned to his native province after leaving the army, but after the death of his parents he felt no attachment to it either. Before his mother died in 1801, he had promised her to provide for his sister by leaving her his inheritance, and though he would not condemn serfdom as such, he was relieved to be rid of his own serfs: "I gave up the peasants like a burden that weighed on me. I love humanity, but I don't know how to rule people." In the fall of 1802 he returned to Moscow, lost his remaining money at cards, and spent his last five rubles on a bottle of wine to share with a friend. Another friend then obtained for him a teaching position in the Ukraine, where he spent three years, after which he came back, again penniless, to Moscow. He hoped to reenter government service, but his application was rejected, and he resumed his work for the theater.[80]

The turning point in Sergei Glinka's life came in 1806, when for the first time Russia seemed directly threatened by Napoleon, and he volunteered for the militia. When the French occupied Vienna in 1805, he had been certain they would one day enter Moscow, he recalled. The conviction that the fatherland was in danger galvanized his energies. Napoleon now appeared to him a figure of almost mythical proportions, impelled to ever new wars of conquest by a mysterious and uncontrollable inner urge. To this rootless young man with his confused search for a purpose in life, the patriotism of the militia represented the end of his quest: a revelation, a quasi-religious experience that completed the epiphany begun with his voyage eleven years earlier. "In an extraordinary year," he remembered with deep emotion, "amidst the Russian people, I came to know the soul of our warriors." His eyes had been opened: "I felt ashamed that, up to now, spinning round in some mysterious world, I had known neither the spirit nor the real way of thinking of the Russian people." However, "time, with powerful force, brought out the Russian spirit before the face of our fatherland and before the face of Europe. [That spirit], as we shall see later, led me toward a new life." Disillusioned by the ancien régime, Glinka found meaning in the nation, as did so many of his contemporaries in France after 1789 and in Germany in 1813. Unlike many of them, however, he would draw *conservative* conclusions from his romantic nationalism, using it to transfigure, rather than attack, the old order.

The war permitted Glinka to devote himself to this new cause. His plays seemed to match the public mood. When he visited Petersburg that autumn, his historical drama *Natal'ia, the Boyar's Daughter* was being staged there. "The boxes, the pit—everything was full," he remembered with pride. The actors "performed with lively and sincere voices; the applause was thunderous. Everything there merged with the course of the events of the time. My drama featured war and conflagration, and selflessness for the Russian land." He also completed his play *Mikhail, Prince of Chernigov,* about Russia's struggle against the Mongol invaders, a topic with obvious contemporary overtones.[81] He brought the same zeal to inspiring the peasants as he did to mobilizing aristocratic patriotism. Traveling between St. Petersburg and Moscow, he passed through a village where the peasants were close to blows over the question of who among them would have to join the militia. "Your blood and your life are needed by the fatherland," Glinka admonished them (in his later retelling). "I, my friends, have neither house nor home, neither wife nor children; I myself earn my daily bread by the sweat of my brow, and I have sworn an oath to serve the fatherland and to die for it." He explained that the militia had been created "for our land, for our fields, for the graves of our fathers, for everything that God has endowed our Russian land with and that He commands us to preserve and maintain in it." The effect of this speech was, it seems, that "the peasants were wiping away tears, and the tears also were not freezing in my eyes." The peasants cheered him and wished him good health. Their words, he wrote decades later, "echo even now in my memory and in my heart."[82]

Glinka's self-appointed mission was thus to unite the nation. His patriotic theater and oratory recalled the French Revolution, as did the Roman-sounding vow to die for the fatherland and his later work on the *Russian Messenger*. What made his efforts so similar to those of the French was the insistence on reaching across social divides and drawing his audience into active participation in a mass experience that stressed raw emotion, not cool logic, and that equated patriotism with heroic self-sacrifice. It is telling that many leading revolutionaries, like Glinka, had professional ties to the theater or journalism.[83] Even the militia was, in contrast to the professionalized army he had left, a kind of *levée en masse*. A Glinka and a Camille Desmoulins were products of the same culture, of the same longing for a catharsis that would create a Rousseauesque society of purity and innocence. Variations in personality and national circumstances determined whether this cast of mind resulted in a radical or conservative orientation.

Although he never in fact saw combat, Glinka served in the militia with great enthusiasm. "Death for the fatherland is sweet," he wrote to Derzhavin, whom he had met as a cadet, "and what does life mean in days when power-hungry monsters, after plunging humanity into the abyss of unbelief and depravity, are driving it at their whim across the frenzied waves of ruin and death?" Anti-Napoleonic patriotism fused in his mind with broader concerns. "What benefit did we derive from our sham enlightenment? Did it increase our happiness, in the sense of a moderate, familial life in the community of kin and friends[?]" he asked. No, he answered himself, of course not. The *philosophes,* who "wanted to overthrow the altars of God and the faith," had "shaken the laws and morals of the Russian land. Glory to those who will resurrect Russia in Russia!—that is, who will renew the love, the exclusive love for simple morals, the faith and God."[84]

He was a man alienated from his society. Since his fellow nobles ignored the values he had internalized as a cadet, he searched for them elsewhere, and found them in the common people; the respect he had been taught for the peasantry encouraged him in this. He had been deprived of a secure identity by his education and by his estrangement from the rural life and service career typical of his class. He compensated for this void in his life by identifying with the Russian nationality, and specifically with those traditional and popular manifestations of it that were farthest from his own experience. Not unlike Alexander I, who later sought refuge in religious mysticism, Glinka wished to live by a strict ethical code but lacked the knowledge and intellectual rigor to fathom the relationship between his ideals and reality. In his personal life he was capable of great selflessness, but his romantic nationalist views on society at large, though held with intense determination, were often simplistic. Given the glaring flaws of his society, he shifted his loyalty backward in time to pre-Petrine Muscovy, when the moral values taught at his cadet corps had supposedly been reality and Russia was still unafflicted by the "sham enlightenment" that had robbed so many nobles, including himself, of their Russian identity. Like Shishkov, Glinka idealized a mythical past free from moral corrosion by cynicism or spiritual doubt. He rejected the Enlightenment belief in progress, substituting for it the notion of a past golden age of social harmony. This harmony had been the product, he believed, of paternalistic Christian rule by a virtuous tsar and benevolent boyars who reflected peculiarly Russian moral and spiritual qualities. Serfdom was a benign force in this society, since it permitted the nobles to exercise a gentle authority over the peasants. Glinka's mission in life, of which he became fully convinced in 1806–1807, was to reacquaint Russians with this forgotten golden age and thereby help liberate them from their European spiritual fetters. Violence and arbitrariness were to be replaced with altruism and security for the weak and innocent. The nobility, returning to its patriarchal rural roots, was to be morally cleansed of the parasitic ways and decadent luxury that had become customary since its emancipation from compulsory state service by Peter III in 1762. And Glinka's weapon in this crusade would be the monthly *Russian Messenger.*[85]

When he returned to Moscow after the war of 1806–1807, he began for the first time to appreciate the city's significance as the repository of Russia's past and greatness. "In this state of mind I conceived the idea of publishing the *Russian Messenger*." Tilsit, he believed, was only a truce, and the *Messenger*'s purpose would be "to arouse the spirit of the people and summon it to the new and inescapable struggle." An admirer of Rostopchin's *Thoughts Aloud,* he welcomed the count's plan to contribute to the new journal. The two men established close personal relations as well. In February 1808, Glinka came to Voronovo, where he was entertained with reminiscences of Suvorov's campaigns (which also appeared in the *Russian Messenger*) and the days of Paul I.[86] Rostopchin loved talking about these subjects, and Glinka likely listened avidly.[87]

The considerable impact that Glinka's *Russian Messenger* had on contemporaries resulted from the journal's exuberant glorification of the pre-Petrine heritage and the Russian national character. This editorial stance permitted some criticism of modern social ills (noble cruelty toward serfs, bureaucratic despotism, and so on) because these abuses, strikingly absent in Russia's idealized past, could be blamed on West European influence. Prior to the reign of Peter the Great, the *Messenger* asserted, Russia "was hardly second to any country in its civil institutions, legislation, purity of morals, family life and all that makes for the prosperity of a people that honors its ancestral customs, its fatherland, its tsar and God."[88] His exploration of Russia's past was hampered, however, by his own ignorance. His essays reflected his European upbringing: he tended to superimpose on Russian historical characters anachronistic patterns of thought and behavior drawn from European history. Thus Zotov reportedly taught his pupil, the future Peter the Great, according to the precepts of Condillac and Pestalozzi, and Ermak, who initiated Russia's conquest of Siberia, was likened to Scipio Africanus. Like Shishkov, Glinka searched for Russian substitutes for the great figures of Western culture, and the Westernized education that he had himself received now struck him as one of the sources of Russia's ills. Russian tradition became a vast panorama of goodness and virtue.[89] Although this understanding of history was superficial, it was more than many of his readers had, and many of them shared the European lenses through which he viewed the national past. That, and the current Francophobic mood, accounted for his journal's success among readers who had been raised in the European tradition and were astonished to discover that their own country had a past worth exploring.[90]

Glinka published his list of subscribers for 1811,[91] the fourth year of the *Messenger.* By then he had 171 subscribers in Moscow, 531 in other provinces, and 12 whose residence he did not specify. They included great aristocratic dynasties (some of them later linked to the Decembrists) and prominent individuals such as Labzin and former foreign minister Nikita Panin (though not Rostopchin, with whom Glinka had quarreled). The *Messenger*'s geographic range extended as far as Irkutsk, Arkhangel'sk, Riga, and Tiflis. The church was represented by a metropolitan, four bishops, five archimandrites, two archpriests, a priest, two ecclesiastical academies, and three seminaries. Three noble assemblies subscribed, as did at least five secular schools and even the Moscow dance club. On the other hand, only Admiral Shishkov and nine others subscribed in St. Petersburg, a fact that suggests how much official distrust and cultural antipathy Glinka's anti-Napoleonic glorification of Muscovy aroused on the Neva. In 1808, Napoleon's ambassador even complained to Alexander I about the publication's anti-French content, but the state took no decisive action against Glinka.[92]

He especially spoke to, and presumably for, an audience of rural and Moscow nobles, for most of his subscribers lived in the city, the nearby agricultural provinces, the Ukraine, and along the Volga. This impression is borne out by the numbers for 1813.[93] Of the 386 subscribers with identifiable places of residence outside Moscow, 165 lived in the densely settled south-central provinces where servile agriculture predominated;[94] in Orel province alone, the *Messenger* was received in each of the ten district *(uezd)* capitals. At least 69 subscribers lived in areas west and north of Moscow, and another 55 along the Volga between Nizhnii-Novgorod and Astrakhan', where economy and society were similar. However, in the provinces where nobility and serfdom were less prevalent or that were not ethnically Russian, the numbers were much smaller: Arkhangel'sk (4 subscribers), Petrozavodsk (none), the Baltic provinces (none), the North Caucasus (1), Siberia (11).

The social background of the 1813 subscribers (it was not indicated for 1811) confirms this picture of Glinka's audience, for 451 indicated noble status. Of these, 136 were identified simply as *blagorodiia* (nobles) and 197 as *vysokoblagorodiia* (majors or colonels and their civilian counterparts), but 75 were *vysokorodiia, prevoskhoditel'stva,* or even *vysokoprevoskhoditel'stva,* indicating the rank of general or its equivalent. Another 41 subscribers were *siatel'stva* (nobles who held the title "count" or "prince"), and two were members of the imperial family (the emperor's brothers Nikolai—the future Emperor Nicholas I—and Mikhail); one subscription even went to the Hermitage, where the emperor's own library was located. At the other end of the social scale, 52 subscribers were merchants, and one Grigorii Sokol'nikov, of frigid, remote Iakutsk in northeastern Siberia, even belonged to the *meshchanstvo,* the urban lower class. Glinka's audience thus was broadly representative of the literate public, with the exception of clergymen, who (perhaps because the *Messenger* usually ignored religious topics) ordered only nine subscriptions. He reached mostly rural nobles (people similar to Shishkov's family) who had retired from the service with a respectable mid-level rank, but also a number of important officials, and he was read by nonnobles as well. We should keep the profile of Glinka's readership in mind when thinking about the social base of Russian conservatism.

It is difficult to determine his publication's impact. His press runs of six or seven hundred pale next to the five thousand of the Interior Ministry's *Northern Post.* On the other hand, journals such as the *Messenger of Europe* and the *Son of the Fatherland* were considered quite successful for printing one to two thousand copies,[95] so on that scale Glinka's numbers were respectable. Also, in a market where periodicals frequently went under after only a few issues, Glinka succeeded in publishing for over a decade, which attests to the loyalty of his readers. Furthermore, the *Russian Messenger* was not a paper one gave a cursory glance and then threw away. To begin with, at 15 rubles per year for out-of-town subscriptions, it was not cheap. More importantly, it was not a news publication, so it did not quickly become outdated. Provincial nobles presumably added each new booklet to their modest family library, perhaps lending it to friends or neighbors. One imagines that all or most of a household's literate members at least perused it during their long, uneventful months in the country, and its ideas probably informed their conversations with others who had not. Also, among the subscribers were schools and noble assemblies, and the copies in their libraries and reading rooms might pass through many hands. Thus the audience whom Glinka's work actually reached must have been far greater than the number of subscribers.

The *Russian Messenger* propagated Glinka's favorite themes of Russian greatness and moralizing sentimentalism. For example, the December 1811 issue (to which the list of 1811 subscribers is appended and which is a book 124 pages long) contains poetry by Glinka and by a reader, an excerpt from a chronicle about the Cossacks (with Glinka's own highly laudatory commentary), a review of a recent French book on the importance of religion, an analysis of a Muscovite chronicle from the Time of Troubles in the early seventeenth century, a short allegorical play condemning subservience to fashion, letters from readers describing particular families in dire financial distress, and letters from just such unfortunates, thanking other readers for sending them aid. Always the theme was the patriotism, wisdom, and kindness possessed by Russians of all eras and classes, so long as they remained loyal to ancestral ways and did not succumb to the evil temptations of the modern world.

Many literati held a low opinion of Glinka's work, as they did of Shishkov's. Batiushkov, for instance, considered Glinka to be "like the preacher of a crusade" and wondered: "Can one love ignorance? Can we love morals and customs from which centuries separate us, and, what is more, an entire century of enlightenment? . . . These patriots and ardent declaimers don't love or don't know how to love the Russian land." Zhukovskii likewise rejected "crude rapture à la Glinka."[96] Vigel', on the other hand, noted with satisfaction that Glinka "consistently extolled everything national and consistently reviled everything foreign," and he found that the *Messenger* performed a valuable service, especially for readers in the provinces. Shishkov was full of admiration: "It is with great pleasure that I read the *Russian Messenger,* which does not keep repeating the words *esthetics, education, enlightenment* and so forth [i.e., code words of the New Style] but always talks about genuine and pure morality." He applauded Glinka for "paying no heed to the fact that such writings of his displease many whose heads have been turned by the *new ideas;* he . . . sows the seeds of a right thinking . . . without trying to guess the future and without knowing whether the rain will drench them, or the sun warm them."[97]

Glinka was determined to preserve the *Messenger*'s independence from the powerful of society. Princess Dashkova showed an interest in writing for it, but Glinka objected to the Anglophile and Germanophobe tone of her articles and their collaboration soon ended. The same fate befell Rostopchin. After the fiasco with his play *News* early in 1808, Rostopchin had dashed off two furious letters attacking the play's audience. Glinka refused to publish them, arguing that they went too far in insulting the public. Rostopchin thereupon angrily renounced their collaboration. To this, Glinka responded coolly that he refused to cater to the whims of anyone. Their partnership was thus dissolved within a few weeks of its beginning (it would revive briefly at the end of 1809 and resume in full force only in 1812). Arakcheev, with whom Glinka's relations were generally good, once requested that the *Messenger* publish a series of letters flattering to himself from various individuals. Glinka politely but firmly declined. When he later told General Miloradovich about this, the general exclaimed, "And you did that with so frightening a man?"—to which Glinka responded, "What is a frightening man?" The *Messenger* was, after all, "battling . . . the giant of our time," Napoleon, and Glinka took this crusade too seriously to permit others to manipulate it. Quite possibly his account of these events is embellished, but there is no reason to doubt his wish to be the independent conscience of his fellow Russians, not a tool of the absolutist state. Other journalists attacked him as a xenophobic obscurantist, but he was undeterred, and the years between Tilsit and 1812 were so full of meaning and activity for him that attacks did not unduly disturb him. After his wedding in 1808, he was also a happy family man and felt at one with the common Russian on his walks about town: "Since people in Moscow knew me, they spoke to me without hesitation and openly. In a word, I lived among the people and shared in the life of the people."[98]

In his spare time, Glinka worked on other projects, including a history of the French Revolution that he published in 1809, *Mirror of the New Paris*.[99] It was a logical companion to the *Russian Messenger:* the latter glorified Russia; the former pilloried the degeneracy of France. The book reveals the familiarity with French and classical culture that he had acquired at the cadet corps, but his breathless accounts of revolutionary horrors brim with hostility and moral indignation.

In the introduction, he laid out his theory of the French Revolution. Between 1788 and 1793, he argued, Paris, the "capital of taste, intellect, *fashion* and enlightenment," had turned into "a den of monsters and villainy." The reason for this metamorphosis lay in "morals and passions. Passions gave to luxury power over virtue, to flippancy [power] over reason; it was passions that introduced horror and death into the residence of taste and fashion." In general, he asserted, "the morals, way of thinking and qualities of people explain the cause and consequence of all social transformations."[100]

The *Mirror* never advances very far beyond this initial premise. Glinka's history begins with a long retrospective on the decline of morals after the death of Louis XIV. All of French society was affected by this decay, he wrote, but it was most pronounced among the aristocracy and at court. Dwindling respect for caste was another ominous symptom. Art played a role as well, since the popularity of Beaumarchais's *Marriage of Figaro,* which mocked "all that is held sacred in society—matrimony, the courts, modesty, etc., etc.," showed that "the minds of the inhabitants of Paris were prepared for a decisive transformation."[101] His portrayal of the revolution itself is relentlessly grim. Louis XVI, though an honest and devoted monarch, was surrounded by yes-men and abandoned by the nobility. The Third Estate's delegates were bookish dreamers with no experience of life's realities, and their Declaration of the Rights of Man was a hoax to mislead the masses and provide a cover for the crimes of Marat and Robespierre; they even took these principles to the bizarre extreme of granting civil equality to Negroes and Jews.[102] The outcome of the revolution was that life in France had become gloomy and anxious; extravagant wealth and bitter poverty had increased, as had greed; people feared each other as possible secret-police informers; and even courtesy toward ladies and the elderly had disappeared. The causes of these horrors were clearly identifiable: *"vengeance, ambition, envy, vainglory, greed* and *lust for power."* Glinka left rather vague the practical significance of these diabolical vices, but they formed an obvious contrast to the virtues of old Muscovy. "Examine the nature of these passions," he wrote, "and then you can predict all that will ensue from them. Moral and political events are foreshadowed with the same precision as natural phenomena." As he wrote in the preface to the second volume, with his usual simplicity and candor: "Our impartial countrymen, when they read the *Mirror of the New Paris,* will be even happier to have been born as Russians and in Russia."[103]

Criticism of society's moral hollowness had been a staple of Russian literature for decades, but the arguments of Glinka, Shishkov, and others were original in two important ways. First, because the Enlightenment had now become associated with revolution, these writers attacked it far more scathingly and uncompromisingly than had their predecessors. Second, in a pan-European cultural atmosphere of romantic Francophobia, they systematically grounded their response to Enlightenment society not in universal notions of morality but specifically in Russia's national past. Thus their romantic nationalism marks a departure from the thought of the late eighteenth century: it was the beginning of the explicit, self-conscious amalgamation of a rejection of the West, on the one hand, with conservative hostility toward changing Russia's sociopolitical structures, on the other. Despite the cultural umbilical cord tying them to Europe, Glinka and Shishkov constituted an essential link between the Western culture of the eighteenth century and the Russian conservative nationalism of the nineteenth.

Aside from Rostopchin and Glinka, the third of the notable Moscow conservatives was Nikolai Mikhailovich Karamzin, the literary nemesis of Shishkov. Although a more profound thinker and a more gifted writer than the other two, Karamzin was not, as they were, a prolific writer of political tracts that influenced public opinion in the years before 1812. For that reason he is less important to this study of Russian conservatism, although his contributions to Russian culture were greater and have been sufficiently recognized by scholars. Given the considerable literature that exists about him, I limit myself here to a broad overview of his background and intellectual development.[104]

Nikolai M. Karamzin

Karamzin was born in 1766 near Samara, by the Volga, in a modest noble family. Pugachev's rebellion ravaged the region during his childhood, the first in a series of upheavals (the French Revolution, the 1812 invasion, and the Decembrist revolt) that impressed upon him society's need for strong government. Life by the Volga was ruggedly patriarchal, and Karamzin, though given to melancholy daydreaming and the reading of French novels, acquired a strong sense of gentry pride and identity. In 1777 he was sent to Moscow, where he attended a boarding school that, much like Glinka's cadet corps, inculcated moral precepts and *sensibilité*. These were also the years of his first contact with Moscow's intellectual life. From 1781 to 1784 he served intermittently in the Preobrazhenskii Guards regiment, and in Simbirsk in 1784 he became involved with freemasonry.

In 1785 he moved back to Moscow, where he began his literary career as a writer and translator for one of Novikov's journals. He admired Novikov's interest in philanthropy and the spreading of "enlightenment" through morally uplifting literature, but he was not attracted to masonic religious views, and he opposed the occultism and withdrawal from the world advocated by the wing of the movement known as Rosicrucianism or Martinism. As he moved away from freemasonry and became interested in English sentimentalist literature, his thinking continued to revolve around ethical questions, and he rejected the rationalism of the *Encyclopédistes*. Like Shishkov and Glinka, he believed in progress through moral improvement, not political or social change. Thus he and Novikov (and Glinka and Shishkov) thought peasants deserved benign treatment, but they did not question the legitimacy of serfdom. Instead, they expected all to be content with their station in life.

In 1789–1790 Karamzin undertook a lengthy trip to Western Europe, which he subsequently described in his *Letters of a Russian Traveler*. He exhibited a sentimental enthusiasm for religious tolerance, the idyllic life of Swiss shepherds, and the notions of liberty and virtue. His lack of interest in politics, however, is apparent from his decision, upon hearing of the French Revolution, to postpone visiting France and explore picturesque Switzerland instead.[105]

Yet the Russian monarchy's repressive policies after 1789 forced him to come to terms with politics and with his own ambivalence toward the French Revolution. The vision outlined in Plato's *Republic* appealed to him in theory: a reign of virtue in which the absence of freedom is the price for absolute happiness. But this conception was unrealistic, he thought. One reason was that it required the abolition of property, the institution that he regarded as the root of social conflicts. Given the impossibility of abolishing it outright, he preferred that it be maintained in a regulated form—through serfdom—rather than in the chaotic freedom of private property. Karamzin's other objection to the Platonic utopia was political. The features of "republican" government that most attracted him were virtue and order, which in turn required a strong government. As a result, Iurii Lotman has argued, he was in principle sympathetic to Robespierre and the early Napoleon and rejected both democracy and tyranny in favor of an authoritarian state governed by wisdom and committed to virtue. However, the turmoil of the French Revolution, Napoleonic aggression, and Paul I's despotism convinced him that a dictatorship of virtue was a utopian dream. These experiences reinforced his tendency to separate morality from politics and reconciled his belief in social progress through education and "enlightenment" (an ideal he considered "republican") with support for the sociopolitical status quo as a prerequisite for that progress. As his brother-in-law Viazemskii later put it, Karamzin was "a republican with his soul but a monarchist with his head."[106]

Serfdom, according to Karamzin, was an essential part of the Russian social order whose abolition could be envisioned only in the distant future, perhaps fifty or one hundred years hence. An enemy of oligarchic political rule by the aristocracy, he nonetheless vigorously defended the gentry's social privileges. Government should be omnipotent within the confines of its own jurisdiction (with the restraint of its own laws preventing it from becoming arbitrary or despotic), so that it could guarantee public tranquillity and security, but it should not interfere in the social spheres of life that were the prerogatives of society. Among these were culture, individual liberty, the distinctive rights and duties of society's existing castes, and national tradition.

Carrying Robespierre's ideas to their extreme, ironic conclusion, Karamzin argued that republican government required an impossible degree of civic virtue and must therefore remain a dream. Instead, from his extensive study of Russian history, he concluded that autocracy, restricted by society's moral code and by laws that the monarch voluntarily prescribed to himself, offered the sturdiest guarantee of good government without tyranny or anarchy. The monarch would act as an honest broker between the disparate interests of society, whose members would know that their civil (but not political) rights were protected by his laws, and would be free to pursue their own moral self-improvement. Progress would come through the gradual spread of "enlightenment" and through the revival of Russia's national language and traditions, at the expense of a culture based on indiscriminately imitating foreigners.[107]

Karamzin's opinions on European affairs early in Alexander's reign broadly resembled those of his friend Rostopchin. Both applauded Napoleon for restoring stability in France, and his rise confirmed Karamzin's belief in the virtues of autocracy. His views on foreign policy, like his support for absolutism, were driven largely by pragmatic considerations. He agreed with Rostopchin that Russia's *raison d'état* argued against military intervention in Europe, and he did not clearly take sides in the war that erupted between Britain and France in 1803.[108] However, he did not share Rostopchin's Machiavellian enthusiasm for grand foreign policy schemes. Karamzin was by instinct a cautious isolationist who found war distasteful and believed that Russia best served its own interests and honor by avoiding European conflicts. He criticized Paul's military forays, advocated compromise with Napoleon, and worried in 1805–1806 that Alexander had mired Russia in a war from which it could gain little, even in the event of victory. When Russia abruptly became France's ally in 1807, he was dismayed, on grounds that this both endangered Russian security and weakened its credibility among the European states opposed to Napoleon, but he continued until 1812 to favor conciliation with France.[109]

Like Rostopchin but unlike Shishkov, Karamzin considered Russia an integral part of European civilization.[110] Whereas the admiral's fully elaborated conception of Russian culture was backward-looking and isolationist, Karamzin's was rooted in post-Petrine Russia's synthesis with the West. Shishkov saw modern education as morally and politically subversive; Karamzin equated "enlightenment" with progress. Both men opposed the French Revolution and the reforms of Alexander I, but unlike Shishkov, Karamzin did not advocate a static social ideal drawn from the past. As he told a friend, "I am an enemy of revolutions, but peaceful evolution is necessary. It is most possible under monarchical government." Shishkov rejected the possibility of progress; Karamzin believed in it. Karamzin held that Russia's present was generally superior to its Muscovite past, and that the source of its national identity lay not in the ancestral way of life but in timeless principles of monarchical statecraft. Shishkov identified with the people and their culture (as he imagined them), whereas Karamzin identified with the state; Karamzin believed in a dynamic historical process, while Shishkov distinguished only between stasis and decline. These differences have led Mark Al'tshuller to conclude that Shishkov was "a Slavophile, whereas Karamzin, despite his opposition to the tsar's hasty reform plans, was a Westernizer."[111] As he grew older and more conservative, however, Karamzin became increasingly preoccupied with Russia's distinctive national heritage. Especially after Alexander I named him Russia's official historian in 1803, his admiration for the Petrine reforms gave way to a heightened appreciation for Muscovite achievements and to opposition to further Westernization.

Despite broad conceptual disagreements, Shishkov and Karamzin often held similar views on specific issues. Both admired Catherine II but not her successors. They loved theoretical speculation but were products of an essentially apolitical eighteenth-century culture and did not feel at home in the more politicized atmosphere of the nineteenth. Neither took much interest in constitutional questions, and indeed they viewed such concerns as (at best) a distraction from the true business of government or (at worst) tricks employed by people bent on subverting the state. Their conception of state and society was rooted in a tradition of personal power relationships (although Karamzin's interest in legal codification suggests greater sophistication in this area than Shishkov exhibited). Both took autocracy and serfdom for granted as the basis of the social order and could imagine no limitations on either, other than voluntary self-restraint grounded in religion and ethics. In foreign policy as well, they broadly agreed: they condemned Alexander's rashness in first going to war in 1805 and then in 1807 accepting the humiliation of Tilsit (although Shishkov later showed greater enthusiasm than Karamzin for the war of 1812).

Karamzin and Shishkov represented different sociocultural types. Both came from modest provincial families and had ties to freemasonry, but that was the extent of the similarities. Shishkov, who was twelve years older, received a technical education and spent his career in the navy in the capital, while Karamzin was trained in the humanities and lived as a professional writer in Moscow. Shishkov lived a characteristic noble life of state service, uncritical loyalty to throne and altar, and the typical contemporary amalgam of Russian and foreign cultural influences. Only his philological ideas set him apart from his fellows, and even there his moralism, lack of formal training, and idiosyncratic theories reflected his generation's cultural experiences and attitudes. Karamzin was an independent man of letters and a more reclusive personality with only vague religious beliefs. Unlike most nobles, he cared little for service or agriculture and lived almost exclusively for writing. His uncommonly broad education was further enhanced by a lifetime of intellectual pursuits. His thinking about culture and politics reached a much more sophisticated level than Shishkov's; it was also influenced by a different social milieu, since Karamzin hobnobbed with the Moscow aristocracy while Shishkov lived among courtiers and bureaucrats. They were similar in the small direct influence that foreign conservatives had on their thinking. Karamzin appears to have had little interest in the ideas of Edmund Burke (whom he had heard in London) or Joseph de Maistre (whom he knew personally), despite the parallels between his ideas and theirs. But this does not mean, of course, that he was unaffected by the intellectual climate which they and other prominent European conservative thinkers helped to create.[112]

Perhaps the greatest influence on Shishkov was the St. Petersburg of Catherine, where he spent most of his life between the ages of thirteen and forty-two. This environment focused his thinking on the relationship between Russian tradition, which he knew from his rural childhood and medieval literature, and Europe, which he encountered on his naval missions. Karamzin, on the other hand, was educated in Moscow, with its less conspicuous foreign influences, and traveled abroad for the first time (at the impressionable age of twenty-three) just as the French Revolution broke out. Unlike Shishkov, he took a lively interest in the nature of the foreign societies he encountered. After his return, he witnessed the police harassment and arrest of his freemason friends and the strict censorship that affected his own journalistic work. He had grown up in the areas hardest hit by the Pugachev revolt, and he was only thirty when Paul I came to power and provided a further lesson about the nature of power and government. Shishkov, too, witnessed Paul's despotism, but he did not fit it into a systematic theoretical pattern, except perhaps for broad assumptions about morality and human nature.

It is significant that Shishkov's formative years occurred a decade earlier than Karamzin's, in a time when absolutism was unchallenged abroad and autocracy and serfdom unquestioned in Russia. As a result, he took the permanence of these structures for granted, and there was a note of outraged incomprehension in his remarks about those who attacked the ancien régime. Karamzin, on the other hand, had witnessed these challenges at important junctures in his life, and his historical studies further convinced him of autocracy's fragility and the danger of social chaos. His defense of them had a more urgent and anxious air, because unlike Shishkov he realized intuitively that the ancien régime was not invulnerable.

Karamzin, Shishkov, and Glinka contributed to the development of Russian conservatism mainly through literature, an arena in which they could ignore or finesse the glaring disharmony between their ideologies' theoretical conceptions and reality. Rostopchin, on the contrary, was a practical statesman and serf owner who lived in the "real world" of the French-speaking, semieducated, authoritarian elite and its oppressed peasant masses. Even in his theoretical views he was therefore hard and disillusioned, essentially a Karamzin without rose-colored glasses or an ethical agenda. He did not believe (as did Karamzin and basically also Shishkov) that society needed to improve morally as a precondition for harmony and stability. Nor, as a loyal servant of Paul I, did Rostopchin share his friend's fear of despotism and faith in the rule of law. He lacked the same concern for fostering a Russian culture independent from Europe, and wrote and published in Russian only when he wished to arouse xenophobia. His driving force was political ambition, of which Karamzin had none. Unlike the others, who adopted the lofty moral tone that was a legacy of the German *Aufklärung*,[113] he cultivated the elegant, facile wit and sarcastic skepticism popularized by the French Enlightenment, as well as the boorishness of a backwoods landowner. More than any other leading conservative, Rostopchin spoke for the sociopolitical interests and cultural preferences of the Europeanized old regime of the late eighteenth century. That, paradoxically, may have made him the only true "conservative" (in the sense of a defender of the existing order) in the entire group. Yet, theory and attitude aside, Rostopchin and Karamzin agreed on many substantive points, especially regarding the threat to the social order from enemies both external

(Napoleon) and internal (the Unofficial Committee, Speranskii, Alexander I himself) and the deplorable moral character of Russian society: the peasants were drunkards, officials corrupt, and the court filled with hypocrites. Hence their impassioned pleas on behalf of serfdom and autocracy, their hostility to reform and their nakedly selfish defense of noble privileges.[114]

While there was no formal "gentry opposition" movement, there was a vast body of opinion that regarded the preservation of autocracy and of gentry rights as government's most urgent task. This opinion was centered in Moscow; Karamzin was its most profound thinker and Rostopchin its most important political leader. Shishkov and Glinka belonged to a different wing of conservative and nationalist thought. More optimistic than Rostopchin and Karamzin, they saw in the "national spirit" an effective guarantor of the existing order. Rather than merely stave off that order's decline, they believed they could indeed revitalize it with ancestral traditions that survived behind Russia's Westernized façade. Unlike Rostopchin, for example, they argued (when they considered such matters at all) that class tensions and political oppression were aberrations, a misunderstanding among Russians about the essence of their national identity. Consequently, their justifications of serfdom were less cynical than Rostopchin's, and they went through fewer intellectual contortions than Karamzin. They sincerely believed that the peasants were satisfied with their lot, and so they did not experience the fears for the society's stability that tormented Karamzin and Rostopchin.

The significance of the Moscow conservatives lay not only in their shaping and echoing opinions that were widespread among the nobility of the old capital and beyond. These men also had important opportunities to bring these opinions to the monarch's attention through the intermediary of his sister Grand Duchess Ekaterina Pavlovna, as I will attempt to show in the next chapter.

CHAPTER FOUR

The "Demigoddess of Tver'" and the "Lovers of the Russian Word"

Grand Duchess Ekaterina and her husband, Prince Georg of Oldenburg, spent three happy years in Tver' after he took up his governor-generalship in 1809.[1] Mariia Fedorovna twice visited her daughter there, and Ekaterina took trips to St. Petersburg three times during 1810 and 1811. She also frequently corresponded with her brother Alexander I, and they met at least every three months, as Tver' was a convenient way station between Petersburg and Moscow, a route the emperor traveled occasionally. She frequently hosted receptions for local society and became popular for her charming demeanor and friendliness to all regardless of rank or status. At one such event, Alexander even felt reminded of one of his palaces and declared approvingly, "What you have here, sister, is a small Peterhof." Yet provincial life was lonely, and such festivities were not enough to compensate for her isolation. So she sought to dispel her ennui by reading and by cultivating whatever interesting people could be induced to visit from time to time. She was especially attracted to individuals who shared her political outlook, which was nationalistic and conservative. (In 1818, as queen of Württemberg, she wrote that the German constitutions were "nothing but utter nonsense. . . . Good laws that are enforced, there's the best constitution.") Her guests included Joseph de Maistre, General Bagration, and her brother Konstantin Pavlovich. She likewise took an interest in cultural figures, such as the painter Kiprenskii, the poets Batiushkov and Gnedich (perhaps also Shishkov), and various Moscow art patrons and professors. When Baron vom Stein traveled to Petersburg to escape Napoleon, he, too, stopped over in Tver'.[2]

Grand Duchess Ekaterina Pavlovna

Among her habitués was Rostopchin, whom she had probably known since Paul's reign. She had been almost thirteen at the time of her father's death and appreciated Rostopchin's loyalty to him. (Her brother Alexander never openly endorsed Paul's murder, which may be why the memory of their father does not appear to have harmed the two siblings' close relationship.) Rostopchin astutely reminded her of these ties, but he was sincere—after all, he *had* refused to disavow Paul even after 1801, when it might have benefited him politically. The ghost of the murdered emperor, which drove a wedge between Rostopchin and Alexander, formed a link between him and the grand duchess. It also gave him the opportunity to entertain her with his talent as a raconteur. As one unsympathetic witness later recalled, his stories "had great success, and people died laughing at them, even though they told—and in front of whom?—about the tsar-benefactor, who had permitted the storyteller to move up in the world by showering him with favors and honors." After her death, Rostopchin wrote: "I grieve deeply for her for the friendship she showed me, and for the concern I felt for her as a child of Paul's; she was the only one about whom I had no right to complain."[3] This was an honest friendship, but she was also his best hope for a return to imperial favor. "I would be arrogant," he humbly wrote to her, "to imagine that I could distinguish myself before her who inspires amazement and love in all Russians." Nevertheless, he continued, "my devotion to . . . the Father gives me the hope that the perceptive gaze of the Daughter, his equal in mind and heart, might one day be directed at him who until now has been moved only by honor and loyalty."[4]

For several years, Rostopchin's strategy produced disappointing results. Ekaterina arranged for her brother to meet with him during their visit to Moscow in

December 1809 and even convinced Alexander to ask him to report on the state of Moscow's charitable institutions. Rostopchin zealously devoted himself to this really rather modest task, and produced a thoughtful and substantive account.[5] When he arrived in Petersburg on February 9, 1810, to submit his findings, he instantly set in motion the capital's rumor mill. He was known as the protégé of the reputedly influential grand duchess, and it was understood, Sardinia's ambassador de Maistre wrote on February 21, "that she was involved . . . in [his] resurrection." Rostopchin's cocky attitude set tongues wagging, and his new status was clear from the fact that he dined with the emperor twenty-seven times in 1810, whereas until then he had not done so once in all the years since Paul's death (nor would he in 1811). On February 26, the Sardinian envoy marveled at his "triumphant demeanor; he visibly snubbed the Ambassador of France [Caulaincourt], to whom he did not even have himself introduced at Court." Sensing a political shift, "everyone bows down before the new arrival. The Emperor was asking him the other day: 'How are you doing, Rostopchin?' 'Very well, Sire, but I have a pain here' (placing his finger on his cheek). 'How can that be?' 'Sire, it's because everyone kisses me.'" As de Maistre was writing these lines, however, Rostopchin's ambitions had already been humbled. Reacting perhaps to his annoying self-assurance, open contempt for Caulaincourt, and ties to the opposition to Speranskii, Alexander sent him home with merely an honorific promotion (to senior gentleman of the chamber). The emperor specified that no official duties were attached to this new rank, and that he was on leave from state service and free not to live in the capital.[6]

It was during Alexander's visit to Moscow in late 1809 that Rostopchin first introduced Ekaterina Pavlovna to Karamzin. She instantly took a liking to Karamzin, and even sought his appointment as governor of Tver', which would permit her to enjoy his company and, she assured him, would not interfere with his historical studies. (He declined politely.) He first visited her in Tver' in February 1810, and then again in late November or early December.[7] Her relationship with Rostopchin was based on memories of Paul, shared political nationalism, and the gregarious, ambitious personality they had in common, whereas Karamzin appealed to her intellect and cultural patriotism. Indeed, she (like Rostopchin) prided herself on being less "foreign" than others in the aristocracy and the imperial family. When she had first moved to Tver', the governor's wife was overheard saying that it was "truly strange to hear what a good command of Russian the grand duchess has." Ekaterina promptly sought her out and pointedly declared herself "astonished . . . that you found it strange that I, a Russian, speak good Russian?" History also interested her, and she listened with rapt attention as Karamzin read from the manuscript on which he was working; to Western-educated Russians, Karamzin's patriotic and monarchistic history of Russia— like the more simplistic version in Glinka's *Russian Messenger,* which neither Karamzin, Rostopchin, nor the grand duchess appear to have read—was a revelation. The spellbound audience "was afraid, even by an expression of pleasure, to interrupt the reading, which was both skillful and fascinating, [and] listened with imperturbable attention."[8]

Karamzin became something of a mentor for her. In her letters she called him her "teacher" and attempted, evidently under his prodding, to write in Russian. This was a difficult exercise: usually she began a letter in Russian and then switched into French, with a remark such as "This was a great effort; only you could make me do it," or "You make me perform miracles by the desire I have to please you." He sent her Russian books, and she reported to him on her translations and her study of grammar. Her letters give no details on these pursuits, but they reflect her curiosity about Russian culture and, more generally, the degree to which nationalist values were penetrating even the most cosmopolitan sectors of the aristocracy.[9] He visited Tver' again in February, March, June, and November of 1811, usually for a week or two, and other trips were planned but for various reasons had to be canceled. Karamzin wholeheartedly reciprocated the affection shown him by the woman he called the "demigoddess of Tver'."[10]

During his second visit, in the fall of 1810, the two apparently discussed politics, and she asked him to lay out in writing his criticisms of Alexander I's policies. Evidently she explained that she wished eventually to show this essay to the emperor. Richard Pipes argues that the entire episode was arranged by the grand duchess, who used the unsuspecting Karamzin for her own political purposes: it was probably she who took the initiative, because Karamzin (unlike Rostopchin) was averse to polemics and uninterested in state office, he devoted all the time he could to scholarship, and as imperial historian he depended on a salary that could be revoked by Alexander. "What could he have gained from criticizing the tsar and his advisers?" Pipes asks, and answers: "Exactly nothing." Wolfgang Mitter, on the other hand, argues (perhaps more convincingly) that Karamzin and Rostopchin were active in the Moscow "gentry opposition" that hated Speranskii and that encouraged Karamzin to argue its case before Ekaterina and her brother. J. Laurence Black makes a similar argument.[11]

In any event, Karamzin went to work after returning home to Moscow around the beginning of December, and on February 3, 1811, he returned to Tver' with the finished document. He stayed for two weeks, during which Ekaterina familiarized herself with it, and then he went back to Moscow. On February 19, she informed him that the emperor would be coming to Tver' and she wanted the two of them to meet. She did not, however, indicate that she planned to show the essay to Alexander at that time. Karamzin and the emperor met on March 16–19 and dined together several times. Alexander offered him a high government post (which he declined), and, on March 18, they heatedly debated the topic of "autocracy" after a reading from Karamzin's unfinished manuscript on Russian history. Most likely, Karamzin defended his absolutist conceptions against Speranskii's reform plans. (These were known to the grand duchess, who may have discussed them with her friends.) After that conversation, unbeknownst to Karamzin, she passed on his essay to her brother; the author was informed only when he asked to have his manuscript back.

Whether Alexander ever read Karamzin's *Memoir on Ancient and Modern Russia* is not certain, but its basic ideas were surely communicated to him orally by Karamzin himself or by Ekaterina Pavlovna. Since the grand duchess had sworn Karamzin to secrecy, the *Memoir* (unlike Rostopchin's writings) was not supposed to become known to the general public. It was, however, the most systematic theoretical exposition of the gentry opposition's thinking. Therefore an important document, it reflected the opinion of an influential social stratum, and the ideas contained in it were conveyed in some form to the emperor himself.[12]

The *Memoir on Ancient and Modern Russia* was a blistering attack on the policies of Alexander and his advisers, although it cautiously avoided naming the advisers and exempted the emperor from all personal blame. It has been thoroughly analyzed elsewhere,[13] so my intention here is to summarize its ideas in order to place them in the conservative context of the time. The text (about one hundred printed pages) consists of three discrete sections: an introduction covering Russian history from its beginnings until 1801, a survey of events since 1801, and a sketchy set of positive recommendations for the monarch.

Karamzin's view of history was strikingly at odds with Admiral Shishkov's, who believed, with the romantic nationalists, that Russia's identity lay in its *people* and their culture. Karamzin followed an older, Petrine conception in seeing the *state* at the heart of Russia's national existence. After reviewing the greatness of Kievan Rus', the internecine strife of the appanage era, and the restoration of a unified state by Muscovy, the author of the *Memoir* concluded that "Russia was founded by victories and by monocracy, she perished from the division of authority, and was saved by wise autocracy." The country was "a compound of ancient customs of the east, carried to Europe by the Slavs and reactivated, so to say, by our long connection with the Mongols; of Byzantine customs which we had adopted together with Christianity; and of certain German customs, imparted to us by the Normans."[14]

Karamzin thus regarded Russian culture as a product of historical forces, whereas the less sophisticated Shishkov implied that it had somehow emerged, fully formed, out of the mists of the past. They shared a high opinion of Kievan Rus', which Karamzin regarded as having been "of all [contemporary] states . . . the most civilized." However, he attributed the achievements of Muscovite culture in part to its interaction with Europe, an emphasis that Shishkov avoided. To Karamzin, the Time of Troubles proved that autocratic government was vital to Russia, so he hailed the election of Mikhail Romanov as a glorious milestone. Russia began to recognize Europe's "obvious superiority" in things military and diplomatic, in education, and in "the very manners of society," for Europe "had left us far behind in civil enlightenment." Russia began to change, but "by a means of natural evolution, without paroxysms and without violence. We borrowed but as if unwillingly, adapting the foreign to the native, and blending the new with the old."[15]

Shishkov and Karamzin both projected onto the Muscovite past what they wished to see in Russia's future: Shishkov, a tradition of cultural autarky; Karamzin, a fusion of Russian and European culture that would preserve those native elements that remained viable and were emblematic of the national heritage. Following this logic, Karamzin took a stand that had been taboo to Shishkov and Glinka (Shcherbatov's essay *On the Corruption of Morals in Russia,* which had violated the taboo two decades earlier, was not published until 1858)[16] but became increasingly common among conservative nationalists in the nineteenth century: he harshly criticized Peter the Great. A nation's inner strength, he reasoned, derived from patriotism, which "is nothing else than respect for our national dignity." How did it contribute to "enlightenment" that Russians were humiliated by being forced to change their dress and shave their beards? Granted, Westernization had improved Russia's science and technology, and even its occasionally "depraved" morals (a point Shishkov would have disputed), but the country suffered from the cultural divide now separating the nobles from the rest of society (a view shared by Shishkov) and from a profound loss of national pride.

Like Rostopchin, but unlike Shishkov or Glinka, Karamzin stressed this functional aspect of patriotism; what mattered was not the spiritual substance of "Russianness" but rather the integrity of the national identity, whatever its content. The seventeenth century had struck a better balance than the eighteenth, since "our ancestors, while assimilating many advantages which were to be found in foreign customs, never lost the conviction that an Orthodox Russian was the most perfect citizen and *Holy Rus'* the foremost state in the world." However, "would we have today the audacity, after having spent over a century in the school of foreigners, to boast of our civic pride?" Like Shishkov, he saw in this foreign influence a political threat. Russians, who had earlier viewed Europeans as infidels, now considered them brothers: "For whom was it easier to conquer Russia—for *infidels* or for *brothers? That is, whom was she likely to resist better?"[17]

Karamzin argued that, "should we compare all the known epochs of Russian history, virtually all would agree that Catherine [II]'s epoch was the happiest for Russian citizens." He praised her expansionism and wise management of the state, but like Shishkov deplored the moral dissolution afflicting all of society under her rule, as well as the growing corruption, craving for European luxuries, and influence of foreigners, and he contended that her reforms of the state had often been poorly suited to Russian realities. The empire had enjoyed great successes in education, diplomacy, and war, "but we lacked decent upbringing, firm principles, and social morality." Still, her reign had been blissful when measured against that of her son. Unlike his friend Rostopchin, Karamzin regarded Paul I as a tyrant comparable to Ivan the Terrible and recalled the public joy at his death. He condemned the conspiracy against Paul, but mentioning it in writing was in itself a daring act, since the subject remained highly sensitive.[18]

He warned Alexander to resist the temptation of constitutionalism: "'You may do everything, but you may not limit your authority by law!'" Like

Shishkov, Derzhavin, Vigel', and others, he was sympathetic to the "Senatorial Party" of the beginning of Alexander's reign and opposed bureaucratic government by powerful ministers who "wedged themselves between the sovereign and the people" (that is, the nobility) and cut him off from the experienced (and socially conservative) counsel of the Senate. He likewise attacked Speranskii, although not by name. Russia needed a government staffed by, and attentive to, the best minds in Russia yet respectful of the traditional order, he argued. This had been the case under Catherine, when the state had kept to a minimum its role in noble affairs. But now, he complained, it was governed by men whose conception of the state was rooted in a lifeless, authoritarian, legalistic formalism, men "distinguished more for the art of clerkship than for that of statesmanship." "The reforms accomplished so far," he concluded, "give us no reason to believe that future reforms will prove useful; we anticipate them more with dread than with hope, for it is dangerous to tamper with ancient political structures."[19]

His assessment of Alexander's foreign policy was equally unflattering. He agreed with Rostopchin that, in its relations with France before 1805, Russia "had lost nothing and had nothing to fear." Austria had kept France in check and was itself restrained by Prussia. Russia, the "magnanimous arbiter of Europe," could be hurt only if a new war changed the status quo in favor of either Napoleon or the Habsburgs. Karamzin was dismayed that Russia had fought "to help England and Vienna, that is, to serve them as a tool in the quarrel with France, without any particular advantage to herself." Had the Third Coalition triumphed, the victorious Austrians "would have proclaimed us an Asiatic country, as Bonaparte had done," and squeezed Russia out of the circle of European great powers. Having blundered into the war, Russia had the opportunity to make peace on favorable terms before Austerlitz, but "the ways of the Lord are unfathomable: we wanted battle!" These two mistakes were compounded by a third: Tilsit, which entailed the disgraceful alliance with Napoleon, the costly trade war with Britain, an attack on innocent Sweden, and the restoration of a Polish state. "Thus, our mighty efforts, having led to Austerlitz and the Peace of Tilsit, consolidated French hegemony over Europe and made us, through [the Grand Duchy of] Warsaw, the neighbors of Napoleon." The most prudent course of action was now to avoid antagonizing the French, but "what will happen next? God knows."[20]

Various other areas of government policy also came under Karamzin's fire. The militia of 1806–1807 had suffered from inadequate preparation and leadership. The educational reforms had also failed, because the state had simply copied the structure of German universities while ignoring the unique conditions that prevailed in Russia. He criticized the educational requirements for promotion in government service, arguing that, while young officials might be expected to obtain a university degree, "it is unfair to confront an old official with new conditions of service," and it was also unreasonable to expect officials to develop expertise in areas unrelated to their own work. These measures were typical of the bureaucracy's tendency to address problems by simply transplanting foreign institutions without regard to Russian circumstances. Karamzin's lengthy discussion of state finance criticized the management of fiscal and monetary policy as well, especially the recent financial reforms proposed by Speranskii.[21]

Like virtually all Russian conservatives, Karamzin opposed any reform of serfdom. He asserted that, since serfs were descended from both free peasants and slaves and the two were now indistinguishable, the crown could not liberate the serfs without depriving the gentry of their rights over the slaves. Emancipation would be an economic disaster for the peasants, he wrote, because the nobility would retain all the land—its rightful property—and the new tenant farmers would move from place to place in search of more accommodating landlords, thereby interfering with agricultural work and tax collection. Besides, abolishing serfdom meant ending the manorial powers of the gentry, thus saddling the state with the huge task of administering the peasants; the state might not rise to this challenge, the peasants would be abandoned to their vices (especially drunkenness), and anyway corrupt officials would be no kinder to the peasants than the nobles had been. The peasants' moral decline since their enserfment had rendered them unfit for freedom, he claimed. Instead of seeking to liberate the serfs, therefore, the government should content itself with cracking down on abusive serf owners. "In conclusion," he wrote, summarizing in a single sentence the essence of gentry conservatism, "we have this to say to the good monarch: 'Sire! history will not reproach you for the evil which you have inherited (assuming serfdom actually is an unequivocal evil), but you will answer before God, conscience, and posterity for every harmful consequence of your own statutes.'"[22]

He also condemned Speranskii's plan to adopt a modified *Code Napoléon* as Russian law, on the grounds that the code was incompatible with Russia's legal tradition and sociopolitical structure. Like Shishkov and Rostopchin, and so many radicals and conservatives in Europe's overheated politics after 1789, he simply labeled as traitors those who did not share his views: "Is this why we have toiled for one hundred years or so to produce our own comprehensive code, in order now to confess solemnly to all Europe that we are fools, and bow our gray heads to a book pasted together in Paris by six or seven ex-lawyers and ex-Jacobins?" Instead, he suggested compiling Russia's existing laws as the basis for a legal code—precisely the approach Speranskii ultimately used under Nicholas I to create Russia's law code.[23]

Karamzin then offered his own remedies for the problems he had identified. His advice was simple: the legal description of an office mattered less than the character of the officeholder. "Men, not documents, govern," he asserted, and they must be motivated through the judicious use of incentives and deterrents. Catherine II was a model worth emulating, for she had placed her trust in carefully screened lieutenants, not constitutional formalities. "Ask not, how are the laws of a state written? How many ministers are there? Is there a supreme council? But ask: what sort of judges, what sort of landlords are there? . . . Phrases are for newspapers—for governments, there are only principles." The health of the state, he further argued, was inseparable from the well-being of the nobility, which must be made more exclusive, and so the practice of ennobling commoners who had risen in the state service should be curtailed. In fact, certain service ranks should be reserved for nobles: "Noble status should not depend on rank, but rank on noble status."[24] Limiting the emperor's ability to reshape arbitrarily the country's social elite was essential, to Karamzin, if the autocracy was to avoid becoming a tyrannical despotism.

In conclusion, Karamzin summarized his view of society: "The gentry and the clergy, the Senate and the Synod as repositories of laws, over all the sovereign, the only legislator, the autocratic source of authority—this is the foundation of the Russian monarchy." Alexander should "in the future be more cautious in introducing new political institutions, . . . paying more attention to men than to forms." Specifically, he should attend to Russia's fiscal and foreign trade problems, make peace with the Ottomans, and avoid another war with Napoleon, "even at the cost of so-called honor—a luxury only strong states can afford, and one which is by no means identical either with their basic interests or with their self-preservation." Only these measures would restore public trust in the emperor. Meanwhile, "Russia is seething with dissatisfaction. Complaints are heard in the palaces and in the cottages; the people lack confidence as well as enthusiasm for the government, and condemn strongly its aims and policies."[25]

Following the *Memoir* episode, Karamzin continued to assist Ekaterina in her efforts to acquaint herself and her husband with Russian culture, but in the months leading up to the war with France in 1812 he took no further part in political life. Not so Rostopchin, who, stymied in his first attempt to regain imperial favor, also carried on his friendship with her and his efforts to position himself as the spokesman of the "gentry opposition."

Rostopchin showed great skill at identifying and appropriating the major themes of contemporary politics that were effective across old-regime Europe. Nationalist Francophobia, popularized in Russia by Shishkov and others, was one. Conspiracy theories were another: ever since 1789 and with growing frequency, both conservatives and revolutionaries had invoked dastardly plots by secret organizations to explain away inconvenient realities. After 1815, the emperor would become similarly convinced that a *comité directeur* based somewhere in Western Europe must be orchestrating the revolutions dogging his foreign policy. From 1789 to 1815 there were widespread conservative fears about the Illuminati (a short-lived German group that had been suppressed in the 1780s but became synonymous with subversive conspiracy to conservatives across Europe) and other masonic societies, about which little was known and which were widely regarded as revolutionary. "Illuminism," like "Martinism," became a conveniently vague cliché, used indiscriminately against anyone associated with revolution or reform. As with his *Thoughts Aloud on the Staircase of Honor,* it is difficult to determine whether Rostopchin's arguments reflected genuine beliefs or whether he simply adopted the political language of the age.[26] This time, however, he would proceed not through an appeal to public opinion but by the more traditional route of court politics.

In 1810 Rostopchin set out to convince Ekaterina (whose opinion of freemasonry was not unfavorable) of the "Martinist" peril and of the emperor's need to know of the threat. On April 14, he promised her "a history of the corporation of the Martinists in Russia, as I have all the information needed for this. This secret (and hence intolerable) society . . . now rules openly and pursues its goal in safety, even while assuring the Sovereign of its own insignificance." What he brought to Tver' was the *Memorandum on the Martinists,* a French-language history of the Russian freemasons in which he described their alleged conspiratorial activities. Its subsequent fate is unknown, but Ekaterina may have sent it to Alexander in the fall of 1811, since a letter from him indicated that she had raised the subject of "Martinism" in her correspondence.[27]

Around the time when Rostopchin wrote his *Memorandum,* the state itself was taking an interest in the masonic movement, which had revived vigorously after the persecution of the 1790s. Although membership was widespread among the elite and some lodges were politically reactionary, freemasonry's secretiveness and past links to Enlightenment thought aroused intense conservative fears across Europe. Sinister conspiracy theories about godless radicals dated at least as far back as the writings of the French Jesuit Claude-François Nonnotte (who already in the 1760s was warning of evil plots by *philosophes*) and his Italian fellow Jesuit Luigi Mozzi; their most influential exponent was yet another Jesuit, the Frenchman Augustin Barruel, whose readership in the 1790s extended as far as Germany, Great Britain, the United States, the Netherlands, Italy, Portugal and Spain, and who was published in Russia as late as 1905.[28] It was only natural that Russia, with its Francophone upper class, would be receptive to these ideas, especially since their main propagandists wrote in French. Indeed, in 1807 the Committee for General Safety was instructed specifically to investigate such societies, and Speranskii complained that his enemies labeled him an Illuminatus and Martinist.

An interesting illustration of this paranoia is an 1810 memorandum, perhaps intended for the monarch himself, by an officer of his suite, Major Aleksandr Polev. The "most depraved and ambitious among scholars," Polev asserted, had formed secret societies in order to "weaken, in people's opinion, the faith as the foundation of familial and civil unions" under the pretense of combatting prejudice and superstition, and they accomplished this goal with the assistance of the wealthy and the powerful. The masonic lodges, established by "the most impious of these enlighteners," had attracted the young and the foolish with the promise of showing them the path to true wisdom. Having first sworn these dupes to silence "with horrible oaths," they succeeded in presenting any society, law, government, or religion other than their own "as a tyranny worthy of hatred, and they presented the destruction of all of that as an act of kindness toward mankind, and aroused them to pursue and carry out all of this."

By propagating the lie that humanity was one great family, these masonic leaders had supposedly convinced their followers that "love of the fatherland is the same as hatred of the rest of mankind" and that humanity "on the entire globe should be governed by identical laws and should have one ruler"—a freemason, naturally (Napoleon?). In pursuit of this goal, they "filled all the cabinets of sovereigns, senates, *lycées* and military and civil posts with men who disdain the faith, hate the laws and betray their sovereigns and fatherlands." Freemasonry was thus not only a threat to the social order, but its alleged influence in government (Speranskii, for example, was a freemason) served to undermine the state's own legitimacy in the eyes of the public.[29]

As a consequence of these kinds of concerns, Balashov (named minister of police on March 28, 1810) was entrusted with an investigation of the lodges' activities. An enthusiastic freemason himself, he could be expected to be lenient. In a message of August 1810 he reassured the masonic leaders that the authorities had no cause for worry, but explained that "from being secret [the lodges] have become almost open and thereby have given ignorance or malice the opportunity for various attacks on them. Under these circumstances and to block these rumors," the government felt obligated to verify their political reliability. As a result, under new rules issued in the fall of 1811, some lodges were authorized to continue functioning, under police supervision, while others, including the Rosicrucian lodges of Labzin and several others, were banned, though they continued to meet illegally.[30] Perhaps Polev's and Rostopchin's memoranda were instances of the "ignorance" and "malice" referred to by Balashov; they were certainly echoes from a public given to irrational fears about secret societies.

Rostopchin began his *Memorandum on the Martinists* with a brief history of the Russian Martinists, by which he meant the mystical branch of freemasonry, the Rosicrucian tradition brought to Russia by J. G. Schwarz and his associate, "one Novikov, a very intelligent, false, poor, daring and eloquent man." (Ironically, Rosicrucianism had actually originated in Germany as a conservative, anti-Illuminist, antirationalist movement.) After an unobjectionable description of Catherine II's fears about freemasons in general and Novikov's arrest, Rostopchin summarized the findings of the investigation she had ordered: Novikov's lodge had supposedly planned to assassinate her, and the group itself consisted of "a few cunning frauds and thousands of simple-hearted victims" (in fact, the membership was in the teens, although Novikov's periodicals did reach a broad audience). These "weak minds hoped to reach paradise, whither they were being led directly by their leaders, who preached that they should be fasting, praying and practicing charity and humility (while [the leaders] were appropriating [the followers'] wealth) in order to cleanse their souls and renounce worldly goods."[31]

Several prominent freemasons had been among the entourage of Paul I, and one of them, S. I. Pleshcheev, had supposedly given him the idea of exhuming Peter III and reinterring him together with Catherine. Paul, Rostopchin wrote, had intended this as an innocent gesture to reconcile his deceased parents and had not meant to insult the memory of his mother. This curious effort to rehabilitate the late emperor reflects Rostopchin's use of Paul's memory as a basis for his relationship with the grand duchess. He then described his own efforts to discredit the freemasons in front of the emperor, exaggerating his own influence somewhat, since Paul had been turning against them anyway.

He described the modest revival of "Martinism" at the beginning of Alexander's reign, but it was only in 1806, he wrote, when the Moscow nobility was organizing the region's militia, that the group again reared its head. Rostopchin claimed that they had arranged for the election of Admiral Mordvinov, a former marine minister inexperienced in land warfare, to head the militia, evidently in the hope that he would perform poorly. They further allegedly engaged in defeatist rumormongering and even "gave rise to the idea that the form of government needed to be changed and that the nation had the right to elect a new sovereign for itself." Rostopchin particularly criticized the Moscow military governors Tutolmin (1806–1809) and Gudovich (1809–1812) for inadequate vigilance against the Martinists. Rostopchin himself would succeed Gudovich in 1812, and here he was evidently already trying to establish himself as an alternative to him. Sarcastic remarks about Gudovich were standard fare in his letters to the grand duchess as well.[32]

The list of men whom Rostopchin linked to the Martinists included, in St. Petersburg, Mordvinov and Count Razumovskii (who was named minister of education in April 1810 after serving as curator of Moscow University), and in Moscow, the postal director Kliucharev, his assistant Runich, and Lopukhin. Kliucharev, whom Rostopchin persecuted with particular zest in 1812, was here described as "the most inveterate and despicable scoundrel who ever existed," a man supposedly involved with contraband and who opened other people's mail, stole imperial property, and oppressed his subordinates. Lopukhin was "a most immoral man, a drunkard given to depravity and unnatural vices." Another alleged Martinist plotter was the new curator of Moscow University, P. I. Golenishchev-Kutuzov, who, "having been a police informer in Paul's reign, is a stupid and base man who has all the nasty characteristics of the common rabble." There even was a passing reference to Speranskii, obliquely described as a protector of Kliucharev, who in turn "flatters" the powerful imperial protégé. These were only the leaders of "a multitude of sly people" who "conceal their schemes behind a cloak of religion, love for one's neighbor and humility," but who in reality "set themselves the goal of bringing about a revolution so they might play a prominent role in it, like the scoundrels who ruined France and paid with their own lives for the disturbances they provoked." After reviewing the arguments against the Martinists—essentially, that loyal subjects would have no reason to participate in a secret society in the first place—he concluded that they were agents of Napoleon and that "this sect is nothing but a secret enemy of governments and sovereigns."[33]

It may be assumed that the ideas of the *Memorandum on the Martinists,* and possibly its actual text, were communicated to Alexander, who visited Tver' from

May 29 to June 6, 1810. Rostopchin probably piqued the grand duchess's curiosity but did not turn her entirely against the Martinists, since after his visit she asked Alexander for books by Lopukhin.[34] Like other writings by Rostopchin, the *Memorandum* may also have circulated in manuscript form. However, he was unsuccessful in arousing the emperor to combat the freemasons, against whom he embarked on a personal crusade as military governor of Moscow in 1812.

Rostopchin's career therefore remained in the doldrums. In the summer of 1811 he wrote to Labzin (himself a "Martinist"): "I am not suited for anything. First, by today's standards, I am old, and besides, I am honest, diligent and not a Jacobin." He was convinced, he added, that, in the coming fall, Napoleon "will appear in the North as the scourge of the Lord and will start delivering merciless blows."[35] It seems odd that he expected Napoleon to strike so late in the year, given Russia's climate, but he was accurate in expecting war. Perhaps he also understood that such a war would rescue his own political ambitions. Meanwhile, he continued to present himself as the voice of conservative Russian opinion.

Three developments cast doubt upon the future of serfdom: the early reforms under Alexander I, the specter of Napoleon, and Speranskii's little-understood proposals. This question of serfdom, perhaps the most sensitive of all in gentry eyes, was cautiously addressed in an 1808 book, whose Russian version was printed in 1809 but which the censors kept off the market until the fall of 1811:[36] the Polish Count Strojnowski's *On the Landowners' Compact with Their Peasants*. In it the author voiced the hope that Russian nobles would eventually see the need to liberate their serfs (although without giving them any land). On September 11, 1811, Rostopchin's friend Golovin wrote to him from Petersburg that the book "has a remarkable output; the store where this book is sold cannot keep up with the number of requests." Golovin declared that the book "contains not one single new idea" and suspected that the author's intention was "to overthrow and disorganize our government"; in fact, he added, "it appears proven that he is paid by the French government to work at that."[37]

Within a month, Rostopchin—who did not share Shishkov's, let alone Glinka's, idealized vision of peasant virtue—had written a detailed rebuttal. Strojnowski, he asserted, was an ignorant dreamer and his book was typical of the "rantings by foreigners about servitude in Russia." Strojnowski "wrote his book in Polish, whereas I think and write in Russian," he declared, and hinted that the disloyal Pole wanted to detach Poland from Russia. Strojnowski supposedly was on the side of the French Revolution, while Rostopchin would present the perspective of the Russian nobility. He proceeded to criticize Strojnowski's arguments and formulate a defense of serfdom. "The word *freedom* [*vol'nost'*] or *liberty* [*svoboda*]," he wrote, "represents a condition that is flattering but not natural for man, since our life is a continual dependency on everything." This was the case because human interdependence was inherent in society. The power to make peoples happy "is predestined by Providence to those who sit on thrones or who govern peoples." The ancient republics were gone forever, but their phantom

image had led "many of the hungry and naked writers" of the past century, especially Rousseau, to fancy themselves the successors to classical heroes and to
seek to change the world. These writers had created "freethinking" and thereby
"planted the seeds of the French frenzy called the revolution." The urge for freedom from social constraints was illusory and reprehensible; the essence of the social order was authoritarian government, and the desire for freedom was synonymous with sedition.

He went on to present his view on serfdom. While Karamzin's *Memoir on Ancient and Modern Russia* had accurately traced serfdom to the sixteenth and seventeenth centuries, Rostopchin implied that modern serfs were all descended from
medieval slaves. He asserted that unnamed past tsars had already experimented
unsuccessfully with giving the peasants freedom of movement, but always such
freedom "brought disorder to the noble estates and ruin to the peasants themselves,
who, in order to evade taxes, labor and state obligations," lived "like nomadic peoples, and by their ceaseless migration from one place to another lost their last possessions." Emancipation would always produce this same result. The longevity of
any legal arrangement (such as serfdom), whatever its flaws, only proved "either
that it is beneficial or that it could not be replaced with a better one."

He then argued that serfdom actually was a form of social insurance for the
peasants. Some of them, knowing that their masters would not permit their pau-
perization, even exploited the nobles' unfailing generosity. (Rostopchin did not
address the internal contradiction in his argument that serfdom both maintained
social discipline and encouraged peasant laziness.) He gave examples of serfs of
his own who had thus taken advantage of him by feigning poverty, and concluded
that "in general their profligacy, sloth and carelessness boggle the mind." He argued that Russian peasants, who inherited their land and homes, lived better and
more securely than English tenant farmers. The master's power to deprive his
serfs of their property was a red herring, "for ruining the peasant is the most certain means of ruining oneself," and even the rare *pomeshchik* who abused his
peasants behaved like an angel of virtue in comparison with the British, French,
and Dutch overseas: Catherine II ("who caused Russia's felicity during her glorious reign") and Alexander I had actively prosecuted abusive serf owners, while
the West Europeans "in their colonies gave themselves the right to inflict every
possible punishment on their slaves." All things considered, then, serfdom was a
necessary evil, and no evil at all, and even if it was an evil, foreigners were worse
and had no right to criticize Russia.

He then examined the obstacles facing Strojnowski's proposal. Like
Karamzin, he assumed that the land would remain noble property, and warned of
interminable disputes over the peasants' access to fields, waterways, forests, and
so on. Accustomed to the free use of these resources, peasants would refuse to
pay for them, and it would be impossible to arrange for the nobles to purchase
their labor or produce. Yet the real raison d'être for serfdom was the absence of
other means to force the peasants to farm at all. "Agriculture cannot prosper in

Russia if the peasants are free," Rostopchin declared, "because the Russian peasant does not like farming and despises his condition, in which he sees no benefit to himself." Noting that the peasants were ignorant of elementary agronomy as well as lazy, he argued that emancipation would spark a vast exodus to the towns and unmanageable migrations in search of new farmlands in other provinces. The seasonal departure of men to work in the towns, and the end of the practice of serf owners' arranging the marriages of peasants who had difficulty finding a spouse, would lead the population to dwindle (not increase, as Strojnowski had argued). Factories and livestock raising would grind to a halt, as would the collection of head taxes.

The peasants themselves would not long enjoy their freedom, for a new class of wealthy peasants would begin to oppress their fellows. The nobles would no longer be able to help the peasants in times of need, and any litigation between nobles and peasants would inevitably be decided in the nobility's favor, since the judges were drawn from the gentry. Yet the courts and other authorities would be of little use in defending the nobility's legitimate interests, since the state would be incapable of administering "ten million people who are intoxicated and unruly from freedom." Like Karamzin, Rostopchin pointed out that the rural population was being governed by the nobility at no cost to the state and that there was currently no substitute for the serf owners in this regard.

Furthermore, he argued, the advocates of peasant freedom "sentenced to death by starvation" the vast number of house servants who would have no place under the new order. These people had no skills or trade to support themselves and their families, and few actually rendered any services to their masters, but they survived by their masters' charity: "House servants cause great expense, but we do not as yet reckon in the foreign way, and the phrase 'After all, he's human' feeds a million people." Again, he fended off foreign criticism by arguing that the Russian character rendered serfdom more humane than the greedy, heartless "freedom" of Western countries, and he contended that nobles who liberated serfs under the Edict on the Free Farmers had done so merely to evade their responsibilities toward old or disabled peasants, not as a gesture of humanitarianism.[38]

Apparently thought was given to printing Rostopchin's essay, but the authorization was not granted, and it circulated only in manuscript form.[39] There is no evidence that he showed it to Karamzin or Ekaterina Pavlovna, but his friendship with them and his desire to use his writings for maximum political effect make it likely that they knew it. The ideas in it are reminiscent of Karamzin's arguments in the *Memoir;* this similarity shows the political affinity between the two and, probably, that they articulated the views of an entire stratum of Russian nobles. Like Karamzin's *Memoir,* Rostopchin's rebuttal of Strojnowski was apparently forwarded to the monarch,[40] but nothing is known of Alexander's response.

There were objections against this point of view. The future Decembrist Nikolai Turgenev, for instance, apparently read Rostopchin's text (or another attributed to him) in the spring of 1812, after returning from his studies in Göttingen.

Outraged, he complained that Rostopchin *"does not know the issue"* and confused help for "the most useful class of the people in the state" with "the freedom and independence that were preached by power-hungry republicans and enthusiasts of philosophy." He rejected the claim that Russian well-being was "founded on slavery" and added that Rostopchin "argues badly for our prosperity with examples of how poor the destitute are among other peoples."[41] Despite isolated critical voices like Turgenev's, however, Rostopchin spoke for many. As Michael Confino has argued, a distrustful, condescending view of the peasants—without the idealizing gloss added by Glinka or even Shishkov—was commonplace among the nobility. Serfs were seen as petty liars and hypocrites with a predilection for parasitic living at the lord's expense. At best, they might be naïve and childlike. Their laziness was believed to be the cause of both their poverty and the backwardness of agriculture in general. Anything that loosened their ties to the manorial economy—especially work outside the estate, that is, the migration to cities that Rostopchin warned would likely result from emancipation—indicated "dissoluteness" and "immorality." In the nobles' assumptions, a peasant was a brutish creature whose limited mind held no thoughts worth knowing; this conviction confirmed nobles' own sense of superiority and made possible their serene acceptance, unclouded by moral qualms, of the institution of serfdom. Rostopchin's emphasis on the benefits of bondage for the serf himself, however, reflected the changed atmosphere of the early nineteenth century, when abolitionists argued that the peasants' low moral character was in fact an evil consequence of serfdom, not simply a justification for preserving it.[42]

That Rostopchin was not alone is indicated by the other writings similar to his that circulated at the same time. One of these, shorter and less sophisticated, argued that, in the matter of serfdom, the issue at stake was "whether Russia would be or not be." Its author equated emancipation with the French Revolution, anarchy, and godlessness, and like Rostopchin he argued that Russian peasants were better off as serfs than the poor in Europe. He warned of all manner of social and economic disasters threatening Russia, made the point that its serfs were happier than the emancipated Polish peasants now dying for Napoleon in Spain, and also accused Strojnowski of being an agent of Napoleon, who, despairing of ever triumphing over Russia, was seeking to subvert it from within: "No! It is not at all love for humanity or the desire to benefit Russia that guide your pen, but the secret envy that gnaws at all foreigners when they gaze upon Russia's glory and greatness, its strength and prosperity."[43] This, of course, was a theme already popularized by Shishkov and Rostopchin: insufficient enthusiasm for Russian "tradition," whether cultural or sociopolitical, opened one to being labeled a tool of Russia's French enemies.

The public identified Rostopchin with the "gentry opposition" to such a degree that antigovernment tracts penned by others began circulating under his name. For instance, a letter to Alexander I passed around in manuscript form in the spring of 1812 purported to have been written by Rostopchin on behalf of the

people of Moscow, "to present to you the disastrous condition of the entire state
and the danger menacing your own person from the premeditated and almost accomplished betrayal of the crowd that surrounds you." At the letter's supposed
time of writing (March 1812), the real Rostopchin was in St. Petersburg, where he
and the emperor were arranging his appointment as military governor of
Moscow.[44] He had avoided obvious, personal attacks on Speranskii even in his
Memorandum on the Martinists, and by this time Speranskii was already on his
way into exile. Attacking him and bullying the emperor therefore made no sense
at all for Rostopchin. The letter, however, bluntly warned the monarch that Speranskii and his assistant Magnitskii "and their accomplices have sold you out to
your sham ally," Napoleon, who was allegedly preparing to invade Russia. In addition, Speranskii was deliberately burdening the Russian people with unbearable
taxes (probably a reference to the special tax levied on the nobility, which the nobles bitterly resented). Therefore, the letter demanded: "Allow me [i.e., Ros-
topchin] to approach the capital and cut short the plot hatched by the beasts of
prey that surround you." It ended on a crudely menacing note that would never
have occurred to the skillful Rostopchin: "This letter is the last, and if it remains
without effect," it threatened, "then the sons of the fatherland will find themselves compelled to move on the capital and insistently demand both the revealing of this crime and a change of government." The regime took such matters so
seriously that the Committee for General Safety investigated the case and identified, among others, two men who had been circulating the letter and making
copies. They were officials of modest rank (levels nine and twelve on the Table of
Ranks), which suggests that the influence of this and other manuscript texts extended well beyond the elite circles frequented by the likes of Rostopchin.[45]

Rostopchin's chief ally and patroness was Ekaterina Pavlovna, whose political
influence is difficult to gauge. Foreign diplomats, as we have seen, thought her
very influential and possibly even a threat to the emperor, and the importance of
her close personal relationship with Alexander was amplified by her ties to conservative circles whose views she presented to the monarch. Karamzin's *Memoir*
reached Alexander through her, and Rostopchin's *Memorandum on the Martinists* may have, too. She arranged for the emperor to hear Karamzin's opinions on
the proper nature of autocracy, and she persistently promoted Rostopchin's career, at least from 1809 on.[46]

While her views on domestic affairs were conservative, she also held belligerently nationalistic opinions on foreign affairs that could be utterly out of touch
with reality. During the Tilsit conference, for instance, when Russia was negotiating from a position of weakness, she insisted that extending Russia's borders to
the Danube and the Vistula (which would require despoiling its Prussian allies)
was the only acceptable condition for an alliance with Napoleon. She echoed
Rostopchin's views that Russia should carve up the Ottoman Empire because a
strong German buffer was not required and that power considerations alone
should guide foreign policy. "I want Russia to be unapproachable, unassailable,

inaccessible," she wrote to her brother. "I want it to be respected not in words but in fact, because it certainly has all the resources and the right to be respected." At the same time, she told Alexander: "Never in my life will I get used to the idea of knowing you to be spending your days with Bonaparte," whose "displays of fawning over the Russian nation are so many tricks, because this man is a combination of cunning, personal ambition and falsehood."[47]

Her meetings with Alexander involved political discussions and sometimes even had a formal agenda. For instance, while planning the 1811 visit during which he met Karamzin, he sent her a fifteen-point program covering foreign policy, military preparations, and even Speranskii's report on his official activities, including "different ideas about institutions to be created." Speranskii's plans to reform the central government were also submitted to her: in the summer of 1811 Alexander sent her "the printed proposals for the new organization of the Senate according to the great plan that you know and of which we have often spoken." He also included, for her husband, the planned reform of the ministries: "Since this letter is for him as much as for you, I ask you both for your advice on all these items."[48] Whether she "leaked" these plans to her Moscow friends is not known.[49]

She deeply disliked Speranskii, who in turn made little effort to accommodate her. When he refused her request to promote her husband's secretary to a higher rank without the examination required by law since 1809, her conservative friends were quick to agree with her annoyance. Rostopchin remarked to her, "How dare this worthless priest's son turn down the sister of his Sovereign, when he should have deemed it a favor that she asked for his mediation," and informed the emperor directly of Moscow's irritation with Speranskii.[50] It did not mollify Ekaterina that, in 1810, Speranskii dissuaded Alexander from appointing Karamzin as minister of education.[51] She complained as early as that year that Speranskii was a "criminal, but my brother doesn't even suspect it," and her husband agreed: "How can one keep such a villain near oneself?" Speranskii was aware of the hostility of the Tver' salon,[52] and his opposition to Karamzin's appointment and the stalled career of Rostopchin may have reflected fears for his own political survival. Perhaps, also, Alexander's failure to implement Speranskii's reform plans was due in part to opposition from the grand duchess and her husband.

The bond of affection that linked Ekaterina with her brother, and her frankness in presenting her opinions, are evident from their frequent visits and correspondence, although some of the more intensely emotional outbursts in his letters surely reflect romantic literary influence. What is less clear is the influence of her political views. Various circumstances suggest that it should not be overestimated. To begin with, she was an elegant and charming woman, and Alexander loved such company and entertained platonic relationships with ladies ranging from Queen Louisa of Prussia to his wife's maid of honor, Roksandra Sturdza.[53] With them he found refuge from the burdens of state and could bask in the glow of his power and charisma without being drawn into personal or political commitments.

He kept his options open by listening to competing sources of advice without clearly endorsing any one approach. After Tilsit, he let Rumiantsev promote the French alliance while he himself undermined it. Speranskii was the main proponent of domestic reforms and Arakcheev the enforcer of discipline, but the emperor also solicited counsel elsewhere; thus General Filosofov proposed an ambitious plan to distribute land more equitably among the peasants in order to shore up serfdom and protect the social order.[54] It stands to reason that Ekaterina was a useful link to the Moscow-based gentry opposition. However, as has been pointed out, there were basic philosophical differences between her and the emperor: he was an idealist and a mystic who distrusted himself and others; she was more pragmatic and psychologically less complex. In domestic affairs her instincts were more conservative than his, while in foreign policy they were more nationalistic.[55] Advisers showed Alexander the available options, permitting him to reach his own decisions. There is no evidence that she was more influential than others. In 1807 she was interested in marrying the Austrian emperor but was unable to overcome her brother's opposition.[56] In 1810, Karamzin, her candidate for the post of minister of education, was turned down, and his *Memoir on Ancient and Modern Russia* led to no noticeable changes in policy; her railings against Speranskii likewise had no immediate effect. Her attempt to revive Rostopchin's fortunes also miscarried, and his *Memorandum on the Martinists* failed to induce a serious crackdown on the freemasons.

The "demigoddess of Tver'" was not, therefore, the powerful *éminence grise* that some foreign diplomats suspected. However, her salon was a conduit that allowed the voice of the Moscow conservatives, and of the gentry whose fears they both shaped and echoed, to reach the Winter Palace. In the relatively stable years until 1811, Alexander I could afford to ignore them. Amidst the crisis of 1812, however, it became apparent that he knew their concerns and was prepared to regard Rostopchin as their leader and give in to their wishes. In that sense, the efforts of Rostopchin, Karamzin, and Ekaterina Pavlovna paid off handsomely.

While Rostopchin, Karamzin, and Glinka shaped the conservative scene in Moscow, broadcasting their views in aristocratic salons, the press, and informal visits with the imperial family, a separate oppositional current arose in St. Petersburg. Its central figure was Admiral Shishkov, and in keeping with the character of the capital, it was quasi-bureaucratic in form. This opposition was less outspoken but in its own way as critical of the regime as the conservatives in Moscow and Tver'. Shishkov shared their misgivings regarding, for example, the creation of the ministries in 1802, the decision to go to war in 1805, and the treaty of Tilsit in 1807.[57] Yet, given his cautious personality and the political atmosphere of the capital, he did not vent his frustration in angry brochures and manifestoes. Instead, he devoted himself to his literary pursuits.

This was a retreat, not a surrender. In the ongoing battle between the Old and New Styles, Petersburg was generally in the admiral's camp, while his foes were based in Moscow. Since his defense of the Old Style was a highly political matter, the literary war merely extended the political controversy by other means. His power base lay in the Russian Academy, which he ruled with an iron hand. He brooked no criticism of his writings, which the academy dutifully praised and published, and he used its periodicals, which would have folded without his energetic leadership, to make his case for the Old Style. One effect of his dictatorial methods, however, was that the Russian Academy attracted only writers of whom he approved, and even they were stifled in their creative endeavors. As a result, it did not fulfill its mission of leadership in the literary world. Zhikharev, who preferred the New Style but personally knew and liked Shishkov, was shocked to see its membership roster. It included a few major authors and several prominent officials, but not some of Russia's best writers (such as Karamzin and Ozerov). "I cannot understand how people are found in it who are not at all known in literature or, worse yet, who are known for their lack of talent."[58]

Around 1804–1805, Shishkov also began to organize literary soirées with three of his friends: Dmitrii I. Khvostov, the former overprocurator of the Holy Synod;[59] Mikhail N. Murav'ev, the deputy minister of education and curator of the Moscow educational district;[60] and Derzhavin. (Shishkov and Derzhavin became friends only around this time.)[61] The four would meet regularly at the home of one of them to read and discuss their works. They belonged to the same generation as Shishkov (Derzhavin was born in 1743, Shishkov in '54, Khvostov in '56 and Murav'ev in '57)[62] and, like he, had come of age before both late-eighteenth-century culture and the separation of the bureaucracy from the intelligentsia began to eat away at the sociocultural foundations of the old regime. They were less concerned than Karamzin, Rostopchin, or Glinka with the safety of the old order, and accordingly less conscious of the need to articulate a defense for it. After all, the youngest member of their group (Murav'ev) was still six years older than the dean of the Moscow trio (Rostopchin), while Derzhavin was twice Glinka's age. The two groups were on opposite sides of the divide that separated two generations: those who had grown up accustomed to what Talleyrand wistfully called the "sweetness of life" before 1789, and those who had still been young and impressionable when Louis XVI mounted the guillotine.

At the beginning of 1807, Shishkov turned these informal gatherings into public events that attracted a sizable portion of the St. Petersburg literary elite. The first was held at Shishkov's home on Saturday, February 2, and was attended by about twenty people, mostly writers, but also Labzin, the imperial aide-de-camp P. A. Kikin, and Colonel A. A. Pisarev of the Semenovskii Guards regiment. Labzin and Shishkov had been acquainted at least since the 1790s; Shishkov's Orthodox beliefs do not appear to have affected his relations with the renowned mystic.[63] Similar Saturday gatherings were held three times in February, four times in March, and once in May 1807, after which the group adjourned for the summer. Petersburgers prominent in culture and politics attended these gatherings, including the military governor Viazmitinov; Minister of Education Zavadovskii; the senators Rezanov and Salagov; Olenin, the director of the Public Library and president of the Academy of the Arts; and the retired general and former aide-de-camp to Potemkin, S. L. L'vov.[64]

A range of literary abilities and generations was represented here. Dmitrii Khvostov, for instance, was considered so bereft of talent as to be the laughing-stock of the literary world,[65] while Ivan Krylov and Nikolai Gnedich were known as writers of great ability and stature. The age structure of the group is also interesting. Except for Derzhavin, the core members of the group, who organized and hosted the meetings (Shishkov, Murav'ev, Zakharov, and the two cousins Khvostov), had all been born in the 1750s. The others were usually younger. Of twenty of them (excluding the two whose birth dates I could not discover), one was born in 1739, two each in the 1740s and 1750s, five in the 1760s, four in the 1770s, five in the 1780s, and one in 1790.[66] Of those born before 1760, only Gorchakov was a writer, while those born after 1780 were all writers. The six who made up the core were all longtime members of the Russian Academy (in fact, Shishkov was the most junior among them, except for Murav'ev, who seems to have dropped out of the literary meetings before 1807), and of twenty-two others, nine were current or future members. Since Labzin, the two senators, Zavadovskii, Viazmitinov, and the generals Kikin and L'vov were not academicians, the proportion of academicians among the writers in the group was even higher (nine out of fifteen).[67]

Shishkov was thus reaching out to a younger generation. As Zhikharev was told when the meetings were first planned, absolutely "all men of letters who have been introduced to the master of the house by one of his acquaintances have the right to attend and read their works"; however, "young people who . . . appear promising will even be invited, because these soirées are being established primarily with the object of making their works known." The partisan nature of the gatherings was apparent in the exclusion of followers of the New Style (Zhikharev noticed "a kind of insulting indifference to the Moscow poets") and in the prevalence of academicians. Shishkov wanted not only to encourage young talent but also to draw the rising generation into his camp. As one result, younger writers often found the soirées, like the Russian Academy itself, tedious and of limited literary value.[68]

Like the academy, the literary evenings drew both writers and officials, as well as people such as Colonel Pisarev who were both. This peculiarity was apparent by the third session, which, Zhikharev noted, "did not resemble a literary soirée. The people who were there! Senators, overprocurators, gentlemen of the chamber and even the governor himself." Characteristically, at the very first meeting, participants discussed politics as much as literature. The recent battle at Preußisch-Eylau provoked heated debate: Kikin and Pisarev, both officers, thought the war should be continued, while Labzin and A. S. Khvostov favored peace. Shishkov remained noncommittal, at least in young Zhikharev's presence, volunteering only that Russia should proceed with caution and that he had utter confidence in the emperor's judgment. Zhikharev's notes suggest that the mood was not mainly oppositional, perhaps because he was not privy to all that was said. Still, unlike Ekaterina Pavlovna's salon, this was not primarily a forum for expressing dissatisfaction with the government. Instead, it provided a place where the conservative literary elite could meet with like-minded representatives of bureaucracy, court, and army, and where Shishkov and others of the older generation could disseminate their views on Russian culture and (implicitly) politics.[69]

The soirées resumed after the summer, against the background of the discontent caused by Tilsit and the Continental System.[70] As he had explained in his *Treatise on the Old and New Styles,* Shishkov viewed politics and culture as inseparable, and the public mood after 1807 encouraged him to revive his simmering feud with the New Style. The result was a series of angry polemics and rebuttals in 1808–1811.[71] In this atmosphere, Shishkov's and Derzhavin's literary gatherings took on a political character even if politics per se was not the main topic of conversation. They continued to attract much the same audience. There were also some new faces, including Karamzin's friend, the poet Dmitriev, who became minister of justice in 1810. Other frequent guests were Shishkov's friends Bakunin (the civil governor of St. Petersburg), General Kutuzov (the hero of 1812) and Admiral Mordvinov, who assisted Speranskii in working out his fiscal reform plan and was named to the State Council; Mordvinov advocated making the government more responsive to the needs of the nobility but rejected any thought of tampering with serfdom. Aside from these state dignitaries of Shishkov's own generation, there was also Pavel Stroganov (born in 1774), formerly of the "Unofficial Committee," who opposed the French alliance, and such hopeful young literati as S. I. Viskovatov (born in 1786) and Aleksandr Sturdza and Sergei Aksakov (both born in 1791).[72]

Like the Moscow conservatives, the Shishkov-Derzhavin group had ties to the imperial family. Empress-Mother Mariia sympathized with their views and invited writers linked with the group to read from their works at her suburban residence at Pavlovsk. Ambassador Savary complained to Napoleon in 1807 that St. Petersburg's elite regularly made pilgrimages there to attend her salon, and her patronage gave the views of Shishkov and his friends greater public exposure and credibility.[73] On the other hand, because of the political nature of his activities, Shishkov (like Rostopchin) was heartily disliked by Alexander I. When the State Council was created in 1810, Mordvinov and M. M. Filosofov were named to it. Mordvinov offered to ask the emperor to appoint Shishkov, but Shishkov requested that he not do so. Then Filosofov (who did not know Shishkov personally) came to see Mordvinov, who was staying at Shishkov's house, and asked the host why he was not also a member of the State Council. Evidently, these two senior officials of Shishkov's generation thought him fit for such a high position. Without telling Shishkov (according to Shishkov's version), Filosofov went to the emperor to ensure that this seeming anomaly be rectified. However, as he later told Shishkov, "I noticed in [the emperor] such an ill disposition toward you, that, when I strongly insisted, he finally told me that he would sooner agree not to rule than to make you a member." Even Shishkov was shocked at the depth of Alexander's hostility. Like Rostopchin, he was thus barred from office (although without having solicited it) and pursued his literary interests instead. He was unpopular at court, and the emperor turned down his request to have his collected works published by the navy, but in his discontent he reflected the mood of a nobility increasingly frustrated with the monarch's policies.[74]

As Vigel' recalled, the French menace weighed heavily on society, and religion and patriotism seemed to be among the few forces capable of resisting it. Increasingly, speaking French was deemed unpatriotic, so "aristocratic ladies began, in French, to extol the Russian language, to indicate the desire to learn it and to feign that they knew it."[75] Rostopchin abandoned his elegant French for a self-consciously popular Russian when appealing to such instincts, and Ekaterina Pavlovna worked to improve her own Russian skills. Rostopchin's character Bogatyrev, Glinka's *Russian Messenger,* the patriotic dramas of Glinka, Derzhavin, and Ozerov, and the teachings of Shishkov were welcomed by a public anxious to protect its certainties and way of life by grounding them in a socially conservative sense of national identity.

In 1810, in response to this mood, the Shishkov-Derzhavin group decided to turn their gatherings into a formal organization whose readings would be open to the elite of the capital. This was a remarkable step, for older conservative nobles and officials did not normally create formal associations to promote an even implicitly political point of view, let alone an oppositional one, and it bespoke their estrangement from current policy and willingness to organize along ideological lines. Although the new group was far from a political party, it represented a hesitant step away from a world divided wholly between a private and an official sphere and toward a civil society in which politics went on in structured, autonomous organizations not based on kinship or patronage.

After discussing various alternatives, the members decided to name their new organization the Symposium of the Lovers of the Russian Word. It was to consist of four sections, each of which had a chairman (Shishkov, Derzhavin, A. S. Khvostov, and Zakharov), four or five active members, and between three and five associate members who would become active members should a seat open up. It also had four curators (Mordvinov, Minister of Justice Dmitriev, Minister of Education Razumovskii, and the latter's predecessor, Zavadovskii) and thirty-three honorary members.[76] To Karamzinists such as Vigel', this structure (which reminded him of the State Council) was senseless, as the different sections lacked separate purposes. Moreover, it seemed symptomatic of the absurdity of the Symposium in general: "It had the appearance more of a governmental office than of a learned body, and even in the allocation of positions they followed the Table of Ranks more than that of talents."[77]

This charge was not entirely fair, since the division into sections made it easier to organize the soirées that the Symposium planned in meticulous detail. In a sense, though, Vigel's analysis was accurate: the proponents of the Old Style objected to the studied informality and egalitarianism of the New, and favored a sharp distinction between the forms appropriate for daily life and those befitting a solemn occasion such as a literary reading. They propounded the conception—essential to the old regime in general and the Russian service state in particular—of a society where all relationships were based on a single, all-pervasive hierarchy. Nothing could have been farther from the Symposium's sense of rank and decorum than the spectacle of a tearful Sergei Glinka spontaneously haranguing a crowd of peasants, or Rostopchin impersonating a country bumpkin. The pomp and formality of the Symposium were meant to emphasize the special dignity of literature, like the awe that the pomp of monarchy both expressed and evoked. The Old Style was partly a generational phenomenon, and it preached regard for age, tradition, and precedence. This was reflected in the Symposium's hierarchical structure, since active members tended to be older, better known, and higher ranking in the state service than the associate members. Also, many members were career officials to whom respect for bureaucratic forms was second nature; in their eighteenth-century universe, state service and literature were not yet separate worlds.[78]

The Symposium was joined by most of Shishkov's earlier literary circle and boasted an impressive array of literary talent. As Al'tshuller points out, it included "the most talented writers of the older generation" (Derzhavin, Krylov, Shishkov), "the major writers of the 'second rank'" (Shakhovskoi, Shikhmatov, Kapnist, Gorchakov, Nikolev, Karabanov), serious scholars (Ermolaev, Vostokov) and "talented youth" (Grech, Olin, Zhikharev, Bunina, Gnedich).[79] Interestingly, there was almost no overlap between the Symposium's membership for 1811 and Glinka's subscriber list for the same year; evidently, Shishkov's following among sophisticated Petersburg officials and writers differedly markedly from Glinka's readership among nobles and merchants in Moscow and the provinces.

Like Shishkov's earlier group, the Symposium was to be more than just a gathering of writers and scholars. The curators, whose function was honorific, were current or former government ministers, and the list of honorary members read like a Who's Who of the Russian elite. Besides two bishops, it included Viazmitinov, Balashov, Minister of the Interior Kozodavlev, and the overprocurator of the Holy Synod, Golitsyn. Quartermaster-General (effectively the army's chief of staff) Volkonskii was also an honorary member, as were the curators of the St. Petersburg and Moscow educational districts, the administrator of the Committee of Ministers, the director of imperial theaters, and two State Council members. Although they played no active role, their names lent the Symposium additional political weight. When Derzhavin added Karamzin to the list, Shishkov retaliated by enrolling Rostopchin and others whom Derzhavin disliked. These and other out-of-towners did not, however, participate in the group's proceedings. Lastly, bowing to distasteful political necessity, Shishkov added Speranskii and his lieutenant Magnitskii to the roster, although the Symposium members strongly opposed the policies for which the two men stood.[80]

The group's organizers had hoped that the emperor would confirm their charter in November 1810, but as Al'tshuller puts it, he "was in no hurry to allow large assemblies of writers suspected of being in the opposition." Dmitrii Khvostov heard that "at the sovereign's table, when the new Symposium was being discussed, it was said that instead of the word *bilet* [ticket] it intended to use the word *zval'tso* [a fabricated Slavonic neologism meaning 'little invitation']. This caused general mirth and the Symposium remained unconfirmed." By mid-February, however, the Symposium had gained approval from the emperor and could begin operating.[81] The significance of the delay is not entirely clear; perhaps Alexander wanted to convey his displeasure without, however, inviting a confrontation by refusing confirmation outright.

The first public reading began at 8 P.M. on March 14, 1811, "in the presence of two hundred most select persons" admitted by invitation only. The scene in Derzhavin's house by the Fontanka was solemn and festive. The ladies wore evening gowns and the gentlemen appeared in uniforms bedecked with medals and ribbons. As Aleksandr Sturdza later recalled, the hall, "of average size and lined with beautiful yellow imitation-marble columns, appeared even more graceful in the brightness of its luxurious lighting." For the guests "there were, around the hall, ascending rows of well-designed seats," while "a huge oblong table, covered with delicate green cloth, was set up in the middle of this house of the muses. At the table sat the Symposium members under the chairmanship of Derzhavin, upon whose nod the absorbing and often exemplary reading aloud commenced and alternated." Some guests at the readings, which lasted two or three hours, had come (in K. S. Serbinovich's recollection) "out of a feeling of patriotism, even if not out of literary conviction." That sentiment of patriotism was a powerful force, and it was not only Sturdza who saw the Symposium as educated society's answer to the 1806–1807 people's militia, in which Russia had gathered its strength to repulse Napoleon's aggression.[82]

Nobody had volunteered to give the inaugural speech, so Shishkov accepted the task.[83] His address, thirty-eight printed pages long and replete with lengthy quotations from Russian writers and poets, restated the basic position of the Old Style: that a culture must be rooted in its national language and not imitate that of foreigners. He effusively praised Catherine II, the idol of conservatives, but invoked Alexander I only to argue that the Symposium was in conformity with the tsar's own views, since his educational reforms and the Symposium were both helping to spread enlightenment in Russia. He asserted that Russian was among the world's oldest languages, in no way inferior to Greek or Latin, and capable of expressing any concept or emotion, and he singled out folk language as an important resource of the national culture. (Even his critics respectfully acknowledged his work to promote the appreciation of folk language and poetry.)[84] Without attacking foreign cultures or languages, he appealed to Russians to learn more about their own, for otherwise, he warned, their nation's inner vitality would wither.[85] This was the same pathos that had pervaded his *Treatise on the Old and New Styles*. Shishkov, unlike Rostopchin with his character Bogatyrev, carefully avoided pseudopopular vulgarisms or xenophobic hysteria. The notion of dignity undergirded his conception of his role: the dignity of Russian letters, which motivated the Symposium's formalistic structure; the dignity of the language, which could not tolerate the intentional use of vulgar speech for cheap effect; and the dignity of patriotism, which must not be exploited merely as a political tactic.

He considered his speech a success. "They listened to my address with rapt attention: complete quiet and silence reigned during the reading." The audience was then treated to some entertaining fables by Krylov, and "the Symposium meeting concluded with everybody pleased. Everyone praised it." People were so favorably impressed that "without the members insisting, a subscription was then set up to support the Symposium." Countess Stroganova assured Shishkov that the sheer bulk of his speech's text had at first led her to worry that she would be bored but that, in fact, it had been so interesting that she would gladly have listened to another two hours of it.[86] He was pleased that the soirée seemed to have convinced many ladies to take a greater interest in the national language and literature. The following day he visited the countess and saw Krylov reading his ever-popular fables to the guests. Joseph de Maistre dropped by, surveyed the scene, and told Shishkov in French, "I see something new and unprecedented: people are reading in Russian, a language that I don't understand and only rarely hear being spoken in aristocratic houses!" Shishkov, naturally, was delighted.[87]

The monthly public readings continued to attract large crowds. At the second, held on April 22, 1811, there were "no fewer than three hundred of the best people in the city, among which number there were many ladies." The interest shown by women was particularly gratifying, since Shishkov had long maintained that the charms of French-speaking ladies led even the most Russian-minded men astray,[88] and the Symposium's stated goal was therefore to "develop in the public, and especially among ladies, a taste for Russian literature." A year later, public interest had not diminished, for three hundred guests appeared for the reading on February 23, 1812. In an apparent bid to attract interest outside the capital, the Symposium decided, in the winter of 1812, to send its literature (its proceedings were published as *Readings in the Symposium of the Lovers of the Russian Word*) to the governors of twenty-one provinces. The number and social standing of the audiences in the capital, and the Symposium's efforts to reach the provincial public as well (which likely enjoyed some success, since its members and patrons in Petersburg had social ties to the provinces), suggest that the Symposium had developed into a significant forum for the development and expression of elite opinion in the capital and perhaps beyond.[89]

Outside reactions to the Symposium naturally depended on the observer's political and literary views. Shishkov sent Mariia Fedorovna and her daughter Anna Pavlovna a transcript of the first evening. The empress-mother responded sympathetically and apparently authorized him to communicate her best wishes to the

Symposium's membership, which in return acknowledged her greetings "with the deepest gratitude." The emperor, on the other hand, demonstratively snubbed the group by turning down an invitation to a public reading. When, after a meeting with Alexander, Derzhavin announced publicly that the emperor would attend the reading after all, the monarch embarrassed him by telling him through Balashov: "I did not give you my word; you disobeyed."[90]

The partisans of the New Style were variously amused and appalled. Vigel' declared that the guests at the session he had attended "understood absolutely nothing" but "did not display—and perhaps did not even experience—boredom; they were inspired by the idea that they were doing a great patriotic deed, and this they did with exemplary selflessness." "Woe was only unto those," he sneered, "who did understand and were obligated continually to hold back their yawns." The purpose of the event seemed to be political: "fashionable society assumed that the triumph of our national literature must precede the triumph of faith and fatherland." Others were equally unflattering. After the first two Symposium sessions, Aleksandr Turgenev noted that "the aristocratic public is congregating in large numbers" but "it is of no use, because the members, for the most part, are unfit even to be watchmen on Parnassus." And Karamzin, the principal (if usually unnamed) target of the Old Style's attacks, wondered simply: "Why do these gentlemen refuse to leave me alone?"[91]

The sections of the Symposium took turns organizing the 1811–1812 readings, each of which primarily featured presentations by the section then on duty, discussed and approved in advance by that section. The inaugural reading, in March 1811, was organized by Shishkov's section, the second by Derzhavin's on April 22, and the third by A. S. Khvostov's on May 26. After the Symposium had dispersed for the summer and early autumn, which nobles often spent in the country, Zakharov's section organized a reading on November 11.[92]

Then it was the admiral's turn again. It was typical of Shishkov that out of fiery conviction he had drafted a provocative speech, "but I dared not read it" for fear of angering the monarch. So he took the unusual precaution of securing the formal approval of all four sections for his address at a meeting on December 4, and then gave the speech at the reading held on the fifteenth. The audience first was read a letter conveying the emperor's thanks to the Symposium for sending him the third issue of its *Readings*. Alexander had apparently been in no hurry, since the *Readings* had been published in the summer and the November soirée had mentioned no response from him. Another possibility, however, is that Shishkov wanted the letter read at this meeting to stress his good relations with the court even as he risked antagonizing it again with the evening's speech, which was published in that issue of the *Readings*.[93] He was nervous about this address; as he saw it, it was a political gamble. Twelve days later, describing the evening to a friend, he wrote that "the more than four hundred guests," who included "the clergy and the most distinguished persons of both sexes," had barely fit into the hall. With his usual candor, he added, "I confess that I was somewhat shy about beginning to read; I thought not everyone would share my sentiments and perhaps many would consider some truths to be too bold."[94]

He opened his talk—which would later be published as the *Treatise on Love of the Fatherland*—by asserting that loving one's country was a divinely inspired instinct, as natural as loving one's parents; therefore, "a man who considers himself to be a citizen of the world, that is, as not belonging to any nation, does the same as though he did not acknowledge having a father, mother, kin or tribe." Such a man would be abdicating his humanity and lowering himself to the level of animals. Patriotism, Shishkov argued, was more powerful than any other love. He gave fourteen pages of examples, citing classical figures and then (as Glinka was likewise fond of doing) showing their counterparts in Russian history. Themistocles was similar to Patriarch Filaret (the father of Mikhail Romanov), for example, and Epaminondas resembled Peter I's general Golitsyn. Shishkov wanted to illustrate the point that a true patriot is willing to make sacrifices on the battlefield, risk persecution by foreign enemies, accept certain death, and even defy the laws of his own people in defense of his nation. None of these heroes had been monarchs, and all had exhibited individual moral courage. It was not difficult to recognize the reference to people like Shishkov himself, who stood up to his own rulers to warn that the fatherland was in danger. His Russian patriots had confronted Tatars and Poles; the implication was that Alexander I should likewise resist Napoleon.

While he condemned those who did not love their country, he considered a more insidious and serious problem to be those who strayed from patriotism out of weakness. "Take away from us the blindness that makes us see a beloved person as perfect," he said, and "the mind will begin to reason, the heart will grow cold, and soon this person, who before was above comparisons, will cease to seem unique in the world, and will become, first equal with all, and then actually worse than others." "The same," he asserted, "is true of the fatherland." This syndrome had affected some in Russia, who despised anything Russian and admired anything foreign. While he condemned the kind of pride that led man to rebel against God and virtue, a nation needed the sort of national pride that motivated people to work unselfishly for their country. If a people recognized itself as inferior in a particular area of thought or activity, it should seek to uplift itself by its own means, not lose heart and rush to imitate foreigners.

Only patriotism could steel a people against an invader, and enemies could sap its strength by undermining its spiritual cohesion and attachment to its own identity, "a means more certain than swords and guns." Indeed, "little by little it imposes moral fetters, so it can later impose real chains as well." If one people so entranced another that it "did not love its country, its customs, its language, its handicrafts, its amusements, its costume, its food, its air, and if it found all this to be not good at home and better abroad"—that would be a "disparagement worthy of pity." Patriotism inspired people to defend their country's honor, traditions, and interests. A proud people was a friend to all nations, but only so long as they did not seek to conquer it through cunning or violence—a transparent reference to Russian Francophiles and Tilsit.

What, Shishkov asked, were the wellsprings of Russian national pride? He identified three factors. The first was the Orthodox faith. Religion was the ultimate source of morality, and hence of social peace, equity, and loyalty to one's country; and faith in God and eternal life gave men the strength to face the horrors of battle. People who knew nothing of the true faith might be capable of some of these qualities, but those who had deliberately rejected it could never rise above selfish passions. Only if the young were raised to love their faith could they love their monarch, their country, and humanity.

It followed, he reasoned—this was the second point—that youth needed to be educated by its compatriots. Even the best-intentioned foreigner, though possibly a source of useful technical instruction, would raise young Russians to love the foreigner's own country and customs, and they would cease to be Russians themselves. But what would happen if the foreigner harbored "bad morals, a penchant for unbelief, for willfulness, for universal citizenship, for the new and ruinous philosophy, for those deceptive words of government by anarchy, loyal betrayal, philanthropic torture of people and fettered liberty?" The consequences of such an education could be averted only if Russia undertook more vigorously to develop its own educators and if they received greater respect than they currently enjoyed. In case of doubt, however, ignorance was preferable to a bad education: "Better a simple man with common sense and good morals than a learned one with depraved thoughts and a bad heart."

The third source of patriotism was respect for language and literature. Karamzin, in an essay from 1802 on patriotism, had already argued that love for one's own language was a sign of national self-respect.[95] Shishkov took this idea further by arguing that language and letters were the "people's soul, the mirror of its morals, the faithful indicator of its enlightenment and the incessant advocate of its deeds." If a people's thinking was mendacious, its language could not convey truth. Language was "the criterion for the people's mind, soul and qualities. It cannot prosper where the mind obeys the heart and the heart obeys blindness and error." This was obviously another attack on the French and their language and books; besides, the "newspeak" of the French Revolution, like that of the Petrine reforms, had established an obvious connection between linguistic and political change. A virtuous people's language expressed and encouraged virtue. A shared language was also the essential bond that defined and united a nation. If people lost respect for their language, they lost respect for their nation as well.[96]

The speech lasted about ninety minutes. Shishkov had earlier been anxious about the audience's response, but "the success surpassed my expectation, and there I saw that, however morals might have been corrupted, the truth does not cease to live in the hearts of men." His bellicose tone, his broadside against the alliance with France, and his equation of patriotism with military glory and the rejection of the West struck a responsive chord. D. I. Khvostov, though personally unimpressed, observed that "the members of the Symposium were ecstatic." De Maistre had apparently come to the reading out of curiosity, but the audience was so excited that he could find no one to explain to him the cause of all the commotion.[97] Shishkov's critics, however, were outraged by this challenge to their patriotism. Thus Batiushkov, wounded in battle in 1807, bitterly complained to Petr Viazemskii about the Symposium's "ignorance" and "shamelessness": its members were talentless mediocrities who, "covering themselves with the shield of love for the fatherland (for which, in practice, I was always prepared to spill my blood, and they, ink) . . . persecute common sense"; and they were boring to boot.[98]

Shishkov's speech abounded with the nationalistic pathos, classical allusions, and praise of patriotic self-sacrifice that were staples of late Enlightenment culture across Europe. Although they could be used to defend an old regime, they had also been invoked, most famously, by the revolutionaries in France, and Shishkov and his friends sensed, at least intuitively, that they were negotiating a "slippery slope." In its ideological program the Symposium was, of course, worlds removed from the Jacobin Club, but was not the nature of the forum itself significant?

It appears that the Symposium's leaders saw the danger and sought to defuse it. Public oratory might have been a feature of revolutionary politics, but Shishkov's declamation was presumably staid and dignified rather than dramatic and rousing. Mass public gatherings could be politically volatile, but the Symposium's guests (selected from the "best people" only) came strictly by invitation, and the soirées' proceedings were carefully scripted in advance. Any spirit of egalitarianism within the Symposium that might even implicitly have challenged a social order based on rank and birth was countered by the society's emphatically hierarchical structure. Its leaders strove to involve the emperor and his family, officials, and courtiers in order to head off suspicions of political disloyalty. And yet, one gains the impression that these efforts to reconcile an autonomous public opinion with the old regime succeeded only in part, for both the monarch and the upper-class public treated the Symposium as a manifestation of opposition to his policies.

On March 17, 1812, Speranskii was suddenly dismissed as state secretary and sent into exile. His dismissal was due to the increasingly vocal public hostility to his policies, to reform in general, and to the rapprochement with Napoleon. The Continental System, the taxes on the nobility, the examinations required for promotions in state service, suspicions that the priest's son Speranskii was an enemy of the nobility, the ominous vagueness of public knowledge about the reforms he was proposing, the feeling of humiliation after Tilsit—all these grievances were deposited on his doorstep, although in some cases only because of critics' reluctance to blame the emperor directly. Mariia Fedorovna and Ekaterina Pavlovna were hostile to him as well, as were de Maistre, Stein, and other foreigners opposed to Alexander's foreign policy. Balashov, too, and other senior officials were involved in the intrigue.[99]

That hostility had left Alexander precariously isolated. Absent an immediate foreign threat, he felt able to resist domestic pressures; by 1812, however, the prospect of war made it imperative to heal the rift with the nobility, so Speranskii had to be dismissed and reform suspended. The courtier Count Gustav Armfelt, one of the participants in the intrigue, articulated this with particular bluntness: Speranskii must be accused of treason and "sacrificed, guilty or not; it's indispensable to rally the nation behind the head of state." This was essential, for "the war we will fight with Napoleon is no ordinary war, and, to avoid defeat, it must of necessity be made into a national war." "Listen to the public," he added. "What a fury it is in: a conspiracy has been uncovered—that's exactly what we need."[100]

De Maistre had the impression that the nobility, and even the mass of the population (who were groaning under burdensome taxes), were delighted with Speranskii's fall. In Penza (where many read Glinka's *Russian Messenger*), this event was "celebrated as the first victory over the French," Vigel' recalled. People congratulated each other and wondered only "how it was possible that the criminal, the betrayer of the state, the traitor, was not executed, and was merely removed from the capital and excluded from the affairs of state!" Speranskii's dismissal fully achieved its purpose and renewed the nobility's confidence in the emperor and his policies.[101]

That this was a victory for Rostopchin and Shishkov, the emperor himself made clear. Rostopchin had arrived in the capital on March 12 to request that Alexander assign him to his retinue. He later recalled that "the sovereign received me very well" and spoke of his determination to fight Napoleon to the death. Five days later, Speranskii was dismissed (Rostopchin denied prior knowledge of, let alone involvement in, any plot against him). Two weeks after Rostopchin's arrival in the capital, the emperor, apparently after a discussion with Ekaterina Pavlovna, appointed him military governor of Moscow. He initially declined the position, asking instead to join the emperor's suite. Ekaterina and Alexander first cajoled him, without success, and then Alexander simply ordered him to take the post offered.[102]

Shortly after Speranskii's dismissal, which apparently surprised Shishkov, the admiral was summoned to the emperor. Nervous, he went to the palace. Since Speranskii had been removed, and Mordvinov had also asked to be relieved of his duties, what shock might be awaiting Shishkov, given Alexander's low opinion of him? Instead, he was told: "I have read your treatise on love of the fatherland. Since those are your sentiments, you can be useful to it. We apparently will not be able to avoid war with the French; we need to levy recruits; I would like you to write the manifesto for that." Shishkov promptly drafted the manifesto in his grand, archaic style. Alexander accepted the draft, and the authorities soon reported from the provinces that the population was responding favorably to the text. As a result, on April 9, Shishkov was appointed to succeed Speranskii as state secretary (the other candidate considered for the position apparently had been Karamzin) and was instructed to join the emperor's military headquarters in Vilna in April.[103]

Yet these appointments were less than a triumph for the conservatives. The appointees did not receive key positions of power: Rostopchin was kept away from the imperial headquarters altogether, and Shishkov inherited only Speranskii's title, not his influence. The significance of their new positions lay in their function as liaisons between emperor and people, a task at which, paradoxically, they seemed quite skilled. Moscow had long been a hotbed of opposition, and discontent might intensify if a French invasion was at all successful. With his dictatorial demeanor and local ties, Rostopchin was ideally suited to preserve public tranquillity there. Furthermore, he had proven his ability to communicate through his writings with sections of the population beyond the aristocracy; the same was true of Glinka, whose *Russian Messenger* now began receiving imperial subsidies.[104] Shishkov, meanwhile, had demonstrated in the Symposium his mastery of patriotic pathos. His language in the *Treatise on Love of the Fatherland* was precisely what the government needed in order to pitch the war to the masses, and he was therefore assigned the task of writing the emperor's public pronouncements.

By appointing Rostopchin and Shishkov, Alexander had made a powerful gesture of reconciliation to the conservatives who identified with them. His action had broken visibly with the policies of Speranskii and Tilsit and co-opted the most prominent conservative leaders. In addition, he had recruited propagandists with a proven ability to discuss current affairs in language intelligible to the humbler strata of the reading public. From now on, instead of criticizing Alexander's policies, Shishkov, Rostopchin, and Glinka used their resources and credibility to justify his regime's actions to the population.

CHAPTER FIVE

The
"War for the Fatherland"
A People's War?

Napoleon's invasion in 1812 sparked a debate in Russian "society" over the purpose of the war, behind which loomed fundamental disagreements over the nature of Russia's sociopolitical order. One question concerned the character of the war. Was it a conventional contest between rival monarchs or an all-or-nothing effort to save Russia from national subjugation and social chaos? And was it imperative to mobilize all the nation's resources, human and material, given that Napoleon could draw on the wealth and manpower of most of Europe?

The notion of a *levée en masse* inspired mixed feelings among the likes of Shishkov and Rostopchin. On the bright side, it suited their nationalism and hatred of Napoleon to see the people united against the Corsican; however, battle-trained peasant militias, armed with pitchforks and muskets and slogans of liberation, were the stuff of a serf owner's nightmares. De Maistre spoke for many that autumn when he wondered whether "this armed people, which has proved itself so brilliantly, [will] return peacefully to its original state?" These peasants, now "changed into veritable guerrillas who know only how to kill"—would they "turn back into docile serfs"? The specter of a serf revolt haunted nobles across Russia. Vigel' observed this in Penza, a provincial town remote from the war zone, and in the capital, John Quincy Adams found that it was "what most touches the feelings

of all the Russians with whom I have conversed on this subject." Yet these appre-
hensions proved groundless. There were cases of insubordination, sometimes
linked to a mistaken belief that militia service freed one from servitude, and
Napoleon, to pressure Alexander I to make peace, encouraged rumors that he
would proclaim emancipation,[1] but by and large the peasants remained loyal and
even joined in the struggle against the French.

The other issue troubling conservatives—and everyone else—was the nature
of Russia's war aims. Once the *Grande Armée* had been defeated, should Russia
turn a war of national defense into a campaign to destroy the Napoleonic empire?

The first question, about the character of the war, was especially problematic,
for conservatives were deeply ambivalent about the notion of a *narodnaia voina,*
a "people's war." Rostopchin distrusted the masses and (much like the tsarist
government of 1914–1917) sought to both stymie and manipulate their desire to
participate in the war. Glinka, by contrast, reveled in the unity of an otherwise
painfully divided society as it faced a common national enemy (an attitude reminiscent of the "spirit of August 1914"). Shishkov occupied an intermediate position. As usual, he was more benign than the suspicious Rostopchin but did not
share Glinka's naïve exuberance. Rostopchin saw as his mission the prevention
of mass unrest and "Martinist" subversion, while Glinka experienced 1812 as the
apotheosis of the "Russian spirit." Shishkov viewed the entire war as a necessary
but repulsive affair, onerous to him (an "old man" of nearly sixty, he had to follow Alexander's headquarters as it crisscrossed Russia and Central Europe) and
perilous for the empire.

All three realized that mass participation made 1812 a phenomenon unprecedented in recent Russian history. Glinka expressed this feeling when he invoked
the Time of Troubles (1605–1613), the last occasion when Russia had faced such
a powerful external threat. The novelty of 1812 flowed from the French Revolution, which had replaced small, reluctant, professional armies with large and enthusiastic forces based on conscription. The nation, from being a bystander in
war, had become a decisive actor. The victories of the revolutionary armies and
Napoleon, the swift collapse of Prussia in 1806, and the successful Spanish resistance against the French all made this clear. When, after the disaster at Jena and
with the French armies advancing into Prussia, the Berlin police president announced that "the king has lost a battle. Now the citizenry's first duty is to remain
calm," he unwittingly made clear how counterproductive the dynastic state's effort was to exclude the nation from the war.[2] Only with the nation's full support
was victory possible. In Russia, however, "the nation" was the enserfed peasantry, and mobilizing it threatened both social stability and the division of labor
among social classes that was supposed to legitimize serfdom in the first place.

Conservatives tried variously to resolve this dilemma. Rostopchin appealed to
xenophobia and fear of masonic conspiracies in order to deflect popular discontent from the nobles and the serf system. Glinka hoped that the war would revitalize the social compact by showing the nobles that their own serfs, not foreign

aristocrats, were their true kinsmen. He appealed to Russians' pride in their history and to popular monarchism to bridge the divide between the classes. Such solidarity across class lines might release similar energies in Russia as in France after 1789, except that the cause would be a conservative sense of national harmony, not the overthrow of the old regime. Glinka even hinted at the kind of universalism that shaped both the French Revolution and, later, the Holy Alliance: to the French republicans' belief that *la Grande Nation* was destined to bring *liberté, égalité, fraternité* to a European continent in thrall to despotism and superstition,[3] he opposed the proto-Slavophile notion that Russia's Christian virtue would rescue Europe from the barbarism of the Enlightenment. Shishkov advocated a traditional, isolationist version of these ideas. Unlike Glinka, he had no use for social change and did not favor a Russian campaign to liberate Europe. However, he agreed that the war was cultural and spiritual as well as military, and he used imperial proclamations to denounce cultural Francophilia. Like Glinka, he believed that the war should bring about a reconciliation between classes as the nobles returned to their national roots. However, he emphasized preserving the structures of the old regime, whereas Glinka was more interested in its capacity for moral change.

What all three sought to do, albeit in different ways, was to convince Russians that the old regime was essential to their national identity. Their invocations of history, praise for the national character, ridicule of the French, even the archaic language of Shishkov's manifestoes, all aimed at making this point. True Orthodox Russians, they argued, were loyal to tsar and country, obeyed their lords, and hated the invaders. The people were to rise, not (like the French in 1792) in the defense of universal principles of liberty and popular sovereignty, but rather (like the Spaniards, or the Prussians in 1813) to fight for the right to live traditionally Russian lives, which included the "right" to serfdom and autocracy. A century after Peter I's reforms, it was implied, tsar and nobility were resuming their traditional role of leading "Holy Russia." In response to the Enlightenment rhetoric of Napoleon, conservatives declared the Europeanized old regime of the Petersburg autocracy to be the heir to Kiev and Muscovy, while equating *Imperator* Alexander I—the frustrated reformer, half-German and Francophone—with the pious tsars of old. In this way the conservatives launched a tradition that grew ever stronger in the last century of imperial Russia and reached its apogee after 1881: the idea that the European old regime of the eighteenth century, dressed up in Muscovite rhetoric and symbolism, represented Russia's true identity and its special path into the future.[4]

Rostopchin's view of the strategic situation was at first ambivalent. At times he exhibited a robust confidence, as when he wrote to the emperor: "Your Empire has two powerful defenders in its expanse and its climate. . . . The Emperor of Russia will always remain formidable in Moscow, terrible in Kazan', and invincible in Tobol'sk." He also argued optimistically that the masses, unsullied by foreign influences, would rise up against the invaders. He asserted that the people of

Moscow so hated the French that he needed to protect innocent foreign residents from angry mobs. Therefore, he concluded, the enemy's propaganda of liberty had no appeal for Russians. Yet he worried about the military situation. Though aware of the benefits of drawing the enemy into Russia's vast interior, he was alarmed at the steady Russian retreat and ceaselessly pleaded with the emperor not to yield more territory. The possibility that Moscow might fall particularly alarmed him, since he expected such a setback to deal a terrible blow to Russian morale.[5] He worried that the empire was politically unstable and might collapse in the absence of good news from the battlefield. Although he questioned the nobility's selflessness and patriotism, he particularly feared trouble from two other quarters—the plebeian masses and the "Martinists"—which his administration sought to prevent through a combination of demagogy and repression. These concerns led to the most famous (or notorious) episodes of his tenure as governor: his propaganda campaign and the Kliucharev-Vereshchagin affair. Both have received scholarly attention in the past but are worth revisiting for the insight they offer into Rostopchin's political philosophy and style of government.

Rostopchin's propaganda activities, in 1812 as before, were based on two assumptions: that the brutish, volatile masses required tight supervision, and that he was ideally suited to provide it because he intuitively understood them and could (literally and figuratively) speak their language. In 1812, he appeared in public in as many places and as often as possible and made himself available to citizens wishing to see him; as he later boastfully recalled, "Two mornings were all I needed to show off and convince most Moscow residents that I was indefatigable and that they were seeing me everywhere." Though he never ceased to marvel that the people "are always inclined to some kind of foolishness when they gather in a crowd," he enjoyed manipulating that trait for his own ends. He later recalled that "persons of all ages and ranks, all of them idlers drawn by the wish to find out something positive" about the progress of the war, gathered in the mornings at his residence when he received couriers from the army. The crowd tried to guess the tenor of their reports from his expression as he read them, so he made a point of looking cheerful even when the news was bad (as it usually was that summer). The onlookers had no idea, he remembered with satisfaction, "that I was a talented pantomime, and had, in my youth, excelled in the art of acting."[6]

Regarding Moscow itself, Rostopchin fretted about mass panic as the French drew nearer. To dispel the public's fears, he regularly issued news bulletins that were printed in the *Moscow News* and posted around the city. These took two forms: some simply reproduced official army communiqués or imperial proclamations more or less verbatim, while others, written by the governor in his trademark colloquial style, summoned the people to hate and despise the French.[7] One of these appeals, for instance, featured the fictional *meshchanin* (man of the urban lower class) Karniushka Chikhirin leaving the tavern after a few drinks and cursing the French. (The character's name is derived from *chikhir'* ["strong red wine"] and means "drunkard.")[8] Most of the text was devoted to his stream-of-consciousness rantings, complete with popular vulgarisms, phonetic spelling, and virtually no punctuation. He taunts Napoleon, "Your soldiers are little dwarves and dandies," and ominously describes the fate of past Swedish, Polish, and Tatar invaders: "And beneath the mushrooms are their bones well your force too will go to its grave."

Propoganda leaflet issued by F. V. Rostopchin in Moscow in 1812. The text reads: "The Moscow *meshchanin* [man of the urban lower class] and veteran Karniushka Chikhirin, after drinking one glass too many and hearing people saying that Bonaparte wanted to come to Moscow, grew angry, cursed all Frenchmen with nasty words, came out of the tavern and, beneath the [imperial double] eagle, began speaking thus."

Elsewhere Rostopchin reminded Muscovites of their mighty defenders before God ("the Mother of God and the Miracle-Working Saints of Moscow"), the world ("our merciful Sovereign ALEKSANDR PAVLOVICH") and the enemy ("our Christ-loving soldiers"). The people needed only "obedience, devotion and faith in the words of their Leaders." He particularly warned them about Napoleon's cunning promises of freedom and social equality: "He promises the soldiers a fieldmarshalship, the paupers mountains of gold and the people freedom, but he will catch all of them by the whiskers, trap them in his vise and send them to their death." Anyone heard repeating the enemy's lies should be reported to the police, he wrote. He concluded by calling himself "a loyal servant of the Tsar, a Russian lord and an Orthodox Christian," thus restating his themes of monarchism, social hierarchy, and Orthodoxy.[9]

Rostopchin faced a volatile mood in the old capital. Morale had risen with Alexander I's visit in July, but after his departure, and especially after the fall of Smolensk (regarded as the main obstacle to Napoleon's advance), the population became nervous. As the Russian army withdrew toward Moscow, Rostopchin worked ever harder to raise the people's spirits, inflating Russian successes, and disseminating misleading rumors. After the battle at Borodino on August 26, for example, General Kutuzov had reported cautiously that heavy casualties were forcing him to retreat, yet Rostopchin asserted in one of his bulletins that Kutuzov was promising not to surrender Moscow.[10] Fear of unrest was never far from his mind. He worried that the exemption from militia service granted to state-owned peasants would arouse the envy of the noble-owned serfs, who were required to serve and who would vent their anger on their noble masters. He later warned the emperor that further retreat would allow Napoleon to stir the people to revolt, since they were demoralized by the loss of Moscow.[11] After the fall of the city, he wrote to Minister of Police Balashov that he had "kept Moscow quiet . . . and protected the state from the seeds of revolt," which had indeed been his chief goal. In 1813 one of his trusted lieutenants, A. Ia. Bulgakov, wrote a pamphlet (under Rostopchin's guidance) in which he defended the governor's methods. He argued that, had the masses known of the desperate military situation and had their opinions not been controlled by the government, there might have been anarchy; this could be avoided only if the people were addressed in their own language.[12]

Rostopchin's attitude toward the popular mobilization brought about by the war was complex. He viewed the masses as instinctively anti-French: "The mood of the people is such that daily it makes me weep for joy," he reported to Balashov a week before Borodino. He tried to prevent lynchings of innocent foreigners, but he also enjoyed indulging popular xenophobia. In early August, for instance, he wrote that his Belgian cook had said that Napoleon was coming to liberate the people, and somebody promptly turned him in to Rostopchin, who had him publicly whipped the following day and then deported to Siberia.[13]

After the fall of the city he appealed to the peasants of the area (on whom Napoleon had to rely for supplies) not to trade with "the enemy of the human race, God's punishment for our sins, the devilish apparition, the evil Frenchman." He described in lurid terms how the French had desecrated churches and graveyards and urged "you Orthodox, loyal servants of our Tsar" to distrust their false promises and defend Holy Russia against the blasphemers. Any subversive implications that might have been read into such appeals were headed off by the definition of a good Orthodox Russian as a "loyal servant of our Tsar." The emperor had always been a (remote and abstract) object of popular affection, but not so the landlords, so he also urged the peasants to resist the impulse to riot against them. Instead, Rostopchin told them to "honor your leaders and landowners, for they are your defenders and helpers and are ready to give you clothing, shoes, food and drink." The nobles' legitimacy came from the emperor, who received it from God: "He is our father and we his children, while the evil Frenchman is an unbaptized enemy. He is prepared to sell even his own soul, he even has already been a Turk, for he became a Muslim while in Egypt." After thus repeating the Holy Synod's claims of 1806–1807 (when it likened Napoleon to the Antichrist), he concluded by calling on the peasants to "destroy the insolent scum, the filthy vermin"; in reward, the emperor will "restore you as you had been before, and you shall live in clover like you used to." Thus the peasants were to fight, on their own initiative, for the restoration of the old regime, and under the leadership of its elites.

Rostopchin regarded the masses as a formidable but mindless force that would crush anything—French armies or Russian nobles—standing in its path. Unlike many nobles in 1812, he felt no spiritual bond with the common people, to whom he preached a bellicose Francophobia but refused, even as Moscow was falling, to open the military arsenal at his disposal. Instead, he saw them as a tiger he must ride if the old regime was to survive the war.[14] Tartakovskii stresses this point in comparing Rostopchin's propaganda with the bulletins disseminated by the army headquarters. The army bulletins provided relatively accurate information and appealed to a sense of civic duty, while Rostopchin's leaflets were misleading and appealed to xenophobia. These two types of propaganda reflected differing attitudes toward the nation and the war. The army bulletins were drafted by re-formist (civilian) officials who saw the people's war effort as a prelude to an eventual abolition of serfdom, and by Kutuzov, who understood the military's need for popular support. Rostopchin opposed the officials and disliked Kutuzov. The army spokesmen considered the peasants fellow citizens with whom one should reason. Rostopchin saw them as boorish *muzhiki,* almost as dangerous to the Russian side as they were to Napoleon.[15]

He also feared the "Martinists." He felt surrounded by them and attributed all criticism of his administration to them. He warned the emperor that they were "your hidden enemies" (June 30) and that "this hellish sect cannot contain its hatred for you and Russia, and its devotion to the enemy" (August 4). "If the armies suffer sustained setbacks and the police have difficulty containing the wretches who are preaching a revolt, I will have a few of them hanged," he vowed (August 13). They were Napoleon's fifth column, he wrote: "If by misfortune your cruel enemy succeeds in undermining the loyalty of your subjects, Sire, you will see the Martinists unveil their plans, which will support Bonaparte's perfectly" (September 19).[16]

His campaign against them took several forms. He denounced distinguished Muscovites to the emperor as traitors,[17] and old Novikov was placed under house arrest. Rostopchin's main target was Fedor P. Kliucharev (director of the Moscow post office), because of a personal feud between him and Rostopchin's friend and lieutenant Adam F. Broker, and because the post office could open private letters; if Rostopchin controlled it, he could prevent complaints about himself from reaching St. Petersburg. The postal director was the local intelligence-gatherer for the interior minister, who reported to the emperor and could strengthen or damage Rostopchin's position in St. Petersburg.

Rostopchin's weapon against Kliucharev was a merchant's son named Vereshchagin, found to have Russian translations of speeches by Napoleon published in foreign papers that were banned in Russia and were intercepted at the post office. Rostopchin declared him a traitor who must be punished with utmost severity; at one point he advised the emperor to sentence the hapless young man to death and commute his sentence (to hard labor in Siberia) only as the public execution was about to take place. Rostopchin denounced him both in a bulletin published in Moscow[18] and in repeated letters to Alexander I. He tried to link

Vereshchagin with Kliucharev, whom he exiled to Voronezh (in arbitrary violation of the service rules) after arresting his assistant Druzhinin and dispatching him to St. Petersburg. In his reports, Rostopchin depicted the postal director as the head of a monstrous, regicidal conspiracy, but the emperor's tepid response to these charges suggests that he understood their absurdity. Indeed, as Kizevetter has pointed out, there was a strange disproportion between the vast scale of the plot Rostopchin alleged and the mere handful of (obviously harmless) "plotters" he actually identified. Vereshchagin himself came to a tragic end, linked ever since with Rostopchin's name because it epitomized the deep unease that his brutal demagogy inspired in other Russian nobles and because Tolstoy depicted it with such damning eloquence in *War and Peace*. Though the details are obscure, this much is certain: Vereshchagin's dossier traveled between Moscow and Petersburg for two inconclusive months; finally, on September 2, in the hours before French troops entered Moscow, Rostopchin turned him over to a frenzied mob to be lynched, an act that deeply offended the emperor himself.[19]

The attack on the "Martinists" was motivated by three considerations. One was crudely political: with his dark warnings of organized subversion, Rostopchin could portray himself as an indispensable guardian of imperial interests. Second, his authoritarian instincts placed him at odds with independent thinkers of any description, and in his contempt for the upper class he usually divided its members into only two categories: spineless nonentities and rebellious "Martinists." That General Kutuzov (who became his archenemy after the fall of Moscow) was a freemason may have further intensified his hostility. Last, he needed scapegoats to blame for Russia's setbacks and to punish as a lesson to others; this followed from his fear of social unrest and his belief in the credulity of the masses.[20]

Rostopchin never wavered in his belief that the French must be defeated, and was willing to go to great personal lengths to achieve this, especially if it kept him in the limelight. His role in the great fire that destroyed much of Moscow remains in dispute, but he did, in a typically theatrical gesture, set fire to his own estate at Voronovo, leaving behind only a defiant message. This scorched-earth patriotism did not fail to impress the French, who, one of their generals recalled, read his note "shuddering with surprise." According to another French general, "It had a profound effect on every thinking [Frenchman], and won the Governor more admirers than critics," even though Napoleon himself "turned the whole thing to ridicule."[21]

As governor-general, Rostopchin continued to act as the self-appointed voice of the Moscow nobility vis-à-vis the emperor. He denounced current policy as well as most senior officials. He demanded that Kutuzov (whom Alexander disliked as much as he disliked Rostopchin) be made commander of the army, only to attack him relentlessly after their falling-out over the military's evacuation of Moscow. There was much self-promotion in Rostopchin's letters to the monarch, but little flattery or hypocrisy. As Kizevetter has argued, Rostopchin had strong political convictions and considered it his duty to stand up to the emperor himself if autocracy and noble privilege seemed threatened.[22] The manner in which he combined demagogic methods with a fierce commitment to Russia's old regime sparked considerable controversy among contemporaries. Some, such as General Bagration, A. P. Obolenskii, and Karamzin, admired him as a great patriot, although Karamzin found his proclamations unpleasantly vulgar and offered helpfully to write them for him. His friend Zhukovskii liked them, however, and Prince Viazemskii, though put off by their rabble-rousing tone, conceded that a more measured style (such as Karamzin's) might have been less effective in stirring the people. Vigel' and M. A. Dmitriev recalled that many nobles had shared these reservations, but both agreed on the effectiveness of Rostopchin's unconventional style. The Turgenev brothers, on the other hand, were appalled at his brutal and demagogic methods (as was Tolstoy in *War and Peace*).[23]

Rostopchin's actions reflected a ruthless pragmatism. He hoped to preserve the social order by redirecting popular aggression from the nobility onto the French and the "Martinists." Unlike some contemporaries, he grasped one important consequence of the French Revolution: total war, waged with every weapon and on every front. So he raided the propaganda arsenal of the revolution: crudely demagogic rhetoric (if his character Bogatyrev was not worthy of Hébert's Père Duchesne, surely Karniushka Chikhirin was), the deliberate fomenting of paranoid conspiracy theories, exemplary public punishment of suspected enemy agents, the use of "controlled" mob violence. It was not that Rostopchin, a cultivated *grand seigneur,* necessarily enjoyed this; however, unlike a Shishkov or a Glinka, he had no ideological scruples about using the most powerful tools available to him.

The diversity of "conservative" views of the war becomes apparent when one examines the emperor's visit to Moscow in July 1812. This story begins with Admiral Shishkov, whose main function as newly appointed state secretary was to draft the imperial proclamations and manifestoes by which the monarch spoke to his people. The confusion he found at the headquarters in Vilna appalled him. It was unclear whether Alexander or General Barklai de Tolli was in charge; a naval officer (Admiral Chichagov) was in command of one of the three armies; and Grand Duke Konstantin knew nothing more urgent than to drill troops on the parade ground. With attitudes toward the impending conflict so casual, Shishkov felt depressed and pessimistic. Once the retreat began, he was most concerned (like Rostopchin) about stemming the spread of defeatism, so he kept urging the emperor to sound defiant. No admirer of Alexander I, he objected to describing the headlong retreat as a calculated strategy, a claim he thought devoid of credibility. Years later he still insisted that not the retreat had saved Russia, but only enemy overconfidence, the fire of Moscow, the guerrilla war, the appointment of Kutuzov, and the brutal winter. None of these had been foreseeable: the retreat itself ought to have doomed Russia, and only divine intervention saved it from disaster.

He thought the emperor's presence at headquarters a mistake, for it undermined Barklai's authority and turned any setback into a personal defeat for the monarch. Perhaps the influence of his friend Kutuzov, who had argued against Alexander's disastrous strategy at Austerlitz, induced Shishkov to distrust the emperor's generalship, as did the petty military formalism that he detested and that Paul I's sons had all inherited. The emperor belonged on the home front, to arouse patriotism and reassure the population. Aware that the monarch (who hoped to erase the humiliation of Austerlitz) would resist the idea, Shishkov prevailed upon Arakcheev and Balashov to second him, and after a few days' reflection, Alexander reluctantly agreed.[24]

On July 11, the imperial party arrived in Moscow, where the emperor hoped to convince the nobility to "volunteer" a portion of its serfs for the militia, and the merchantry to donate money for the war effort. He received a tumultuous welcome upon his arrival,[25] and one of the leaders of the crowd (according to Sergei Glinka) was Sergei Glinka. Early in the morning, upon hearing of the creation of the militia, he had rushed to Rostopchin's residence to be the first man to enlist in the force. He later recalled, still intoxicated with exuberance, that "people felt a serene confidence" when they heard of the monarch's visit. "Not one word of hatred and indignation toward the enemy crossed their lips. All thoughts, all words mingled in a single feeling of love." Already he felt like a popular leader when, "turning to me, they said: *You, your Honor! Lead us!* I cried: *Hurrah! Forward!* And thousands of voices repeated: *Hurrah! Forward.*" "On July 11, 1812," he concluded modestly, "the impetuous spirit of the people made me the leader of its devotion."[26] Needless to say, impetuous popular spirits selecting leaders in a burst of spontaneous patriotic rapture was hardly customary under the old regime, but neither was Glinka a man of the old regime.

The high point of Alexander's visit was to be his address, on July 15, to large deputations of the Moscow nobility and merchantry. To protect the hierarchical sensibilities of the monarchy, the two groups of listeners would be gathered in separate halls of the Slobodskoi palace. However, in Glinka's imagination, this exercise in old-regime caste awareness became transfigured into a glorious patriotic catharsis. He later recalled that, in the nobility's hall before the emperor's arrival, he had improvised a long and impassioned speech (cut short only by Rostopchin's arrival), prophesying the fall of Moscow because "our national chronicles [show] that Moscow is accustomed to suffering for Russia" and because "the surrender of Moscow will be the salvation of Russia and Europe." How much of this is mere retrospective fantasy is, of course, difficult to assess. His memoirs are equally rhapsodic about the assembly of merchants: as during the most glorious moments of the Time of Troubles, "the spirit of Minin [the merchant who helped to oust the Poles in 1612–1613] was resurrected in every townsman."[27]

This was no Estates-General. Alexander I was merely asking for help in a war that depended primarily on the effectiveness of his armies. Yet the events in Moscow that July, otherwise a mere footnote to history, become more interesting when viewed in light of what had occurred in Versailles twenty-three summers earlier. Louis XVI had called the Estates-General to help him resolve his kingdom's crisis, but in a spirit of old-regime hierarchy, dividing them into orders even for such minutiae as attire and seating arrangements. The king and many among the first two orders (clergy and nobility) insisted on this division, knowing it was essential to the integrity of the regime. The radicals among them as well as the Third Estate, however, were swept up in the pathos of "the nation" and insisted on the unification of the three orders. Similar concerns governed the Festival of the Federation in Paris in 1790: from across France, thousands gathered to pledge undying loyalty to *la patrie,* thereby both celebrating the democratic idea of popular sovereignty and affirming a belligerent, heroic sense of national unanimity. As Jean Starobinski points out, the revolutionary fêtes aimed at mobilizing the mass exaltation of the moment in order to solemnly commit the nation to a glorious future; this distinguished them from the vapid, ephemeral fêtes of the aristocracy.[28] Glinka, who likewise hated aristocratic dissipation and would have dearly loved to partake in such a moment of national oneness, projected these feelings onto 1812: Russia, overcoming caste divisions, both rallied behind its monarch and imparted to him its own emotion and sense of purpose. Glinka did not see himself as a revolutionary; yet he was, by temperament and sensibility, a stranger to the stratified world of the old regime.

Shishkov and Rostopchin accompanied the emperor during his meetings with the roughly one thousand nobles and the merchants, and their account of the atmosphere bears out Glinka's. To the merchants Shishkov read the proclamation he had drafted. This was no spontaneous outburst like Glinka's, for Shishkov represented traditional monarchy in all its majesty. "The enemy has crossed Our borders," he solemnly intoned. "He has conceived the malicious intention of destroying [Russia's] glory and prosperity. With cunning in his heart and flattery on his lips he brings to it eternal chains and fetters." General Ségur, at Napoleon's headquarters, was stunned by the violence of these lines, and the merchants responded similarly. Even Rostopchin was impressed, and wrote later on that at this point the crowd "tore their hair, wrung their hands," and "over the noise one could not hear what they were saying, but it was threats, cries of fury and groans. It was a unique spectacle." Continuing his speech, Shishkov demanded that the enemy, "at every step, find loyal sons of Russia, striking him with all their means and strength and heeding none of his tricks and lies." Recalling the heroes of the Time of Troubles, he said, "may he meet a Pozharskii in every nobleman, a Palitsyn in every cleric, a Minin in every townsman." Maintaining social distinctions, he appealed separately to each class, but urged them to "unite, all: with the cross in your heart and weapons in your hands, no human strength can overcome you." He thus viewed the war effort as reaffirming the social hierarchy that Glinka wished to see transcended. It is telling that Glinka's memoirs devote sixteen exuberant pages to the monarch's visit, stressing the spontaneous devotion of the masses to the father of the nation, in Moscow, a setting rich with pre-Petrine history and religious symbolism. Shishkov's, on the other hand, spend under a page on the visit and mention only the speech to the nobility.[29]

Rostopchin, who was also struck by the people's response but did not share Glinka's and Shishkov's confidence in Alexander I's subjects, characteristically saw the visit in terms of propaganda and public order. It had come to his attention, he recalled, that "the Martinists" planned to sabotage the meeting with the nobility by asking "insolent" questions that suggested a critical civic awareness ("How great are the forces of our army? How strong is the enemy's army? What means are available for defense? etc."), so he made it plain that anyone who dared to "cause disorder, and who forgets himself in his sovereign's presence," would at once "begin a very long journey." He lent emphasis to this warning by posting policemen with travel-ready carriages outside the building. The result: "For the entire duration [of the meeting], the braggarts said not a word and behaved as befits well-mannered children."[30]

The contrast between Glinka's and Rostopchin's opinions of the imperial visit conceals an important fact. Glinka's outbursts of July 15 could occur only because Rostopchin judged them opportune; had he spoken differently, he might have found himself en route to Siberia in one of the military governor's carriages. He was the solution to the authoritarian conservatives' dilemma: a free spirit who independently argued the state's point of view. Viazemskii captured the irony in this by calling him "a born popular tribune, but a lawful tribune, a tribune for the government." This position was new for Glinka. As recently as July 11, he had been under official surveillance, obligated to report to the police on his role in the crowd welcoming the emperor. So his wife was understandably alarmed when, on the nineteenth, the fearsome Count Rostopchin sent for him, for the two men had quarreled since December 1809. But the governor magnanimously let bygones be bygones, gave Glinka a medal from the emperor "for your love for the Fatherland" and informed him that, "in the sacred name of the Lord Emperor, I untie your tongue for all that is beneficial to the Fatherland, and your hands with an extraordinary sum of three hundred thousand."[31] During the remaining weeks until the city fell, Glinka—now a government agent—continued publishing the *Russian Messenger,* which carried some of Rostopchin's proclamations and, as we have seen, reached a broad audience.[32] But the war did disrupt distribution, and he later remembered having succeeded in sending out no more than a hundred copies of any one issue that year.[33] He gave frequent speeches in support of the war and vigorously fueled Muscovites' patriotism, if contemporaries' memoirs are to be believed. Viazemskii, for example, noted later that in 1812 Glinka had been "the oracle of the provinces and the Chateaubriand of the Moscow militia."[34]

Only in some regards did Glinka see eye to eye with Rostopchin. Glinka later defended him against charges of having deceived Muscovites with promises that the city would be defended; he also praised his proclamations and rapport with the common people, and credited him with encouraging the peasants around Moscow to fight the French. Yet this support was not unambiguous. He particularly objected in retrospect to Rostopchin's doubts about the loyalty of the masses. This was perhaps their main disagreement, for Glinka believed that the war should unite Russians. His two autobiographical books on the war period continually note the parallel between 1812 and 1612, when Russia, led by the nobleman Pozharskii and the commoner Minin, had expelled Western invaders and freely elected the Romanov dynasty. National pride, solidarity across class boundaries, and "democratic" monarchism were parts of a heroic past that Glinka hoped to see resurrected in 1812. He also condemned Rostopchin's public ridiculing and deportation from Moscow of French residents, which he thought in poor taste, and he later obliquely distanced himself from the governor's propaganda by asserting that "no frenzy of hatred agitated Russia's sons" in 1812.[35] To this point he often returned: Russians formed a nation of love, not hate; their struggle had derived its dignity from their patriotic devotion, so vulgar xenophobia merely sullied the purity of their cause.

At least, this is what Glinka wrote twenty years after the war, once his Francophobia had subsided and he had reasons of his own to resent tyrannical officials. He was not so conciliatory in 1812, in the heat of battle, when he destroyed all his French books and (it appears) roamed the city in his carriage appealing to Muscovites to "give up French wines and drink our national raw vodka!" His *Messenger*, meanwhile, denounced Napoleon as "the progeny of sin, the slave of a false and hellish glory, the scum of nature, the cruel son of Gehenna."[36] Nevertheless, a moral and humanistic impulse undergirded his patriotism, and sharply differentiated him from Rostopchin.

Glinka's memoirs develop his theory of the war as a providential mystery, in which—as in 1612—a patriotic "Russian spirit" moved all Russians, from the emperor to the *muzhiki* ambushing the French in the forests. The estrangement of monarch and people troubled Glinka. He believed that the common people, who rarely distinguished between the natural and the supernatural, between secular and sacred history, were the wellspring of Russia's identity and strength. When monarchs and nobles had abandoned this conception of life for the arid ways of the West, they ruptured their link with the people. Alexander I's triumphant welcome in Moscow suggested that, like a prodigal son, he had returned to his people. Yet it would not do merely to invoke the memory of Minin and Pozharskii: "It was also necessary to call forth the Russian way of life of their time." It deeply disappointed Glinka that this did not occur, and that French culture and ways remained dominant in Russia even in 1812.

The invaders, he believed, had performed a role designed by cosmic forces beyond their ken. Alexander I had triumphed through patience, humility, and love. Napoleon was a "genius," a general greater than Alexander the Great or Caesar, drawn in his youth to a contemplative life but corrupted by power, and God had guided him in the fatal steps of proclaiming himself emperor and invading Russia. A tragic figure, he ultimately came to terms with his failings, and on St. Helena "it was confirmed, in Napoleon's solemn consciousness, that the heavenly word is *the word of life* and *of love*. There Providence refuted the arguments that confuse heaven with the machinations of men." In Moscow,

Napoleon was to meet his destiny; an irresistible force drew him there, to prepare his downfall and punish Russia for her sins, as the barbarians had destroyed the corrupt Roman empire.

That parallel proved the irrelevance of Europe's "enlightenment" to true civilization and morality, for it was Russia in 1813–1814 that saved Europe from itself and gave its civilization new life. After suffering the corrupting influence of the West, Russia would bring reason and moral light to Europe. It was typical of his desire to Russianize the Western myths he had absorbed as a cadet that Glinka substituted Russia's mission to redeem Europe for Europe's self-assigned task of civilizing Russia. Europe in the eighteenth century had sinned by its wars and by abandoning truth and love. As its crimes had grown more egregious, the divine warnings had become more severe, until the disastrous 1812 war that involved armies of many European nations. Europe's hollow "enlightenment," he wrote, resembled a tall ladder: from the pinnacle one plummeted horribly to the basest level of barbarism, as had the invaders of 1812. The horrors of the war, he argued, should finally open Europeans' eyes to their need for spiritual redemption. No slave to consistency, he elsewhere equated Napoleon with the Romans and with Charlemagne; now it was the Russians who were likened to the northern peoples who had ruined both the Roman and Carolingian empires. He was outraged that Napoleon had claimed to protect civilized Europe from the Russian savages: "For the *third time*," he declared, "the North has saved Europe in response to an invasion of the North by Europe; will the North be so magnanimous again? I don't know."

Moscow burned, as Glinka claimed to have foreseen, to save Russia and Europe. He accused Rostopchin of having lied in his 1823 pamphlet *The Truth about the Fire of Moscow,* which charged the French with setting the fire: instead, "*God's judgment* passed over [Moscow] and in it. This was neither the Russians nor the French: this was a *heavenly fire.*" God had smitten aristocratic Moscow: "Our falsehoods burned; our fashions, our splendors, our plots and intrigues; all of this burned, but did it burn up completely?" In 1612, Russia's salvation had been organized in Holy Moscow, but in 1812 the now corrupted city was given up—not to Napoleon but "to God's judgment."[37]

His conception of the people's role in the war has given rise to some misunderstandings. Tartakovskii argues that Glinka did not see 1812 as a "people's war" (one conducted at the people's initiative and under their own leadership) because he linked that notion with the democratic tendencies of the Time of Troubles. Glinka does indeed, in the passage Tartakovskii cites, refer pejoratively to the early seventeenth century; he argues against calling 1812 a "people's war," suggesting instead that monarch, army, and nation together fulfilled a providential mission,[38] so 1812 was a display of social harmony, not of popular independence from authority. Yet Tartakovskii errs in equating Glinka's thinking with that of Rostopchin, to whom the people in arms represented the specter of anarchy. Glinka trusted their loyalty and admired their struggle. His language is telling: "The Russian soul," he asserted later, had "defended the Russian land," so praise for victory was due not only to the army, the emperor, and the icy weather. Unlike Rostopchin ("I have succeeded perfectly in making the peasant despise the French soldier"; "I have saved the empire"),[39] he took no credit for sparking the guerrilla war but respected the peasants' patriotism and desire to defend their homes. To the question of what motivated Russians, he answered: *"the common cause,"* not the ruler or the social order.[40] Rostopchin regarded the "people's war" as, at best, a dangerous military necessity. Glinka considered it an exhilarating spectacle of national solidarity.

Glinka had far-reaching hopes for the changes in society that the war would cause. After the fall of Moscow, his reminiscences tell us, he and his brothers were traveling toward Riazan' in search of Sergei's family. As they rode they naturally discussed the war. They came to a conclusion so remarkable—in the convergence it shows between the "conservative" Sergei and the future Decembrist Fedor—that it deserves to be quoted in full.

> Unusual events also produce unusual transformations in society. On this basis we proposed:
>
> *First,* that the rapprochement of the nobles and the peasants for the joint defense of the Fatherland would also bring them closer together in the moral realm, and that, without the nobles making the peasants into philosophers, they would at least grant them the status of humans.
>
> *Second,* we thought that the owners of thousands of souls would abandon the caprice of the fashions of the capitals and towns, and would begin to live on their estates, so that *management by others* would not ruin their properties and bring suffering to the estimable people who feed humanity and the Fatherland, that is, the farmers.
>
> *Finally,* we imagined that the annihilation of the all-devouring fashions and a change of our spiritless education would bring the souls of all classes of society together and breathe a new life into them.
>
> A utopia, a utopia! A dream, a dream!

Glinka hoped for a social transformation through a moral epiphany among the nobility. Though prudently vague on the issue of serfdom in his memoirs (given the censorship realities of 1836), he apparently hoped to see injustice vanquished without formal changes in the social order. Still, he was closer in spirit to liberals who hoped the "people's war" would end serfdom than to conservatives who wished only to protect the old regime.[41]

After the visit to Moscow, Admiral Shishkov and the emperor had returned to the capital. Kutuzov was put in command of the army, the Russians and French fought the great battle at Borodino, and finally Moscow fell. Shishkov's proclamation on this occasion was fiercely optimistic. He stressed Napoleon's supply problems and casualties and the doubtful loyalty of his foreign troops, gave reasons for hope for victory, and invoked God's blessing for the Russian effort.[42] At Alexander's request, he also drew up a proclamation detailing enemy atrocities in

Moscow. The French, he charged, had lost the sense of honor that moderated war among the civilized; even savages delighted only in looting, not wanton destruction. French acts of vandalism (especially against churches), as well as Moscow's gratuitous destruction and the mistreatment of its remaining residents, stood in glaring contrast to Moscow's past hospitality to the French. These evils showed the moral degeneracy of the French people, which had erupted to full view since 1789. He concluded (like Glinka) that Russians should be thankful for their miseries, which had at last shown them the truth about a culture they had so long admired and emulated. It was time to repent. "The friendship and temptations of a depraved people are more dangerous to us than their enmity and their arms. Let us thank God! Even in His wrath He is a Father to us and looks after our well-being. In bringing calamities upon us, Providence is showing us Its mercy." These were entirely Shishkov's personal views. As he wrote to a friend, regarding those who had attacked his *Treatise on the Old and New Styles,* "At the time, they could clamor so loudly because they could count on the large number who were infected with this spirit, and I was forced against my will to restrain myself"; but "now I would rub their noses in the ashes of Moscow and loudly tell them: this is what you wanted!" He concluded, "God did not punish us, rather He sent us His grace, if our burnt cities make us into Russians." He initially hesitated to show his draft proclamation to the emperor, who (being a cultural Westernizer himself) might take offense. However, Alexander, seemingly traumatized by the war and wracked with metaphysical anxiety, merely remarked, "It's true! I deserve this reproach."[43]

As one scholar has pointed out, Shishkov's manifestoes can be divided into two distinct periods. Approximately until the fall of Smolensk, he sought mainly to defend the government's actions; then, reassured about the patriotism and military potential of nobles and commoners, he urged them to participate actively in the war. He wrote in the style he had advocated since 1803, and his archaic language and lofty, old-fashioned vocabulary, sprinkled with scriptural verses and Slavonicisms, gave the proclamations "a coloring that was not only solemn, but also ecclesiastical and biblical."[44] Shishkov himself thought them one of his lasting achievements. Years later, after copying several quotations from them into an acquaintance's album, he added proudly: "I am old, my sight is dimming, my mind is growing weak; / But perhaps not everything will die forever with me."[45]

From this official pulpit he preached what he had argued for years, and his uncompromising sincerity drew the respect even of his literary rivals. Aksakov later wrote that Shishkov's appointment had been welcomed in Moscow and the provinces (this suggests the reknown his writings had earned) and that the manifestoes, despite their bookish language, "electrified all of Russia" with the "Russian feeling" they conveyed. Nikolai Grech, the young and then-liberal journalist, concurred (somewhat reluctantly), and even the caustic Rostopchin praised the admiral's work. Three decades later, after Shishkov's funeral, Viazemskii mused that, "at the time, we [young New Style literati] ridiculed the absurdity of his manifestoes," yet "the majority, the people, Russia, read them with enthusiasm and emotion, and even now many admire their eloquence; therefore they were appropriate." Karamzin might have written "with greater prudence and art," but would that have been as effective? On another occasion, however, Viazemskii argued that the emperor would never have signed the manifestoes had they been written in French but that his poor grasp of Russian prevented him from seeing the absurdity of their style.[46]

Just as he was a vitriolic polemicist but a gentle person, so beneath his bellicose rhetoric Shishkov actually hated the war, for reasons both personal and political. He detested the privations it imposed, as he wrote to his wife, Dar'ia Alekseevna. "It's very tedious to drag oneself about like this at my age and disposition," he complained in January 1813. He felt too old for this, his health was poor, the roads were muddy, he was often separated from headquarters and trying to find it, he felt useless to the war effort, feared capture by the French, and generally just wanted to go home.[47] He also recoiled at the human toll of this first land war he had ever witnessed. Along the route of the French retreat "my eyes beheld sights so terrible that they filled my soul with somber emotions it had never felt before." He felt a deep sorrow for the unfortunates whom Napoleon had lured to Russia, and this revulsion continued as the war moved to Europe: "How many victims this damned war is claiming!" From Freiburg he wrote to Dar'ia Alekseevna at the end of 1813: "[War] be damned! If you killed all scholars (I consider scholarship inseparable from gentleness), all people would turn into wicked boors; whereas, if you killed all soldiers (that is, the passion for glory and gain), all people would live in peace."

This weariness and disgust, and a natural caution and pessimism that were perhaps growing with age, were central to Shishkov's attitude toward the war. He served with conviction in 1812 and was relieved when it was all over, writing to a friend that "Divine Providence, assisted by Faith and the people's spirit, saved us," and drawing the parallel, popular at the time, with the guerrilla movement in Spain. Russia could be grateful for its rescue and for the chance to cleanse itself of the French cultural contagion. Unlike the young officers who were eager to overthrow Napoleon's "tyranny" and were later drawn to the Decembrists, he had no desire to carry the war into Europe. He argued to Kutuzov that Russia should enjoy its restored security and leave it to the Germans to fight Napoleon if they wished. Kutuzov and Arakcheev evidently agreed, but not the emperor. Shishkov appreciated the welcome extended to the Russian army by the Prussians, whose courage in rising up against the French he admired, but he always wished the war would end. Even when the allies were poised to invade France, he wrote to his wife: "If God were to take mercy on us and tell us to go home, that would be much better. Let their Paris remain whole, and let them revel in the vile glory of having burned Moscow." That would be a moral victory, he added: Russia would have "repaid evil with kindness, not burned a single town or village and liberated all those from their yoke who had come to bring us harm. That is true glory!"[48]

Shishkov laid out these views in a memorandum to the emperor. Russia had reached its key objectives, he argued: French power was shattered, the German buffer restored, and Russian security thereby assured. An invasion of France to oust Napoleon might require vast resources, reconcile the French people and their emperor, end in disaster like Napoleon's Russian campaign, and if unsuccessful, lead to a revival of his empire. Instead, an allied army with only a modest Russian force should patrol France's border and convince its people it was in their own interest to remove Napoleon, since his dreams of empire were dashed and the allies had no designs on France itself. Alexander told Shishkov that he agreed with parts of the memorandum but had no intention of acting on its recommendations.[49] Shishkov was not alone in these opinions, for the allied headquarters in Frankfurt witnessed heated debate on precisely this issue. Alexander I and the Prussian "patriots" (Stein, Blücher, Gneisenau) were visionaries who wished to reconstruct European politics by pursuing the war. On the other side, Metternich and the Austrian and Prussian monarchs, cautious men interested in restoring the balance of power and haunted by the memory of 1792 (when France's revolutionary armies had smashed a powerful invasion force), shared Shishkov's fears. In the end, as Napoleon did not respond to Metternich's peace feelers, the war continued.

Once Napoleon's defeat was certain, Shishkov conceived a more ambitious goal: to roll back the entire Enlightenment. Russia could claim full victory only if it reversed "not so much the physical as the moral changes" caused by the French. This meant that "the revolution's spirit and fire must be extinguished so that not even a spark remains; kings and peoples must be restored to their former dignity; the false teaching of the French demons must be burned in a bonfire in Paris where it was born." Otherwise, "our business will be unfinished and our glory incomplete."[50] His thinking was thus shaped by two opposing impulses. His cautious instincts, strengthened by the horrors of 1812–1813, made him skeptical of fighting for the Germans, whom (aside from the Prussians) he viewed as dubious allies. Once victory was all but certain, however, he was determined to root out the entire Enlightenment in its native soil of France.

Although his patriotic zeal resembled Glinka's, Shishkov was less melodramatic. To Glinka, at least in retrospect, Napoleon was a tragic hero; Shishkov hated him as an aggressor and usurper of a legitimate monarch's crown. He agreed with Glinka's belief that biblical prophesies were coming true in his own time, but shared neither Glinka's grandiose providential vision of the war's significance nor his hope that the peasantry's bravery would be rewarded with a change in its condition. The war proved to Shishkov the old regime's viability. Like other conservatives, he downplayed the popular element in the Russian victory, instead crediting God and the cohesiveness of Russian society. Like Rostopchin, he saw no link between victory and social reform and was similarly concerned, once Napoleon's defeat in Russia became obvious, with disarming the peasant militias and consigning the guerrilla movement to oblivion.[51]

This attitude, treating victory and social reform as unrelated, is illustrated by an episode from 1814. August 30 (Alexander I's name day) was often an occasion for important pronouncements, and the emperor, back in St. Petersburg, wished to express his gratitude to his subjects. Shishkov drafted a document to this effect: all who had assisted the war effort were to be duly recognized, in order of their importance. According to the draft, first, God would be thanked every Christmas. Next, all clergymen would receive a commemorative cross. Then the nobles, troops and certain merchants would be given medals, and the nobles would be urged to live more virtuously and be more solicitous toward their serfs. Finally, the emperor would state that the peasants ("our loyal people") would "receive their reward from God," although in addition there would be no conscription this year or next, given the current wartime size of the army. Shishkov's draft argued that an "ancient tie exists" between nobles and serfs that reflected "their mutual advantage" as well as "Russian morals and virtues"; this "leaves us [Alexander I] free from any doubt" that the nobles (with their "fatherly concern" for the peasants) and the peasants ("fulfilling their filial obligations and duty") would bring each other "into that happy condition in which well-behaved and prosperous families flourish." The nobility was presumably the first estate in the empire, so he had placed it ahead of the army; but the emperor angrily ordered him to reverse their order. When Shishkov returned the next day with a revised draft, Alexander said that his conscience could not accept the characterization of serfdom as "based on their mutual advantage." Shishkov argued in vain that this idea was serfdom's moral foundation, and was left to ponder the monarch's "unfortunate . . . prejudice" against "serfdom, the rights of the nobility and the entire traditional structure and order."[52] This exchange was typical of Alexander's moral antipathy toward the old regime. His conservative view of the "people's war," however, was little different from Shishkov's: the emperor believed that the French had irreversibly alienated the peasants by desecrating their churches, and he said at the end of 1812 that among the peasants "we find once more the morals of patriarchal times, a profound respect for religion, the love of God and a complete devotion to the sovereign!"[53]

Shishkov's cautious attitude toward the war was not shared by all conservatives. Rostopchin, for example, urged the emperor to liberate all of Europe and expand Russia's borders to the Vistula. (However, his private views on the desirability of continuing the war are not entirely clear.)[54] His patroness Ekaterina Pavlovna also saw the war as an opportunity to expand Russian power. Like Rostopchin and Empress Elisaveta Alekseevna (and unlike her mother, Mariia Fedorovna; Konstantin Pavlovich; Arakcheev; and Foreign Minister Rumiantsev)[55] she did not favor making peace after the fall of Moscow, nor did she share her brother's religious fatalism. Instead she asserted that "setbacks come from the mistakes that men make and we should not blame Providence," and she urged him to continue the war because honor and public opinion demanded it.[56] Russia's valiant struggle against the invaders filled her with pride and hope. She favored creating a militia, indicating sympathy for the idea of a "people's war," and declared to Karamzin (in a letter even written in Russian) that "Russia has been the second power in Europe, but now and forever it is the first."[57] With the French expelled from Central Europe, and while she was traveling there in 1813 for reasons both private (to recover from her husband's sudden death in December 1812) and political, she wrote that it was "the grandest thought" that "Russian troops are stationed from the Peter-Paul Fortress [in St. Petersburg] all the way to the Rhine and that men on foot have marched from Kamchatka to Frankfurt." However, Russians should not "let success make us giddy," for "the time has come for the harvest." The payoff for Russia's sacrifices must be the establishment of "its supremacy for the centuries to come. . . . The more I see of others, the more I think [my own nation] is the first."[58]

The war marked both the apex and, for a time, the end of the ascendancy of the romantic nationalists and gentry conservatives. In Moscow, Rostopchin continued to persecute Russians who had collaborated with the French, as well as Martinists real and imagined. Apparently he was increasingly disliked by Muscovites, who blamed him for the miseries of 1812 and resented the government's limited compensation for victims of the Moscow fire. On August 30, 1814, both he and Shishkov were dismissed from their posts.[59] The "War for the Fatherland" was over, so the emperor no longer needed conservative stalwarts who were hostile to his liberal dreams and mystical religion. Now the most powerful monarch in Europe and arbiter of its destinies, he had no use for demagogic xenophobes and unsophisticated isolationists.

Rostopchin remained in Russia until 1815, ailing and embittered by his countrymen's ingratitude, and then retired—to Paris. There he shed his Francophobia and once more became the polished *grand seigneur,* whose caustic *bons mots* entertained the salons where he basked in the glory of having burned Moscow and defeated Napoleon.[60] He returned to Russia in 1823 and died in Moscow in 1826. Ekaterina Pavlovna married the king of Württemberg and relocated to his domains, where she died after a brief illness at the end of 1818. Sergei Glinka lived on for many years, penniless once more and in relative obscurity. His raison d'être as a writer had vanished with the defeat of Napoleon, and his naïve, idealistic patriotism—which had once been ahead of its time—lost its pioneering significance as cultural nationalism gained ground in Russia. He continued publishing the *Russian Messenger* and tried his hand at other literary ventures. Never again, however, was he able to capture the public's imagination, and Russia stopped reading his works long before his death in 1847. Admiral Shishkov likewise fell from grace and power but remained in good health and lived in the capital, where his new seat on the State Council, his position in the Russian Academy, and the relentless intensity of his opinions ensured that the fiery old man's second quasi-retirement, like the first (1801–1812), would be merely temporary. Indeed, after another decade of political hibernation, Admiral Shishkov would return once more to high office for his final battle with the forces of modernity.

The
Mental World
of the
Holy Alliance

In two regards, Russia's victory over Napoleon marks a watershed in the evolution of conservatism under Alexander I. To begin with, the initiative now moved from "society" to the state, so the center of gravity of this study now shifts from salons, literary societies, the theater and the press to the world of the court and bureaucracy. Public opinion continued to play a role, but only insofar as its ideas were shared by the influential individuals on whom I focus in the remaining chapters. Furthermore, the new "conservative" ideas, in part derived from German and English Protestant thought and embodied in the Holy Alliance, had even more ambiguous political implications than did the nationalism of Shishkov and Glinka; and—to a far greater extent than romantic nationalism or gentry conservatism—these ideas resulted from a direct intellectual dialogue with Western Europe. Yet in important ways this post-war conservatism was a continuation of the earlier conservative movement. Not only were there intellectual and personal links between the two, but the same search persisted for a way to purify society morally without damaging its overall institutional framework. This time, however, the conservatives actually controlled the levers of state power and could attempt to implement their ideas. (This chapter addresses neither the origin nor consequences of the Holy Alliance *treaty* but rather the people and ideas on which the Holy Alliance *ideology* was founded.)

The thinkers of this second conservative wave based their ideology on religion. The Orthodox hierarchy itself had strongly conservative leanings, but the religious conservatism that most influenced Alexander's reign was shaped by foreign influences. (Indeed, in none of the other currents of Alexandrine conservatism were there such clear, explicit links between Russian and European thought.) Orthodoxy's spiritual hold over the educated classes had been uncertain ever since Peter I abolished the patriarchate and placed the church under the supervision of a lay official (the overprocurator of the Holy Synod), thereby damaging its credibility with a population that came to see the church as a servant of the state. It has been argued that its status now roughly resembled that of established Protestant churches in other countries and that, because its own philosophical tradition was weak, its schools taught a curriculum influenced by Protestant scholasticism, which further diluted Orthodoxy's distinctive identity.[1]

The uneasy coexistence of "national/backward" and "alien/advanced" elements in the religious sphere mirrored broader trends in Russian life, in particular the linguistic debate. The religious counterpart to the dignified and backward-looking Old Style was traditional Orthodoxy, and the nobility's unfamiliarity with Church Slavonic literature and language had religious consequences, since Church Slavonic was the language of scripture, prayers, and rituals. The New Style—cosmopolitan, elegant, sentimental, informal, at times facile—found its equivalent in the popularity of introspective, extra-ecclesiastical piety in Russia around 1800. Like the New Style, this churchless piety echoed European romanticism and sentimentalism. As Georges Florovsky has written, the age suffered from "an irresponsible heart. 'An esthetic culture of the heart replaced moral precepts with delicate feelings,' in Kliuchevskii's words." This religiosity suited a society whose spiritual hunger, rooted in centuries of Orthodox tradition, persisted even as it no longer found adequate sustenance in the teachings and rites of the established church.[2]

Various forces combined to bring about a revival of faith among the upper classes. To begin with, many took offense at the crude skepticism popularized by the French Enlightenment, which often served as a fig leaf for vice and ignorance. The Enlightenment, for all its intellectual power, seemed silent in spiritual questions. Much of the early intelligentsia (for example, Novikov and Lopukhin), whose Orthodox faith had been undermined by exposure to "Voltaireanism," resolved the conflict through the vague religiosity of the freemasons, a peculiar blend of Christianity and the Enlightenment.[3] From the 1780s on, Russian freemasonry became increasingly mystical and consciously hostile to rationalism, and this trend helped prepare the resurgence of religion. A particularly influential group was the Rosicrucians. They did not consider themselves disloyal to Orthodoxy but their beliefs, influenced by Western mystics (such as Jacob Böhme, Karl Eckartshausen, Emanuel Swedenborg, and Louis Claude de Saint-Martin), stressed inner spirituality and personal communion with God and de-emphasized the dogma, sacraments, hierarchy, and other essential "external" features of traditional Orthodoxy.[4] Another force promoting religion was the impression made by the French Revolution, which discredited the French Enlightenment philosophy that provided the revolutionary rhetoric. As parts of Russian opinion turned against the Enlightenment and the French culture that had given birth to it, the irreligion now associated with the Jacobins fell into disrepute as well.

However, Orthodoxy was poorly situated to take advantage of this revival of faith, because of its estrangement from the upper class. To be sure, the church had undergone its own form of cultural and intellectual Westernization, but its ties to Protestant and Catholic thinking did not bring it closer to a Russian upper class whose rather different Westernization led toward either mysticism or freethinking. Furthermore, the clergy was a hereditary class, so members of the aristocracy did not join the high clergy as in Catholic countries. This social separation of the aristocracy from the clergy had its corollary in the weakness of communication between them: as Donald Treadgold points out, Aleksandr Pushkin ("the greatest of Russian writers") and St. Serafim of Sarov ("the greatest of modern Russian saints") were contemporaries but apparently never knew of each other's existence.[5] The Orthodox Church, often perceived among the elite as coldly ritualistic and intellectually ossified, could offer them only limited spiritual leadership. The paradoxical result was that it came under attack from its own government and aristocracy even as Christianity experienced a remarkable resurgence in Russia. The weaknesses of the church left the more urban, educated strata of the elite to look elsewhere for spirituality. Four currents succeeded best in filling this vacuum: sectarianism, "nontraditional" Orthodoxy, the Awakening, and Catholicism.

The sects, the least important of the four, provided an unusual instance of aristocrats and peasants meeting on peasant-dominated cultural ground.[6] That the sects enjoyed any influence at all among the elite is evidence of the Orthodox Church's weakness, since church and state relentlessly harassed them. Their antiecclesiastical, emotional, mystical beliefs, with their almost Protestant stress on individual communion with God, touched a receptive chord in the upper classes. A striking example is the story of Kondratii Selivanov, the mysterious founder of one of the more bizarre sects, the *skoptsy,* whose male adherents were encouraged to castrate themselves to avoid sin. His followers thought he was God; in addition, like the rebel Pugachev, he declared himself to be Emperor Peter III. All this was so subversive that Catherine II had exiled him to Siberia for twenty years. After his return following her death, he was presented to Paul I and, it appears, suggested that Paul castrate himself, whereupon he was confined to an insane asylum. Despite the eccentricity of his teachings, Selivanov was the object of much public interest after his release in 1802. Noble and merchant ladies came to seek his blessing and hear his prophesies, and even the emperor visited him in 1805.[7]

"Nontraditional" Orthodoxy, defined by a certain autonomy from the church leadership, consisted of two disparate currents. The first resembled sectarianism in its mystical religiosity and its roots in the xenophobic culture of the lower classes. Its most influential representative was Fotii Spasskii, an emotionally unstable, semiliterate monk who railed against foreign abominations seeping into Russian culture and religion and who routinely conversed with supernatural beings. While he formed a striking contrast to the Orthodox Church's learned, conservative bishops and metropolitans, he reminds us of the marginally educated village priests who constituted the vast, pauperized majority of the Orthodox clergy but rarely made an appearance in the salons of the capitals. Like Rasputin a century later, he fascinated the bloodless, culturally rootless, spiritually confused sophisticates of Petersburg (especially the emperor) with his coarse, fanatical "Russianness." The second current was the effort by Western-oriented thinkers (both lay and clerical) to redefine Orthodoxy's role in society. One of these was Aleksandr Sturdza, of whom more will be said later. Another was Filaret (Vasilii M. Drozdov), a young clergyman (born in 1782) whose talent and industry made him rector of the St. Petersburg Ecclesiastical Academy and a member of the powerful Ecclesiastical Schools Commission by the age of thirty. A future metropolitan of Moscow, Filaret was one of the most dynamic figures in the church hierarchy. His eloquent sermons attracted people drawn to mysticism or other aspects of Western theology (including Prince Golitsyn, Labzin, Aleksandr Turgenev, Vasilii Popov, Varvara Turkistanova, and Sturdza, all prominently linked to "religious conservatism"), and he advocated translating the Bible into modern Russian, appalling linguistic traditionalists like Shishkov. Nonetheless, he wanted to renew the church from within, and this distinguished him from the mystics (such as Labzin and Golitsyn) who questioned whether the church had meaning at all.[8]

Filaret's ideas were popular partly because they echoed the mystical, quietistic current in German Protestantism that deeply influenced many leaders of Russian society. Like freemasonry, the German "Awakening" sought to revitalize religion without interposing the church between believer and God, and it rejected dogma and ritual. Its links with freemasonry became apparent in the mystical lodges that flourished under Alexander I, of which the most famous was Labzin's. Like the mystic Saint-Martin, the luminaries of the Awakening argued that the events since 1789 were proof the end was near, and their chiliastic beliefs took root among "awakened" Russians as well. The works of Johann Heinrich Jung-Stilling, for example, enjoyed great popularity, thanks largely to Labzin's translations, while Ignatius Fessler (a Catholic monk who had converted to Lutheranism and directed his own masonic lodge) taught a mystical brand of religion to St. Petersburg seminarians until he was dismissed at the insistence of traditionalist Orthodox clerics.[9]

Russian aristocrats were subject also to Catholic proselytizing, particularly by the Jesuits. Suppressed by the pope in 1773, the Society of Jesus had survived in Russian Poland, where Catherine II protected it because she valued its loyalty to the crown (important in restless Poland) and its educational work. Paul permitted it to establish schools in the Russian capital, where Jesuits educated the sons of some of the greatest families. The Jesuits and many émigrés who had fled the

French Revolution, most notably the ultramontane Joseph de Maistre, worked energetically to spread Catholicism. Among the converts were the wife and daughter of Count Rostopchin, who was dismayed that his own family had abandoned the national faith. De Maistre himself, although only the ambassador of the small Sardinian kingdom, cultivated ties with the emperor and a cross-section of the Russian elite whom he impressed with his brilliance and charm. He frequented exclusive salons, intriguing against Speranskii and on the lookout for potential converts to the Catholic faith; aristocratic women counted prominently among these.[10]

Still, the Awakening had a stronger impact than Roman Catholicism. As a spiritual attitude rather than a formal church, it was compatible with membership in the Orthodox Church and required no formal conversion. In addition, Catholicism had long been associated with Russia's Polish enemies, whereas the Awakening's appeal (like freemasonry's) gained from the prestige of Protestant German and British culture. In Russia it took root as an introverted faith that stressed personal communion with God and, in some instances, personal reading of the scriptures; one's formal church affiliation mattered less than the informal community of the "awakened."[11]

Aleksandr N. Golitsyn. Engraving by Thomas Wright, based on the painting by Karl Briullov.

Its main representative at court was Prince Aleksandr N. Golitsyn. He was an intelligent, gentle, charming, honest man, and it was no foregone conclusion that his name would become synonymous with oppressive religious zealotry. His early outlook on life had been shaped by the court of Catherine II, where he was the playmate of the future Alexander I, so in his youth he became, according to biographer Walter Sawatsky, "an Epicurean and eventually a Voltairean." However, to quote Georges Florovsky, he was his era's "most sensitive and expressive representative. His ability to absorb impressions nearly constituted a sickness." Therefore, when Alexander named him overprocurator of the Holy Synod (a post he held for twenty-one years, longer than anyone else except Konstantin Pobedonostsev [1880–1905]), he read the New Testament—"for perhaps the first time in his life," his friend Peter von Goetze thought—and found religion. "Given over entirely to the world and to all the vices one finds there, he was truly its slave," another of his friends (Princess Turkistanova) wrote in 1813, but "beginning two years ago he has completely reformed his way of life, and at this hour nothing is more orderly than his conduct." As his biographer writes: "He was gradually moving through a Deist and a rationally committed Orthodox position toward an increasing interest in a personal religious commitment." At the same time, Speranskii, himself a priest's son and former seminarian, was also developing a personal, mystical Christianity, to which the Rosicrucian Lopukhin evidently introduced him around 1803–1804.[12] Alexander I was thus surrounded by a group of pious advisers: Golitsyn, Speranskii, and the old mystic and freemason Rodion A. Koshelev, who had personally known the celebrated Saint-Martin. Other members of the imperial family (such as Mariia Fedorovna), though, stayed aloof from these religious currents, and the emperor himself at first was noncommittal.[13]

Reconstructing Alexander's psychology is exceedingly difficult. He was a master of dissimulation who rarely tipped his hand and could surprise those who took his apparent brooding indecisiveness at face value. It seems likely, however, that the trials he had endured since 1801—his role in his father's murder, the collapse of his reform plans, his defeats abroad, the failures of his private life—subjected him to terrible spiritual pressures that reached their climax during the disastrous summer months of 1812. St. Petersburg could not have offered much comfort then: when he had left in April 1812, the people had cheered him on, as had Moscow in July, but when he returned the mood had darkened. Then Moscow fell. On September 15, the anniversary of his coronation, there was such concern for his safety that he traveled down Nevskii Prospekt in a carriage with his wife and mother, not, as was customary, proudly on horseback. Roksandra Sturdza, his wife's maid of honor, later recalled "the glum silence and annoyed faces" of the crowd. "One could have made out the sound of our steps" as the imperial party mounted the stairs to the Kazan' Cathedral—"one spark would have sufficed at that moment to set off a general conflagration." The emperor seemed shaken. Nikolai I. Grech read the mood similarly, although to him it seemed sad rather than menacing: the emperor "was pale and pensive, but not confused; he seemed saddened, yet firm."[14]

In the weeks after the fall of Moscow, as Kutuzov operated with little concern for his wishes and the public was furious at him and terrified of Napoleon, Alexander seems to have undergone a spiritual transformation. Years later, still awed by the miraculous destruction of the *Grande Armée* in the frozen wastes of Belorussia, he recalled: "The fire of Moscow lit up my soul, and the Lord's judgment on the ice fields filled my heart with a warmth of faith that it had never felt before. Now I came to know God as He is revealed by the Holy Scriptures." Golitsyn, himself "awakened" in 1812, with the help of Filaret (Golitsyn's favorite preacher) guided Alexander in his new religion, which became a bedrock of his thought.[15]

Alexander's mystical, chiliastic "conversion" apparently deepened over the next years and was supported by several members of his entourage. Two especially typified the religious revival among the educated and influenced both his religious evolution and his thinking on foreign affairs for the next decade: Roksandra Sturdza and her brother Aleksandr.

Roksandra S. Sturdza.
Lithograph by Weber.
Courtesy of Francis Ley.

In Roksandra Skarlatovna Sturdza we meet the most appealing personality among the religious conservatives and the one who, perhaps more than anyone else, linked the Awakening with "nontraditional" Orthodoxy. Her writings, and her contemporaries' letters and reminiscences, show her to have been a circumspect personality with a sharp yet sentimental mind and an instinct for others' emotional needs that she used to both offer solace and advance her own aims.[16] She was incapable of cynical self-promotion, yet she saw herself and those around her as chosen instruments of divine providence. The Awakening appealed to her romantic sensitivity, which also reinforced her close emotional and intellectual bonds with de Maistre, Sofiia Svechina, Juliane von Krüdener, Jung-Stilling, Franz von Baader, and other Western Christians who likewise searched for a truer path to God. Her faith stressed personal devotion over doctrinal correctness, but she always remained Orthodox and kept a careful distance from the cultish excesses of some contemporary mystics.

Her brother Aleksandr was different in both personal disposition and religious attitudes. His character was lively but hard, his intellect keen yet rigid. Unlike his sister, he had few social skills and gave offense easily. With the melodramatic introspection that contemporary literature had popularized, the adolescent "Aléco" wrote to Roksandra that, "while not entirely devoid of sensitivity, I am often hard, morose, and severe, and above all never expansive," and "my outbursts, though very rare, are extremely violent and suicidal in their effects."[17] Lacking her sentimentality, his more dogmatic mind was also more analytical and less impressionable. Whereas she was skillful in communicating with people, his strength lay in the theoretical dissection and exposition of complex issues, albeit within a rigidly doctrinaire conceptual framework. Her career revolved around the court; he came into his own as a theorist of state policy. His religion mirrored his personality: a proponent, like Filaret, of a vigorously intellectual Orthodoxy worthy of its Greek theological heritage and not distorted by the vagaries of Russian tradition, he was a harsh critic of Catholicism, Protestantism, and all forms of contemporary Western mysticism.

Aleksandr S. Sturdza

Roksandra was born in Constantinople in 1786, and Aleksandr in Iassy in 1791. Their Greek mother, Sultana Mourouzis, was the daughter of Moldavia's ruling prince *(hospodar)*, while Skarlat Sturdza belonged to one of its most powerful clans. A melancholy and pious man, educated in Germany, he moved his family to Russia after Aleksandr's birth to escape the Turks. Two of the children's uncles had risen in the Ottoman service but were executed in 1812 as punishment for the unfavorable Treaty of Bucharest, which one of them had helped negotiate. This family history gave the younger Sturdzas their intense piety, polyglot sophistication, hatred of the Ottomans and Islam, fervent support for Greek independence, and loyalty to Russia as the bastion of Orthodoxy and justice.[18]

The two children grew up in St. Petersburg and at Ust'e, the family's estate in Belorussia. There they underwent three traumatic, formative crises. First, like Lopukhin and many others, Roksandra saw her faith nearly destroyed by rationalism.[19] Like they, she emerged from the ordeal relentlessly hostile toward all irreligion, but the rationalism, social criticism, and introspective sentimentality of the Enlightenment and romanticism left their mark on her and her brother. The second trauma was the death of their sister Smaragda (1803) followed by the suicide of their brother Constantine (1806). Family tragedies, the financial and psychological hardships of émigré life, and the morose disposition that Skarlat had passed on to his offspring, all heightened their tendency toward melancholy resignation. Roksandra acquired a strong sense of responsibility, especially for her elderly father and her brother, for whom she harbored an almost maternal affection.[20] This precocious authority accustomed her to sensing and soothing the pain of others, an ability that would stand her in good stead with Alexander I. She also learned that she could afford no missteps in life. The results were loyalty and zeal in the imperial service, a habit of not letting down her emotional guard, and the absence in her personality of all frivolity.

In the third crisis, during the 1805–1807 war, Aleksandr angrily repudiated his French upbringing and embraced Russian patriotism (as Glinka had earlier), even going so far as to try his youthful hand at writing dramas about Russian history. He was representative of an entire generation of educated Russians—including the future Decembrists—who, in the crucible of the Napoleonic Wars, questioned traditional aristocratic culture and sought a closer bond to the Russian masses and their traditions.[21] Like most observers of Russian letters, he followed the current linguistic debate. He had mixed feelings about the *Treatise on the Old and New Styles,* where, he later wrote, "Shishkov is alternately a superstitious worshipper of the past and an intelligent expert and judge of the Russian language's incalculable richness." He welcomed the criticism of rash innovation and began to learn Church Slavonic, but he found that Shishkov's idiosyncratic etymologies revealed utter ignorance of the Latin and Greek origins of many Russian words. While applauding Shishkov's patriotism, he sensed its intellectual shallowness. Aleksandr Sturdza was drawn, like other young Petersburg literati, into Shishkov's orbit, attended his soirées, and would have joined the Symposium had not his youth stood in the way (he turned twenty on November 18, 1811). Like his enthusiasm for the Russian language, his interest in the Symposium was dictated in part by hatred of Napoleonic France: "While the national peasant militia of 1807 might be called a review of our military forces," he recalled, the Symposium "mobilized the intellectual forces of the educated class, which felt affected and anxious about the immensity of events."[22]

Aleksandr met the poet Gnedich, who translated the *Iliad* and shared his passion for the Greek language. Apparently through him, Sturdza submitted to Shishkov an essay that urged Russians to study Greek in order to cultivate the ties of kinship between their Orthodox nations. The admiral agreed with this idea, accepted the essay, and presented parts of it to the Symposium on March 23, 1812, before an audience of three hundred. Forty years later, Sturdza still recalled the pride he had felt as he sat in the audience that evening.[23]

This association with Shishkov was a passing phase (and Sturdza later was friendly with Karamzin and other writers of that school). Yet it had lasting importance, for it confirmed Sturdza's evolution from a cosmopolitan Francophile into a proto-Slavophile. Although he continued to write mainly in French and actively followed European intellectual life, he became a believer in the superiority of Orthodox Greco-Russian culture over the Latin West. Unlike Paul I, who had hoped to counter the ideological universalism of the French Revolution with a universalistic, chivalric, theocratic conception in which denominational distinctions were irrelevant,[24] Sturdza regarded the gulf separating Eastern and Western Christendom as unbridgeable. Eastern culture's core was, in his opinion, its Orthodox religion, but he also believed that the Russian people (especially the peasants) had exceptional intellectual and spiritual virtues that raised them above other nations. In this sense, he represents a bridge between the romantic nationalist ideas of Shishkov and later nationalists. Like the Wisdom Lovers *(liubomudry)* of the 1820s[25] and the Slavophiles of the 1840s, both of whose views Sturdza antici-pated, he published many of his writings in the periodicals of the historian Mikhail Pogodin, who in turn had been an avid reader of Glinka's *Russian Mes-senger*. The world of Russian conservative thought was a small, even inbred uni-verse, and Sturdza—a friend of Shishkov, Karamzin, and Gogol, and later a fre-quent correspondent of Pogodin—was one of its more active citizens.

He entered the foreign ministry in April 1809 and joined the minister's chan-cellery by September. Since he was an astute analyst and good writer, fluent in Russian, French, German, Italian, Greek, Latin, and Church Slavonic, and a well-read man with broad intellectual horizons, he made a favorable impression on Foreign Minister Rumiantsev. However, the reminiscences he wrote at the time portray him as a bored, frustrated, blasé young man, unhappy in both his service and his social life and contented only when he was alone in a library; this pose of gloom and disenchantment, fashionable among upper-class youth and popular-ized by novelists, was a feature young Sturdza shared with Russian and European contemporaries of all ideological orientations.[26] Around this time he met Ioannes Antoniou Kapodistrias—or in the more common English spelling, Capodistrias—who had fled his native Ionian Islands when they were seized by France after Tilsit. He arrived in St. Petersburg in January 1809 and joined the Russian foreign ministry. He and Sturdza became friends through their service and because Capodistrias, like other Greek émigrés (including Alexander Ypsilantis, the fu-ture initiator of the Greek revolt and a relative of the Sturdzas), frequented the Sturdza household. The then-thirty-three-year-old Capodistrias became a mentor to Aléco Sturdza, whose entire career he shaped. Capodistrias was for Sturdza an object of lifelong, unstinting admiration. For him, meanwhile, the Sturdzas were a source of contacts invaluable to his subsequent career. Also, the two shared the same religious faith, devotion to Greek independence, and interestingly, rever-ence for the Russian people and messianic hopes for its future. Capodistrias also formed a close relationship with Roksandra Sturdza, to whom he subsequently proposed marriage (apparently to her utter surprise; she declined, despite intense pressure from her family and friends).[27]

In 1806, Roksandra Sturdza's parents obtained a court function for her, which, with her characteristic dexterity, she parlayed into an appointment as maid of honor to Empress Elisaveta. The access this gave her to the empress should not be overrated, however, since the empresses Elisaveta and Mariia together had sev-enty such attendants, most of them senior in status to Sturdza.[28] She was also a regular guest at the home of Admiral Chichagov (whose wife had helped intro-duce her at court), where she first met Joseph de Maistre. The young courtier and the elderly diplomat formed a close bond of mutual affection and intellectual respect, and as long as de Maistre remained an informal adviser to the emperor (until about 1812), he was a valuable ally to the discreetly ambitious maid of honor. As Markovich argues, both were exiles who hoped that Russia would help their foreign homelands and their families. Also (unlike Shishkov and Rostopchin), they both regarded the French Revolution as a providential event and believed that Alexander I was the man destined to liberate Europe, the man whom they must serve.[29] Their only major disagreement was over de Maistre's Catholic proselytizing, since she defended Orthodoxy and sympathized with the nondenominational religiosity of the Awakening.

The crisis of 1812 allowed her to become the emperor's confidante. After returning from Moscow, he had inquired about people attached to his court and asked to be introduced to her. When they met, he spoke of the war and bemoaned his own inadequacy, whereupon she assured him of her unwavering confidence. Many of the maids of honor at court had been educated to feel a "hysterical devotion to the monarch,"[30] and Roksandra Sturdza was not immune to these sentiments. Her veneration for both his crown and his person was boundless; she believed he had a vast potential for good that had gone unfulfilled owing only to his irreligious education, and she wished to help him surmount his spiritual troubles. He in turn was receptive to her charm; he was also a suspicious man who appreciated genuine loyalty and affection, especially at a time when external disasters forced him to call on the services of Shishkov, Rostopchin, Kutuzov, and others whom he disliked and whose low opinion of his own abilities he knew. Further reinforcing his confidence was her friendship with Golitsyn and Koshelev, his new religious mentors.[31]

Their bond was closest when she helped to introduce him to the German Awakening. The opportunity arose when Elisaveta Alekseevna set out in late 1813 to visit her native Germany and be nearer Alexander's headquarters. Despite their shared religion and loyalty to their adopted Russian homeland and its emperor, her relationship with Roksandra, though affectionate, was tense; perhaps Sturdza, like Ekaterina Pavlovna, aroused jealousy in the empress, whose husband showed them the attention and trust that he denied her. In any case, the lengthy overland journey to Baden was unpleasant from the first. Elisaveta herself felt painfully ambivalent about returning to her childhood home, and became even more irritable from the festivities she was forced to endure along the way.[32] The animosities within her suite, the pomp that greeted the empress of Germany's liberators (and Baden's prodigal daughter)—Sturdza had always despised these at court. The journey only reinforced her disgust with "the world" and intensified her desire to escape it. They finally reached Heidelberg in February 1814. In Baden that winter, Roksandra Sturdza met two of the most significant religious figures of the age: Juliane von Krüdener and Johann Heinrich Jung-Stilling.

Krüdener is sufficiently well known that a brief overview of her background will suffice.[33] Born in 1764 to a Lutheran family in Livonia, she was married at nineteen to a diplomat twenty years her senior. After her marriage had disintegrated in the 1790s, she lived in France and sought to make a name for herself as a writer. In 1804 she returned to Livonia, where the death of an acquaintance shocked her into finding religion. Her exuberant sentimentality now merged with her newly acquired faith, and as a passionate disciple of Herrnhut Pietism, she came to believe in her own prophetic powers and ability to communicate with God. She visited Herrnhut communities near Dresden, where she met friends of Jung-Stilling, and continued directly to Karlsruhe, where she and Jung-Stilling himself first met in late 1807 or early 1808.

He, unlike Krüdener, was a major figure in "awakened" circles. Born in 1740, Jung-Stilling had worked as a village teacher and then a tutor before being "awakened." For many years thereafter he was a professor of economics and read widely in the literature of the eighteenth century. As his horizons expanded, however, his religious beliefs were shaken. Like Roksandra Sturdza and Lopukhin, he saved his religion from the acid of philosophy; like theirs, his faith was steeled by the ordeal. The French Revolution showed the consequences of the Enlightenment's attack on the Bible, he believed, and he saw the Napoleonic Wars as a harbinger of the Apocalypse. To fulfill his mission of rallying the faithful, he became a prolific writer of religious tracts. In 1803 he entered the service of the grand duke of Baden, which allowed him to devote all his time to this work. The "patriarch of the Awakening" then spent his last fourteen years traveling and writing, impressing upon great and humble alike that the Kingdom of God was near.[34]

Jung-Stilling was well known in Russia. Nikolai Turgenev and Sergei Aksakov read him, Lopukhin corresponded with him, and Labzin translated his works. Elisaveta Alekseevna—who was increasingly pious (although devoted to Orthodoxy, as she was to Russia in general) and was a granddaughter of Jung-Stilling's Badenese patron—may have popularized his book *The Yearning for Home* at court and introduced the emperor to it. Its prophesy that Christendom's salvation would come from the east could have appealed to her Russian patriotism, although in later years she expressed a distaste for mystical writings.[35]

Jung-Stilling was a leading light among German spiritualist mystics, and Krüdener, who was searching for religious guidance, found it to some extent in him. Yet his influence over her was limited by her uncritical fascination with the extrasensory and supernatural, and she associated with self-styled prophets whom he dismissed as charlatans. He distrusted her credulous enthusiasms but was interested in her as a Russian, because "awakened" Germans expected (after 1789 and the French invasion of their country) to seek refuge in the east and there await the Apocalypse, and she gave him his first direct contact to Russia and was sympathetic to his views.[36]

When Roksandra Sturdza first met Krüdener, she was drawn to Krüdener's faith and charity toward the poor but also thought her a victim of her own mystical "chimeras."[37] In early March she met Jung-Stilling, who appealed in equal measure to her piety and her idealization of the simple life. Like de Maistre, the seventy-four-year-old Jung-Stilling became a spiritual father figure to the restless, searching young courtier.[38] She urged her brother to read his *Yearning,* but Aleksandr instead warned her against "German books. Some of them are quite pernicious, their poison hidden under the appearance of exaltation and depth." She responded defensively that she was no "Martinist": she viewed Krüdener as "an interesting phenomenon" and Jung-Stilling as "an excellent man" but promised that her Orthodox opinions were "in no way influenced by theirs."[39] Krüdener, who was now a spiritual adviser to the emperor, attracted the attention of his retinue, including Capodistrias and Aleksandr Sturdza, his assistant. The two and Roksandra visited her in Heidelberg in June 1815, and the two men saw her again in Paris in September. Initially, Aleksandr was as moved by Krüdener as his sister, but soon he dismissed her as a gossip and found her prophesies intolerably gloomy (a strong statement from a man as austere as Sturdza).[40]

Roksandra Sturdza's affirmation of her Orthodoxy seems inconsistent with her glowing descriptions of Jung-Stilling, her lengthy and emotional letters to him and her scheme to establish an ecumenical convent. However, like other "awakened" Christians, she believed that all godly people were alike, whatever their church affiliation, and both de Maistre and Jung-Stilling shared her faith in Russia's providential role and in Alexander I's divine mission to destroy the evil threatening Christendom. She acted as a bridge linking the mystics with the "nontraditional" Orthodox conservatives (such as her brother). She shared the mystics' inner-directed, ecumenical spirituality but not their chiliasm and cultishness. Krüdener she thought too gullible, and "unfortunately" Golitsyn's "reason is not commensurate with his zeal." As for herself, she told Jung-Stilling, "I am attached with my heart and soul to the Church that received me in its arms at my birth."[41]

She soon had an occasion to introduce her new friends to the emperor, whom she had not seen since 1812 and who now took a special interest in her. They talked about religion, and he inquired about Jung-Stilling.[42] Alexander subsequently sought him out, and heard from Jung-Stilling that Roksandra and he had formed a Christian "bond of love and charity." "I asked him to accept me as a third member in this alliance," Alexander told her, "and we shook hands on that." In a tearful scene full of the period's lachrymose sensibility, she gave her consent as well. In an age of sentimental friendships and masonic lodges, such mystical "marriages" among the "awakened" were common in Germany. These could involve more than two people, so there was nothing inherently unusual about Alexander's joining the union of Roksandra and Jung-Stilling. Henceforth they prayed for him and in the words of one historian "took on, in a sense, the role of 'godparents,' entrusted with presenting him spiritually to God and the Savior."[43] In his struggle for a new and perhaps unsteady faith, he could rely on his two allies, and their admiration for him as liberator of Europe was surely welcome also. In addition, they appealed to his escapism. Alexander had, after all, dreamed as a youth of living a simple, bucolic life on the banks of the Rhine. Roksandra Sturdza held similar sentiments and gave them a religious direction: "Nothing removes me farther from God and true greatness," she wrote, than the hollow ostentation of court life, and "I will be happier in a hut with our dear Savior than in palaces with the mighty."[44] This state of mind resembled Alexander's after 1815 and especially after 1820, when he increasingly left affairs of state to Arakcheev; this was reflected in the legend that he did not die in 1825 but lived on in the wilderness as the *starets* (elderly monk) Fedor Kuzmich.

Roksandra Sturdza brought about his acquaintance with Krüdener as well. Like Jung-Stilling, Krüdener played a senior role *vis-à-vis* Roksandra, whom she needed mainly as an audience, and she also hoped to communicate her prophetic insights through Sturdza to the emperor. When Sturdza and the empress's retinue were at the Congress of Vienna, Krüdener sent her a letter filled with obscure prophesies to the effect that Napoleon would escape from Elba and return to France. Roksandra showed it to the emperor, who was astonished when the prophesy came true within months, and he became interested in meeting the prophet herself.[45] Alexander paid great attention to Roksandra during the Congress of Vienna. She reported to Jung-Stilling, not without a touch of pride, that she had "even exhibited to him a frankness that may be incautious, for the truth always enrages those who are not accustomed to it." As she saw it, she sacrificed herself, despite her distaste for "the world," to guide her beloved monarch to the truth. This was a fundamental belief of the Awakening: the Christian was to seek inner peace in the communion with God and other believers and by avoiding "the world," but also to submit to His will and spare no effort in doing His work.[46]

While keeping herself in the background, Sturdza worked tirelessly for her brother's advancement. In the fall of 1812, he was a diplomatic official in the army of Admiral Chichagov, who had requested his services because he knew his education and talents. When Aléco grumbled about his ungrateful chief, and about government service in general, his sister urged him to speak to the admiral and make his case.[47] Still, he left the army late in 1812 and, after almost being assigned to the Ministry of Education, resumed service only in 1814 as a junior diplomat involved in the preparations for the Congress of Vienna. There, too, he was bored and disillusioned. Again she pushed him on, in a letter that illustrates how she linked ambition with ideology and how the idea (found in freemasonry as well as the Awakening) of leadership by a small elite of the chosen shaped her worldview. "Don't be too modest," she urged. "People need to know that you are aware of your superiority; that is the only means for leading men. They need to be dominated, and you have to start from there if you want to be useful to them."[48] With tact and persistence she promoted his career. Thus, in 1814, she made a point of mentioning him (and his new chief, Capodistrias) to the emperor, with the disclaimer that she asked no favors because "I can count on his talent for his advancement." Aléco may have required more encouragement, because he complained that Krüdener (perhaps at Roksandra's prodding) "keeps obsessing me with talk about my alleged calling, which, she says, consists of not leaving the Emperor." Aleksandr, like his sister, was of two minds about state service. He detested its tedium and humiliations, but he took the initiative in causes dear to his heart. For instance, while only an assistant to Capodistrias, he submitted to the emperor a memorandum on the oppression of the Greeks, which deeply preoccupied him for many years.[49]

On February 25, 1815, the empress and her suite left Vienna for Munich. While Napoleon's last campaign was unfolding, Roksandra met the third of the religious figures who would so deeply influence her in Germany. In contrast to Krüdener and Jung-Stilling, Franz von Baader was a Catholic. Reading Saint-Martin and Böhme had deepened his mysticism and his ties to the Awakening. In him, as in Krüdener and Jung-Stilling, Sturdza found a kindred soul whom she brought into contact with her government. She sent to Golitsyn a memorandum in which Baader outlined ideas that later formed the core of the Holy Alliance: essentially, that society must combine freedom and love on the basis of the Christian faith. Like the emperor, the Sturdzas, and other "awakened" Russians, Baader argued that revolutions occurred when despotism misused religion to oppress society, but that the revolution itself, if not guided by Christian love, would also become despotism. Despotism and godlessness were synonymous, in his opinion, and true liberty, equality, and fraternity could be found only in Christianity. This was also the thinking of Roksandra and the emperor, who were drawn to "republican" ideals but gave precedence to spiritual improvement over institutional reforms. It was consistent with their opposition to the old regime and the revolution, both of which had strayed from the true path of the Gospel. As Max Geiger has argued, the Awakening produced a peculiar ideology in which notions of a Christian theocracy combined with liberalism, idealism, and romanticism.[50]

So it was no surprise that Baader and his ideas were warmly received. Aleksandr Sturdza wrote that his "religious genius and intellectual ability are truly prodigious," Capodistrias found spiritual comfort in his presence, and Golitsyn (who promised to forward his memorandum to Alexander I) engaged him to report regularly to St. Petersburg on German intellectual and religious life.[51] An important similarity of Baader's thought with that of "awakened" Russians was his desire for a unification of Catholicism, Protestantism, and Orthodoxy. Orthodoxy, he argued, had been more successful than the Western churches in preserving the original substance of Christianity from both papal despotism and Protestant rationalism. These arguments (almost identical to Aleksandr Sturdza's in his defense of Orthodoxy) echoed the views of many Russians[52] who wished to restore a universal church as the foundation of European society but had also internalized the Orthodox tradition.

Roksandra Sturdza formed a crucial link between the Russian court and Germany's Russophile religious thinkers.[53] Krüdener and Jung-Stilling saw Alexander I and his empire as liberator and haven until the Judgment Day, while Baader came to consider Orthodoxy the cure for the ills of Western Christianity. He articulated some of the ideas of the Holy Alliance, whereas Jung-Stilling and Krüdener set the tone for it with their peculiar form of piety. These influences, Geiger points out, shaped four important elements of the Alliance.

One was its ecumenism, which contrasted with the Catholic orientation of de Maistre and others who saw in religion a pillar of the social order. Instead, in a consciously symbolic gesture, the Alliance was created jointly by the leading Orthodox, Protestant, and Catholic monarchs of the Continent (Alexander I, Frederick William III of Prussia, and Francis I of Austria); the same dream had motivated Roksandra's plan for an interfaith convent. The second element was the insistence on atonement for the transgressions of both the old regime and the revolution. Reactionaries and radicals shared the guilt for humanity's woes, which Shishkov or Rostopchin ascribed to the latter only; in contrast to the romantic nationalism of Shishkov or Glinka, the Awakening did not consider the past a model for the future. Instead, it awaited with anxious anticipation the utter transformation of a world that had at last repented of its sins. Third, the Alliance echoed the slogans of 1789, and the spirit of the masonic lodges and the "circles" of the "awakened," in demanding solidarity between social classes. In the face of God's judgment, there could be no caste snobbery, and both Krüdener's work among the poor and Alexander I's support for constitutions in France and Poland and for plans to reform serfdom reflected this idea.[54] Finally, the Alliance hoped to institutionalize brotherly love in international relations; Russia's renunciation of revenge against France was evidence of this Sermon-on-the-Mount philosophy.

Were these people "conservative"? The answer is a qualified yes. Baader regarded the French Revolution as a dialectical response to despotism. Krüdener condemned post-1815 society as "a web of iniquities, a tissue of lies," and asked of the German governments that obstructed her work: "Of what use to us are so-called enlightenment and liberal ideas if one no longer dares to feed the pauper, or clothe him, or house him, or defend his rights, or comfort him with the Gospel in hand?" Yet her social criticism was meant to strengthen the chiliastic community of the "awakened" by showing the corruption of "the world," not to argue for structural reform of society.[55]

Roksandra Sturdza was also ambivalent. "At the bottom of my soul I am a republican," she told the emperor, for she hated the nobles' arrogance toward commoners and status consciousness toward each other. She also opposed serfdom (a view anathema to Shishkov or Rostopchin) and praised Alexander I for ending it in Livonia. Without him, "the system of reaction would have exerted its baneful influence" everywhere in 1814–1815, but he had "shown the nations the limit of their hatreds and vengeance." Her friend Svechina called her "you, my friend, who were full of hope for the regeneration of Europe, who believed in the reign of liberal, just, generous ideas." In this context, "liberal" (like "regeneration," "just," or "generous") denotes a moral aspiration, not a reform program, for Sturdza gave little importance to constitutional issues. Thus, she viewed the reformers Novosil'tsev and Czartoryski (of the "Unofficial Committee") as pretentious nonentities whose ideas the emperor, himself raised on the "philosophic chimeras of his age," had shared "with all the ardor of a young and passionate soul," not the wisdom of a Christian statesman. With the archconservative de Maistre, on the other hand, she "agreed on everything," except religion.[56] The Napoleonic Wars were important above all metaphysically, and the Waterloo campaign appeared to Roksandra as "this terrible and decisive struggle of good against evil." She believed, in the elitist spirit of the romantic era, that the strong reigned supreme in a world where most were weak. Accordingly, echoing Glinka, she called Napoleon and Alexander I "models, the one of ancient grandeur and the other of Christian virtues," and contrasted them with the petty cynicism of unreformed old-regime leaders, of whom she singled out Metternich and Talleyrand for their plotting against the Russian emperor's peace efforts after 1814. In the cosmic struggle of good and evil, good exhibited certain "liberal" features, particularly the rejection of serfdom, despotism, and caste snobbery. Yet these were but signs of the Christian humility and solidarity whose triumph Roksandra and her friends hoped to see after the downfall of Napoleon. As for laissez-faire economics, a charter of civil rights, or other liberal concerns—these were trivial issues when the world was groping toward a new morality and a new compact with God.[57]

While the Holy Alliance took shape in the emperor's mind in Europe, however, the groundwork was being laid in St. Petersburg for a far-reaching transformation of domestic policy as well. The religion of Roksandra Sturdza and her friends was the quietist German spirituality of the Awakening, but the activism of English Nonconformity also influenced Russia. While most European state churches were under siege in an age of secularization, the Nonconformist churches in the Anglo-Saxon world experienced rapid expansion. One symptom was the growth of Protestant missionary organizations, in particular the British and Foreign Bible Society (BFBS). Founded in 1804, within a decade and a half it had branches in France, the Netherlands, the United States, Hungary, and various German and Scandinavian states, though Metternich not surprisingly banned it from Austria as subversive.[58] The aim of the emphatically nondenominational BFBS was to disseminate the Bible in various languages, without commentary, to avoid sectarian conflicts. Soon it was operating in the Caucasus, Finland, and Russia's Baltic provinces; but only in September 1812, with Napoleon in Moscow, did it establish a chapter in St. Petersburg.

It was warmly received there by Protestant clerics and some officials, especially Viktor Kochubei (of the "Unofficial Committee") and Interior Minister Kozodavlev. The emperor approved the Russian Bible Society (RBS) in December and it first met in Golitsyn's house on January 11, 1813. It was to deal only with non-Orthodox peoples of the Russian Empire, respecting the Holy Synod's monopoly on publishing Bibles for the Orthodox in Church Slavonic. Soon, however, in light of those Bibles' bulk and prohibitive cost, Golitsyn (who presided over both the RBS and the Synod) arranged for the RBS to print a cheap edition of the Church Slavonic Bible as well, and the Synod began taking active part in the work of the RBS. In 1816, Alexander I asked the RBS to publish the New Testament in the Russian vernacular. This project, entrusted to the Holy Synod under Filaret's guidance, was informed by the same ideas that shaped Alexander's own faith and his Holy Alliance foreign policy. Alexander's goal was the regeneration of society on the basis of a spirituality that, though ostensibly nondenominational, came close to Protestantism in deemphasizing ecclesiastical forms and stressing the Bible-reading Christian's personal communion with God. The Orthodox Church, a vital pillar of the Russian nation's historical identity, was legally downgraded to the level of a first church among equals, and the state began zealously enforcing religious tolerance toward the heterodox.[59]

The RBS leadership included Kochubei, Kozodavlev, Koshelev, Education Minister Razumovskii, and Krüdener's brother; Russia's leading Orthodox, Catholic, and Protestant clerics; and Labzin, its premier mystic.[60] As in Shishkov's Symposium, the members were representative of the state and ecclesiastical elite and were drawn both by the RBS's theology and by the prominence of its leaders, with the added attraction of imperial patronage. While affiliation with the Symposium required a modicum of political courage because of its vaguely oppositional tone, the Bible Society's links to the court made membership a shrewd career move even for people whose faith was less than fervent. The RBS attracted a disparate group of people, ranging from optimistic progressives to gloomy reactionaries and opportunist hypocrites. The third group—opportunists—is best illustrated by the career of Mikhail Magnitskii, of whom more will be said later. Typifying the first two groups were Osip P. Kozodavlev and Dmitrii P. Runich.

Born on March 29, 1754 (three weeks after Shishkov), Kozodavlev had attended Leipzig University together with Aleksandr Radishchev and Skarlat Sturdza during the years 1769–1774. He then served with the Senate, the Academy of Sciences, and finally the Commission on the Establishment of Popular Schools, where he remained until 1797. In these positions he showed great zeal for education: he favored creating universities open to all classes (a radical notion in a noble-dominated society) and argued that the language of instruction should be Russian despite the prevalence of German instructors, an idea in line with the cultural nationalism of Shishkov or Karamzin. Also, anticipating Speranskii, he believed that the bureaucracy should be an education-based meritocracy, not a caste preserve of the nobility.[61]

From 1797 on Kozodavlev was an influential member of the Senate and made a name for himself as a man of rare sophistication. Intent on promoting the rule of law, he shared Radishchev's hostility to serfdom, support for a free press, and desire to fight superstition and ignorance. Perhaps because of his progressive yet nationalistic views, he was the only friend of Karamzin's friend, Minister of Justice Ivan Dmitriev, in the committee of ministers. Kozodavlev became deputy minister of the interior in 1808 and minister in 1811. His economic policies, until his death in 1819, aimed at developing manufacturing by removing obstacles to its growth and encouraging society to "buy Russian." The main hurdle, he believed, was regulation. Asked why foreign plants grew well in Russia's greenhouses while Russian manufacturers had difficulty copying successful foreign products, he exclaimed: "Because the bureaucracy does not interfere with the design of greenhouses."[62]

Kozodavlev was attracted to the Bible Society. Like the Sturdzas and the German mystics, he thought the French king had helped cause the revolution, so the old regime was no foundation for the future. The RBS's individualism (encouraging every believer to read the Bible), support for mass literacy (required for Bible reading), and cultural nationalism (publishing the Bible in Russian) may have appealed to him. The RBS was also a joint private–governmental venture, analogous to the cooperation he sought to foster between state and industry. Finally, he disliked regulation in religion as well as economics, so presumably the society's ecumenism attracted him (although he later opposed the intellectual authoritarianism and intolerance that it began to exhibit).[63]

Among his duties was editing the *Northern Post,* his ministry's semiweekly newspaper. It carried Russian and foreign news, but among its chief purposes was boosterism: it relentlessly extolled Russia's language, literature, and manufacturing in its columns. Much of the information published there came from postal officials (who were subordinate to his ministry).[64] It was through this connection that he first met the man who would become one of the most notorious figures of Russian conservatism, Dmitrii Runich.

Born in 1778 and raised in Moscow, Runich began his career at the embassy in Vienna, where, according to word reaching Labzin, "[his] entire life is passed with merry-making and [his] only purpose is the pursuit of pleasure and amusements."[65] In 1805, he was named deputy to Moscow's postal director, Kliucharev, a veteran freemason and friend of Novikov, with whose circle Runich and his father were likewise associated. Yet he felt lost without the guidance of his friend, the charismatic and despotic Labzin (who lived in St. Petersburg), and wrote him that he yearned desperately to "rest near you from the dissipation of Moscow life and enjoy love and harmony in [your] fraternal association." "Forgive me," he begged abjectly, "scold me, beat me, only don't stop loving me and lending me strength in my weakness with your counsel."[66]

Like many contemporaries, Runich was tormented by a "Voltaireanism" that he could neither shed nor live with. A half-century later, he would still awaken suddenly at night and recall in terror the "blasphemous songs" of his youth. As he struggled in vain to banish the gremlins from his mind, it dawned upon him what tortures lay in store for the departed sinner: for all eternity he would be forced to contemplate the repulsive details of his crimes. At least until 1806, this "Voltaireanism" wrestled with the mystical faith communicated to him by Labzin, Novikov, Lopukhin, and probably others as well. In the end, his metaphysical anxieties, together with the frustrations of his service life, drove him to find solace in a gloomy, mystical religiosity.[67]

Dmitrii P. Runich

Runich's fortunes changed overnight when, on August 10, 1812, Rostopchin did him the unintended favor of deporting Kliucharev and left him in charge of the post office. Henceforth he reported directly to Kozodavlev; this was the true beginning of his career. He now joined a circle of devout Christians with ties to the Bible Society and who were readers of Glinka's *Russian Messenger,* although they did not always share its sunny confidence in human nature and the Russian people.[68] One was Kozodavlev, a member of the RBS's governing board. Another was Vasilii M. Popov (born in 1771), Kozodavlev's assistant in the postal administration since 1809 and director of his chancellery since June 1811, who became one of the RBS's two secretaries in 1813 (Aleksandr Turgenev was the other). A lonely widower raising three daughters, and a man of limited intellect and of mystical faith, Popov later figured prominently in some of the more outlandish episodes of the history of Alexandrine mysticism. Peter von Goetze, who worked with him and had a low opinion of him, recalled him as "a small, shoulderless figure with a simplemindedly pietistic expression on his face," who concluded prosaic, routine RBS meetings on Bible distribution by gazing at the ceiling and sighing: "God, great are Thy miracles." Runich may have known Kozodavlev and Popov earlier, but only their correspondence after Kliucharev's removal seems to have created a close rapport between them.[69]

A postal director's duties were important. To begin with, Runich was responsible for monitoring the private mail that passed through his station. This was a significant source of intelligence for the authorities, which is why Kozodavlev gently complained in 1815: "The excerpts you provide are so dry and so few in number. I hope you will now increase your attention to this and capture much of the news that is being written from Petersburg to Moscow." Runich also served as the minister's eyes and ears. Kozodavlev urged him to write, explaining that he based his reports to the emperor about conditions in and around Moscow on accounts relayed by Runich, to whom local postmasters reported. Runich was expected to expand sales of the *Northern Post* and serve as liaison with manufacturers—reporting their opinions, sending samples of their work, conveying the minister's views, promoting Russian industry in local society, and so on. In general, Kozodavlev seemed satisfied with his work.[70]

On April 14, 1813, only three months after its inaugural meeting, Runich wrote to Kozodavlev requesting admission to the Bible Society. His request was granted, and henceforth his official correspondence, especially with Popov, also contained RBS business and metaphysical reflections. They had corresponded on religion before and had sent each other religious literature, but accession to the RBS sealed a friendship with Popov (and presumably Kozodavlev) that apparently constituted a mystical "marriage" like that between Roksandra Sturdza, Jung-Stilling, and Alexander I.[71] Popov wrote to him: "I am glad to have come across a man with whom I can speak openly about the religious truths that I feel. Others, of course, would consider this hypocrisy or madness; you even have to worry about exposing the Word of God to insults of some sort."[72] Here we see the mentality of the "awakened" Russians of the Bible Society: their sense of persecution, their zeal for the sacred cause, and the quasi-masonic sense of brotherhood uniting the select few who had seen the light and stood apart from their benighted fellows.

Popov's faith was fed by an intense preoccupation with sin. He told Runich, "The *certainty* about man's fall and the complete depravity of our moral nature, and the *uncertainty* about one's own strength to do good, are the basis of the Christian teaching." However, as the Bible Society taught, the scriptures alone—without further explanation—could bring redemption to those who read them. He saw no need even to render them into modern Russian, for (like Shishkov) he regarded Church Slavonic as a form of Russian and believed in the effectiveness of the Bible's power regardless of its archaic language.[73] He called for its widest distribution, to spread virtue and shore up the social order. Thus he told Runich of Livonian villagers ("boors and troublemakers") who, after hearing preachers, had become "industrious, orderly in their way of living, sober and obedient to their landlords and to any authority": in a word, they were "similar in many ways to the first Christians of Apostolic times." Even nobles who were "insensitive to the grandeur and power of this" could "see the benefit to themselves" that arose from their peasants' faith. "Are there not," he concluded, "visible miracles even today?"[74] This shows the socially conservative orientation of Popov's faith, already implicit in his emphasis on sin and humility. It also demonstrates why he was more typically conservative than the Sturdzas. Both Roksandra and Aleksandr found their religious convictions to conflict with serfdom and favored its abolition. Even Glinka thought serfs ought at least to be treated with kindness. Popov, on the other hand, drew no sociopolitical conclusions at all from his beliefs. That Kozodavlev made him one of his chief assistants is testimony to his willingness to let shared faith take priority over basic ideological disagreements.

Runich did not share Popov's devotion to the Bible Society and was depressed by the politicking he observed in the Moscow branch, whose director he was.[75] Furthermore, his beliefs differed from his friend's. He alarmed Popov by asserting that modern religious writings were more important for salvation than the Bible, and Popov and Kozodavlev chided him for not making sufficiently clear, in a speech to the RBS's Moscow branch, that the RBS's goal was the distribution of Bibles without commentary. When Popov sent him foreign religious tracts, he promptly translated them and arranged for their publication. Popov feared they might be mistaken for Bible Society publications and warned that the RBS's adversaries "call us Martinists and such." He also objected on principle to overconfidence in religious questions: "How do we know which of the loyal followers of Christ's teaching thinks better than another?"[76] While Popov advocated *sola scriptura*, Runich, in keeping with his ties to "Martinism," put greater stock in modern writings. His library contained at least seventeen volumes by various mystical writers, as well as such titles as *The Mystery of the Cross, The Key to the Mysteries of Nature, The Hermetic Polar Star, A Brief History of Freemasonry*, and Labzin's journal, the *Messenger of Zion*.[77] What Runich and Popov had in common, of course, was that their religious conceptions differed from those of the Orthodox Church, which had historically defined Christianity for Russia. Social and political conservatives though they were, their religious views, the true inspiration of their ideology and policies, radically challenged centuries of Russian tradition.

Unlike others, Runich did not experience faith as a liberation from anguish. Popov was committed to the Bible Society, which he considered the key to human happiness. Aleksandr and Roksandra Sturdza, who were endowed with warmer personalities, a better education, and far richer intellects than Popov's, saw the seeds for a better future in the goodness of the Russian people, the truths of Orthodox and "awakened" religion, and the divine mission of Alexander I. Runich's outlook, on the contrary, was arid and perpetually pessimistic. "Man is born evil," he wrote lugubriously, and "love for one's fellow man is nothing more than a magnificent dress that is embroidered with gold and silver but covers a skeleton eaten away by maggots." He felt (along with the Sturdzas, Glinka, and Shishkov) that in 1812 Russia was punished for her sins, and he considered Napoleon's escape from Elba to be a further warning.[78] Like Glinka, the Sturdzas, Shishkov, and other proto-Slavophiles, he took a dim view of the upper class. But—unlike the others—he also attacked "the extreme depravity of our common people." The brutishness of the rural masses was a point to which he returned again and again in his memoirs. The peasant "lives only to satisfy his physical needs and to enjoy a freedom that he seeks in a vegetative life." This contempt, influenced perhaps by his father's role in suppressing the Pugachev revolt, shaped his view of the "people's war" of 1812. The villagers were natural xenophobes, and when the French violated their property, they retaliated with barbaric cruelty. "Patriotism had nothing to do with it." What had truly defeated Napoleon, however, was providence, not nature or man.[79] Yet Russia's primitiveness was also its strength, for the vast distances and the people's ignorance and ethnic disunity would prevent revolution for centuries to come. Unlike Glinka or Shishkov, he considered old Muscovy "barbaric." Peter I had left Russia "a country that was not civilized in the European way, but savage; yet it was a virginal country, whose rulers could easily guide it in this direction or that." However, when the monarchy undermined religion, the entire nation experienced a moral decline. Russians, he concluded, were in no way prepared to govern themselves, for the peasants were too primitive, the Westernized nobility was morally corrupt and politically disloyal, and in general "the Russian people has not yet emerged from its childhood. One cannot yet speak with it about freedom."

Runich thus occupied an uncomfortable middle ground between the nativists and reformers of the day by rejecting the positive in both. Shishkov (whom he regarded as a pretentious, ignorant mediocrity) and his disciples acknowledged the dignity of the people, for whom Runich had only contempt. The reformers desired civic equality and the rule of law, while Runich considered drastic reforms neither possible nor desirable, let alone necessary. Instead, in the historicist logic common among Western conservatives and argued by Aleksandr Sturdza as well, he wrote that "constitutions are neither given nor taken by force; they must mature and appear in the world in due time." That due time, he felt, had still not arrived in Russia even as he was writing these reminiscences around 1850.

He advocated a negative policy of restraining both the barbarism of the poor and the decadence of the elites. The task fell to religion, an area where Runich shared neither the traditionalists' faith in Orthodoxy nor Popov's belief in the power of the Gospel. Unlike the Sturdzas, he was no great admirer of Alexander I, either. Even freemasonry, in its revived form after 1801, met with his disapproval, for it seemed to be led by men ignorant of masonic teachings, and during meetings "the masonic brothers were attentive only to ensure that their glasses were never empty." Labzin's lodge had been a rare exception, he recalled, and the ideals of freemasonry retained his admiration even if its concrete manifestations after 1801 did not. Runich's thinking, therefore, was both pessimistic and repressive. Since he had a European's disdain for the Russian masses and their Muscovite heritage, and a Russian conservative's distrust of Westernized aristocrats, he could look to no class or ideology as a source of hope for the future. The only milieu in which he felt at home was the mystical wing of freemasonry, where European culture, aristocratic manners, nonecclesiastical religiosity, strict sociopolitical conservatism, and a sense of Christian brotherhood were cultivated. Yet this environment did little to prepare him to deal with the great issues of Russian life. In a Moscow postal director, such reactionary sterility was of little consequence. When he became curator of the St. Petersburg educational district, however, it would acquire considerable importance.[80]

From the first, the Bible Society was greeted with distrust by the foes of freemasonry and religious change. Their war against it provided the drama of conservative politics after 1815. Within a year of joining the RBS, Runich inadvertently offered a preview of battles to come, for his promotion of non-Orthodox religious works handed others a stick with which to beat the Bible Society, which, as Popov warned, was widely suspected of "Martinism." The first enemy to cross Runich's path was Rostopchin—an unreconstructed *Polizeistaat* conservative with little tolerance for associations of foreign-inspired, self-important do-gooders, who had just demonstrated his power and ruthlessness by illegally expelling Kliucharev, Runich's chief, from Moscow.

Rostopchin warned, even after France's defeat, of the danger posed by Napoleon's "enthusiasts, that is, the Illuminati, the Martinists and the sectarians." The Bible Society appeared to be just such a group, and he wrote to the minister of police that he expected "nothing positive from this organization," for the well-to-do already owned Bibles and the illiterate had no use for them. Runich caught his eye because he headed the Moscow RBS branch and, perhaps, because any postal director not under Rostopchin's thumb seemed a threat to the military governor. Rostopchin reported to the emperor that autumn about the "grumblers and doubters here," among whom he included Runich. "They gather together stupidities, add their ideas, and pass their uncertainties into the stupidity of others." Rostopchin gave one of the other grumblers "a dressing-down," which left Runich "a little worried for himself."[81] When (in September 1813) Runich obtained approval to publish a translation of a religious text issued by the London-based Tract Society, Rostopchin responded (the following March) by ordering the seizure of all unsold copies, once again acting without legal authority since censorship was the bailiwick of the education ministry; he argued, however, that the book contradicted Orthodox dogma on the sacrament of baptism and caused dangerous commotion among the Old Believers. Given the sympathy Runich and his father had exhibited for the Old Believers, it was not implausible to associate him with them.[82]

Rostopchin's action aroused a storm of protest, revealing both the Bible Society's clout and its limitations. Runich appealed to Golitsyn, his chief in the RBS; and the curator of the Moscow educational district (the chief censor), a fanatical Rosicrucian, filed a complaint with his own superior, the minister of education. The bishop of Moscow likewise reported to Golitsyn (this time as overprocurator of the Holy Synod) that he found Runich's booklet consistent with church teachings. Topping off the list of officials defending Runich was the influential Kozodavlev, who also argued his man's case.[83] Yet Golitsyn, although he assured Runich that the tract was unobjectionable from the church's standpoint, refused to take that stance when submitting the dossier to the emperor. Instead, echoing Kozodavlev's and Popov's admonitions to Runich, he stressed that the Bible Society was unrelated to the Tract Society (Rostopchin had sought to link the two) and published only the scriptures.[84] Evidently, Golitsyn feared the power of conservative Orthodox circles and hoped to keep the RBS out of the controversy. The case lingered, with Alexander I away in Europe and preoccupied with foreign policy. By September 1814, Rostopchin had been dismissed, and a relieved Runich rejoiced that at last "the terror of deportations, knouts and gallows has disappeared!" Within a few weeks, the ban on his book was lifted as well.[85]

The Awakening's powerful impact in Russia was due in part to a cultural mood that was captured in literature by the sentimentalists but that also permeated the world of young aristocrats, people who associated emotional refinement with elite culture and gained fulfillment from poetry and the cultivation of elevated feeling, not service.[86] These attitudes characterized many religious conservatives as well. The letters of Alexander I and his sister Ekaterina, of Roksandra Sturdza and both her brother and Jung-Stilling, and of Runich and Popov, spoke a strangely intimate, almost amorous language. Not surprisingly, this note was absent from the letters of Shishkov and Rostopchin, men of an earlier generation and strangers to sentimentalism.

Sentimentalism encouraged the forming of intensely emotional bonds, in contrast to the formalized, hierarchical etiquette governing contemporary life. This led to close friendships between men and women (Roksandra Sturdza's ties with de Maistre, Capodistrias, Alexander I, and Jung-Stilling, and Krüdener's with the emperor) where propriety was guaranteed by the religious and moral zeal of the people involved. Another consequence was the popularity of masonic lodges, in which men formed friendships across boundaries normally fixed by service rank. The Bible Society was emotionally akin to a lodge, and the friendship of Runich with his superiors, Popov and Kozodavlev, illustrates this solidarity among "brothers" regardless of formal rank. Related psychologically to these phenomena was the antirationalist search for a religion based on individual emotion, rather than on scholastic theology or historical tradition. The Bible-centered faith of Popov, the mysticism of Runich and Labzin, and even the reformism of Filaret all illustrate the power of this impulse. This also was in some measure a generational phenomenon, a fact that helps explain Shishkov's and Rostopchin's hostility to it.

The popularity of the Awakening tied into the Russian nobility's intellectual superficiality. Like "Voltaireanism," it was rendered fashionable in part by the ease with which it could be acquired. Traditional theology demanded extensive training, but Russia offered even nobles few opportunities for formal education in religion and philosophy; to be "awakened," on the other hand, required only the proper attitude. Yet the Awakening also reflected the turmoil of an age when ancient certainties about the social order came crashing down. The horrors associated with the revolutionary and Napoleonic regimes, both of which outsiders linked with secularism, brought on a profound crisis of confidence in rationalism. This disillusionment (adumbrated in the Rosicrucian lodges well before 1789) was most striking among those who came of age around the time of, or after, the fall of the Bastille.

The leaders of the Awakening were of the "prerevolutionary" generation: Jung-Stilling was born in 1740, Koshelev in 1769, and Labzin in 1766. The most zealous followers, however, were younger people (Alexander I, the Sturdzas, Runich) who searched for guidance from those of their elders who had reconciled faith with Enlightenment and romantic attitudes, attitudes that included an introspective individualism and the belief that the Kingdom of God—a religious counterpart to the Jacobins' "republic of virtue"—was imminent.[87] The belief in the supremacy of the individual over institutional tradition and in emotion (not formal learning) as the key to the truth, and the hope to see ultimate certainties realized in the near future, were telling psychological traits of the age that passed into the Awakening.

In the long run, however, these factors did not amount to a coherent approach to ordering society or even religion itself. Russians responded variously to the Awakening. Some, like the Sturdzas, remained loyal to the Orthodox Church, which they sought merely to energize with foreign ideas. Others, like Popov, switched to the Protestant position of accepting only the Bible as truth. Runich adopted a faith that allotted great importance to nonscriptural works. "Awakened" religion's wide umbrella could accommodate almost any political opinion. The Sturdzas opposed serfdom; Runich did not. They were sympathetic to representative government, which he opposed. Kozodavlev favored industry and a free press; Aleksandr Sturdza had grave doubts about both. Sturdza believed in the peasants; Runich despised them. Sturdza admired the religious culture of Muscovy, an era Runich thought barbaric. Kozodavlev believed in free speech, religious tolerance, and public education; Runich supported none of these.

These differences of opinion over questions of fundamental importance must be kept in mind if we are to understand the decade after 1815. Although the struggle with the traditional conservatives consumed much of the religious conservatives' energy, their own failure to reconcile their conflicting views left them unable to put forward a viable program for the spiritual renewal for which they yearned.

CHAPTER SEVEN

The Holy Alliance Experiment

It is a stubborn cliché that after 1815 Alexander I single-mindedly opposed change abroad and reform attempts at home, and that his displays of religious faith were either a manipulative political tactic or proof of an unbalanced personality. In this view, conservatives were either obsequious courtiers or incorrigible obscurantists, and it is telling that many historians found Arakcheev, Magnitskii, and Krüdener worthier of study than more intelligent, enlightened figures.[1] It is only more recently that James Flynn, Judith Cohen Zacek, and others have challenged this one-sided interpretation.

In fact, the period 1815–1825 began as a time of experimentation, with the emperor and his advisers seeking to defeat the forces of revolution without lapsing into a sterile policy of coercion. Religion, in this context, was no mere fig leaf for reaction, nor was it a doctrine of quietist escapism; instead, it frequently served as a guide to reformist activism. This was a fascinating moment in the history of Russian conservative thought and policy, for the imperial government did what Shishkov and others could only dream of: use the powers of the state to mold the consciousness of Russia and even Europe.[2] Ultimately, however, the effort foundered—on its own internal contradictions, its incompatibility with key state interests, and its lack of a base of support other than the emperor and a few officials and intellectuals—and it gave way to precisely the statist reaction that its visionaries had hoped to avoid.

In the preceding chapter, I dwell principally on the way these religious views took shape and penetrated the Russian elite through the interaction of Russian and European ideas and events. In the present chapter, I will explore the program for Russian foreign and domestic policy that Aleksandr Sturdza—one of Alexander I's most interesting but least known advisers—and others articulated on the basis of these beliefs, and discuss the political controversies this program aroused among the various factions of Russian conservatives.

Sturdza's political and social thought is best understood in the broader context of the Enlightenment's impact on Russia. As Marc Raeff has argued, the German *Aufklärung,* much more than the French *Lumières* or the British Enlightenment, shaped Russian culture around 1800, and German Pietism in particular inspired several important impulses in Russian thought. These included an individualistic, activist, introspective religiosity (in contrast to the deism or skepticism of many French *philosophes*); an emphasis on ethics and on man in his "organic" social context, rather than the stress on individual liberation often found in Britain and France; a belief in the importance of moral, Christian education, oriented toward the needs of the community rather than toward the emancipation of the individual; and a strong faith in the state to promote these goals.[3] These ideas came together in Aleksandr Sturdza, whose work in foreign policy (like the roles of Golitsyn, Magnitskii, Sturdza himself, and others in ecclesiastical and educational affairs) illustrates the emperor's desire after 1814 to base his policies on his religious beliefs. The foreign policy component of this strategy was the Holy Alliance, whose premier thinker was Sturdza. A man who was at once doctrinaire, thoughtful, and sharply analytical, he could offer the monarch an intelligent Holy Alliance perspective on any given issue. Alexander liked to surround himself with advisers of different ideological orientations, including in the arena of foreign policy. After 1814, Russian foreign policy was dominated jointly by Nesselrode, who supported Metternich and the Restoration order, and Capodistrias, who was more sympathetic to liberal aspirations.[4] The emperor could thus hear out a variety of opinions and always had a range of alternatives to current policies.

Capodistrias and Sturdza typify the ambiguity of the terms *liberal* and *conservative* in the early nineteenth century. Like Alexander I, they believed that men of goodwill must find a middle road between revolutionary upheaval and reactionary stagnation. Capodistrias favored constitutionalism as an insurance against revolution and believed that nations had a right to political self-determination. He also supported the Holy Alliance's high-minded effort to introduce greater morality into international relations. He and Sturdza broadly agreed in these areas, yet with important differences in emphasis. Capodistrias stressed the progressive and secular implications of these ideas: he argued forcefully, for instance, for the desirability of constitutional governments in Europe, and he criticized Metternich and others for ignoring the social tensions that caused revolutionary crises in the first place.[5] Sturdza, on the other hand, stressed the need for strengthening religion as a remedy for society's moral disequilibria, a focus that gave his opinions a decidedly more conservative bent. He argued that Western man must stop rebelling spiritually, return to a humble obedience to God, and disavow the innovations of the eighteenth century. The embodiment of the ideal society he envisioned was the Holy Alliance: a league of Christian states, safeguarding national traditions yet bound together by the solidarity of their common faith. Much of his work in Russian foreign policy between 1815 and 1821 was devoted to implementing this vision of Europe's and Russia's future.

More than any of the other subjects of this study, Sturdza devoted his career to implementing a complex and in some ways profound ideological program. Nothing he did makes sense outside of that context. His views remained consistent throughout his adult life and can be reconstructed from fragments that survive in many different sources: private letters, government position papers, propaganda tracts written for the state, essays published under his own name, essays that he wrote but kept in his files, and other documents written during the reigns of Alexander I and Nicholas I, in state service and in retirement.

Sturdza regarded religion as the core of national identity (in contrast to Shishkov's language-centered conceptions or Karamzin's emphasis on the autocracy).[6] He harbored a deep theological hostility to Islam that received added political militancy from his hatred of the Ottoman Empire as the oppressor of the Balkan Christians; but he also took an ambivalent view of the West. He considered Europe a community, and his polyglot education, interest in European political and intellectual life, and frequent travels linked him to it. Yet he was also sharply critical of its Christianity, and this *problématique* was central to his worldview. To Sturdza, the very splendor of Latin civilization was a deviation from the simple truths of early Christianity, to which the Orthodox East, with its perhaps less sophisticated secular culture, had remained faithful. Throughout his adult life he engaged in polemics to enlighten the West about the true nature of Orthodoxy.[7]

A state's tranquillity, he thought, depended on the society's internalized sense of morality, its extragovernmental institutions and historical traditions, not on external coercion by the state; here he shared the outlook of contemporary conservatives such as Franz von Baader, Adam Müller, and Edmund Burke.[8] Unlike Shishkov or Rostopchin, he distrusted the police state of the eighteenth century, which he blamed for the French Revolution and whose resurrection he feared during the Restoration. The essential trait of that state, as he saw it, was that it lacked the moral basis that alone could legitimize its power, and the repression it practiced aggravated society's spiritual ills.

The original Christian Church, he postulated, had found the proper balance between liberty and conformity, democracy and authority. Through their councils, its patriarchs had exercised power wisely without lapsing into despotism; as a result, Christians had internalized the Church's teachings and were able to govern themselves without resort to force and violence. This tradition survived in the Orthodox Church and the societies it governed. The Catholics, however, had broken with the Church over the popes' craving for power, and there began the moral decay of the West. Rome's despotic arrogance had shaped the character of the state in the West as well; papal tyranny had then engendered spiritually anarchistic Protestantism, while royal tyranny led to revolution. Like de Maistre and Bonald, though with an added antipapal bias, Sturdza argued that authority and liberty, church and state, were in conflict in the West, and so—Sturdza agreed in this with Glinka, although his own reasoning was far more complex—God had brought about the French Revolution to punish the West for its wickedness.[9]

Russia, by virtue of its Orthodox heritage, was free of these vices, according to Sturdza. (In this he agreed with the romantic nationalists, though not with the statist conceptions of Karamzin.) However, two aspects of Russian life worked against spiritual harmony. To begin with, he confronted the problem that the patriotic monarchists Shishkov and Glinka refused to face: Peter the Great's reforms had destroyed the integrity of Russian life, splintered its society and rendered it imitative, and helped introduce despotism into Russia. The arguments and the sheer vehemence with which Sturdza condemned Russia's Westernization anticipate Chaadaev (minus his pro-Catholic bias)[10] and the Slavophiles, suggesting that these later thinkers were not merely following Europe-wide intellectual currents of the 1820s, 1830s, and 1840s but were also carrying on an autonomous and highly articulate Russian tradition. Furthermore, he wrote, Russia's moral and human development was stymied by serfdom, which, like any despotism, corrupted both master and bondspeople, and which needed to be abolished. Finally, he argued directly to the monarch that the proper structure for a modern state was a constitutional monarchy with unchangeable "basic laws" and a parliament acting in a consultative role.[11]

Sturdza was thus no reactionary who pined for the "sweetness of life" under the old regime, and he had only contempt for Metternich and others who seemed bent on restoring it. Instead, like Glinka or the French radicals of the late eighteenth century, he worried about a morally decayed social order and had hopes it might be spiritually regenerated and humanity's historic ills cured. He hoped that this goal could be accomplished through a judicious combination of liberty, repression, and education—all applied by a state acting on behalf of the people and in the name of what Robespierre might have called "virtue." The trustee of this divine mission was Alexander I, and its charter, the Holy Alliance, committed its signatories (i.e., most European monarchs) to govern their domestic and international affairs according to the principles of the Gospel.

Some societies, he argued, were better prepared than others to cope with this challenge. He believed in the innate moral superiority of agrarian over commercial societies and regarded less "advanced" societies as more sane, harmonious, and politically stable. Outside of Russia, Spain and Greece seemed to offer compelling evidence for this idea. The similarities between (Catholic) Spain, his beloved Greece, and Russia could hardly have escaped him: a glorious past, economic backwardness, the arrogant condescension of other Europeans, and a fervent nationalism tinged with religious zeal and shaped by a history as an outpost on Christendom's Muslim frontier. It was no coincidence that Russia and Greece had been immune to the revolutionary fever before 1815, nor that Russia and Spain—"two religious peoples"—had defeated Napoleon.[12]

Toward Great Britain, Sturdza, like many Continentals, harbored both cool admiration and deep animosity.[13] Its foreign policy repelled him. He took London to task in his memoirs for placing its desire for naval supremacy ahead of great power cooperation, he accused British business of encouraging the rebels in Spanish America, and he identified Britain (and France) as the center of a revolutionary conspiracy undermining order in Europe. His angriest complaint was that London used the Greeks after 1821 to promote its own cynical agenda. He praised Britain's system of government for ensuring stability and freedom but attributed this success to British society's conservative values and secure strategic location, and cautioned that this system had evolved over many centuries and under unique circumstances, so it could not serve as a model for other societies. He was impressed with the religiosity of the British but highly suspicious of their Protestantism, just as his praise for the virtues of the merchantry was more than compensated by his moral distrust of urban society. Behind Britain's façade of piety and sound government, Sturdza sensed social tension, political subversion, heresy, and an inclination to manipulate other nations.[14]

France, naturally, was the object of Sturdza's abiding hostility. Even so, he preferred the land of 1789 and Napoleon to Russia's erstwhile British allies. Several factors may explain this paradox. He belonged to a pan-European aristocratic culture whose mecca was Paris. Most of his writings (official as well as personal) were in French, whereas he did not know English, and his childhood tutor had been a Frenchman. He had visited France but not Britain, his social circle included Frenchmen but no Britons, and he was much more familiar with French than English literature. Catholicism was more akin to Orthodoxy (and less identified with rationalism) than Protestantism, especially the Awakening of the early nineteenth century. The Bourbon regime had his and Russia's full support, and there were French thinkers, such as Chateaubriand, to whom he felt intellectually close;[15] British politics and thought were terra incognita by comparison. Finally, France was more amenable than Britain to Russian diplomatic influence, Alexander I disliked the British government, and Capodistrias favored closer Russian ties with France. All of these factors presumably made Sturdza more forgiving of French than of British sins.

With no non-Orthodox country did Sturdza feel a greater affinity than Germany. Most of his foreign travels took him there, his second wife was German, and Roksandra (maid of honor to Russia's German-born empress) married a German and settled there temporarily; among his friends were Stein and Baader. There the old regime was still alive, and the conservative, introspective piety that characterized the emperor and Sturdza was more common there than elsewhere in Europe. Even Germany's political fragmentation appealed to him, for it permitted the variegated spirit of its people to reveal itself more fully than in tightly centralized Britain or France.[16] This romantic idealization of Germans' native spontaneity is indicative of several aspects of his thinking. As a Russian and Greek patriot, he believed nations should assert their own cultural identity rather than permit it to be dictated by foreigners, and he also held that the "people," in particular the peasants, were closer to nature, God, and Truth than were the more decadent people of the cities. He criticized papal authoritarianism as well as the Petrine reforms,[17] because such heavy-handed behavior, whether by tsars, popes, or revolutionaries, meddled with the world as God had created it. To respect the natural diversity of social classes and structures, of local cultures and traditions, was to respect the work of God.

After 1815, he wrote pamphlets and articles defending the Holy Alliance, as part of a propaganda campaign directed by Capodistrias (Nesselrode doubted the usefulness of such methods) that paid unofficial "literary agents" abroad to generate press coverage favorable to Russian policy. This work drew on Sturdza's skill as a polemicist who presented his government's views convincingly because he shared them.[18] He also worked with the administration to help integrate his recently annexed Bessarabian homeland into the Russian Empire. His main sphere of activity, however, was Russian diplomacy. From 1816 on, as head of Capodistrias's chancellery, he drafted correspondence with Russian ambassadors and foreign cabinets, memoranda on Russian policy toward France, and other important documents. He was respected as an expert on Europe and a theorist on international affairs. For example, in February 1818, he was asked to brief Grand Duke Mikhail on Prussian affairs for his upcoming European tour, presumably because of his reputation as an authority on Germany.[19]

It was this function as analyst of German politics that precipitated the greatest crisis of Sturdza's career, caused an international uproar, and perhaps almost cost him his life. In the fall of 1818 he attended the international congress at Aachen and, with imperial approval, wrote a confidential memorandum on German affairs that was circulated among allied delegations and ended up being leaked to the press, causing an uproar among German liberals and nationalists.[20] In this *Memorandum on the Present State of Germany* Sturdza argued that, since Germany's political turbulence and spiritual malaise could not be resolved so long as its universities remained hotbeds of radicalism, the governments should suppress universities' autonomy. Similarly, the deplorable state of the press in Germany, he asserted, resulted from the failure of past governments to curb irreligion and rationalism. Educational reform would eventually change people and thereby eliminate the abuses of the press as well; the present, however, called for tough censorship measures, whose uniformity throughout the German lands should be enforced by the German Confederation.

Once published, these proposals provoked a storm of protest that deeply embarrassed Alexander I and his German allies. Especially to Germany's nationalist intellectuals and students—who already feared that the patriotic and liberal hopes aroused by the 1813 "War of Liberation" were being stymied by Metternich's German Confederation—Sturdza's memorandum represented unacceptable interference in German affairs by a reactionary foreign power.[21] In Russia Sturdza's memorandum was unpopular, too, for reasons both political and ideological. There was grumbling over the damage to Russia's image abroad; Sturdza's friends Aleksandr Turgenev and Viazemskii accused him of being fanatical and remote from reality; and the repressive Karlsbad Decrees of 1819 would prompt Nikolai Turgenev to remark that the Germans had decided to "sturdzify" their universities. This criticism was typical of the common but mistaken tendency to link Sturdza (and the idea of the Holy Alliance) with Metternich and the Restoration order. In fact, in a memorandum to Capodistrias, Sturdza roundly condemned the Karlsbad Decrees, arguing that the German Confederation, by censoring only *political* dissent (but not immorality or irreligion) and enforcing only *political* orthodoxy at its universities, was seeking to shore up anachronistic despotisms, rather than accepting the political reforms the times demanded and working to reeducate society in a Christian spirit.[22]

After Russia's "literary agent," playwright August von Kotzebue, was assassinated by a radical German student in March 1819, Sturdza, who was still in Germany and certain he was next on the list, fled back to Russia. He felt abandoned and betrayed by his government, which had allowed the impression to persist that the *Memorandum* expressed merely his personal views. In addition, he was bitter at being labeled a reactionary and believed that Kotzebue's murder had vindicated his warnings about German student radicalism.[23] By late spring he had obtained leave to return to Ust'e, his family estate, and nurse his health, especially his ailing eyes; Nesselrode expected him back in the capital by late autumn, but Sturdza had told Viazemskii of his intention to remain at Ust'e "as long as possible" and planned to spend the winter there. Evidently, he was offended at the way Nesselrode and the emperor had treated him since Aachen, and he liked to think of his sulking semiretirement as a withdrawal from a sinful world. Roksandra, however, forever concerned with her brother's career and the mysterious intentions of divine providence, disapproved of his plans. She pointed out that the Belorussian countryside during the winter was unlikely to restore his health, and further argued: "We live in a time when one must not abandon state affairs when one serves a Christian Sovereign and is oneself a Christian. . . . Evil is making such progress that no one must leave his post when his conscience does not order him to leave it." She regarded Germany as a volcano on the brink of a violent eruption and felt certain that the *Memorandum* had helped alert governments to the danger. Aléco, she wrote, should swallow his pride and return to his duties.[24] Indeed, the European crisis of revolution and reaction was far from abating: the months from August 1819 to February 1820 saw the adoption of the Karlsbad Decrees, the assassination of the heir to the French throne, and the Six Acts and the Cato Street

Conspiracy in Britain. Full-scale revolution, meanwhile, loomed on the horizon in Spain and Italy.

So Sturdza wrote to Petersburg that although his poor health was keeping him at Ust'e he would still gladly serve, and he was entrusted with drafting a propaganda brochure (commissioned by the emperor) to review international events since Aachen. It was intended for publication abroad, anonymously or under a pseudonym, and was not to be traceable to the Russian government. Evidently, despite the *Memorandum* debacle, Alexander I still had confidence in him.[25] In a letter that accompanied the official instructions, Capodistrias made clear that he trusted Sturdza's judgment: "Feel free with regard to the design. You are the master of the terrain. Build as you like. And it will be very good." He wrote that the emperor, Sturdza, and he all favored a policy that sought a middle way between revolution and reaction and that Sturdza would have no difficulty dispelling misconceptions about Alexander's thinking, which some mistook for "the source of liberal ideas" while others thought it "that of absolute power." Alexander's thought "is neither the one nor the other," Capodistrias explained to Sturdza. "It is made up of pious and religious sentiments and is informed by the experience of all times and, above all, that of our century." The outline instructed Sturdza to divide the report into two sections. In the first, he was to analyze the unrest in Europe and Latin America, assigning blame to both governments and peoples. In the second, he would investigate the ideological split of Europe into a liberal and an absolutist camp; the positive and negative elements in both parties were to be noted and the need for a synthesis of the two conceptions pointed out.[26]

The first section of the *Overview of the Year 1819* (the paper's working title) was completed by mid-December of 1819.[27] It was an articulate statement of Sturdza's thinking, arguing that the major European states (except Russia) were perilously unstable and allocating the blame evenly between the ineptitude of monarchs and the dogmatism of their critics. Overall, Alexander was satisfied; while some points required revision, Capodistrias assured Sturdza that these "concern not the idea, but a few turns of phrase."[28]

The requested changes were indeed not fundamental, but they amounted to more than "a few turns of phrase." Sturdza was asked to mellow his criticism of the Congress of Vienna. Having received no guidelines in this question, he had judged it severely, arguing that the statesmen had not been bold enough in "the creation of a new world" and had conducted too much selfish horsetrading. The emperor and Capodistrias found this too harsh and thought the obstacles they and the other peacemakers had faced in 1815 deserved more consideration. Sturdza was likewise told that he had not fully grasped the complexity of the German situation. He had written that the German governments had dealt with the revolutionary challenge in a vacillating and reactive way, a problem aggravated by the country's political disunity. Recent events, he argued (his earlier memorandum condemning the decrees notwithstanding), had made the Karlsbad Decrees necessary, and they were a useful test of the federal system.[29] This apparent consensus,

Capodistrias objected, was a dangerous illusion; the German Confederation's recent measures were intended only to serve Austrian and Prussian interests. The Russian government had sensed this, and its lack of enthusiasm for these measures "has aroused great uneasiness in the troubled consciences of the chancellor of Prussia and Prince Metternich." Capodistrias seemed concerned that the *Overview* might reflect favorably on his archrival, Metternich. It also appears that he rejected Sturdza's metaphysical dogmatism and his advocacy of censorship and educational repression as answers to political turbulence. He feared that Sturdza's document might be misused by schemers such as Metternich, who could adopt his rhetoric and practical suggestions without sharing his Christian ideals. Besides, the original instructions had mentioned "freedom of the press as a necessary condition of a people's political and civil freedom"—a view hardly compatible with the spirit of the Karlsbad Decrees.

The second section of the *Overview* examined the conflict between left and right in contemporary Europe. In keeping with the instructions and with his own thinking, Sturdza found fault with the shrill partisanship of European commentators; if people were less self-righteous and narrow-minded, he argued, they would find more common ground. The current division was an extension of the religious split of the sixteenth century, he wrote, in language suggesting that he associated the Reformation with liberalism and Catholicism with absolutism. Earlier religious conflicts, however, had at least been tempered by respect for God's will; modern secular hatreds knew no restraints at all. While "we cordially detest all types of fanaticism," he concluded, the most dangerous was the one that "has no brake or moderator in itself, and that wants to have all or nothing because it aspires to nothing outside the boundaries of human industry, the pleasures of pride, and the covetousness of this world."

He analyzed the two ideologies of the day: "absolute power" and "liberal ideas." The society of the future, he wrote, would include elements of both. Extreme monarchists were condemned to failure, but advocates of constitutionalism would also have to understand that reform of the social order could emanate only from "government." The real difference between limited and absolute governments lay not in the degree of freedom they allowed—for monarchies (e.g., Great Britain) could tolerate liberty, and republics (e.g., Venice) tyranny—but in that republics presupposed a virtuous citizenry, monarchies a virtuous ruler. In these troubled times, both were in short supply. Furthermore, in times of crisis absolute power was necessary: representative government could thrive only in peacetime. From this Sturdza concluded that, while absolute government was indispensable to society, it could and should incorporate some of the advantages of the representative system. These features needed to be kept in the proper perspective, since individual rights often clashed with those of classes; trial by a jury of one's peers required uncommon virtue and "enlightenment" in the mass of society; legislative control over taxation was limited by executive control over the policies that shaped the government's budget; and there could never be complete freedom of the press.

True freedom, freedom from passions and vice, came from man's voluntary submission to God, and here forms of government were irrelevant. This was the core of Sturdza's thinking. However, abuses of governmental power could be more effectively resisted by the corporate orders of traditional monarchies than by the individualism of constitutional states, where confidence in the constitution undermined corporate solidarities. The formal guarantees that legislatures could offer were paltry next to the historically evolved solidity of traditional societies, as exemplified by the ancient institutions of Great Britain.

A free press was unacceptable because printed statements were not speech but actions, and should be regulated accordingly, he argued, and went on to discuss two means of restraining the press. The first was preventive censorship. Unfortunately, this system could place great authority in the hands of abusive or inept censors, and its guidelines could fail to keep pace with the needs of society. Still, censorship was not "a mere negation" but rather "a perfectible institution." The second system, practiced in Britain, tempered freedom of the press with libel suits once writings had been published. This system clogged the courts and capriciously produced verdicts that ranged from frequent leniency to occasional excessive severity. "The excess of license," he wrote, "sooner or later produces the need for arbitrary repression." In this system, the press could act as a check on abuses of power by the state. Therefore, under representative government, freedom of *political* speech might be desirable, but censorship was still needed for religious, moral, scientific, and literary writings; thus the two systems for controlling the press might converge. The same rules governing the right to vote should also regulate who benefited from freedom of political speech, and anonymous publications should be banned. (The last point is not without irony, since the *Overview*'s true author was to remain secret.)

Finally, Sturdza addressed the role of religion. Only Christianity, with its teachings about moral obligations, could restrain despotism *and* rebellion. Only a return to Christ and a retreat from ideological dogmatism could show Europe the way out of its labyrinth. Such a return required a re-Christianization of education and a commitment to educating each social class according to its station in life, rather than depriving the poor of the consolations of religion in order to give them third-rate secular schooling instead; that kind of educational philosophy had created "that spiritual poverty that reduces the pauper to the condition of the beast—and often inspires him with its furies." The ideal Sturdza envisioned was the "Christian State," where religion was the foundation of a polity whose formal mechanisms might evolve but were ultimately of secondary importance. Its laws and institutions would be "calculated for man's weakness and his dignity; for the need to avoid, when possible, conflicts between the wants and the duties of the human condition; finally for the importance of encouraging no talent that corrupts." Its foreign policy would be based on the brotherhood of Christian peoples. Its social classes would respect each other's status, and while "honest merit can achieve everything" in this society, people do not in fact aspire to everything, "out of respect for public tranquillity." Its government would be free from corruption and church interference, while the church in turn would be independent of the state and would be governed by "the holy assembly of its shepherds" (one of the traditional features of Orthodoxy). "Finally," he wrote, "to define our entire thought with one stroke: in a Christian State (which is the highest point of perfection of social life), '*faith, learning* and *authority,* far from being mutually antagonistic, tend to establish and preserve between them a constant and salutary harmony.'"[30] In this sentence, the last of the *Overview,* Sturdza used a phrase he had formulated in 1818 in the published instruction drafted for the Academic Committee of the Main Schools Administration. This borrowing indicates the extent to which the *Overview* reflected his own thinking and the extent to which he viewed foreign and domestic policy through the same ideological prism. It also risked revealing at least the author's nationality (although his name had not appeared on the printed version of the instruction), especially since, as he put it, the instruction "was translated and was bitterly censured by the subversive papers of Europe."[31]

Capodistrias wrote to him that the second section of the *Overview* was "perfect." Capodistrias had supplied a general outline and had laid out what the spirit of the discussion should be;[32] still, the bulk of this section reflected Sturdza's thinking. The views it expresses on the press, religion, education, and the Christian State all recur in others of his writings. On education, in particular, this document presents the same ideas he promoted within Russia. This suggests how much he thought in ideological and universal, not empirical or national, terms. In addition, the *Overview* illustrated his ambivalence about the struggle between conservatives and liberals. On almost all substantive points, he sided with the conservatives. Yet his professed neutrality was more than a propaganda device, for he genuinely condemned the upper classes of Europe, who, he believed, had given up the moral high ground in a squalid pursuit of wealth and power; by encouraging godless rationalism, they were sawing off the limb on which they sat.

The rapid pace of events that winter rendered the *Overview* moot. On January 20, 1820, Capodistrias wrote that his plans to publish it in Switzerland were being held up by Alexander's slowness in reviewing it. By February 6, he was satisfied with Sturdza's revision of the first section and was waiting for the monarch to finish reading the second. As of February 28, Alexander had still not finished reading it, nor had he by March 19. But by then the *Overview* had been overtaken by events, so publishing it no longer seemed advisable. Sturdza was informed of Alexander's satisfaction with his work, but it was relegated to the imperial archives.[33]

When revolution broke out in southern Europe, the government turned to Sturdza for advice. In early April 1820, Capodistrias asked for his thoughts on the Spanish revolution and the general instability of Europe: "What should they *do* or *not do,* these Governments?"[34] Sturdza argued, characteristically, that, after 1815, King Ferdinand VII was guilty of failing to restore the health of Spain's ancient institutions in alliance with his people. The recent liberal reforms of his state were, of course, absurd and doomed to collapse; but how might Spain affect other countries? Now was the time, he counseled, for other powers to stand firm to prevent the disease from spreading. That meant, above all, preserving the crown as the true locus of power in European governments. He was pessimistic about the prospects for containing the threat but suggested the following: states whose ancient institutions had collapsed (like Spain) should promote reforms based on the familiar triad of *"faith, learning, and authority."* Others (like Russia) that had escaped disaster should avoid reform and instead should focus on wisely administering justice and finances and infusing public education with religion, since failure in these areas was the cause of all revolutions. "Everything else is secondary."

As for the international situation, Sturdza doubted that conventional diplomacy could contain the spread of revolution and warned against intervening between a nation and its king and thereby wounding its national pride. He concluded, in light of the profound differences between the great powers, that it was impossible to establish a unified system through which they could join together to oppose revolution; at best they might be able to offer each other armed assistance. This memorandum he submitted to Alexander I, who agreed with its ideas and requested that Sturdza develop further its implications for Russian domestic policy.[35]

A week later, he dispatched a second memorandum from Ust'e containing practical steps Russia might take. The problem now, as he saw it, was that the European powers were trapped between the Scylla of humiliating the embattled Spanish king with their nagging criticisms and the Charybdis of resorting to brutal intimidation (which had failed spectacularly against France in the 1790s). Instead, they should insist only that the Spaniards strike from their constitution the provisions granting the Cortes (the Spanish parliament) a voice in the making of international treaties, since these clauses threatened the continued validity of all international agreements the Spanish crown had concluded in the past. If the Spaniards refused to comply with this legitimate demand (which had the added advantage of not embarrassing their king politically), the other powers should cut off relations with them. Sturdza's advice on Spain met with imperial approval, and Alexander I ordered that both memoranda be given to his emissary to Spain as supplemental instructions.[36]

Sturdza saw his fears confirmed when revolution spread to Italy: only now, when the Neapolitan rising of July directly threatened its interests, was Vienna willing to take action. The Russian government, having decided to attend the congress at Troppau, turned to Sturdza for advice.[37] His language, as usual, was religious and gloomy (as was apparently Alexander I's own frame of mind): "Everything coincides to make the most fearless observer tremble, because the sum of so many calamities, stirred up, so to speak, by the frenzy of the forces of the abyss, is at the same time, make no mistake about it, a punishment sent from on high." Absent divine intervention at Troppau, Sturdza doubted that the infinite spread of "disorder" could be stopped. The allies' feeble initial response to the Spanish revolution was indicative of their general passivity, he charged, and Alexander needed to either take the lead in dealing with Naples or refuse any direct Russian participation in an intervention. Sturdza considered the most likely scenario to be an armed invasion of the Kingdom of the Two Sicilies. He urged the emperor to see to the establishment of effective government there, even though that would involve a parliament, rather than permit a restoration of the previous unstable authorities that would effectively leave the kingdom under Austrian domination. Such a policy would punish the rebels, discourage future revolutions, and demonstrate the cohesiveness of the alliance.[38]

Before this memorandum had even reached him, Capodistrias dispatched a request that Sturdza received during the night of October 9–10, 1820. In it, the emperor addressed broad political and moral issues arising from the current European crisis and asked how the ideas of the Holy Alliance treaty might be implemented to resolve them. Sturdza later recalled the effort he made in his response to keep his proposals as concrete and practical as possible. His purpose, he wrote, had been to prove that the Alliance was in fact relevant to reality and could be applied to the present "without, as we were accused, injecting poetry into the realm of policy." All of his suggestions would prove completely realistic, provided the governments made a bona fide effort to implement them.[39] In his memorandum, he noted that the failure of the powers even to take the firm stand he had recommended toward the Kingdom of the Two Sicilies left him in doubt about their willingness to act in concert for "a general reform of social and political institutions according to God's law." Still, he would draft a model of a Europe governed according to Holy Alliance principles. As preconditions, he posited that monarchs who had signed the Holy Alliance treaty for the sake of political expediency would now support it out of sincere conviction and that the steps he proposed would be effective at once throughout Europe.

First, he suggested domestic measures. All criticism of the established church was to be banned and the state was to cease intervening in church affairs, so it would become the mediator between the ruler and the ruled: the cohesion of society would be maintained by the priest, not the constable. Once the church's quasi-theocratic monopoly in *spiritual* matters was secure, *politics* could be reorganized according to constitutionalist principles, although Sturdza avoided the vocabulary of popular sovereignty; thus political speech was to be regulated only by laws allowing post facto prosecution of authors, whereas religious speech would be controlled far more stringently, through preventive censorship. (This was the combination of the two systems he had advocated in the *Overview of the Year 1819*.) Since the legitimacy of monarchy and property rested on the same foundation, the latter was inviolable: "Thence derives the principle of a free and periodic deliberation of the Sovereign Authority with the Trustees, not of the national Authority, which does not exist, but of the legitimacy of the national patrimony." Rulers should convoke such assemblies according to their own traditional laws, and not modify the "fundamental laws" of their society without consulting them. These laws, he was quick to add, had been created not by the will of the people but by God. Aside from the fundamental laws, rulers were to keep their absolute powers. Sturdza thus stood "enlightened absolutism" on its head: rather than grant religious and intellectual freedom to a society regimented by the police state, he would allow a free polity to govern itself so long as it submitted to the discipline of the church.

In international relations, the Holy Alliance would "substitute the State of Family for the State of Nature among nations"; this idea reflected the same concept of voluntary cooperation and Christian self-restraint that he expected within society. The "State of Family" among nations involved, to begin with, mandatory mediation in international conflicts, with war being legal only if mediation failed. All states were to guarantee each other's territorial integrity, just as monarchs and parliaments were to guarantee one other's independence. Such corrupt practices as secret societies, espionage, and permanent lotteries were to be abolished, and on the seas Europeans were to take joint action against piracy and ensure that all voyages of exploration be used to spread Christianity. Last, special tribunals, presided over by clergymen, should give Christians the option of settling disputes according to religious precepts and without adding to the burden on the regular courts.

However, even if the five great powers were to be in full accord on these measures, there would remain "the malicious activity of that innumerable mass that wants change or death." Sturdza offered thoughts on four ways to deal with incorrigible malcontents. The first was to develop overseas colonies (to which they would presumably be removed). The second was a war to permit the hotheads to let off steam, for which the obvious choice was a campaign against the Barbary pirates: this would bring Christianity to North Africa and divert Europe's destructive energies, although probably at the cost of high casualties. Third, since subversives were organized to a frightening degree while the friends of peace and order were not, monarchs should organize a "party to defend religion, morals and the law." Fourth, such a party would form almost spontaneously in the event that the ideas of the Holy Alliance were implemented. Although reflecting each country's peculiarities, these groups would also be universal, insofar as the Alliance's principles were universal, and would constitute a check on possible monarchical violations of the new Christian social compact. This idea was the opposite of Karamzin's notion that Russia required autocratic government, and it made explicit what Shishkov and Glinka had only hinted at: that civil society should take upon itself the task of enforcing the laws that, in Europe and especially in Russia, absolutist bureaucracies had traditionally considered their special preserve.[40]

Alexander I was so impressed that he requested that Sturdza come to Troppau in person. Sturdza declined on grounds of ill health but continued to offer written advice. He urged the emperor and Capodistrias not to get bogged down in the details of the Italian question, but rather to seize the opportunity to promote a general spiritual and political renewal of Europe.[41] Personally, he took a dim view of Russia's allies. France, Austria, and Prussia had greeted the Spanish revolution "with inexplicable indifference" that could only encourage revolutionaries elsewhere, especially in the Kingdom of the Two Sicilies. He had no doubt that a timely hard line by the major powers would have forced Spain to back down and prevented the troubles in Italy. However, Russia had stood alone, in the face of both the secret societies of London and Paris (the supposed sponsors of the upheavals) and the allies' "insouciance" and "bad faith." Russia could rely only on itself.[42] Sturdza argued that an Austrian proposal for a great power treaty on suppressing revolution, if carried out, would merely make the powers into tools of Austrian policy. He also distrusted Vienna's plans for restoring "order" in the Two Sicilies without introducing reforms there: Russia might let Austria proceed on its own, but it should not participate in such a bald-faced, cynical assertion of the interests of the rulers against the ruled. He preferred an informal agreement recognizing governments and peoples as allies in the defense of order, while the Austrian idea, on the other hand, would "deepen the confrontation" between them and weld all the malcontents of Europe and (Latin) America into a united front. His alternative was an agreement guaranteeing Europe's current borders and political institutions as well as existing principles of international law (which the Spanish constitution violated, for example); providing for troops to enforce these stipulations; and proposing a conference to perfect the European system on the basis of the Holy Alliance. However, he repeated, actual violations of international law were the only acceptable justification for intervening in the internal affairs of other states. Privately incensed at the allies, especially Austria, he felt that Russia was sacrificing its dignity and the cause of humanity to the phantom of allied unity. Rather than reason with Vienna, Russia should have offered a plan of collective action and, if necessary, proceeded alone.[43]

When the congress moved to Laibach at the end of 1820, Capodistrias again asked Sturdza about the general outlook for the negotiations. His prognosis was glum. He questioned the ability of large conferences to settle problems, writing that the assembled monarchs would be better off returning home, and lamented the imbalance of forces between "the old and the new Systems." Reliable allies of the old were Russia, Prussia (itself dangerously close to constitutionalism), and Austria—and, if one "searched for allies with a microscope," Denmark, Hanover, Saxony, Hessen, Sardinia and the papacy. Lined up against them were Britain, France, Sweden, Spain, Portugal, Bavaria, Württemberg, Baden, the Netherlands, the Two Sicilies, and the Americas. Besides sheer numbers, the "constitutional party" also owned the world's lingua franca (French), and dominated finance, commerce, naval power, and science. Religion was a feeble barrier to "this frantic movement toward a general emancipation," especially since the new revolutionaries themselves, unlike their Jacobin predecessors, had learned to utilize the language of faith. Given this frightening progression of evil, Sturdza considered a peaceful settlement with

Naples to be a brief, but vital, respite in what looked like a losing battle against the forces of revolution.[44]

To what degree did Alexander I and Sturdza share the same ideological views, and how did the emperor receive his adviser's ideas? Both men were religious, convinced of Russia's messianic role, and ill at ease with European politics after 1815, for they hated revolution but sympathized with constitutionalism. However, the emperor saw constitutionalism as an alternative to the old regime and tried to implement it in France, Poland, and Finland, whereas Sturdza rejected modern liberalism and looked back nostalgically to premodern conceptions of representation. Their views on foreign policy also differed, for Sturdza, a Russian and Greek nationalist, deeply distrusted the West. He approved of the Holy Alliance but was reluctant in 1820 to make Russia an instrument for the realization of Metternich's schemes. While he strove to use Russian power to cleanse the West, he also sought to shield Russia from Western religious and political ideas.

Alexander was at once a rationalist and a mystic, and these influences were in permanent conflict in him; to Sturdza, both rationalism and mysticism testified to the modern disharmony between God, society, and man. His old-fashioned gospel demanded that man accept tradition and fate. He did not object to parliaments or free speech per se (representative institutions were part of traditional polities, and free political speech was a threat only when subjects had received an irreligious education), so long as they neither obstructed the restoration of a godly society nor represented a corrosive rationalism. He always sought to distill from his ideas broad, universal verities. Thus he advocated similar educational and censorship measures for both Russia and Germany, and the Holy Alliance appealed to him as a holistic cure for contemporary society. Yet his approach to these matters, as Carl Brinkmann has pointed out,[45] was curiously wooden and unimaginative, and his practical suggestions were long on censorship but short on most anything else.

Unlike Alexander, Sturdza felt no ambivalence in his ideology, whose diverse components formed a cohesive whole. Such integral convictions were attractive to one as intellectually and emotionally changeable as Alexander (especially when their conclusions coincided with his own). Sturdza also offered an alternative to the moderate pragmatism of Capodistrias and the Metternichian realpolitik of Nesselrode. As a result, Alexander continued to favor him after the *Memorandum* scandal and, as mentioned, even requested his presence at Troppau. It probably helped that Sturdza was neither a careerist nor a member of a faction and hence had no ulterior motives in offering his views. Indeed, his sulking "exile" in Belorussia in 1819–1821 and his absence from Troppau suggest the opposite, that he was a man of honest conviction.

Sturdza's advice had little immediate, tangible effect. For example, his proposals for implementing the Holy Alliance were warmly received by the monarch but then vanished in the maze of more concrete issues discussed at Troppau.[46] After all, he was suggesting political change at home—a step to which Alexander never resolved himself—and a foreign policy whose basic assumptions made no sense to Russia's allies. His counsel's significance lay not in its proposals for action but in its perceptive analysis and its ideological certainties, which appealed to an emperor faced with bewildering political challenges and consumed with metaphysical anguish. As Capodistrias put it to Sturdza, "His Majesty . . . finds in [your memoranda] the ideas, or rather *the inspirations, that issue from his heart* and occupy his thought" (emphasis added).[47] Sturdza spoke, as had the "Unofficial Committee" and Speranskii, for the idealist in Alexander I; he, too, discovered that the emperor's interest in his ideas did not signal a willingness to take risks by carrying them out.

In domestic policy, Alexander's final decade was a puzzling mix of despotism and sporadic reform attempts, neither of which reveals much about the dynamics of conservatism. The "liberalism" of the reform attempts was a nostalgic tribute to the happier days of the beginning of his reign, while repression represented a capitulation before apparent necessity. The regime's meager ideological content is evident from the fact that Arakcheev, an unreflective executor of orders, was at once lord of the military settlements (which united the humiliations of serfdom with brutal military discipline) and author of a plan to abolish serfdom. Conservatism was creative mainly in the fields of religion and education. Golitsyn, Runich, Popov, Sturdza, Filaret, and others, who formed a cadre of ideologues dedicated to a domestic version of the Holy Alliance, did not aspire to impose martial discipline on society. Instead of a nation of automatons, they hoped to breed a generation willing to accept, of its own free accord, an only marginally modified version of the old regime.

Such was the mission of the two symbiotic institutions that gave Golitsyn vast power over Russia's cultural life: the Russian Bible Society and the "Dual Ministry." As early as August 10, 1816, he was named acting minister of education, and on October 24, 1817 the Dual Ministry (of Spiritual Affairs and Popular Enlightenment) came into being. It absorbed the Ministry of Popular Enlightenment, the Department of Religious Affairs for Foreign Confessions (already run by Golitsyn), and the Holy Synod, also headed previously by him and now run by Prince P. S. Meshcherskii. The ministry's task—to make religion the basis of Russian life—harmonized with the Bible Society's purpose, and they shared the same leadership: Golitsyn headed both, while Popov and Aleksandr Turgenev, the RBS's secretaries, became the chiefs, respectively, of the ministry's Department of Education and Department of Religious Affairs. Popov had already served under Golitsyn in the Synod in 1804, so they had long experience working together. In keeping with Bible Society ecumenism, the Orthodox Church was reduced to equal status with other churches, and the Holy Synod communicated with the emperor only through Turgenev and Golitsyn.[48]

The Dual Ministry, like the Bible Society, suffered from deep internal divisions that were not immediately recognized but ultimately led to the demise of both. Broadly speaking, three currents existed in the Dual Ministry–RBS complex: pragmatists, Orthodox, and mystics. First the pragmatists, then the Orthodox were squeezed out by the mystics. This left the mystics in command, but their lack of a solid base of support made their position untenable in a changing political environment.

The master of this structure, Prince Golitsyn, was an old friend of Alexander I. Unlike the obedient Arakcheev, he was a man of strong views, to which he sometimes won over the monarch. Tact, charm, and the concordance of his views with Alexander's ensured his political survival. That both had been "awakened" created a bond between them, and Golitsyn—like Sturdza in his memoranda—could speak his mind openly because he naturally thought as the monarch did. As with many of his generation, a superficial education had equipped Golitsyn with pleasant manners but little formal knowledge. The deleterious consequences became apparent in his official activities, since overseeing religious administration and education, which included control over censorship, required a trained intellect the prince lacked. This ignorance had fateful effects when combined with the religious zeal that he developed after his appointment to the Synod (not only his snuffbox but even the dish from which his dog ate was adorned with religious motifs), for he combined the hazy thinking of a mystic with the rigidity of a Russian bureaucrat. Untrained in theology, he was easily swayed by fervent believers and mystics, such as Jung-Stilling, Baader, Labzin, and Ekaterina Tatarinova. His religious judgment inspired no trust from Roksandra Sturdza, who was otherwise his friend, and her brother likewise worried about the influence of mystics over him.[49] The same problem arose in education: lacking secular schooling, and never having attended a university himself, he was susceptible to the influence of obscurantists.

In typical "awakened" fashion, Golitsyn, though he remained a practicing Orthodox Christian, accepted the irrelevance of confessional differences and enforced toleration for all churches. This meant, in practice, that the government promoted the dissemination of mystical and "awakened" literature to encourage a universalist Christian spirit but forbade proselytizing and polemics among churches. This policy placed Orthodoxy at the greatest disadvantage, given its traditional role as the state religion, but it also struck at the Jesuits. In secular matters as well, censorship was expected not only to forestall subversion but to promote a specific vision of life. Writing on constitutionalism and serfdom was forbidden, regardless of one's position on these matters, as Golitsyn's biographer points out: "literature was to serve the needs of the current mood of the government, it was to be part of the teaching arm of the government, a tool of propaganda."[50] Golitsyn sought actively to shape the nation's spiritual life, not merely to shield throne and altar from criticism. Since the Awakening was an intensely personal experience, he sought the friendship of others who shared his beliefs (the Sturdzas, Speranskii, Labzin, Filaret, and others) and placed great trust in the competence of people who harbored—or at least displayed—that faith.[51] This concern for piety, rather than for professionalism and ideology, was the cause of the conflicts in the Dual Ministry's leadership.

Among the moderate pragmatists around him were Aleksandr Turgenev and Sergei S. Uvarov. Turgenev was unusual for his substantial education, obtained at the universities of Moscow and Göttingen. After returning to Russia in 1805 he held various official posts and, starting in 1810, assisted Golitsyn at the foreign-confessions administration. Their ties were strengthened by Turgenev's role as Bible Society secretary, so his being named to head the Department of Religious Affairs was a logical next step. Turgenev's religious beliefs were moderate and ecumenical, and he preferred the company of New Style writers to that of priests. He could be an opportunist; queried by his friend Viazemskii about his seeming devotion to religion (when most careers were made in the military or the civil service), Turgenev replied that "monastic champagne is no worse than military champagne." Although a capable administrator, he lacked the power base to act as a liberal restraining force on Golitsyn.[52] Uvarov, the curator of the St. Petersburg educational district since 1810, was among the few senior officials whom Golitsyn had "inherited" from a previous administration. He was intelligent, arrogant, ambitious, and unpopular, but no mystic. In a spirit more Bonapartist than "awakened," he wanted to create a strong system of education to foster a great culture, and thus preserve social stability, while preparing Russia for a constitutional future without serfdom. Like Sturdza, he saw himself as a man of the center, equally hostile to all extremists. Though his gradualism, his waiting for history to run its course, marked him as no "liberal," his long-range hope was for Russia to emulate Britain and other Western countries.[53]

Like Turgenev, Uvarov belonged to the Arzamas Society of Obscure People (Arzamas is a provincial town whose name was part of a complicated literary joke), a kind of anti-Symposium. The youth and sparkle of its members (Viazemskii, Zhukovskii, Vigel', the Turgenev brothers, and Vasilii and Aleksandr Pushkin, among others) differed markedly from the geriatric leadership of Shishkov's Symposium. Its ironic name suggested a contrast to the Symposium's self-importance, and its democratic spirit and humorous pursuits—such as mock eulogies for the intellectually "dead" Symposium members—stood out against its rival's decorous ceremony and quasi-bureaucratic formalism. The Symposium's atmosphere still recalled the eighteenth-century symbiosis of aristocracy and state service, while "Arzamas" already anticipated the intelligentsia culture of the nineteenth.[54] "Arzamas" did not hew to one political philosophy, and among its members were both future Decembrists (e.g., Mikhail Orlov) and future senior imperial officials (Dashkov, Bludov, Uvarov, Aleksandr Turgenev). However, pre-Decembrist Russian culture was split between backward-, inward-looking thinkers, such as Shishkov and Rostopchin, who saw political theorizing as inherently subversive, and others, such as Speranskii and Karamzin, who were fascinated by creative political and social thought. "Arzamas" was a stronghold of the latter type. This broad consensus left much room for disagreement over republicanism and constitutional monarchy, over whether Russia could be transformed in one radical blow (as many Decembrists thought) or only through the gradual unfolding of historical forces (the opinion of Uvarov and others). Aleksandr Sturdza was friendly with many of the group's members; although his religious beliefs set him apart, his youth, intelligence, literary interests, worldliness, and interest in political thought created a bond between him and them. Uvarov's and Turgenev's culture and erudition, and their ties to the talented minds of "Arzamas," clearly distinguished them from the likes of Popov or Golitsyn, preparing the ground for major confrontations, within the Dual Ministry, with Runich and Magnitskii.

Ideological moderates of Uvarov and Turgenev's sort were, however, an endangered breed in a Dual Ministry increasingly under the sway of religious mystics and obscurantists. One of the latter was Runich. As late as January 1816, Kozodavlev had praised his work as postal director, but only a month later (on February 11), for reasons that are unclear, Runich was sacked and also lost his position as Moscow Bible Society chief. These setbacks were devastating, if only because of the financial implications for his large family. His only hope was that his friend Popov, now at the Dual Ministry, might come to his rescue.[55] Runich was soon negotiating with Golitsyn, who considered him for "the position of director of one of the [Dual Ministry's] departments." Only Popov and Turgenev held such a title, so he may have been a candidate for Turgenev's job. Golitsyn's interest was, as Popov explained, "a sign of particular confidence, not only in your abilities but even more in the Christian principles that have been apparent in your words and conduct so far."[56] The litmus test was not competence but ideological conformity, and there Turgenev may have been deemed lacking.

Turgenev did have enemies. As Peter von Goetze, his loyal assistant, wrote later, his chief had been the target of "fanatics who make piety into a business and seek to use it for their personal gain, and who . . . regard all means as permissible that promote their goals." These "fanatics" found him slow to harass clerics whom they disliked, Goetze asserted, and generally saw him as an obstacle to their influence. Quite possibly, Popov and others were pushing Runich's candidacy in order to oust Turgenev and consolidate their control. This plot (if it was indeed that) failed, and by the following spring, Popov informed Runich that "circumstances have changed somewhat . . . with regard to your placement." Instead of receiving a directorship, he was named to the Main Schools Administration (the governing body of the Department of Education, with about ten members) and its Academic Committee, which screened textbooks and other educational materials.[57]

In his new position, Runich found an ally for his obscurantism in Mikhail L. Magnitskii (born in 1778), who has acquired a remarkable notoriety in modern scholarship.[58] A genial, bright, well-mannered man,[59] highly educated (at Moscow University) and well versed in Enlightenment thought, he had been Speranskii's chief assistant, which did not, however, reflect any reformist convictions. Exiled along with his chief in 1812, he was able, by 1817, to obtain the governorship of Simbirsk. Exquisitely attuned to the shifting political winds, he established Bible Society chapters across "his" province and took care that Golitsyn—who was forever on the lookout for other repentant sinners like himself—was kept *au courant* of the ex-freethinker Magnitskii's spiritual regeneration. To prepare his comeback, he offered to inspect the troubled university in Kazan' (up the Volga from Simbirsk), one of five that had been founded at the beginning of the reign and the only one operating under the coarse frontier conditions of eastern Russia. Administrative and academic problems made a review advisable and the piety that the Simbirsk governor exhibited impressed Golitsyn, so he accepted the offer, and the "inspector" arrived in Kazan' in early March 1819.

What followed is a melancholy and well-known story. After a whirlwind visit, Magnitskii arrived in Petersburg in early April and reported: Kazan' University's efforts at moral and religious education were so hopeless that it should be closed down altogether, an option allowed by Golitsyn's instructions. The Main Schools Administration showed no stomach for this, however; Uvarov even drafted a vigorous dissent. The emperor rejected the report as well, instead reluctantly accepting Golitsyn's alternative proposal of making Magnitskii curator of the Kazan' educational district (which gave him a seat on the Main Schools Administration) and entrusting him with the university's "reform." With his habitual single-mindedness, Magnitskii set out to enforce "morality" at Kazan', compelling many of the foreign faculty to resign and drastically curtailing the others' ability to teach by imposing grotesque standards of religious and ideological correctness. In Petersburg as in Kazan', Magnitskii became a merciless foe of "freethinking" and all other manifestations of the "spirit of the times." Intelligent and aggressive, he soon held a dominant position in the administration, where he enlisted Runich—who seemed dim and colorless by comparison—as his ally. Their brand of religion resembled Golitsyn's, which strengthened their influence. Jointly, Magnitskii and Runich were able to force Uvarov from his post as St. Petersburg curator in 1821; they replaced him with Runich, who did to that university what Magnitskii had done to Kazan'.[60]

These developments reflect the difficulties that Alexander I's government encountered when it attempted to impose religious controls on a society whose ancestral traditions had been corroded by a century of Westernization. It was not that the idea of state-enforced religious conformity as such was unique to Russia—in Prussia in the 1790s, for example, Frederick William II and his minister Johann Christoph Wöllner had similarly tried to combat the modern spirit of rebellion by strengthening religion, resulting in widespread public discontent and embarrassing excesses by obscurantist officials.[61] However, Wöllner at least had enforced Protestant ecclesiastical orthodoxy, presumably generating some support in the church hierarchy. In Russia, on the other hand, where the elite was culturally far less identified with the national church than in Prussia, the Dual Ministry and the Bible Society—already estranged from the more progressive elements in public opinion—were becoming identified with heterodox religious views, and this antagonized even ecclesiastical traditionalists. Old Believers and sectarians became officially associated with the RBS. Mystical literature was published, sometimes at imperial expense and dedicated to Alexander, bypassing ecclesiastical censorship (about sixty such titles came out between 1813 and 1823). Labzin and his journal *Messenger of Zion* epitomized the mystical trend in the Bible Society, although the *Messenger* was finally banned in 1818 under Orthodox pressure.[62]

Another important mystic was Ekaterina Tatarinova (born in 1783). She was, like Juliane von Krüdener, a Lutheran of Baltic German descent. After her own marriage had dissolved (like Krüdener's) and her only child had died, she devoted herself (again like Krüdener) to prayer, Bible reading, and charitable work, despite her modest means. She began holding prayer meetings in the residence granted her by the monarch in the Mikhailovskii castle that were attended by officials, guards officers, and other members of the elite, all of them captivated by her charisma. These included Alexander I, Golitsyn, Koshelev, and her fanatical disciple Popov. At the meetings, songs and dances patterned after the *skoptsy* and prophesy while in a kind of hypnotic trance were customary, with one "prophet" apparently speaking continually for thirty-six hours. These gatherings added to the politically damaging association of the Dual Ministry and Bible Society with mysticism.[63]

Despite their bizarre antics and appalling excesses, however, the significance of these mystics and obscurantists should not be exaggerated. For example, Roksandra Sturdza was far more rational than Krüdener, and because of her ties with German religious thinkers and the Russian court and bureaucracy she was a more important historical figure than the colorful baroness. Similarly, the academic purges that Magnitskii and Runich organized at Kazan' and St. Petersburg were not repeated at the universities of Moscow and Dorpat and thus did not fully represent Dual Ministry policy.[64] The RBS, also, was not just a tool for reactionary mystical obscurantists, for it worked to render the Bible into Russian and disseminate it among the people—projects that won the approval of many Orthodox hierarchs. Besides, along with the Bible Society, Russia had imported British Protestant social activism: an Imperial Philanthropic Society was founded, as was a Prison Reform Society, both headed by—who else?—Golitsyn. To promote the literacy sought by the Bible Society, Alexander and Golitsyn encouraged the Lancastrian school system, which tried to circumvent teacher shortages by having advanced students teach their juniors. All these groups, like the RBS itself, though technically private, enjoyed extensive state support, shared many members and leaders, and arose from a concern for the people's physical and spiritual well-being.[65] To dismiss all of this as "obscurantism" is to distort a complex historical phenomenon.

Aside from mystics like Popov and secularists like Uvarov, the Dual Ministry also had officials linked to the Orthodox Church, such as Aleksandr Sturdza. Working at once with Capodistrias and Golitsyn, he personified the common ideological basis of post-1815 foreign and domestic policy, but he had serious reservations about the direction of the Dual Ministry. Already in January 1817 he had confided to Roksandra that Golitsyn was "in pathetic thralldom to a man who has always inspired a well-founded revulsion in you": perhaps Labzin, whom he intensely disliked. He hoped that the monarch would "not succumb to the spell of [his] false doctrine," which represented "a different sort of despotism than the papacy, but still its goal is to seize the key to the sanctuary and subject the scepter to its orders." As for mysticism in general, "God protect us from ever taking the illusions of our senses for revelations."[66] He nonetheless became more deeply involved with the Dual Ministry. In 1817, he joined the Main Schools Administration and reluctantly accepted a position in its three-member Academic Committee early in 1818. He wrote the guidelines for this committee, whose early sessions he dominated, and attended several Main Schools Administration meetings between March and August 1818, but after his German debacle he remained at Ust'e and came back to the capital only in fall 1821. Thus he was away as the administration became increasingly dominated by Magnitskii and Runich; for example, he missed the discussion of both the former's report on Kazan' and the latter's purge of St. Petersburg University.[67]

Owing to his absences and his other duties, the Academic Committee's guidelines were his principal contribution to educational policy. They mandated that religious texts conform strictly to Orthodox teachings, that government's divine origin be stressed and that natural law be replaced with a morality derived from religion. History and metaphysics were to confirm the teachings of Christianity, and the natural sciences were to be taught as practical subjects, without encouraging philosophical speculation that might challenge the scriptures. The guiding principle was that secular instruction not inadvertently undermine religious belief.[68] As James Flynn has pointed out, Sturdza gave the Dual Ministry a general philosophy, but no details for its implementation; these were left to Magnitskii, Runich, and their colleagues.[69] Like his proposals of the same year in the *Memorandum on the Present State of Germany,* Sturdza's sweeping suggestions provided no protection against outright obscurantism. His ideas for Germany were realized to a degree by the Karlsbad Decrees; his Russian ones, by Magnitskii at Kazan'. No doubt Sturdza himself would have been less primitively coercive than Metternich or (especially) Magnitskii, but he was nevertheless reluctant to dissociate himself from their educational policies.

Aleksandr and Roksandra Sturdza personally liked Magnitskii, although they apparently became closely acquainted only after 1834 in Odessa. Aleksandr took at face value Magnitskii's abrupt, convenient ideological reversals of 1817–1819 (when he found religion) and 1824 (when he betrayed Golitsyn) and concluded that "Magnitskii was never anxious to please, and instead especially prized the treasure of his conscience and his faith, which he had won and assimilated after a difficult inner struggle with the passions and errors of the years of his youth."[70] Yet he did not always agree with the crude repressiveness of Magnitskii and his ilk.

One example was the case of Johann Baptist Schad, a German professor at Khar'kov University who had been expelled from Russia because his teaching was found immoral and anti-Christian; Sturdza wrote to Golitsyn (to no avail) that Schad had been the victim of a conspiracy at Khar'kov. He also disapproved of Runich's handling of the Petersburg professors affair in 1821, although he agreed that their teachings were reprehensible. When Golitsyn sent him the documentation on the case, Sturdza decided that "both sides were wrong," and he returned "a few comments" but otherwise refused to get involved.[71]

Another case in particular revealed the ideological fault lines in the Main Schools Administration. Professor Aleksandr P. Kunitsyn, a critic of absolutism and serfdom, had published a textbook on natural law. Based on the lectures he had given in his years at the Tsarskoe Selo *lycée,* it contained an old-fashioned exposition of the theory of the social contract.[72] Trouble began when the *lycée*'s director so liked the book that he asked that it be presented to the emperor himself. The Academic Committee and the Main Schools Administration read it, were horrified that innocent boys had been exposed to such material, and devised a curriculum of their own. As a skeptical Sturdza put it, they wished to turn natural law into "practical theology."[73] Since Sturdza was in Ust'e, Golitsyn mailed him the relevant papers in September 1820. Sturdza agreed with his colleagues' condemnation of the book (apparently drafted by Runich)[74] but argued that their proposal distorted the discipline's purpose: studying society independently of religion. He proposed to retain natural law's autonomy even while reconciling it with religion.

The aim of natural law was to "make students conscious of the inability of our reason, not only to organize societies, but even to understand the fundamental principles of humanity's civil life without the help of Revelation." Reason, conscience, and will—all contaminated by sin—were no basis for the social order, so pagans and infidels sought to ground the social order in the teachings of their false religions, while philosophers concocted the supposed original "state of nature" for the same purpose. Society could be founded only on religion or its functional equivalent. A course on natural law should have two parts. The first would debunk the existing theories and prove that no "state of nature," followed by a democratic devolution of power from the individual to government (or its usurping by despots), had ever occurred. Instead, monarchy had always prevailed, as an extension of the paternal authority instituted by God. The second part would provide a correct interpretation of natural law, proving that nonmonarchical government was an aberration from the historical norm and only submission to God's law protected society from man's evil and destructive impulses.[75]

Sturdza sent his opinion to the Main Schools Administration, where on February 10, 1821, Kunitsyn's book, and natural law in general, was discussed in a five-hour meeting. Those present reviewed Runich's opinion, that the book was "nothing but a collection of dangerous pseudo-theories that were rendered fashionable by the unfortunately notorious Rousseau and that have agitated and still agitate the hotheaded champions of the *Rights of Man and the Citizen* in both the past and the present century." Since the book insulted the Bible and the divine institutions of monarchy, matrimony and parental authority, its use in schools was incompatible with the Dual Ministry's mission. In fact, Runich wondered in light of these damning facts: "On what grounds is it absolutely necessary to introduce the teaching of this science in the first place?"[76] The meeting concluded with the decisions that the book should be banned from schools and all current natural law textbooks sent to Petersburg for review; a new curriculum ought to be developed, along the lines of Sturdza's proposal, and Golitsyn promised to ban Kunitsyn from all schools under his jurisdiction. These decisions were approved by all members except Magnitskii and Runich, who insisted on the "complete insignificance of the sham science of Natural Law, not to mention [its] obvious harmfulness." They demanded that its teaching "be banned at once, without further delay, throughout the entire State."[77] And within a few days they submitted these opinions in writing.

The opinions written on the Kunitsyn affair illustrate well the divisions in the administration. Runich and Magnitskii wanted to abolish this allegedly subversive discipline altogether. Uvarov (who had missed the meeting and whose political clout was waning) pleaded for mercy, arguing that Kunitsyn was a valuable scholar and teacher; he declined to comment on the book or natural law as such, except to say that of course no subversive teachings should be tolerated. Sturdza sympathized with the Magnitskii-Runich faction's suspicion of modern philosophy, but also shared with Uvarov a concern for protecting scholarship against obscurantism. Turgenev captured the essence of the difference between Sturdza and Magnitskii when he said that Magnitskii "would like to become a Sturdza, but has neither his talent nor his good faith."[78]

Sturdza's reservations about current religious policies were greater still. He saw the Orthodox Church as coming under attack from two directions: the mystics and the Catholics. Of the mystics, he singled out Labzin, whose *Messenger of Zion* denigrated the "external" church (as opposed to the "inner" church of the soul). The *Messenger* was influential in official circles and was distributed to schools and universities around the empire by order of the Main Schools Administration. The rector of the St. Petersburg seminary had protested to Golitsyn about Labzin, but to no effect. In 1818, however, a conspiracy of sorts was brewing. One Stepan Smirnov wrote an Orthodox polemic against Labzin, which was given by Sergei Shikhmatov (a devoutly Orthodox young naval officer whose poetry Shishkov admired) to Sturdza, who confronted Golitsyn with it. Golitsyn, shocked by his protégé's theological transgressions, agreed to no longer grant his journal exemption from ecclesiastic censorship. Labzin knew that the *Messenger* would never pass the Orthodox censors and reluctantly discontinued publication.[79] Sturdza argued that the "masonic lodges, Martinists and pseudomystics of Catherine's time"—all of them "religious anarchists" whose mouthpiece was the *Messenger of Zion*—hoped to subvert Orthodoxy. The Russian Bible Society had been founded in blind imitation of the British, without concern for the needs of the Orthodox Church, and while favoring dissemination of the Bible, he feared the RBS was spreading Protestantism. Also, although he supported translating the Bible into Russian, he opposed the way the RBS carried it out, including Labzin's involvement. The Dual Ministry was tainted by its link with the Bible Society. Both had the same questionable leaders: Golitsyn, of whom Sturdza was personally fond but whose "religious devotion [was] more intense than enlightened"; Popov, whose "feeble intellect" was "pathetically clouded by a spirit of sectarianism"; and Turgenev, whose faith seemed "shaky." While Sturdza liked the ministry's broad aims, he thought it a grave mistake to undermine Orthodoxy's status as *the* established church; he had made this clear to Golitsyn as early as July 1817, when he was first shown the manifesto creating the Dual Ministry.[80]

Likewise, despite his admiration for de Maistre, Sturdza denounced Catholic proselytizing, which he considered to be as dangerous as the mystical influence in government and among sections of the Orthodox clergy. As early as 1816, he had written a polemic against Roman efforts to convert Russia.[81] These efforts had aroused such suspicion in the Russian government that the Jesuits had been expelled a few months earlier from Moscow and Petersburg (although they still operated their academy at Polotsk). Sturdza drafted a defense of their expulsion for the Russian government paper *Le Conservateur Impartial,* referring to the long history of Catholic assaults on Orthodoxy, arguing that they had exhausted Russia's boundless patience by their proselytizing. He also drafted a statement on their expulsion in 1820 from the remainder of the empire. Capodistrias had told him to focus on the question of their proselytizing, without—as Golitsyn had—raising more general issues, but Sturdza found restraint difficult. Once again, as at Aachen in 1818, he submitted a text that Alexander I found unacceptable for reasons of diplomatic propriety. What was finally published was severe enough, but, Capodistrias noted, the emperor had "deemed it appropriate to cut and modify a few passages in order to ensure that the piece remained strictly historical in character."[82]

Sturdza was a thoughtful man whose view of his own church was not always flattering. As he later recalled, many contemporaries had heard "the human heart cry out in the desert, rushed to search for inner holiness, did not find it, and turned to strange and diverse doctrines, exclusively because they found no one to guide them." The church had failed them. As a result, among the upper classes "mysticism prevailed, practitioners of magnetism were active, or fashionable Western theologians insinuated themselves, while poisonous schisms . . . lured the common people into the abyss of depravity or impiety." Of course, "the ship not made by [human] hands survived; but . . . the pilots were asleep at the helm and did not notice the storm or worry about submerged rocks."[83]

This concern with the leadership role of the clergy was what motivated Sturdza's interest in ecclesiastical education. He admired Speranskii and Golitsyn for their reforming work in this area and thought that better educating priests was the key to dealing with peasant morality, sectarianism, and an eventual abolition of serfdom. It was the church's mission to convert the non-Christian peoples of the empire, and so he proposed a seminary to provide the requisite language training. This task was urgent, he argued, because Orthodoxy must reach the benighted masses before they were touched by Western "enlightenment" or heterodox missionaries. Bible Societies were helpful here insofar as they promoted the spread of *Orthodox* Christianity, but they "would attempt in vain to seek the power and glory of the Apostolate. These *worthy* institutions might easily stray from the true path if God does not soon send them a mighty Ally. This Ally and guide is the Church."[84]

The need to strengthen the church was always on Sturdza's mind. More than thirty years later, shortly before his death, he wrote that the Old Believers had left the church out of ignorance and "spiritual hunger" and should be treated kindly, whereas sectarianism was a real threat. "Police measures offer little hope," he found. The evil should be fought through mass education for both boys and girls, a spiritual rapprochement between the higher clergy and the common people, and Orthodox missionary efforts among the peasants. Improving priests' education and ending the practice of rotating bishops frequently between dioceses were causes he similarly advocated. Most fundamental, however, was that the peasants receive proper religious instruction, that is, be made literate; otherwise the entire effort would be fruitless.[85] Like Golitsyn, Labzin, and Runich, he believed that the Russian Orthodox Church required an infusion of ideas from elsewhere. However, whereas the "awakened" sought these ideas in the Protestant West, Sturdza believed they must come from the Orthodox East, particularly Greece. His writings about Orthodoxy consistently reminded his readers that it was not just a Russian religion, and his family cultivated friendships with Greek as well as Russian clerics.[86]

His philhellenism and Orthodox cosmopolitanism led to Sturdza's final break with the government. In February 1821, while Capodistrias and Alexander were conferring with Metternich at Laibach and Sturdza was suggesting means to implement the goals of the Holy Alliance, his cousin Alexander Ypsilantis, a Greek in the Russian army, invaded Moldavia and Wallachia with an improvised army and declared the Balkan Christians free from Ottoman rule. There ensued massacres of Christians by the Turks and of Turks by the Balkan Christians. Ypsilantis's force was crushed, but soon Greece was in full rebellion.[87] For Sturdza, this was potentially a dream come true. He thought that Ypsilantis had no right to serve another country while in Russian uniform, but the rebels' cause itself had his full support. Yet he saw at once the political dilemma: he wrote to Capodistrias that Russia had a duty to rescue its fellow Orthodox Christians and to tell Europe's monarchs "that the cause of the Christians of the East must never be confused with that of the revolutionaries of France, Italy and Spain." Indeed, these were "tributaries, not subjects, Christians, oppressed and decimated a thousand times, who are taking arms in defense of their life, their property, their honor and—dearer than all the rest—their faith." This issue struck at the heart of his conception of the Holy Alliance: "Equating the Greeks with the radicals of other countries would mean placing the Christian Governments on a par with the Ottoman Porte."[88] Greece and the hope for Russian intervention increasingly absorbed his energies. After returning to St. Petersburg in October 1821, he wrapped up his work on Bessarabia and continued to work on Dual Ministry affairs, but his heart was no longer in it. His political star, like Capodistrias's, was sinking rapidly. While Roksandra—whose influence with Alexander I had also waned—pleaded with the monarch to both protect her brother's career and help the Greeks, Sturdza himself wrote to Alexander of "the dual nature of the peril facing our Holy Church. On one side, its enemies [the Turks] strike at it openly; on the other they [the Russian mystics] quietly undermine and disrupt it. . . . The sword or the snake, it makes no difference: everywhere the unchanging permanence of the Church irritates the gaze of our false friends or our declared enemies."[89]

Russia's inaction before the tragedy unfolding in the Balkans was the ultimate failure of the Holy Alliance, which Sturdza had envisioned as a vehicle for propagating the ideals of a Christian polity, not as a mutual aid society for reactionary tyrants. Abandoning Christians to the vengeance of infidels in the name of legitimism and the balance of power was the *reductio ad absurdum* of this conception, and it naturally caused him deep bitterness. Conditions at home likewise offered little cheer, for the domestic incarnation of the Alliance seemed intent on cutting Russia loose from its Orthodox moorings and casting it adrift with the Bible Society, Labzin, Tatarinova, and other flotsam and jetsam of foreign pseudoreligion. Out of favor, worried about his wife's health and his own deteriorating right eye (which three operations had failed to restore), he obtained permission to go to Odessa in the spring of 1822. There he continued to draw his earlier salary but "did not enjoy the consolation of receiving the least testimony of the Emperor's satisfaction" with his years of work on Bessarabian and educational matters. In 1823, finally, Aleksandr Sturdza formally tendered his resignation.[90] The mystics in the Dual Ministry, and the legitimists in foreign policy, had triumphed, and the Holy Alliance was dead.

The secularist conservatives who had earlier dominated the public debate were generally appalled by the policies and ideas of the religious conservatives after 1812. Intellectually the most significant was Karamzin, who published the first eight volumes of his *History of the Russian State* in 1818. This, the first scholarly history of Russia ever to reach a broad segment of the reading public, was both a nationalist manifesto and a defense of the autocratic state. He despised Golitsyn's "ministry of enlightenment, or [more accurately] of obscurity," whose fusion of religion with education was likely only to "increase the number of hypocrites"; unlike the "hypocrites," he remarked sarcastically, "I myself look toward Heaven at times, but not while others are watching." Sturdza was a friend of his and of the young literati of "Arzamas,"[91] but Karamzin distrusted his religion and regretted "that he is ruining his mind with mystical *nonsensology*."[92]

A much harsher critic of the new policies was Admiral Shishkov. While Karamzin served up his criticisms with self-deprecating humor and a measure of reticence, Shishkov was characteristically blunt and unforgiving. After the Symposium gradually died once the end of the Napoleonic Wars had removed its raison d'être, he remained the head of the Russian Academy and worked to expand its ties to scholars in other Slavic nations; here his role continued to be constructive.[93] His political views, however, were increasingly reactionary. In 1814 he had been named to the State Council, which discussed proposed legislation. In this consultative role he could hardly shape state policy (in fact, he complained that the only fruit of his labors seemed to be to increase the number of his enemies),[94] but it did allow him to offer a conservative alternative to current policy. Unlike Golitsyn or Sturdza, he saw no need whatsoever for the ancien régime to change in light of the events of 1789–1815. If anything, these events had proved that it needed to be shored up further. He opposed even the minor reforms of serfdom that Alexander I was considering and to which the Sturdzas were sympathetic. Instead, as when a modest reform bill was introduced in 1820, he favored preserving nobles' unrestricted control over their serfs, including the right to sell peasants individually or without land. The power of the masters appeared to him as indispensable for social order. "The people are a river," he told the State Council, "that flows peacefully within its banks; but increase the water in it and it will overflow them, and nothing will stop its fury." Therefore, "the people's prosperity requires restraint and obedience." Russia, he maintained, was blessed: in addition to its military triumphs, it had been spared the turmoil afflicting the rest of Europe. "Is not this a sign of good-naturedness and of a still unsullied purity of morals?" he asked rhetorically. "Why changes in the laws, changes in customs, changes in our way of thinking? And where do these changes come from?" Naturally, from "the very countries where this unrest . . . and these doctrines, that are disseminated under the guise of intellectual freedom and that arouse the impudence of the passions, are most prevalent." Russians could "see about ourselves the grace of God. The hand of the Almighty protects us. What more could we desire?" To protect Russia, he had argued in 1815, he saw no better weapon than censorship. The printing press was a dangerous invention that facilitated the spread of evil doctrines, and lax censorship numbered among the chief causes of the unrest in Europe since 1789. After all, "not the number of books is beneficial, but their merit; it is better not to have any than to have a thousand bad ones."[95]

Yet Shishkov was ambivalent about Runich's purge of St. Petersburg University. Caught between his conservative beliefs and his sense of fairness, he sympathized with no one. About the interrogation of the professors in the fall of 1821, he later recalled that "they were subjected to the sort of strange and oppressive questions that might be asked by the superstitious when they are invested with strength and power"—hardly a vote of confidence in Runich. Still, "they gave the same kinds of answers, such as alternately bold and frightened freethinkers might give to a judge questioning them and whom they had previously ridiculed." The professors argued that "they were now being condemned for the same thing that earlier, *under the system of liberalism,* had been encouraged and for which they received ranks, medals and rewards. An unfortunately unassailable truth!" It was unreasonable to prosecute them for teaching what they had been told to teach, he concluded, but vigilant censorship was needed to prevent such "freethinkers" from infecting more young minds in the future.[96]

Like Sturdza, Shishkov hated the Bible Society, which he regarded as a British scheme to destroy all other churches. However, he did not share Sturdza's belief that education could improve people; he had greater confidence in the morals of illiterate peasants than the morals of the aristocracy and was convinced that educating the peasants would have terrible consequences. Also, unlike Sturdza, he vehemently opposed translating the Bible from Church Slavonic into modern Russian.[97]

Shishkov and Sturdza represented fundamentally different types within Russian conservatism. The aging admiral firmly believed that the French Revolution had been an aberration that could be reversed with repression and common sense. To those who asserted that changing times required changes in society, he retorted that where "government is firm and laws sacred, they rule the spirit of the times, but it does not rule them." He wanted to bring society to its senses and restore it to the harmony that had existed before 1789. Tellingly, he argued that serf unrest was a recent phenomenon without deep roots in the Russian past—a remarkable statement from a man who could remember the Pugachev revolt.[98] If Shishkov embodied the robust (albeit naïve and anachronistic) confidence of the eighteenth century, Sturdza represented the anxious sophistication of the nineteenth. Thirty-seven years younger than Shishkov, he understood that the ancien régime was obsolete. The time had come for a synthesis of medieval Christianity with the progressive social thought of the Enlightenment, he believed. Hence his opposition to serfdom, his faith in mass education, and his involvement in the philanthropic organizations associated with the Bible Society. In one regard, though, he thought like a man of an earlier age. As we have seen, Runich—who in this stood for many others—could not reconcile his education with religion and concluded that faith and reason were mutually exclusive. Aleksandr Sturdza apparently underwent no such crisis (unlike his sister) and saw the root of all theological evil in ignorance. To him, religion was in part an intellectual pursuit, and so the true faith would thrive among an educated population. Like Runich, he was wary of secular philosophy, but he never stopped believing that Russians required more, not less, education.

The 1820s were a transition period in the ideological development of the Russian state. The decade began with the religious conservatives in the Dual Ministry and the Bible Society at the height of their power. Then followed a traditionalist reaction, identified with the names of Arakcheev, Shishkov, and Fotii Spasskii. Finally, after the death of Alexander I and the dismissal of his lieutenants, Nicholas I inaugurated the authoritarian, statist policy of "Official Nationality."

Around 1820–1821, the Holy Alliance–Dual Ministry policies began to unravel. Revolution in Southern Europe and unrest in 1820 in one of his own guards regiments led Alexander toward Metternich's view that the only alternatives were reaction or revolution. Capodistrias and Sturdza, who had attempted to give the Holy Alliance a constructive meaning, left the government in 1822. When Uvarov was replaced by Runich as St. Petersburg curator and Sturdza resigned, the Dual Ministry lost two of its most able members. The ideological shift was apparent in the state's growing intolerance for displays of autonomy in "society," even when these were conservative or followed a mystical orientation. When Krüdener came to the capital to lobby for Russian intervention in Greece, the emperor ordered her home to Livonia. In 1822, all masonic lodges were banned, Labzin was sent into exile for insulting Arakcheev, and Tatarinova's circle was evicted from the Mikhailovskii castle. As Vienna's ambassador reported, even Golitsyn was losing credit with a monarch consumed by fear of revolution.[99]

Aside from Alexander's disenchantment and the hemorrhage of talented leaders, the religious policies came under assault from other quarters as well. Karamzin and Shishkov spoke for many in their suspicion of the Dual Ministry. Powerful Orthodox interests shared Sturdza's and Shishkov's view that Orthodox preeminence needed to be restored, and so Golitsyn faced a growing number of enemies in the upper clergy, especially Metropolitan Serafim of St. Petersburg. At court, Arakcheev plotted against his rival, Golitsyn, while Magnitskii prepared to jump ship and participated in the intrigue against his chief. According to Semen B. Okun', the Bible Society's ties to Britain became a political liability once Russia began pursuing a more strongly anti-British policy in the Balkans. These pressures came to a head in May 1824 and resulted in Golitsyn's dismissal from office, the dissolution of the Dual Ministry, the eventual abolition of the Bible Society, and the appointment of Shishkov as minister of education.[100]

Golitsyn's ouster, though gentler than Speranskii's twelve years earlier (he kept one of his less significant posts and retained the emperor's personal confidence), was the work of a similar coalition of opportunists (then Balashov, now Arakcheev and Magnitskii) and defenders of conservative interests (noble spokesmen such as Rostopchin, church hierarchs such as Serafim). In 1812, Alexander had learned about public disgruntlement through the semiclandestine literature attacking Speranskii. In the 1820s, the messenger was the monk Fotii Spasskii, an ascetic who considered himself on a divine crusade against false religion. His merciless pronouncements in the salons (where he publicly anathemized Golitsyn), as well as to Alexander himself, did much to undermine the minister's standing.[101] Since the Dual Ministry and the Bible Society represented neither the vested interests nor the traditional cultural attitudes of any significant section of society, their political survival, like that of such earlier reformers as Speranskii, depended on the monarch's support. In the end, as after Speranskii's ouster in 1812, it was Shishkov, the embodiment of social, cultural, and political traditionalism, who was chosen as the successor, to symbolize an end to experimentation.

The following years were spent liquidating the legacy of the Dual Ministry. Popov and Turgenev were dismissed, as was Magnitskii (and, after Alexander's death, Arakcheev), and the Bible Society was placed under the control of Metropolitan Serafim, who was determined to abolish it. The Orthodox Church recovered its primacy and the state ceased to patronize the works of mystics. With the premature death of Alexander I in November 1825, the driving force behind the mystical policies disappeared.[102] Nicholas I, who took no interest in the religious-political experiments that had fascinated his brother, devoted his colder and more pragmatic mind to defending the autocracy. Shishkov shared Nicholas's hostility to the "spirit of the times," yet he was out of place in a world of burgeoning universities and newspapers, where cultural nationalism was so accepted that it was no longer even controversial and where the growth of a critical intelligentsia created a climate in which he felt a stranger.

Shishkov made an effort to implement some of the ideas he had advocated before 1824, attacking mysticism and secret societies, proposing a restoration of Orthodox primacy and strict censorship measures (but not attempting to manipulate public opinion—that idea was too modern for him). He helped to ensure that prayers were no longer printed in modern Russian and took part in issuing the "cast-iron" censorship statute of 1826, which was so restrictive that Glinka, briefly employed as a censor at this time, complained that "even the Lord's Prayer could be interpreted as a Jacobin speech" under the new law (it was repealed in 1828). A belief in simple truths motivated Shishkov's unimaginative approach to an increasingly complex world, but it also accounted for his sense of fairness, as when he sympathized (helplessly) with persecuted professors at Vilna or argued (in vain) for basing the Decembrists' sentences on a formula that would have softened their punishment.[103]

Owing to his age and temperament, he was a timid and ineffective administrator who preferred polemics to politics, although he was active in encouraging Slavic studies at Russian schools and universities. When, in 1828, seventy-four years old and in bad health, Shishkov tendered his resignation, he argued wearily, if defiantly, that he had been "forced to shoulder this burden, which, owing to my old age and even more to the difficulty of circumstances, was beyond my strength." Yet "devotion to faith and throne sustained me," and despite the "hatred of many, I rose up boldly and strongly against the evil spread by the liberal doctrines and books. . . . Perhaps my efforts, despite all the opposition I faced, were not entirely without success."[104] He also requested that Nicholas retain him as head of the Russian Academy.[105] The academy, and its work to codify the language and thereby purify Russia's morals, had been his greatest preoccupation for much of the quarter-century since he had published his *Treatise on the Old and New Styles of the Russian Language* in 1803, and he hoped to spend the last years of his life pursuing this crusade.

None of the major conservatives discussed in this study had successful government careers under Nicholas I, though most lived another twenty to thirty years after Alexander's death. Clearly, the new emperor had no desire to pursue the avenues of romantic nationalism, religious conservatism, or gentry conservatism (in any case, Karamzin and Rostopchin both died in 1826). Of Alexander I's civilian advisers, Nicholas retained the legitimist Nesselrode to guide his foreign policy and Uvarov and Speranskii—heirs to the tradition of enlightened absolutism—in domestic affairs, but he sacked Arakcheev and took no interest in the likes of Golitsyn. The time for grand experiments, from the Bible Society to the military settlements, was over. So, what became of the Alexandrine conservatives after 1825?

Popov remained a loyal follower of Tatarinova even after she was banned in 1830 from holding further prayer meetings. In 1837, however, a disgruntled servant revealed to the police that Popov was participating in religious meetings and abusing one of his three daughters for refusing to take part in Tatarinova's rituals, beating her with a cane several times weekly while reciting lengthy prayers; he also starved her and forced her to sleep in an unheated shed. There the poor young woman was finally discovered by officials, looking, as Peter von Goetze heard from witnesses, "like a skeleton made only of skin and bones, and whose body had been beaten bloody." Tatarinova's circle was broken up by the authorities and she was sent to a nunnery, while Popov was dispatched to a monastery near distant Kazan', where he died in 1842.[106]

Runich was relieved of his position as St. Petersburg curator in June 1826. He apparently lived out his years in retirement, writing reminiscences in which, distancing himself from his earlier views, he attacked the Bible Society and the Dual Ministry and defended Speranskii. He died in St. Petersburg, impoverished and lonely, in 1860.[107]

Several of our protagonists moved south to settle by the Black Sea. Magnitskii was dismissed from state service in 1826, after being found guilty of misappropriating funds, and was forced to leave the capital. He settled first in Reval and then in Odessa, where he lived until his death in 1855.[108]

Prince Golitsyn held various court positions, none of them influential, under Nicholas I. The loss of his eyesight forced him to retire, and in 1842 he took up residence in his Crimean villa, where he died two years later.[109]

Roksandra Sturdza and her husband, Count von Edling, lived in Germany until 1819, when they felt compelled to leave in the aftermath of the fracas over her brother's *Memoir on the Present State of Germany*. After traveling in Italy and Austria, they moved to the Sturdza family estate in Belorussia and, finally, in 1824, settled on the extensive Bessarabian lands that Alexander I had granted her at Manzyr', not far from Odessa. Manzyr', previously a wilderness, became a combination of an experimental farm (employing only free labor) and a Christian commune, complete with a school, a church, and an infirmary. This satisfied Roksandra's urge for rustic distance from "the world," as well as her ideal of Christian philanthropy; and the proximity of her brother's family and the work of caring for "her" people at Manzyr' compensated for the lack of children of her own. In addition, she was active raising money for the victims of the war in Greece. When Alexander I died in 1825, she rushed to Taganrog to comfort Empress Elisaveta, who was reluctant to see her but nonetheless found solace in her presence. Following Edling's death, she traveled for the first time to Paris and Constantinople, the centers of her French and Greek cultural worlds. After a prolonged illness, she died in Odessa, fifty-eight years old, on January 16, 1844.[110]

Aleksandr Sturdza spent several years in Western Europe after leaving government service in 1822 but returned to the Russian foreign ministry during the Russo-Turkish War of 1828–1829. He finally retired to Odessa in 1830, where he lived with his wife and daughter and was active in civic and charitable causes. He wrote prolifically, including his reminiscences and works on religious and cultural topics. He also maintained a keen interest in Balkan affairs and regarded the Crimean War as a religious struggle between Orthodoxy and Islam. On June 7, 1854, he suffered an apoplectic stroke at Manzyr' and died in the evening of June 13. His daughter consoled herself with the thought that at least he would be spared the disappointment of the unfavorable progress of the war with the hated Turks.[111]

Admiral Shishkov became a widower in 1825, when his wife of many years succumbed to breast cancer.[112] He himself was sickly and in need of a nurse, and was also a sociable man who loved company. So, a year later, he remarried. This caused much commotion in Petersburg society and irritated his friends, in part because his new wife, a Catholic Pole, was suspect to the authorities and surrounded the old admiral (who was also minister of education) with her countrymen. As Peter von Goetze pointed out, though, the fact that he married first a Lutheran and then a Catholic, neither of them of Russian descent, indicates the contrast between his belligerently nationalist, Orthodox polemics and his benign, tolerant private nature.[113] During the 1830s Shishkov wrote his memoirs and occasional diatribes against the modern world, entertained friends and guests, and remained active in the Russian Academy, which became so identified with him that it was taken over by the Academy of Sciences after his death. His eyesight began to fail, he became completely blind, and when Aksakov saw Shishkov again at the end of 1840, he thought he had before him a "human corpse, immobile and mute." When his physical condition permitted, however, the admiral still exhibited the lucidity he had shown of old.[114]

He died on April 9, 1841, at the age of eighty-seven. The funeral was held on April 15, a Tuesday, at half past nine in the morning. He was buried near General Suvorov in the Monastery of St. Aleksandr Nevskii. Among those honoring his memory by their presence was Emperor Nicholas I, the fourth Romanov monarch whom Shishkov had served since entering the navy seventy-three years before.[115]

Conclusion

The Russian conservatives of Alexander's reign resembled other rebels of that age, such as the Prussian reformers and French revolutionaries. All of them wished to regenerate the nation as well as protect vested interests, to encourage both a powerful state and a free society. And they all met with a similar fate, for Nicholas, Frederick William, Napoleon, and the restored Bourbons promoted their varying degrees of modernization with a heavy-handed authoritarianism that doused ideological flames with cold political logic. The statist pragmatists made the hard choices that the visionaries of the left and right had evaded. After the upheavals came decades of oppressive quiescence.

For Russia's conservatives, it had been an exciting yet ultimately frustrating time. In an effort to realize their ideas, they had opposed the bureaucratization of government, attempted to rule literature through the Russian Academy and public opinion through the Symposium, and sought to reshape the nation's spirituality by governmental fiat. But it was in vain. Their experiments were short-lived because they depended on a fickle public mood, challenged powerful interests (in the case of the Bible Society), or foundered on internal contradictions (in the case of the Dual Ministry). More broadly, when the conservatives had a program other than protecting vested interests, their essentially spiritual concerns did not translate readily into concrete policies, and so they tended to trust in the wisdom of individuals rather than impersonal administrative mechanisms: thus a "good tsar" was to shoulder the burden of power while society pursued moral introspection, and the Old Style, the Holy Alliance, and Old Russia were metaphors for a process of regeneration within the soul of the individual. This revulsion for politics foreshadowed the Slavophiles, but also distinguished the Alexandrine conservatives from the bureaucrats of the era of Nicholas I.

Moreover, the very concepts on which Alexandrine conservatism was based lost relevance after 1825. Gentry conservatism, for one, was doomed. In the absence of a discourse of "rights" in the Russian service state, the nobles had invoked ancestral custom and the monarchy's need for their support in order to justify their privileges. However, the modernizing bureaucracy existed precisely to uproot antiquated customs and free the crown from dependence on others. Furthermore, recent developments (the end of compulsory noble service, the French Revolution, the Decembrist revolt, and the emergence of a critical intelligentsia) called into question the nobility's usefulness and loyalty to the crown, and convinced monarchs in Russia and across Europe to strengthen state authority, even at the expense of class privilege. As Russian political life became dominated by bureaucrats and *intelligenty,* to the detriment of the nobility as a class,[1] the institutions and prerogatives that nobles had once taken for granted (possession of serfs, privileged access to education,[2] positions in the bureaucracy) became fair game. Gradually, the privileges defended by gentry conservatives were eaten away by social changes that were abetted and even encouraged by the crown.

The romantic nationalism of Shishkov and Glinka fared little better,[3] again in part because it failed to satisfy the needs of the autocracy and its modernizing supporters. The Old Style did not prevail, although it did contribute to the formation of modern literary Russian. More important, Europeanization continued apace: in the half-century after 1825, serfdom was to be abolished, the state bureaucratized, education expanded, the judiciary reformed, conscription introduced, railroads built, manufacturing encouraged—all in a futile effort to arrest Russia's slide into backwardness. Social stability, justice, and cultural growth were pursued, not by returning to ancestral ways but by combining repression and Europeanization.

The ideas of the Holy Alliance came to naught as well. Golitsyn's policies were scuttled by traditionalists who equated any departure from Orthodoxy with subversion, while Aleksandr Sturdza's program was defeated by the tensions between its own different components. Traditionalists had no use for his theological intellectualism while mystics and Catholics disagreed with his zeal for Orthodoxy. Legitimists objected to his support for the Greeks, while he himself opposed the liberals who joined him in that attitude. Sturdza's glorification of rural life and attachment to the backward, unstable Orthodox societies of Southeastern Europe, finally, blinded him to the sociopolitical dynamics of his era and to Russia's real security needs;[4] indeed, Russia's backwardness and Balkan commit-

ments caused the Crimean debacle at the end of Sturdza's life and would ultimately destroy the Russian Empire in World War I.

The most fruitful policies of the early nineteenth century, in terms of their contribution to prolonging the life of the imperial regime, were those associated with
Kozodavlev and Uvarov. In the Petrine tradition of modernization "from above,"
the former advocated industrialization, while the latter sought to strengthen the
state by endowing it with a modern culture.[5] Both contributed to a century-long
effort to keep monarchy and nobility afloat by jettisoning parts of the ancien
régime that they imagined were expendable ballast.

This policy failed in the end because it generated pressure for ever more extensive change. Economic development, the migrations between city and country,
and the spread of modern communications conspired with the loosening of the
bonds between peasant and lord, and between noble and state, to hollow out the
vital structures of the regime. The long-term effect of such incremental change
can be observed in the German experience, which represented, after all, the best-
case scenario for those who desired the fruits of modernization without the pain
of revolution. By 1914, William II was obligated to curry favor with industrialists
and bankers, the petty bourgeoisie, and a Reichstag filled with Social Democrats,
whereas the power of the Junkers—long ago stripped of their serfs and most legal
privileges—was but a shadow of their grandfathers'. Absolutism was gone, a host
of civil liberties had been recognized, and the crown could only hope that the
peasants and middle classes would not vote socialist. Although elements of the
old regime would "persist" (to borrow Arno Mayer's term) until 1914 and beyond
in Germany,[6] news of this persistence of remnants of noble power would have
been cold comfort to a Rostopchin or a Shishkov. In retrospect, the German nobles' tenacious survival may appear remarkable; from the perspective of 1825,
however, the disappearance of the old way of life would have seemed far more
noteworthy. The power of socioeconomic change doomed efforts to control it.
The conservatives of the Alexandrine era sensed this to a greater extent than the
reformers. They hoped that Russia might stave off such change, but they did not
believe that change could be used to the advantage of the ancien régime.

The change that the conservatives feared was associated with Europe, from
which they wished to insulate Russia henceforth. Yet they were themselves products of Russia's Westernization, so they needed to explain why Europeanization
had once been good but had subsequently become bad. Were the suspected reform plans of Alexander I not a logical extension of those of earlier Romanovs?
Of course, Catherine II—unlike her son and grandson—had not threatened noble
privileges. More broadly, however, the very notion of Westernization seemed to
have carried less explosive implications before the French Revolution; only a few
conservatives (including Aleksandr Sturdza) saw enlightened absolutism and revolution as part of a continuum. Though the troubles of the present were understood to be rooted in the Westernized old regime, the solutions proposed by conservatives testified in themselves to the impact of Western thought, even where

their content was ostensibly anti-Western. Romantic nationalist fantasies about Muscovy, as well as Sturdza's vision of a morally cleansed Orthodox Russia at the heart of a Christian European commonwealth, were a kind of ideological import substitution that replaced French with Church Slavonic and classical antiquity with Muscovy. By reviving isolated elements of a poorly understood Russian past, they hoped to stabilize a status quo that was, in reality, but a passing phase in Russia's ongoing Europeanization. They thus combined valid insight into the corrosive effects of social and cultural change with a blindness to the deeper forces governing Russian history. As a result, though their warnings about the future were perceptive, they offered no constructive remedies. Their negative suggestions—repression and censorship—were only palliatives, and the positive ones—the Old Style, the Dual Ministry, and so forth—failed because they did not recognize the root of the problems afflicting the old regime.

Despite these shortcomings, conservative thinkers made significant contributions to Russian culture. To begin with, they promoted the development of a civil society involved with public affairs, whether through Rostopchin's pamphlets, Glinka's *Russian Messenger,* the Symposium, or the Russian Bible Society. They also encouraged a more humane attitude toward the peasantry: Shishkov regarded its culture as a cure for the evils of Westernization;[7] Glinka rhapsodized about the solidarity of classes in 1812; and Sturdza wanted to abolish serfdom and promote universal literacy. Finally, they strengthened Russia's sense of cultural identity: Glinka and Karamzin introduced readers to pre-Petrine history, Shishkov publicized Russia's Slavic heritage, and Sturdza, its ties to the Orthodox world.

Taken together, these influences contributed to a sea change in Russian thought. The impetus toward further Europeanization, which peaked around 1801–1815, began to wane. Just as the artificially Slavonicized Russian of the eighteenth century had been declared by Shishkov to be an age-old tradition, so the European *Polizeistaat,* frozen in the late eighteenth century, came to be regarded as quintessentially Russian by Nicholas I and even Alexander III and Nicholas II. What developed in the intellectual sphere was the notion of a conservative Russian exceptionalism, rooted in Karamzin's belief in autocracy, Shishkov's concern for Slavic identity, and Sturdza's defense of Orthodoxy.[8]

This anticipated "Orthodoxy, Autocracy, Nationality," the slogan to be coined by Uvarov under Nicholas I. The difference lay in the meaning of these concepts. Autocracy for Karamzin was the keystone of a traditional society dominated by the nobility; to Uvarov, it implied rule by a modernizing bureaucracy. Shishkov wanted Russia to return to its cultural and spiritual roots; Uvarov hoped that a *modernized* Russian culture could cement the empire's stability.[9] As for Orthodoxy, Sturdza saw it as the word of God; Uvarov viewed it as a tool to strengthen society's cohesion. What distinguished Alexandrine conservatism from Nicholas's "Official Nationality," then, was its limited concern for raison d'état. This preserved its intellectual integrity, but it also prevented conservatives from reconciling theory and practice, for they were more concerned with the spiritual changes they hoped to realize than with the institutions that were actually to effect them. The policies of Nicholas and Uvarov, on the contrary, joined the quest for modernity with an emphasis on nationalism, and lent the entire undertaking a statist and authoritarian orientation. This gave "Official Nationality" a degree of effectiveness and political viability that the earlier attempts had lacked, but at the price of repressing civil society and sacrificing intellectual and moral integrity to political expediency.

The conservatives examined in this study were broadly representative of the European culture of their time. Gentry conservatism, romantic nationalism, and religious conservatism were powerful forces across Europe. In some cases, particularly among the religious conservatives, the Russians engaged in a direct dialogue with their Western counterparts; in others, they developed similar ideas because they shared a common culture with the West. They also helped lay the foundations for later right-wing thought. Out of the prepolitical culture of the Russian Enlightenment they created self-consciously conservative conceptions that served as touchstones for subsequent thinkers. Their experience demonstrated the difficulty inherent in creating a conservative ideology in post-Petrine Russia: Glinka's appeal to Russian history undercut Rostopchin's defense of noble prerogatives, while Golitsyn's policy of Christianization was opposed by the Orthodox Church. Where cultural and religious traditions (the foundation of conservative thought) so blatantly conflicted with the interests of the ruling elites (conservatism's social base), no unified conservative ideology was possible.

The early conservatives supplied essential ingredients for the different, often mutually antagonistic conservatisms that came into being in late imperial Russia. Reforming bureaucrats, such as Sergei Witte and Petr Stolypin, carried on the tradition of enlightened absolutism, under an ideological veneer of conservative nationalism. Reactionary statists, such as Konstantin Pobedonostsev, countered that the state must prevent, not abet, social change.[10] Finally, there was a conservatism rooted in civil society, where the ideas of Shishkov on Slavic tradition, Glinka on Old Russia's social harmony, and Sturdza on the moral superiority of Orthodoxy all lived on in the thinking of the Slavophiles and their successors.[11]

The conservatives of the age of Alexander I, as we have seen, never fully came to terms with the Petrine legacy. Nor has the fundamental tension within Russian conservatism—between defenders of post-revolutionary vested interests and advocates of prerevolutionary cultural traditions—been resolved by the revolutions of Lenin, Stalin, and Gorbachev; if anything, the destruction of the imperial regime and the monstrous scale of Russia's subsequent upheavals seem only to have deepened the split between the spokesmen for regime interests and the guardians of ancestral virtue. On one side of this divide, it has been difficult for the Soviet and post-Soviet elite—the beneficiaries of the Stalin and Gorbachev revolutions—to justify their power and privileges as deriving from ancient tradition, notwithstanding the Soviet-era glorification of tsars and imperial military glory as well as the post-Soviet efforts to revive the symbolism of the imperial past by renaming streets and cities, changing the state emblem and flag, rebuilding churches, and so forth. The elite's effort to ground its status both in the distant past and in a discourse of progress (whether of the socialist or capitalist variety) is reminiscent of attempts by prerevolutionary regime conservatives to pose as both modernizers and heirs to Muscovite tradition. On the other side, a representative of cultural traditionalism in the romantic nationalist-Slavophile vein is Aleksandr Solzhenitsyn, perhaps modern Russia's greatest conservative thinker and moralist, who was relentlessly persecuted by the Soviet regime and responded with bitter hatred toward both the communist state and its present-day successor, the Yeltsin regime in the Russian Federation.[12] As long as traumatic historical discontinuities such as those precipitated by Peter the Great and Stalin dominate the Russian consciousness, such tensions and ambiguities will likely remain at the center of conservative thought and politics in Russia.

Notes

INTRODUCTION

1. As one scholar has put it: "Before 1789 conservatism, as a positive, self-conscious political outlook, was unknown [in France]. . . . By 1793, however, a new, revolutionary ideology had led to attacks on all the principal pillars of stability: property, social hierarchy, religion, monarchy. None of these, or their justification in the nature of things, could any longer be taken for granted. They now needed to be defended, both in theory and in practice." W. Doyle, *The Oxford History of the French Revolution,* 422. The same point can be made about the rest of Europe as well. Herzen's comments are found in A. I. Gertsen [Herzen], *Sobranie sochinenii v vos'mi tomakh,* 5:247–48. (Unless otherwise indicated, all translations used in this text are mine.)

2. Cited in N. Ia. Eidel'man, *Mgnoven'e slavy nastaet. . . : God 1789–i,* 8, 183–84, 238. The literature on the Petrine reforms is too vast to be surveyed here. To take only two examples from the past decade, Cynthia Whittaker argues that "Peter's reforms add up to a revolution" and represent a "transformation from a medieval to a modern concept" of the relations between monarch, state, and society ("The Reforming Tsar: The Redefinition of Autocratic Duty in Eighteenth-Century Russia," 83), while Evgenii Anisimov blames Peter's "uncompromising,

radical, even revolutionary" reforms for introducing totalitarianism in Russia (*Vremia petrovskikh reform,* 11–12).

3. An excellent discussion of this issue is Marc Raeff's *The Well-Ordered Police State: Social and Institutional Change through Law in the Germanies and Russia, 1600–1800.* The success of Peter's efforts is called into question, however, by some scholars. See J. LeDonne, "The Eighteenth-Century Russian Nobility: Bureaucracy or Ruling Class?"; M. Confino, "A propos de la notion de service dans la noblesse russe aux XVIIIe et XIXe siècles"; G. Freeze, "Handmaiden of the State? The Church in Imperial Russia Reconsidered."

4. Marc Raeff argues that post-Petrine Russians lived simultaneously in two different seventeenth-century worlds: the state adopted seventeenth-century European conceptions of government, while the population clung to Muscovite cultural tradition ("Seventeenth-Century Europe in Eighteenth-Century Russia? [Pour prendre congé du dix-huitième siècle russe]").

5. The psychological similarity between the Decembrists and the entourage of Alexander I is also noted by N. Riasanovsky, *A Parting of Ways: Government and the Educated Public in Russia 1801–1855,* 98–99.

6. Gertsen, 5:215.

7. L. Hunt, *The Family Romance of the French Revolution,* 25; S. L. Baehr, "Regaining Paradise: The 'Political Icon' in Seventeenth- and Eighteenth-Century Russia," 162, 158–64. See also the recent articles by C. Schmidt, "Aufstieg und Fall der Fortschrittsidee in Rußland," esp. 7–13, and C. H. Whittaker, "The Idea of Autocracy among Eighteenth-Century Russian Historians."

8. J. Starobinski, *1789, Les Emblèmes de la raison,* 145. D. Smith, "Freemasonry and the Public in Eighteenth-Century Russia," 34.

9. Iu. M. Lotman, *Besedy o russkoi kul'ture,* 62–64.

10. K. Epstein, *The Genesis of German Conservatism,* 461–65. R. Hole, "British Counter-revolutionary Popular Propaganda in the 1790's," in C. Jones, ed., *Britain and Revolutionary France: Conflict, Subversion and Propaganda.*

11. M. Boffa, "La Révolution française et la contre-Révolution," in F. Furet, ed., *L'Héritage de la Révolution française,* 98.

12. F. Furet, *La Révolution française de Turgot à Napoléon,* 1:36; Epstein, 33–34.

13. F. Schnabel, *Deutsche Geschichte im neunzehnten Jahrhundert,* vol. 1, *Die Grundlagen,* 106.

14. Lotman, 378.

15. M. Raeff, *Origins of the Russian Intelligentsia: The Eighteenth-Century Nobility,* 111; S. O. Shmidt, "Obshchestvennoe samosoznanie noblesse russe v XVI–pervoi treti XIX v.," 18–20.

16. On this subject, see G. Marker, *Publishing, Printing, and the Origins of Intellectual Life in Russia, 1700–1800.*

17. The relationship between Enlightenment culture, the state, and "public opinion" in this period has been much discussed in the context of Western and

Central Europe. For a recent analysis of two classic works on this subject—by Jürgen Habermas and Reinhart Koselleck—that directly addresses these issues, see A. La Vopa, "Conceiving a Public: Ideas and Society in Eighteenth-Century Europe," esp. 89–98.

18. For a study of such patronage networks, see D. Ransel, *The Politics of Catherinian Russia: The Panin Party,* and J. LeDonne, *Absolutism and Ruling Class: The Formation of the Russian Political Order 1700–1825,* 19–21.

19. S. B. Okun', *Istoriia SSSR 1796–1825. Kurs lektsii,* 305.

20. A. Mayer, *The Persistence of the Old Regime: Europe to the Great War,* 4.

21. For examples of this approach in the cases of France and Italy, see S. Schama, *Citizens: A Chronicle of the French Revolution,* 184–94, as well as the works of Hunt and Furet, and L. Riall, *The Italian Risorgimento: State, Society and National Unification,* 16–17.

22. E. Hobsbawm, *The Age of Revolution 1789–1848,* xv.

CHAPTER 1:
ADMIRAL SHISHKOV AND ROMANTIC NATIONALISM

1. Starobinski, 68–76, 96. Schama, 162–74, 798–99. Hunt, 121, passim. E. James, *The Franks,* 239.

2. E. Hobsbawm and T. Ranger, eds., *The Invention of Tradition,* 2–14. For a cogent discussion of romantic nationalism, see the stimulating essay by Thomas Nipperdey, "Auf der Suche nach der Identität: Romantischer Nationalismus," in his *Nachdenken über die deutsche Geschichte,* 110–25.

3. See M. Raeff, *Comprendre l'ancien régime russe: Etat et société en Russie Impériale. Essai d'interprétation,* 137.

4. On Shcherbatov, see A. Walicki, *The Slavophile Controversy: History of a Conservative Utopia in Nineteenth-Century Russian Thought,* 21–32.

5. AIRLI, 10,102, l. 83 ob. (Full archival references are given in Works Cited.) Others give the date as March 16, 1753: A. S. Shishkov, *Zapiski, mneniia i perepiska,* 1:1 (editor's note); P. von Goetze, *Fürst Alexander Nikolajewitsch Galitzin und seine Zeit. Aus den Erlebnissen des Geheimraths Peter von Goetze,* 316.

6. *Entsiklopedicheskii slovar',* s.v. "Shishkovy." For Shiskov's personnel file, see RGAVMF, 406/7/17, l. 1335 ob.

7. On the history of Shishkov's memoirs, see A. G. Tartakovskii, *Russkaia memuaristika XVIII–pervoi poloviny XIX v. Ot rukopisi k knige,* 197–200.

8. P. Dolgorukov, *Rossiiskaia rodoslovnaia kniga,* 4:221–22. Dolgorukov apparently was unaware of the fifth son, Gerasim, identified in *Russkii biograficheskii slovar',* s.v. "Shishkov, Nikolai Petrovich."

9. As of 1719, in this area, 67.8 percent of peasants had been serfs of nobles. P. Kolchin, *Unfree Labor: American Slavery and Russian Serfdom,* 30. In 1777, 32 percent of Russian serf owners owned under ten "souls," and 30.7 percent owned

between ten and thirty. A few, of course, owned many thousands. J. Blum, *Lord and Peasant in Russia from the Ninth to the Nineteenth Century*, 367. In the early 1800s, the owner of under twenty "souls" was "regarded as impoverished." Kolchin, 165.

10. On this aspect of noble life, see Raeff, *Origins*, 122–24.

11. He was a few years younger than Aleksandr and lived until 1813. *Dekabristy: Biograficheskii spravochnik*, ed. S. V. Mironenko and M. V. Nechkina, s.v. "Shishkov, Aleksandr Ardalionovich." Three of his four children were raised by the childless Aleksandr Shishkov and his wife.

12. AIRLI, Kartoteka B. L. Modzalevskago, card 1861. AIRLI, 265/2/3108, l. 37, Shishkov to Dar'ia Alekseevna, Dresden, May 4, 1798. AIRLI, 13,852, O. P. Kozodavlev to Shishkov, St. Petersburg, February 28, 1813. Dolgorukov identifies Dmitrii's second wife as Countess Vera Tolstaia (p. 222).

13. See the letter by him in RGIA, 1673/1/250.

14. D. Riabinin, "Aleksandr Ardalionovich Shishkov 2-i, 1799–1833," 44. AIRLI, Kartoteka B. L. Modzalevskago, card 1861. *Russkii biograficheskii slovar'*, s.v. "Shishkov, Nikolai Petrovich."

15. A. S. Shishkov, *Sobranie sochinenii i perevodov*, 12:270. On the differences between Moscow and St. Petersburg society, see the beginning of chapter 3 in the present study.

16. V. Ia. Stoiunin, "Aleksandr Semenovich Shishkov: Biografiia," pt. 1, 237–38.

17. See M. Raeff, "Les Slaves, les Allemands et les 'Lumières.'"

18. A. L. von Schlözer, *Obshchestvennaia i chastnaia zhizn' Avgusta Liudviga Shletsera*, 101, 165. See also *Sbornik Imperatorskago Russkago Istoricheskago Obshchestva (SIRIO)* 4 (1869): 14, and 8 (1871): 337; Dolgorukov, 219–22; H. Neuschäffer, *Katharina II. und die baltischen Provinzen*, 400–5; Goetze, 245, 283.

19. See H. Pohrt, "August Ludwig Schlözer und die russische Sprache," in *Literaturbeziehungen im 18. Jahrhundert: Studien und Quellen zur deutsch-russischen und russisch-westeuropäischen Kommunikation*, ed. H. Grasshoff, 372.

20. Pohrt, in Grasshoff, 358–74. M. Sh. Fainshtein and V. V. Kolominov, *Khram muz slovesnykh (Iz istorii Rossiiskoi Akademii)*, 65. For Shishkov's library, see RGIA, 1673/1/111, l. 30 ob. The book was *Nestor. Russische Annalen in ihrer Slavonischen Grundsprache verglichen, übersetzt und erklärt*, vol. 3 (Göttingen, 1805).

21. See RGAVMF, 406/7/17, l. 1335 ob.

22. On his experience being shipwrecked in Sweden in 1771, see Shishkov, *Sobranie*, 12:314–27. On his voyage around the Mediterranean in 1776–1779, see his *Zapiski admirala A. S. Shishkova, vedennyia im vo vremia puteplavaniia ego iz Kronshtada v Konstantinopol'* and his "Russkii puteshestvennik proshlago veka za granitseiu (Sobstvennoruchnyia pis'ma A. S. Shishkova 1776 i 1777 g.)."

23. RGIA, 1673/1/2, ll. 1 ob–2.

24. Shishkov, *Sobranie*, 12:1–32. Shishkov, *Zapiski, mneniia*, 1:1–2.

25. *Russkii biograficheskii slovar'*, s.v. "Shishkov, Aleksandr Semenovich." Stoiunin, "Shishkov," pt. 1, 252–53. K. G. Bolenko, "'Kleine Kinderbibliothek' I. G. Kampe v perevode A. S. Shishkova."

26. Iu. K. Iakimovich, *Deiateli russkoi kul'tury i slovarnoe delo*, 55. *Russkii biograficheskii slovar'*, s.v. "Shishkov, Aleksandr Semenovich."

27. RNB 862/3, ll. 78–81, copies of letters to P. A. Zubov, A. G. Orlov-Chesmenskii, and P. A. Rumiantsev-Zadunaiskii, n.d.

28. Akademiia Nauk SSSR, Institut russkoi literatury (Pushkinskii Dom), *Slovar' russkikh pisatelei XVIII veka*, vol. 1 A-I, s.v. "Golenishchev-Kutuzov Ivan Logginovich," by M. P. Lepekhin.

29. AIRLI, 265/2/3109, Shishkov to L. I. Golenishchev-Kutuzov, June 2, 1820.

30. Shishkov, *Zapiski, mneniia*, 1:3. *Slovar' pisatelei*, s.v. "Golenishchev-Kutuzov Loggin Ivanovich," by M. P. Lepekhin. AIRLI, 358/1/149, ll. 4–5, Shishkov to Katerina Il'inishna Kutuzova, Kladovo, February 2, 1813. S. T. Aksakov, *Sobranie sochinenii v chetyrekh tomakh*, 2:287.

31. V. P. Semennikov, "Literaturno-obshchestvennyi krug Radishcheva," in *A. N. Radishchev: Materialy i Issledovaniia*, 215–47. Shishkov was also an honorary member of a masonic lodge in 1780–1781. See T. Bakounine, *Répertoire biographique des franc-maçons russes (XVIIIe et XIXe siècles)*, 534–35.

32. A. G. Cross, *N. M. Karamzin: A Study of His Literary Career (1783–1803)*, 58–60. Semennikov, in *A. N. Radishchev*, 215–47. *Slovar' pisatelei*, s.v. "Antonovskii Mikhail Ivanovich," by V. E. Vatsuro. Iu. M. Lotman and B. Uspenskii, "Spory o iazyke v nachale XIX v. kak fakt russkoi kul'tury ('Proisshestvie v tsarstve tenei, ili sud'bina rossiiskogo iazyka'—neizvestnoe sochinenie Semena Bobrova)," 181–82, 194.

33. I. de Madariaga, *Russia in the Age of Catherine the Great*, 521–31.

34. A. Monnier, "La naissance d'une idéologie nationaliste en Russie au siècle des lumières," 268–69, 272.

35. The poem is discussed in M. Al'tshuller, *Predtechi slavianofil'stva v russkoi literature (Obshchestvo "Beseda liubitelei russkogo slova")*, 37–38.

36. Nipperdey, *Nachdenken*, 120.

37. RGIA, 1673/1/2, ll. 1 ob–2. Shishkov, *Zapiski, mneniia*, 1:5–6.

38. Shishkov, *Sobranie*, 14:143–54 (written 1794–1796).

39. Shishkov, *Zapiski, mneniia*, 1:9–10.

40. Madariaga, 588. RNB, 862/4, pp. 20–79, 97–104.

41. Shishkov, *Zapiski, mneniia*, 1:13–21.

42. Ibid., 1:4, 11, 22, 26. As of 1840 he owned the villages of Markova, Ostashkova, Bory, and Rucheika, with approximately five hundred male "souls," in Bezhetsk *uezd*. This district was adjacent to Kashin and may have been detached from it after he was granted the serfs. RGIA, 1673/1/5 l. 12. In 1834, only 3 percent of Russian serf owners owned over five hundred such "souls," while 84

percent had one hundred or fewer, so Shishkov was a wealthy man. This was still a far cry from, say, Count N. P. Sheremetev's 185,610 male and female serfs. Blum, 368, 370.

43. Shishkov, *Zapiski, mneniia,* 1:36–42.

44. Ibid., 1:43–46, 49–52. AIRLI, 265/2/3108, ll. 8–11, 15–18, 31–37, Shishkov to Dar'ia Alekseevna, Vienna, January 11, 1798, and Dresden, February 3, March 25, and May 4, 1798.

45. AIRLI, 265/2/3108, ll. 5 ob, 8–11, Shishkov to Dar'ia Alekseevna, Vilna, December 20, 1797, and Vienna, January 11, 1798.

46. Already in 1777, when he found French graffiti defacing a chapel in Greece, he regarded this as proof of the unique baseness of the French character. Shishkov, *Zapiski admirala,* 29.

47. See, e.g., Shishkov, *Zapiski, mneniia,* 1:63–66.

48. LeDonne, 141–42. See also E. N. Marasinova, "Russkii dvorianin vtoroi poloviny XVIII v. (sotsio-psikhologiia lichnosti)," 23, and H. J. Torke, "Continuity and Change in the Relations between Bureaucracy and Society in Russia, 1613–1861," 466.

49. Shishkov, *Zapiski, mneniia,* 1:79–80. Shishkov, *Sobranie,* 14:177.

50. Cited in N. K. Shil'der, *Imperator Aleksandr Pervyi: Ego zhizn' i tsarstvovanie,* 2:6.

51. In fact, Alexander I himself liked to refer to this group (jokingly) as his *"Comité de salut public." Russkii biograficheskii slovar',* s.v. "Kochubei, Viktor Pavlovich," 371.

52. Shishkov, *Zapiski, mneniia,* 1:81–86. Stoiunin, "Shishkov," pt. 2, 502–3.

53. Shishkov, *Zapiski, mneniia,* 1:40. On his irritation with the new tsar, see also M. Al'tshuller, "An Unknown Poem by A. S. Shishkov."

54. Kolominov and Fainshtein, 44–45. Shishkov, *Zapiski, mneniia,* 1:87–95.

55. N. Ia. Eidel'man, *Gran' vekov: Politicheskaia bor'ba v Rossii. Konets XVIII–nachalo XIX stoletiia,* 71–85. Shishkov, *Sobranie,* 2:462.

56. S. P. Zhikharev, *Zapiski sovremennika,* 2:178, entry for March 10, 1807. See also the many naval books in Shishkov's library. RGIA, 1673/1/111.

57. On eighteenth- and early-nineteenth-century Russian memoirs in general, see Tartakovskii; also M. A. Kriuchkova, "Russkaia memuaristika vtoroi poloviny XVIII v. kak sotsiokul'turnoe iavlenie."

58. On Shishkov as a private person, see: Aksakov, 2:266–313; Goetze, passim; O. Przecławski, "Aleksandr Semenovich Shishkov, r. 1754 †1841 g. Vospominaniia O. A. Przhetslavskago," 383–402. Karamzin later wrote that "Shishkov is honest and courteous, but dim" (letter of February 14, 1816, cited in A. A. Kochubinskii, *Nachal'nye gody russkago slavianovedeniia. Admiral Shishkov i kantsler gr. Rumiantsov,* 238 n. 1). See also F. F. Vigel', *Zapiski,* 1:199.

59. She was born in 1756. AIRLI, Kartoteka B. L. Modzalevskogo, card 1821.

60. Aksakov, 2:277–79, 289.

61. P. A. Viazemskii, *Polnoe sobranie sochinenii*, 9:195, diary, April 15, 1841.

62. M. I. Sukhomlinov, *Istoriia Rossiiskoi akademii*, 7:206; Kochubinskii, 28.

63. Indeed, the field of comparative linguistics, which was fundamental to the romantic nationalism of which Shishkov was an early representative, was just coming into being and was the preserve of academic specialists, not amateurs. See "Old Languages, New Models," in B. Anderson, *Imagined Communities*.

64. Sukhomlinov, *Istoriia*, 7:204–5. Kochubinskii, 28. In the case of this particular etymology, however, Shishkov's much-scorned theory was apparently correct. D. N. Cherdakov, "Semantika slova i razvitie russkogo iazyka v kontseptsii A. S. Shishkova," 38. In general, modern scholars such as Al'tshuller, Lotman, Cherdakov, and Fainshtein have presented Shishkov's linguistic and literary work in a more favorable light than did such prerevolutionary writers as Sukhomlinov and Kochubinskii.

65. See, for example, his letter to the Czech linguist Václav Hanka, April 28, 1823, in Shishkov, *Zapiski, mneniia*, 2:392.

66. Remark by Shishkov's friend Sverbeev, quoted in I. A. Chistovich, *Rukovodiashchiie deiateli dukhovnago prosveshcheniia v Rossii v pervoi polovine tekushchago stoletiia*, 241.

67. Goetze, 284.

68. Shmidt, 26.

69. This background to the linguistic debates is based largely on Lotman and Uspenskii. An opposing view—that the debates were a vehicle for discussing current events, and that actual language questions were of secondary importance—is presented in N. N. Bulich, *Ocherki po istorii Russkoi literatury i prosveshcheniia s nachala XIX veka*, 1:120.

70. Lotman and Uspenskii, 203.

71. Ibid., 170.

72. J. Bonamour, *A. S. Griboedov et la vie littéraire de son temps*, 22. On Karamzin's literary development, see Cross, *Karamzin*.

73. Bonamour, 24, 28.

74. Lotman and Uspenskii, 228, 230–32, 237–38. E. N. Kupreianova, "Frantsuzskaia revoliutsiia 1789–1794 godov i bor'ba napravlenii v russkoi literature pervoi chetverti XIX veka," 97–98.

75. Bulich, 1:120–27.

76. Shishkov, *Zapiski, mneniia*, 2:5.

77. Bonamour, 88. Lotman and Uspenskii, 184. H. Rogger discusses some of the eighteenth-century background to these ideas in "The Russian National Character: Some Eighteenth-Century Views."

78. See also M. Al'tshuller, "*Rassuzhdenie o starom i novom sloge rossiiskogo iazyka* kak politicheskii dokument (A. S. Shishkov i N. M. Karamzin)," 214–22.

79. Shishkov, *Sobranie*, 2:1–3, 10–12, 23–29, 33–49.

80. Lotman and Uspenskii, 231. Novikov already had blamed women for

spoiling the Russian language (ibid.), as did Shishkov. AIRLI, 358/1/216.

81. Shishkov, *Sobranie,* 2:122–29, 251–53.

82. For the argument that Shishkov was merely using political arguments to bolster his underlying literary and linguistic case, not the reverse, see P. Garde, "Šiškov et Karamzin: deux ennemis?" 282.

83. Al'tshuller, *Predtechi,* 34–38, 341. Kolominov and Fainshtein, 46. Lotman and Uspenskii, 246. The quotation is from Al'tshuller, *Predtechi,* 38.

84. Aksakov, 2:295. Goetze confirms that "for years" Shishkov charged the peasants no quitrent (289), although Przecławski reports him receiving such payments in the late 1820s or 1830s (388). Shishkov's letters to his wife suggest that he did collect some money but was a solicitous landlord. AIRLI, 265/2/3108, ll. 8–11, Vienna, January 11, 1798.

85. Bonamour, 31. Sukhomlinov, *Istoriia,* 7:557. P. Shchebal'skii, "A. S. Shishkov, ego soiuzniki i protivniki," 196. Stoiunin, "Shishkov," pt. 2, 525.

86. S. Ia. Rumovskii to P. I. Sokolov, October 16, 1803, cited in Sukhomlinov, *Istoriia,* 7:189. Sukhomlinov, *Istoriia,* 7:188–89, 513–14, 556. Bulich, 1:140–41. On Derzhavin's and Krylov's coolness, see V. F. Khodasevich, *Derzhavin,* 210; Al'tshuller, *Predtechi,* 60; Kolominov and Fainshtein, 46. On the other hand, P. A. Kikin became such a fervent convert to the Old Style that, in his copy of the *Treatise,* he inscribed "Mon Evangile," which testifies to the pervasiveness of the French language even among so-called Slavophiles. Aksakov, 2:284. RGIA, 733/118/29, P. Zavadovskii to Shishkov, November 11, 1803.

87. Shishkov, *Zapiski, mneniia,* 2:5. "Pis'ma A. S. Shishkova grafu Dmitriiu Ivanovichu Khvostovu," 33–35, Shishkov to D. I. Khvostov, St. Petersburg, January 29, 1805.

88. Shishkov to N. S. Mordvinov, December 19, 1805, in Al'tshuller, *Predtechi,* 32–33.

89. Viazemskii, 9:145. Vigel', 1:199–200, 2:9. Batiushkov to N. I. Gnedich, Moscow, late April, 1811, in K. N. Batiushkov, *Sochineniia v dvukh tomakh,* 2:164. Aksakov, 2:267. Shishkov to Bardovskii, June 20, 1811, in Shishkov, *Zapiski, mneniia,* 2:316–17. Karamzin appears only to have skimmed the book, and refused to issue a response, despite the entreaties of his friend I. I. Dmitriev. M. A. Dmitriev, *Melochi iz zapasa moei pamiati,* 60.

90. Apparently the review by Kachenovskii in *Severnyi Vestnik,* 1804, chap. 1, 17–29 (cited in Bulich, 1:135–37).

91. Aksakov, 2:266–68. *Arkhiv brat'ev Turgenevykh,* ed. E. I. Tarasov, 1:97–98, 281–85, 361, 401, N. I. Turgenev, diary entries, Moscow, March 4, 1808, and Göttingen, April 15/27, 1809; N. I. Turgenev to A. I. Turgenev, Göttingen, July 10/22, 1810; N. I. Turgenev, diary entries for November 1810.

92. Lotman and Uspenskii, 185–86, 190–91. Bulich, 1:133–34.

93. Shishkov, *Sobranie,* 2:422–23, 432–34, 437–47, 458–59.

94. Ibid., 459.

95. Ibid., 459, passim.

96. Stoiunin, "Shishkov," pt. 2, 534. Shchebal'skii, 214.

97. Lotman and Uspenskii, 175. Shishkov, *Sobranie,* 2:462.

98. Prince Viazemskii argued that "Shishkov was not so much a conservative as an old believer." Viazemskii, 10:288.

CHAPTER 2:
GOVERNMENT POLICY AND PUBLIC OPINION

1. Khodasevich, 198–99. G. R. Derzhavin, *Zapiski,* 7, 777, 787–88, 812.

2. Derzhavin, *Zapiski,* 811–14. Shil'der, 2:115.

3. See W. Augustine, "Notes Toward a Portrait of the Eighteenth-Century Russian Nobility."

4. Shil'der, 2:53. O. Narkiewicz, "Alexander I and the Senate Reform," 135–36. D. Christian, "The 'Senatorial Party' and the Theory of Collegial Government, 1801–1803," 302–14. Shishkov, *Zapiski, mneniia,* 1:87.

5. Vigel', 1:148–54, 160–61.

6. Marchioness of Londonderry and H. Hyde, eds., *The Russian Journals of Martha and Catherine Wilmot,* 194, Catherine Wilmot to Anna Chetwood, Troitskoe, September 24, 1805. E. Haumant, *La culture française en Russie (1700–1900),* 119–28, 172–82, 189, 196–97. Vigel', 1:96. G. M. Fridlender, ed., *Velikaia frantsuzskaia revoliutsiia i russkaia kul'tura,* 12–14, 69–70. A. G. Cross, "Russian Perceptions of England, and Russian National Awareness at the End of the Eighteenth and the Beginning of the Nineteenth Centuries." L. Ignatieff, "French Emigrés in Russia after the French Revolution. French Tutors."

7. S. N. Glinka, *Zapiski Sergeia Nikolaevicha Glinki,* 194.

8. For examples of this, see J. de Maistre, *Œuvres complètes,* 9:156, letter to Rossi, St. Petersburg, April 18/30, 1804; and Nikolai Mikhailovich, *Imperatritsa Elisaveta Alekseevna, supruga Imperatora Aleksandra I,* 2:125, letter from Elisaveta Alekseevna to her mother, St. Petersburg, April 5/17, 1804.

9. N. I. Kazakov, "Napoleon glazami ego russkikh sovremennikov," 32–40.

10. Maistre, 9:241, letter to Rossi, St. Petersburg, September 28/October 10, 1804.

11. A. I. Mikhailovskii-Danilevskii, quoted in Kazakov, 32.

12. See D. A. Zharinov, "Pervye voiny s Napoleonom i russkoe obshchestvo," *Otechestvennaia voina i russkoe obshchestvo, 1812–1912,* 1:200.

13. See also N. A. Troitskii, *1812: Velikii god Rossii,* 211–12.

14. Zhikharev, 1:117, 131, 133–34, 138, 144, 153, entries for September 7, October 9, 18, 22, November 2, 25, 1805.

15. Shishkov, *Zapiski, mneniia,* 1:95.

16. Zharinov, in *Otechestvennaia voina,* 1:202–3. Maistre, 10:16, letter from de Maistre to Count de Front, January 4/16, 1806. Zhikharev, 1:160, entry for November 30, 1805. Vigel', 1:231, 259. M. Kukiel, *Czartoryski and European Unity 1770–1861,* 70–71. C. von Stedingk, *Mémoires posthumes du feld-maréchal*

Comte de Stedingk, 2:150–51, letter from Stedingk to the king of Sweden, April 8/20, 1806. Zhikharev, 1:222–26, entry for March 4, 1806. Nikolai Mikhailovich, *Elisaveta,* 2:176–77, letter to her mother, St. Petersburg, December 11/23, 1805. Zhikharev, 1:161, entry for December 2, 1805. Haumant, 253–55. See also Eidel'man, *Mgnoven'e,* 217, on the post-Austerlitz revanchism of future Decembrists.

17. Zhikharev, 1:242, entry for May 18, 1806; 2:5, entry for August 25, 1806; 2:6, entry for September 6, 1806.

18. Stedingk, 2:241, letter to the king, October 25/November 4, 1806. On the shock produced in Russia by the Prussian defeat, see Vigel', 1:269–70. F. von Schubert, *Unter dem Doppeladler: Erinnerungen eines Deutschen in russischem Offiziersdienst, 1789–1814,* 93.

19. Bulich, 1:168–71. Shil'der, 2:362–64.

20. Shil'der, 2:364–67. Stedingk, 2:272–73, letter to the king, St. Petersburg, January 29/February 12, 1807.

21. Kazakov, 38–39. See V. G. Sirotkin, "Napoleonovskaia 'voina per'ev' protiv Rossii," and "Russkaia pressa pervoi chetverti XIX veka na inostrannykh iazykakh kak istoricheskii istochnik."

22. See, e.g., Zhikharev, 2:40, entry for November 30, 1806.

23. Zharinov, in *Otechestvennaia voina,* 1:206–10. I. V. Lopukhin, *Zapiski,* 167–88.

24. Quoted in Zharinov, in *Otechestvennaia voina,* 1:207.

25. Shil'der, 2:354–58, 157–58.

26. Maistre, 10:348, letter to Rossi, St. Petersburg, March 9/21, 1807, and 10:362–66, letter to Rossi, March 19/31, 1807. Zhikharev, 2:233, 262, 299. On the dearth of reliable news in Moscow, see D. Obolenskii, ed., *Khronika nedavnei stariny. Iz arkhiva kniazia Obolenskago-Neledinskago-Meletskago,* 72, letter from Iu. A. Neledinskii-Meletskii to E. I. Nelidova, Moscow, March 4, 1807. Stedingk, 2:321–22, 329. Russian Foreign Minister Budberg officially informed Stedingk of the peace terms on August 6, 1807. Ibid., 2:330–31.

27. Shil'der, 2:207.

28. Wilmot, *Russian Journals,* 250–51, 299–300, Catherine Wilmot to Anna Chetwood, St. Petersburg, July 15, 1807, and Martha Wilmot, diary entry, July 18, 1807. N. F. Dubrovin, "Russkaia zhizn' v nachale XIX veka," pt. 1, 488.

29. Shishkov, *Zapiski, mneniia,* 1:95.

30. See Glinka, *Zapiski Glinki,* 182. For Rostopchin's view that Russia was fighting for British interests, see chapter 3 of this study. Batiushkov began hating the Germans even as he was fighting the French. Batiushkov, 2:68, letter to N. I. Gnedich, Riga, March 19, 1807. Vigel' was insulted, in 1806, that Russia had been "hired" by the "proud islanders" to do their fighting. Vigel', 1:259–60. On the public hostility to Bennigsen, the Russian commander in 1807, see Dubrovin, "Russkaia zhizn'," pt. 1, 499–500. See Bonamour, 67, on the touchy nationalism of such young liberals as Nikolai Turgenev.

31. Okun', *Istoriia,* 168. Dubrovin, "Russkaia zhizn'," pt. 1, 493.

32. Quoted in Dubrovin, "Russkaia zhizn'," pt. 8, 478.

33. Quoted in ibid., pt. 1, 508.

34. P. K. Grimsted, *The Foreign Ministers of Alexander I: Political Attitudes and the Conduct of Russian Diplomacy, 1801–1825,* 151–82. K. Stählin, *Geschichte Rußlands von den Anfängen bis zur Gegenwart,* 3:131.

35. On Russian hostility to the alliance policy, see, for example, Al'tshuller, *Predtechi,* 160; Maistre, 11:136–37, 12:60, letters to Rossi, n.d., n.pl., and St. Petersburg, August 15/27, 1811; Vigel', 1:286; Dubrovin, "Russkaia zhizn'," pt. 9, 56.

36. Ch. F. Adams, ed., *John Quincy Adams in Russia, comprising portions of The Diary of John Quincy Adams from 1809 to 1814,* 69, entry for November 16, 1809 (NS). (Dates given according to the Western calendar are identified here as "NS," or New Style.) The diplomat was the Westphalian ambassador Baron Bussche Hunnefeldt. R. Savary, *Memoirs of the Duke of Rovigo, (M. Savary,) Written by Himself: Illustrative of the History of the Emperor Napoleon,* vol. 2, pt. 2, 97–100, 112–13. "Politicheskaia perepiska generala Savari vo vremia prebyvaniia ego v S. -Peterburge v 1807 g.," 41–43, 80, 86, 140, report sent to Paris on August 24, 1807 (NS); Savary to Napoleon, St. Petersburg, September 23, 1807 (NS), and to Champigny, St. Petersburg, October 18, 1807 (NS).

37. Dubrovin, "Russkaia zhizn'," pt. 8, 480–82. M. A. Dodelev, "Rossiia i voina ispanskogo naroda za nezavisimost' (1808–1814)."

38. See, e.g., Dubrovin, "Russkaia zhizn'," pt. 13, 242, Moscow postal director F. P. Kliucharev to Minister of Police A. D. Balashov, January 13, 1810; and Maistre, 11:406, to King Victor Emmanuel, February 26/March 10, 1810.

39. There were forty-five cases of peasant insubordination in 1801–1805 and thirty-eight in 1806–1810. I. Ignatovich, "Krest'ianskie volneniia pervoi chetverti XIX veka," 49, 68.

40. Dubrovin, "Russkaia zhizn'," pt. 1, 507–8.

41. R. Savary, "La cour de Russie en 1807–1808. Notes sur la cour de Russie et Saint-Pétersbourg, écrites en décembre 1807 par le général Savary," 403. On her power struggle with Alexander in 1801, see *Voprosy istorii Rossii XIX–nachala XX veka. Mezhvuzovskii sbornik,* 3–15. On her personality, see Nikolai Mikhailovich, *Elisaveta,* 1:277 and 2:9. Irène de Vries de Gunzburg, *Catherine Pavlovna, Grande-Duchesse de Russie, 1788–1819,* 12–13, 20–21. On her view of Czartoryski, see Nikolai Mikhailovich, *Imperator Aleksandr I. Opyt istoricheskago izsledovaniia,* 1:47, Mariia Fedorovna to Alexander I, April 18, 1806. On her and Konstantin's opposition to Erfurt, see Maistre, 11:137, de Maistre to Rossi, n.pl., n.d.

42. Savary, "La cour de Russie," 404. Nikolai Mikhailovich, *Elisaveta,* 2:9. Obolenskii, 1–80.

43. Savary, "La cour de Russie," 402–3. See also Nikolai Mikhailovich, *Elisaveta,* 2:8, 29–31, and 2:167–68. Elisaveta Alekseevna's letter to her mother, Kamennyi Ostrov, August 1/13, 1805. L. Pingaud, "L'Impératrice Elisabeth

Alexiéivna, d'après des documents nouveaux." E. Amburger, *Geschichte der Behördenorganisation Rußlands von Peter dem Großen bis 1917,* 400. M. Stepanov and F. Vermale, eds., "Zhozef de Mestr v Rossii," 590.

44. Nikolai Mikhailovich, *Elisaveta,* 2:326, letter to her mother, St. Petersburg, April 30/May 12, 1809. Also ibid., 2:215–17.

45. Ibid., 2:256–57, letter to her mother, Kamennyi Ostrov, August 29/September 10, 1807.

46. Vries, 8–9, 30–31. For an example of the captivating impression her appearance made, see Zhikharev, 2:323, entry for May 28, 1807. On her relationship with Elisaveta, see Nikolai Mikhailovich, *Elisaveta,* 2:215.

47. Vries, 28–29.

48. Various diplomats reported such rumors. Stedingk, 2:356, letter to the king, St. Petersburg, September 28/October 10, 1807. Nikolai Mikhailovich, *Aleksandr I,* 1:401–2, Saint-Julien to Metternich, March 29/April 10, 1810. "Politicheskaia perepiska," 58–59, 82, Savary to Napoleon, St. Petersburg, September 9 and 23, 1807 (NS). Caulaincourt is quoted in N. A. Elenev, *Puteshestvie vel. kn. Ekateriny Pavlovny v Bogemiiu v 1813 godu,* 77. Adams, 93, diary entry for January 9, 1810 (NS). Maistre, 11:175, letter to Rossi, St. Petersburg, December 16/28, 1808.

49. S. Bogoiavlenskii, "Imperator Aleksandr I i velikaia kniaginia Ekaterina Pavlovna," in *Tri veka. Rossiia ot smuty do nashego vremeni,* ed. V. V. Kallash, 172–73. Nikolai Mikhailovich, *Correspondance de l'Empereur Alexandre Ier avec sa soeur la Grande-Duchesse Catherine, Princesse d'Oldenbourg, puis Reine de Wurtemberg 1805–1818,* xxii. On the search for a husband, and on Prince Georg, see I. N. Bozherianov, *Velikaia kniaginia Ekaterina Pavlovna, chertvertaia doch' Imperatora Pavla I, gertsoginia ol'denburgskaia, koroleva virtembergskaia, 1788 †1818,* 13–28. For the view that this marriage was a political move for her, see Nikolai Mikhailovich, *Elisaveta,* 2:569, Elisaveta Alekseevna to her mother, St. Petersburg, December 9/21, 1812, continued on December 20, 1812/January 1, 1813. For an enthusiastic description of her, see Maistre, 11:163–64, letter to Rossi, St. Petersburg, November 10/22, 1808.

50. Quoted in Nikolai Mikhailovich, *Elisaveta,* 2:570, Elisaveta Alekseevna to her mother, St. Petersburg, December 9/21, 1812, continued on December 20, 1812/January 1, 1813.

51. Stedingk, 3:97–98, letter to the king, St. Petersburg, May 31/June 12, 1810.

52. A. A. Kizevetter, *Istoricheskie ocherki,* 381. K. Whiting argues that Arakcheev should not be considered "reactionary" since he had no ideological agenda beyond personal loyalty to the monarch. Whiting, "Aleksei Andreevich Arakcheev," 307–22. See also M. Jenkins, *Arakcheev, Grand Vizier of the Russian Empire.*

53. Kizevetter, *Ocherki,* 372–74.

54. Vigel', 1:282–83, 2:5.

55. Maistre, 11:40–41, letter to Rossi, St. Petersburg, January 20/February 1, 1808.

56. V. I. Semevskii, "Padenie Speranskago," *Otechestvennaia voina i russkoe obshchestvo*, 2:227. This is also the source for the Kochubei quotation.

57. For example, he wrote to his sister: "Pray never through the mails if there is anything important in your letters. . . . However, through the *Feldjäger* you can speak to me in all openness. That is the rule that I will also follow." Nikolai Mikhailovich, *Correspondance*, 60, letter to Ekaterina Pavlovna, St. Petersburg, 1811.

58. On Russian propaganda and censorship policies after Tilsit, see Sirotkin, "Napoleonovskaia 'voina per'ev,'" 142, and his "Russkaia pressa," 84–85.

59. See M. Raeff, *Michael Speransky: Statesman of Imperial Russia, 1772–1839*, 1–28, 49.

60. Derzhavin, *Zapiski*, 807. Vigel', 1:154–57.

61. From the memoirs of V. I. Bakunina, quoted in Shil'der, 2:306. On these decrees and the public response to them, see Raeff, *Speransky*, 64–65; Amburger, 55–65; Dubrovin, "Russkaia zhizn'," pt. 10, 262, 267. On the problems of the educational system, see J. T. Flynn, *The University Reform of Tsar Alexander I 1802–1835*, e.g., 73–75.

62. Quoted in Semevskii in *Otechestvennaia voina*, 222.

63. From the memoirs of de Sanglin, quoted in Shil'der, 3:366.

64. On the reform of the ministries by Speranskii, see Raeff, *Speransky*, 108–16. On the broader plans for reform of the central government, see ibid., e.g., 152–53; on his civil law code, 65–70; on his financial reform, 82–105. These reform plans, like those of the "Unofficial Committee," have been the subject of much debate. The thrust of Marc Raeff's highly influential work is that they aimed only to streamline the administration and turn Russia into a *Rechtsstaat*. Other scholars, however, have argued that both the "Unofficial Committee" and Speranskii actually pursued fundamental changes in Russia's social structure and constitutional order. G. Vernadsky, "Reforms under Czar Alexander I: French and American Influences," 53–54. D. Christian, "The Political Views of the Unofficial Committee in 1801: Some New Evidence," 250–51, and "The Political Ideals of Michael Speransky," 203. J. Gooding, "The Liberalism of Michael Speransky," 402–3, and "Speransky and Baten'kov," 400.

65. Dubrovin, "Russkaia zhizn'," pt. 12, 24.

66. Ibid., pt. 11, 458–61.

CHAPTER 3:
THE MOSCOW CONSERVATIVES

1. G. I. S., "Naselenie S. -Peterburga v 1808 g.," 870–72.

2. R. Pipes, *Karamzin's Memoir on Ancient and Modern Russia: A Translation and Analysis*, 19.

3. Viazemskii, 7:82–83.

4. Quoted in ibid., 7:82.

5. Wilmot, *Russian Journals,* 213–19, letter from Catherine Wilmot to her sister Alicia, Moscow, February 18, 1806 (NS).

6. *Entsiklopedicheskii slovar',* s.v. "Klub." Zhikharev, 1:194, 1:291, entry for January 23, 1806, and editor's note.

7. *Entsiklopedicheskii slovar',* s.v. "Moskva."

8. Vigel', 1:116.

9. Viazemskii, 7:84.

10. Vigel', 1:116–17.

11. Viazemskii, 7:83–84.

12. See also Dubrovin, "Russkaia zhizn'," pt. 3, 244–47, 263–64. Raeff, *Speransky,* 171.

13. The most thorough biography of Rostopchin appears to be A. El'nitskii, "Rostopchin, graf Feodor Vasil'evich," in *Russkii biograficheskii slovar'.*

14. Viazemskii, 7:501, 504.

15. Nikolai Mikhailovich, *Elisaveta,* 2:627, letter to her mother, Kamennyi Ostrov, June 12/24, 1816. K. A. Varnhagen von Ense, *Werke in fünf Bänden,* 3:138. See also the discussion of Rostopchin's personality and family life in D. Schlafly, "The Rostopchins and Roman Catholicism in Early Nineteenth Century Russia," 49–58.

16. A. F. Rostopchin, ed., *Matériaux en grande partie inédits pour la biographie future du Comte Théodore Rastaptchine, rassemblés par son fils,* 480, Rostopchin to P. D. Tsitsianov, Voronovo, April 15, 1804. *Arkhiv kniazia Vorontsova,* 8:53–54, 76–77, 93–94, 112, 135–36, letters to S. R. Vorontsov, St. Petersburg, July 8, 1792; July 6, 1793; May 28, 1794; September 14, 1795; February 22, 1796. El'nitskii, in *Russkii biograficheskii slovar',* 240–44. A. A. Kizevetter, *Istoricheskie otkliki,* 67–71. V. N. Golovina, *Souvenirs de la Comtesse Golovine née Princesse Galitsine 1766–1821,* 94–95.

17. "I have never believed that Russia needed to fear any French government. The distance between the two countries, the gigantic strengths of our empire, its physical location and the aegis it presents to other sovereigns are so many guarantees of its commanding existence. It has nothing to fear from coalitions." *Arkhiv kniazia Vorontsova,* 8:288–89, Rostopchin to S. R. Vorontsov, Voronovo, June 30, 1801.

18. M. de la Fuye, "Rostoptchine, Chancelier du Tzar Paul Ier," 13. "A Russian don Quixote" was Napoleon's description of Paul. Eidel'man, *Mgnoven'e,* 179. See also Kizevetter, *Otkliki,* 82; R. E. McGrew, *Paul I of Russia 1754–1801,* 315–16; H. Ragsdale, *Détente in the Napoleonic Era: Bonaparte and the Russians,* 36–40, 118–19; and M. de la Fuye, *Rostoptchine: Européen ou slave?* 87, 92. This entertaining book reveals more about French views of Rostopchin and "Slavs" in general than about the count himself, and never answers the intriguing question posed in the title.

19. Fuye, "Rostoptchine," 14. On his activities under Paul, see El'nitskii, in *Russkii biograficheskii slovar'*, 244–57; D. N. Bantysh-Kamenskii, *Slovar' dostopamiatnykh liudei russkoi zemli*, vol. 3 (1847), 110–20; Kizevetter, *Otkliki*, 72–82.

20. Jenkins, 74–80. El'nitskii, in *Russkii biograficheskii slovar'*, 256–57.

21. A. F. Rostopchin, *Matériaux*, 463–64, 495, letters to P. D. Tsitsianov, Voronovo, September 17, 1803, and October 25, 1804. *Arkhiv kniazia Vorontsova*, 8:298, 294, letters to S. R. Vorontsov, Voronovo, January 15, 1802, and November 10, 1801.

22. A. F. Rostopchin, *Matériaux*, 470, 489, 475, Voronovo, December 2, 1803; Kozmodemiansk, July 8, 1804; and Voronovo, February 4, 1804. *Arkhiv kniazia Vorontsova*, 8:299, letter to S. R. Vorontsov, Voronovo, July 3, 1802.

23. *Arkhiv kniazia Vorontsova*, 8:307–8, Voronovo, August 23, 1803.

24. Ibid., 8:295, 292, letters to S. R. Vorontsov, Voronovo, November 10 and June 30, 1801. Bulich, 1:186–87.

25. Quoted in R. B. Holtman, *The Napoleonic Revolution*, 123.

26. *Arkhiv kniazia Vorontsova*, 8:96, letter to S. R. Vorontsov, St. Petersburg, May 28, 1794.

27. Ibid., 8:466, letter to A. R. Vorontsov, Voronovo, August 23, 1803.

28. A. F. Rostopchin, *Matériaux*, 479, 484, 485, letters to Tsitsianov, Voronovo, March 30, May 26, and June 12, 1804.

29. Quoted in Haumant, 252.

30. *Arkhiv kniazia Vorontsova*, 8:308, letter to S. R. Vorontsov, Voronovo, August 23, 1803.

31. A. F. Rostopchin, *Matériaux*, 507–8, Voronovo, March 20 [1805].

32. Fuye, "Rostoptchine," 2.

33. L. Rostoptchine, *Les Rostoptchine*, 28. Wilmot, *Russian Journals*, 105–6, diary entry for June 12, 1804 (NS). See also p. 144, entry for June 21, 1805 (NS). Bulich, 1:186, 188. Bantysh-Kamenskii, 114.

34. B. L. Modzalevskii, ed., "Pis'ma grafa F. V. Rostopchina k A. F. Labzinu," 419–20, 422–25; letters of Gatchina, October 8, 1800; Voronovo, June 21 [1804]; Moscow, December 22 [1810] and January 12, 1811. N. S. Tikhonravov, *Sochineniia*, vol. 3, pt. 1, 322. G. Vernadskij, "Le césarévitch Paul et les francmaçons de Moscou," 277–85.

35. F. V. Rostopchin, "Zapiska o Martinistakh, predstavlennaia v 1811 godu grafom Rostopchinym velikoi kniagine Ekaterine Pavlovne," 78–79.

36. B. L. Modzalevskii, ed., "K biografii Novikova. Pis'ma ego k Labzinu, Chebotarevu i dr. 1797–1815," pt. 1, 21–22, Novikov to Labzin, Tikhvinskoe, n.d. [1799–early 1800s].

37. Ibid., pt 2, 21, 25–26, Novikov to Labzin, Tikhvinskoe, February 12, 1804; copy of a letter from Rostopchin to Novikov, Voronovo, March 21, 1804; Novikov to Labzin, Tikhvinskoe, April 18 and May 2, 1804. Modzalevskii, "Pis'ma k Labzinu," 421–22, Voronovo, March 27 [1804]. The date of this letter

is incorrectly given as 1802 (pointed out in a note to Modzalevskii, "K biografii Novikova," pt. 2, 24). See also S. P. Mel'gunov's review of the Novikov-Labzin correspondence published by Modzalevskii ("Eshche o Rostopchine," 239–40, reprinted in Mel'gunov's *Dela i liudi aleksandrovskogo vremeni,* vol. 1).

38. Zhikharev, 1:148, entry for November 12, 1805. A. F. Rostopchin, *Matériaux,* 521, letter to Tsitsianov, Moscow, December 15, 1805.

39. A. F. Rostopchin, *Matériaux,* 525, letter to Tsitsianov, Voronovo, January 24, 1806.

40. El'nitskii, in *Russkii biograficheskii slovar',* 257. Mel'gunov, *Dela i liudi,* 129.

41. Kizevetter, *Otkliki,* 146–49.

42. "Pis'ma grafa F. V. Rastopchina k Imperatoru Aleksandru Pavlovichu," 419–20.

43. "Reskript Aleksandra I grafu Rostopchinu po povodu pis'ma ego o slukhakh i bezporiadkakh v provintsii," 634, letter dated January 2, 1807.

44. Kizevetter, *Otkliki,* 149.

45. Lopukhin, 171, 180. Alexander's letter was dated January 16, 1807. On Lopukhin, see also A. Lipski, "A Russian Mystic Faces the Age of Rationalism and Revolution: Thought and Activity of Ivan Vladimirovich Lopukhin."

46. Bonamour, 54.

47. "Mysli vslukh na krasnom kryl'tse," in F. V. Rostopchin, *Sochineniia Rastopchina (grafa Feodora Vasil'evicha),* 5–18.

48. Bulich, 1:190. G. D. Ovchinnikov, "'I dyshit umom i iumorom togo vremeni . . .' (O literaturnoi reputatsiei F. V. Rastopchina)," 151.

49. Dmitriev, *Melochi,* 241.

50. A. F. Rostopchin, *Matériaux,* 431, letter of April 15, 1807. *Entsiklopedicheskii slovar',* s.v. "Klub."

51. B. N. Bochkarev, "Konservatory i natsionalisty v Rossii v nachale XIX v.," *Otechestvennaia voina i russkoe obshchestvo,* 2:206. J. D. Popkin, "Journals: The New Face of News," in *Revolution in Print: The Press in France 1775–1800,* ed. R. Darnton and D. Roche, 335.

52. El'nitskii, in *Russkii biograficheskii slovar',* 260. Glinka later wrote that *Thoughts Aloud* "spread to both mansions and huts and was almost like a harbinger of the great year 1812." Glinka, *Zapiski Glinki,* 223.

53. F. Furet and D. Richet, *La Révolution française,* 216.

54. Rostopchin, *Sochineniia Rastopchina,* 255–98.

55. K. Pokrovskii, "Graf F. V. Rastopchin i ego komediia 'Vesti ili Ubityi zhivoi,'" 19. Kizevetter, *Otkliki,* 103–6. S. P. Mel'gunov, "Kritika i bibliografiia. *A. Kizevetter. Istoricheskie ocherki,*" 410. The book being reviewed was actually *Istoricheskie otkliki; Istoricheskie ocherki* was an earlier work by Kizevetter.

56. The cult of the ancient martyr St. Mauritius (generally believed to have been a black African) was popular across early modern northeastern Germany, and the "black-head corporations" *(Schwarzenhäuptervereinigungen)* that Baltic

Germans formed in his honor survived long after the Middle Ages as honorary guilds for young, unmarried merchants. Russians who traded with the Baltic Germans may have noticed this custom and, perhaps, mockingly associated a "Moor's head" with Germans in general. For this information I thank Tapio Salminen, who cites Paul Johansen and Heinz von zur Mühlen, *Deutsch und Undeutsch im mittelalterlichen und frühneuzeitlichen Reval* (Cologne 1973), 66. I also thank Michael Harscheidt and Hans-Martin Moderow for their assistance in this question.

57. Rostopchin had demonstratively failed to include Bennigsen in the pantheon of Russian military leaders glorified in *Thoughts Aloud,* and he was dismayed when Shishkov added the general's name in his version of *Thoughts Aloud.* El'nitskii, in *Russkii biograficheskii slovar'*, 260.

58. Rostopchin, "Vesti, ili Ubityi zhivoi," in *Sochineniia Rastopchina,* 40–42, 60–61.

59. Memoirs of N. V. Sushkov, quoted in Ovchinnikov, 152.

60. A. M. Gordin, *Pushkinskii Peterburg,* 38.

61. Glinka, *Zapiski Glinki,* 234. Rostopchin, "Pis'mo Venikova k Sile Andreevichu Bogatyrevu," in *Sochineniia Rastopchina,* 137–38. For details on the people who felt insulted by the play, see Pokrovskii, "Rastopchin," 9–11.

62. "Oh, les Français! Histoire tirée des faits modernes," in A. F. Rostopchin, *Matériaux,* 74–75.

63. *Arkhiv kniazia Vorontsova,* 8:139, letter to S. R. Vorontsov, Sophie, May 1796.

64. Bochkarev in *Otechestvennaia voina,* 208. Bulich, 1:174–79. Al'tshuller, *Predtechi,* 140–44.

65. Glinka, *Zapiski Glinki,* 221–22.

66. See Lotman, 335–38, on this aspect of the Decembrists' psychology.

67. Glinka, *Zapiski Glinki,* 1–25.

68. See J. L. Black, *Citizens for the Fatherland: Education, Educators, and Pedagogical Ideals in Eighteenth Century Russia,* 77–83; A. N. Eroshkina, "Deiatel' epokhi prosveshchennogo absoliutizma I. I. Betskoi"; and Lotman, 79.

69. Schama, 380.

70. Among the Decembrists and their friends educated at the cadet corps were Kondratii F. Ryleev, Andrei E. Rozen, Fedor N. Glinka (Sergei's brother), and various others. See N. N. Aurova, "Idei prosveshcheniia v 1-m kadetskom korpuse (konets XVIII–pervaia chetvert' XIX v.)."

71. Glinka, *Zapiski Glinki,* 63, 66. Glinka's articles in his *Russian Messenger* frequently cite Russian folk sayings as evidence of the Russian people's profound, intuitive wisdom. (See, e.g., *Ruskoi Vestnik* [July 1811]: 16–43.) Glinka also repeatedly makes allusions to names from Greek and Roman history, usually to suggest that particular figures from the Kievan or Muscovite past were comparable to them in virtue and greatness.

72. Glinka, *Zapiski Glinki,* 116–17, 40–41, 112–13.

73. RGIA, 777/1/876, ll. 35 ob–36.

74. See Eidel'man, *Mgnoven'e,* 147–49.

75. Glinka, *Zapiski Glinki,* 127–36, 142.

76. Ibid., 146, 153–64, 175.

77. Ibid., 166, 175, 182, 194.

78. RGIA, 777/1/876, ll. 35 ob–36.

79. Glinka, *Zapiski Glinki,* 177–79, 184.

80. Ibid., 184–93. For a survey of his writings, see *Russkii biograficheskii slovar',* s.v. "Glinka, Sergei Nikolaevich."

81. Glinka, *Zapiski Glinki,* 195–96, 211, 216–17, 203. A letter he wrote on January 29, 1807, to D. P. Runich from Smolensk province, shows the relationship he saw between his writing and his militia service: "'I behold the troubled time of our fatherland's [word illegible] / My friend! how onerous it is to take on this life's burden!' This voice of my Mikhail is also the voice of my heart. As long as we are not told: 'Be at rest!,' until then I shall see neither Moscow nor Petersburg. . . . O, cara Patria!" (RNB, 656/13, ll. 3–3 ob).

82. Glinka, *Zapiski Glinki,* 204.

83. Schama, 168, 379.

84. Derzhavin, *Zapiski,* 6:202, Glinka to Derzhavin, Moscow, March 21, 1807.

85. Bochkarev in *Otechestvennaia voina,* 209–10. I. V. Popov, "Preddekabristskaia publitsisticheskaia kritika o patriotizme," in *Pisatel' i kritika. XIX vek: Mezhvuzovskii sbornik nauchnykh trudov,* ed. I. V. Popov, 5–9. See also F. A. Walker's highly interesting article, "Reaction and Radicalism in the Russia of Tsar Alexander I: The Case of the Brothers Glinka."

86. A contribution by Rostopchin to the first issue of the *Russian Messenger,* a pseudonymous letter to the editor written in the spirit of *Thoughts Aloud,* is reproduced in Tikhonravov, vol. 3, pt. 1, 371–72.

87. Glinka, *Zapiski Glinki,* 220–26.

88. *Ruskoi Vestnik,* no. 3 (1808): 42, quoted in Bulich, 1:213. To appreciate the pervasiveness of these themes—the glories of pre-Petrine morals and culture (Glinka approvingly quoted Shishkov's writings on language) and the idyllic relationship between peasants and lords whose Russian virtues had not been corrupted by the West—in Glinka's works, consider the references to them in just the first two issues of the *Russian Messenger* for 1811: January, 3–24 ("Luk'ian Stepanovich Streshnev"), 31–49 ("Otryvki o vnutrennei promyshlennosti i o snoshenii onoi s nravstvennost'iu"), 56–71 ("Pouchitel'naia Gramota Tsaria Alekseia Mikhailovicha . . . o Bozhiem gneve i ob uchrezhdenii posta"), 91–104 ("O vospominanii velikikh Muzhei"), 105–16 ("Mysli Ippolita Fedorovicha Bogdanovicha o Slavianakh"); February, 1–27 ("Nravstvennyia svoistva Tsaria Feodora Alekseevicha"), 28–34 ("Derevenskaia chestnost'"), 35–52 ("Mysli o perevode K. B. G., s primechaniiami Izdatelia R. Vestnika"), 52–62 ("Poslanie k Chinovniku-poselianinu"), 62–80 ("Vypiski i zamechaniia iz khitrosti ratnago

dela, ili Voinskago Ustava, izdannago v tsarstvovanie Tsaria Alekseia Mikhailovicha, 1647 goda"), 81–90 ("Ot'ezd *Mody* iz Moskvy, ili perepiska Mody so Vkusom"), 91–107 ("Blagodeianie"), 108–26 ("Zamechaniia na odno mesto iz knigi: Sravnenie svoistv i del Konstantina Velikago s svoistvami i delami Petra Velikago"). Even when he discussed Peter the Great, Glinka usually stressed his loyalty to Muscovite tradition.

89. Bulich, 1:212–16. Popov, 7–9.

90. For examples of this phenomenon, see Dmitriev, *Melochi,* 103, and Viazemskii, 2:337. The conservative historian Pogodin later wrote to Glinka: "Your *Russian Messenger* of 1808 . . . awakened in me the first feeling of love for the fatherland, the Russian feeling, and I am eternally grateful to you." Ibid.

91. *Ruskoi Vestnik,* no. 1 (1811), continued in no. 2 (1812).

92. Bulich, 1:211–12.

93. *Ruskoi Vestnik,* nos. 3 (March 1813), 6 (June 1813), 11 (November 1813), 12 (December 1813).

94. Orel, Kaluga, Tula, Riazan', Tambov, Penza, Khar'kov, Voronezh, and Kursk (based on the provincial boundaries of 1850).

95. A. V. Zapadov, ed., *Istoriia russkoi zhurnalistiki XVIII–XIX vekov,* 100–101, 119–20.

96. Batiushkov, 2:17 and 2:111, notebook for 1810–1811 and letter to N. I. Gnedich, Khantonovo, November 1, 1809. V. A. Zhukovskii, *Sobranie sochinenii v 4–kh tomakh,* 4:481, letter to A. I. Turgenev, Belev, December 4, 1810.

97. Vigel', 1:346. Viazemskii also noted the *Russian Messenger*'s popularity among provincial readers. Viazemskii, 2:338. Shishkov, *Zapiski, mneniia,* 2:319, Shishkov to Bardovskii, St. Petersburg, July 19, 1811.

98. Glinka, *Zapiski Glinki,* 229–35, 239–52.

99. S. N. Glinka, *Zerkalo novago Parizha, ot 1789 do 1809 goda.* These two volumes actually cover only the period until the Terror; it is not clear whether the projected four subsequent volumes were ever written.

100. Glinka, *Zerkalo,* 1:1.

101. Ibid., 2:11, 1:22, 2:6, 1:32–33.

102. Ibid., 1:73–76, 116–17, 132–34, 1:55, 1:98–99, 2:43, 2:94–96.

103. Ibid., 2:22–27, 37, unpaginated preface.

104. See A. G. Cross, "Karamzin Studies: For the Bicentenary of the Birth of N. M. Karamzin (1766–1966)." Some of the most valuable monographs in Western languages are J. L. Black, *Nicholas Karamzin and Russian Society in the Nineteenth Century: A Study in Russian Political and Historical Thought;* W. Mitter, "Die Entstehung der politischen Anschauungen Karamzins"; Pipes, *Karamzin's Memoir;* and Cross, *Karamzin.*

105. Pipes, *Karamzin's Memoir,* 31–32. See also L. G. Kisliagina's "The Question of the Development of N. M. Karamzin's Social Political Views in the Nineties of the Eighteenth Century," in J. L. Black, ed., *Essays on Karamzin: Russian Man-of-Letters, Political Thinker, Historian, 1766–1826,* 91–104.

106. Iu. M. Lotman, "Politicheskoe myshlenie Radishcheva i Karamzina i opyt frantsuzskoi revoliutsii," in Fridlender, ed., *Velikaia frantsuzskaia revoliutsiia,* 59–66. For another interesting discussion of this subject, see G. Dudek, "Die Französische Revolution im Urteil N. M. Karamzins" (Viazemskii is quoted on 350). Mitter, 202.

107. Pipes, *Karamzin's Memoir,* 45. R. Pipes, "Karamzin's Conception of the Monarchy," passim. Cross, *Karamzin,* 205–10. Mitter, 213–24.

108. A. G. Cross, "Karamzin and England."

109. Mitter, 230–34. Cross, *Karamzin,* 210–15. J. L. Black, "N. M. Karamzin, Napoleon, and the Notion of Defensive War in Russian History."

110. The generalizations about Karamzin's and Rostopchin's thinking that I make in the remainder of this chapter are based in part on the writings of the two men I discuss in the following chapter.

111. Al'tshuller, *Predtechi,* 41–45. Pipes, *Karamzin's Memoir,* 51.

112. Ibid., 33, 89.

113. Raeff, "Les Slaves," 550.

114. A. A. Kizevetter, "N. M. Karamzin," 25. The similarities and differences between Karamzin's and Speranskii's views have been much discussed. See Shil'der, 3:34; Pipes, *Karamzin's Memoir,* 84; A. N. Pypin, *Izsledovaniia i stat'i po epokhe Aleksandra I,* vol. 3, *Obshchestvennoe dvizhenie v Rossii pri Aleksandre I,* 277; Black, *Karamzin,* 79–80.

CHAPTER 4:
THE "DEMIGODDESS OF TVER'" AND THE "LOVERS OF THE RUSSIAN WORD"

1. For an idyllic description of their conjugal life, see Bozherianov, 45–48.

2. E. A. Pushkin, ed., *Pis'ma velikoi kniagini Ekateriny Pavlovny,* 9–11 (quotation from Alexander I), 73, letter to Karamzin, Stuttgart, November 1/13, 1818. Vries, 44–46, 50. F. P. Lubianovskii, "Vospominaniia," 504. Bozherianov, 44, 46. Black, *Karamzin,* 73. Did these comings and goings reflect her political ambitions? Bogoiavlenskii (175) and Pipes (*Karamzin's Memoir,* 69) both assert this. Vries argues that she was merely seeking to relieve the boredom of provincial life.

3. "Pis'mo grafa F. V. Rostopchina k velikoi kniagine Ekaterine Pavlovne," 374, Moscow, April 14, 1810. Lubianovskii, 502. *Arkhiv kniazia Vorontsova,* 8:360, Rostopchin to S. R. Vorontsov, Paris, January 26, 1819.

4. "Tri pis'ma grafa F. V. Rostopchina k Velikoi Kniagine Ekaterine Pavlovne," 759, Moscow, March 24, 1810 (also quoted in Bozherianov, 31).

5. El'nitskii, in *Russkii biograficheskii slovar',* 261.

6. Maistre, 11:402, letter to King Victor Emmanuel, St. Petersburg, February 21/March 5, 1810. Nikolai Mikhailovich, *Aleksandr I,* 2:720. Maistre, 11:416, letter to King Victor Emmanuel, [St. Petersburg] February 26/March 10, 1810. El'nitskii, in *Russkii biograficheskii slovar',* 261. On the failure of Rostopchin's

comeback, see Maistre, 11:493, letter to Rossi, St. Petersburg, September 14/26, 1810.

7. Bozherianov, 37. Pushkin, *Pis'ma,* 5. Pipes, *Karamzin's Memoir,* 70.

8. She is quoted in Pushkin, *Pis'ma,* 9. Lubianovskii, 501–3.

9. Pushkin, *Pis'ma,* 43, 45, 38, 40, 51, 55–56, letters to Karamzin, Tver', July 3, 14, April 25, May 25, October 13, 1811, and January 4, 1812. Bozherianov, 43. See also her letters in N. M. Karamzin, *Neizdannyia sochineniia i perepiska,* 1:87–124.

10. *Pis'ma N. M. Karamzina k I. I. Dmitrievu,* ed. Ia. Grot and P. Pekarskii, 149, 137, Tver', June 3, and Moscow, February 19, 1811.

11. Pipes, *Karamzin's Memoir,* 70–71. Mitter, 259–62. Black, *Karamzin,* 73.

12. Pipes, *Karamzin's Memoir,* 70–75.

13. Ibid., 75–86. Mitter, 236–58. Black, *Karamzin,* 73–78.

14. Pipes, *Karamzin's Memoir,* 110–11.

15. Ibid., 104–5, 111, 120.

16. Walicki, *Controversy,* 21–22.

17. Pipes, *Karamzin's Memoir,* 120–24.

18. Ibid., 130–37.

19. Ibid., 139, 147–56.

20. Ibid., 141–47.

21. Ibid., 156–61, 167–82.

22. Ibid., 162–67.

23. Ibid., 182–90.

24. Ibid., 101, 192–200.

25. Ibid., 204–5, 140.

26. Pypin, 309–10. Mel'gunov argues that Rostopchin's campaign against the freemasons reflected mainly his political opportunism but that he had also been aroused against them by his Jesuit acquaintances. *Dela i liudi,* 134. On the Illuminati, see Epstein, 87–104.

27. Letter from Rostopchin to Ekaterina, Moscow, April 14, 1810, p. 374. On her view of freemasons as honest and pious, see her letter to Alexander I, Tver', February 8, 1810, in Nikolai Mikhailovich, *Correspondance,* 28. Alexander mentions freemasonry in ibid., 60, Alexander to Ekaterina, St. Petersburg, December 18, 1811, which Semevskii (in *Otechestvennaia voina,* 231) cites as proof that she sent him the *Memorandum.* The editors of *Russkii Arkhiv* give 1811 as the date of the *Memorandum;* there is neither an explicit date nor any internal evidence, although the absence of references to the state investigation of freemasonry in 1810–1811 suggests that it may have been written earlier. Perhaps they, and Semevskii, were unaware of the 1810 Rostopchin letter and used as evidence the 1811 letter from the tsar, or they had other evidence. Or, possibly, the letter from Rostopchin to Ekaterina was written in 1811 and misdated in *Russkii Arkhiv* as 1810.

28. J. Herrero, *Los orígenes del pensamiento reaccionario español,* 35–45,

183–218. A. Elorza, "Hacia una tipología del pensamiento reaccionario en los orígenes de la España contemporánea," 374. Epstein, 503–4.

29. ARAN, 100/1/198, ll. 483–483 ob. This document does not identify the intended reader and gives only the name and rank of the author; but Polev wrote two memoranda to Alexander I in 1812, which describe him as an officer of the emperor's suite. RGVIA, 474/1/1223. On Speranskii, see *Masonstvo v ego proshlom i nastoiashchem,* ed. S. P. Mel'gunov and P. I. Sidorov, 2:176.

30. Ibid., 2:176–181.

31. Rostopchin, "Zapiska o Martinistakh," 75–77. On the Rosicrucians, see Epstein, 104–11. E. I. Tarasov (Mel'gunov and Sidorov, 2:1) lists sixteen members of Novikov and Schwarz's Moscow Rosicrucian lodge and adds that there were "several other" members.

32. Rostopchin, "Zapiska o Martinistakh," 78–79. Mel'gunov and Sidorov, 2:150. Kizevetter, *Otkliki,* 86–87.

33. Rostopchin, "Zapiska o Martinistakh," 80–81.

34. Nikolai Mikhailovich, *Correspondance,* 30, editor's note, and 34, Alexander to Ekaterina, Tsarskoe Selo, June 27, 1810.

35. Modzalevskii, "Pis'ma k Labzinu," 428, Moscow, June 12 [1811].

36. *Arkhiv brat' ev Turgenevykh,* 3:433–34, editor's note.

37. A. F. Rostopchin, *Matériaux,* 436.

38. F. V. Rostopchin, "Zamechanie grafa F. V. Rastopchina na knigu g-na Stroinovskago," 203–16.

39. A. F. Rostopchin, *Matériaux,* 437, Golovin to Rostopchin, St. Petersburg, October 23, 1811. See Rostopchin, "Zamechanie," 193 (editor's note), on the difficulty of identifying which of several extant manuscripts on this subject was written by Rostopchin.

40. *Ostaf' evskii Arkhiv kniazei Viazemskikh,* 1:530, editor's note.

41. *Arkhiv brat' ev Turgenevykh,* 3:191–92, diary entry, Moscow, April 9, 1812.

42. M. Confino, "Le paysan russe jugé par la noblesse au XVIIIe siècle," 51–63. See also J. -L. van Regemorter, "Deux images idéales de la paysannerie russe à la fin du XVIIIe siècle."

43. Anon., "1811. Vozrazhenie neizvestnago na knigu, sochinennuiu grafom Stroinovskim, *O usloviiakh s krest' ianami,*" 195–202. Another version was published as "Vozrazhenie kniazia Volodimira Mikhailovicha Volkonskago na knigu: 'O usloviiakh pomeshchikov s ikh krest'ianami, soch. grafa Stroinovskago, 1811 goda.'" Turgenev's comments on Rostopchin suggest he may have been referring to Volkonskii's text; both circulated as anonymous manuscripts, so confusion was possible. It is clear from internal evidence that "Zamechanie grafa Rastopchina" was written by Rostopchin and "Vozrazhenie neizvestnago" by someone else. See "O grafe F. V. Rostopchine i o sobytiiakh 1812 goda v Moskve," esp. 181–82, on the question of Rostopchin's authorship.

44. El'nitskii, in *Russkii biograficheskii slovar',* 262.

45. "Pis'mo grafa Rostopchina k imperatoru Aleksandru I-mu s donosom na Speranskago." The letter is dated March 17, 1812. A. Vasil'ev, "Progressivnyi podokhodnyi nalog 1812 g. i padenie Speranskago." RGIA, 1163/16/5, ll. 5–5 ob.

46. One of Ekaterina's biographers argues that "Rostopchin's influence on the grand duchess" has been "exaggerated." Vries, 49–50.

47. Nikolai Mikhailovich, *Correspondance,* 19, letter from Ekaterina Pavlovna to Alexander, June 25, 1807.

48. Ibid., 36, 51–52, Alexander to Ekaterina, December 26, 1810, and July 5, 1811. They met in Tver' in early December 1809, May 29–June 6, 1810, and March 14–26, 1811, as well as several times in St. Petersburg. Ibid., 30, editor's note. Other sources suggest that his 1811 visit lasted from March 15–19. Bozherianov, 38.

49. Semevskii (in *Otechestvennaia voina,* 224) suspects that she did.

50. As the tsar told de Sanglin, from "Rostopchin's report about the rumors in Moscow I see that they hate Speranskii there and they suppose that, in the institutions of the ministries and the Council, he was cunningly intriguing against the autocracy" (Semevskii in *Otechestvennaia voina,* 231–32).

51. Bogoiavlenskii, 178. Razumovskii was appointed on April 11, a few weeks after Alexander received Karamzin's *Memoir.* It is not clear whether the two events were related.

52. Semevskii in *Otechestvennaia voina,* 224–25. This is the source for the quotation by Rostopchin about Speranskii. Semevskii cites Lubianovskii's memoirs as the source for Ekaterina's and Georg's remarks on Speranskii.

53. Mel'gunov, *Dela i liudi,* 98–101.

54. M. M. Safonov and E. N. Filippova: "Krest'ianskii vopros v zapiskakh M. M. Filosofova" (in *Voprosy istorii Rossii,* 15–24) and "Neizvestnyi dokument po istorii obshchestvenno-politicheskoi mysli Rossii nachala XIX v."

55. Vries, 49.

56. Nikolai Mikhailovich, *Correspondance,* 9–17.

57. Shishkov, *Zapiski, mneniia,* 1:87, 95.

58. Zhikharev, 2:199, entry for March 18, 1807. Sukhomlinov, *Istoriia,* 7:189–96, 235–36, 557. Kochubinskii, 39–54. Khodasevich, 211–12.

59. For his biography, see D. I. Khvostov, "Iz arkhiva Khvostova," 361.

60. Amburger, 112, 192, 194.

61. Khodasevich, 210.

62. Amburger, 528, 554

63. On the involvement of Labzin's lodge with Shishkov's group, see "Zhurnaly 'Besedy liubitelei russkogo slova'" in V. A. Desnitskii, *Izbrannye stat'i po russkoi literature XVIII–XIX vv.,* 108–9. Zhikharev, 2:117, entry for February 3, 1807, has a list of the people attending the meeting. AIRLI, 263/2/216, ll. 3–4, Labzin to D. P. Runich, St. Petersburg, January 9/20, 1798, mentions Shishkov.

64. Zhikharev, 2:139, 140–41, 177–78, 197, 206, 279. Entries for February 17, March 10, 17, 24 and May 5, 1807.

65. Khvostov, 359.

66. I was unable to determine the years of birth of Rezanov and Iazvitskii. The others: P. V. Zavadovskii, 1739; S. L. L'vov, 1742; S. K. Viazmitinov, 1748; S. I. Salagov, 1756; D. P. Gorchakov, 1758; A. N. Olenin, 1763; P. I. Sokolov, 1764; P. M. Karabanov, 1764; A. F. Labzin, 1766; I. A. Krylov, 1768; P. Iu. L'vov, 1770; P. A. Kikin, 1775; Ia. A. Galinkovskii, 1777; M. S. Shulepnikov, 1778; A. A. Pisarev, 1780; V. F. Timkovskii, 1781; S. A. Shirinskii-Shikhmatov, 1783; N. I. Gnedich, 1784; S. P. Zhikharev, 1788; P. A. Korsakov, 1790. Birth dates are given in the index at the end of Zhikharev, vol. 2.

67. See Sukhomlinov, *Istoriia,* 7:444–65.

68. Zhikharev, 2:109, 208, entries for January 24 and March 24, 1807. Stoiunin, "Shishkov," pt. 2, 525–28.

69. Zhikharev, 2:139, 117–20, entries for February 17 and 3, 1807. See also 1:26, introduction by M. A. Gordin.

70. This discontent was manifested with particular vehemence at the theater. For an evocative description of the response to Ozerov's *Dmitrii Donskoi,* for example, see A. S. Sturdza, "Beseda liubitelei russkago slova i *Arzamas,* v tsarstvovanie Aleksandra I-go i moi vospominaniia," 6. On Shishkov's ambivalent view of the play, see L. P. Sidorova, "Rukopisnye zamechaniia sovremennika na pervom izdanii tragedii V. A. Ozerova 'Dmitrii Donskoi.'" On the nationalist theater of the time, especially by playwrights associated with Shishkov, see Al'tshuller, *Predtechi,* 137–67.

71. Bulich, 1:220–31. Stoiunin, "Shishkov," pt. 2, 537.

72. Aksakov, 2:302. *Entsiklopedicheskii slovar',* s.v. "Mordvinov (graf Nikolai Semenovich, 1754–1845)."

73. Al'tshuller, *Predtechi,* 163.

74. Shishkov, *Zapiski, mneniia,* 1:114–15. RGAVMF, 166/1/2669, ll. 1–3, Shishkov to Ivan Ivanovich [de-Traverse], St. Petersburg, August 31, 1810; letter to Shishkov (no author indicated), n.pl., September 12, 1810.

75. Vigel', 1:359–60.

76. The list of members is printed in Al'tshuller, *Predtechi,* 365–70.

77. Vigel', 1:360–61.

78. Al'tshuller, *Predtechi,* 51, 98.

79. Ibid., 52. The writers of the New Style, who enjoyed ridiculing the Symposium, strongly influenced its image in subsequent scholarship. Al'tshuller's important study seeks to rectify that distorted perception.

80. Khodasevich, 233. Sturdza believed, but was not certain, that he had seen Karamzin at Symposium functions. Sturdza, "Beseda," 5.

81. Al'tshuller, *Predtechi,* 52. Khvostov, 368, entry for late January–early February 1811. Desnitskii, 109, entry for February 21, 1811.

82. Ibid., 112, entry for March 14 [1811]. Khvostov, 369, entry for March 1811. Sturdza, "Beseda," 5–6. Serbinovich is quoted in "Aleksandr Semenovich Shishkov i dve vsepoddanneishiia ego zapiski," 574.

83. Shishkov, *Zapiski, mneniia,* 1:116.

84. Bulich, 1:231–33.

85. Shishkov, *Sobranie,* 4:108–46.

86. Shishkov, *Zapiski, mneniia,* 1:116–17. The subscription is mentioned by Khvostov, 369, entry for March 1811.

87. Shishkov, *Zapiski, mneniia,* 1:117.

88. AIRLI 358/1/216, letter to his niece.

89. Khvostov, 372, 364, entries for April 1811 and November 1810. Desnitskii, 127–28, entries for February 11 and 23, 1812.

90. Ibid., 114, entry for April 10, 1811. RNB, 143/115, ll. 1–2, letters from Shishkov to G. I. Villamov, April 18 and 22, 1811. Khvostov, 371–72, entry for April 1811.

91. Vigel', 1:360. *Arkhiv brat'ev Turgenevykh,* 2:436, letter from A. I. Turgenev to Nikolai I. Turgenev, St. Petersburg, May 2–3, 1811. *Pis'ma Karamzina Dmitrievu,* 139, Moscow, February 19, 1811.

92. Desnitskii, 115, 120, 122, entries for April 22, May 26, and November 11, 1811. See also the table of contents for each issue of *Chteniia v Besede liubitelei russkago slova,* which give an idea of the works presented, in Al'tshuller, *Predtechi,* 372–74.

93. Shishkov, *Zapiski, mneniia,* 1:117–18. Desnitskii, 123–24, entries for December 4 and 15, 1811. The letter with the emperor's message appears in the Symposium minutes after Shishkov's speech, suggesting that the speech was read first.

94. Shishkov, *Zapiski, mneniia,* 2:321–22, letter to Ia. I. Bardovskii, December 27, 1811.

95. "O liubvi k otechestvu i narodnoi gordosti," in N. M. Karamzin, *Izbrannye stat'i i pis'ma,* 96.

96. Shishkov, *Sobranie,* 4:147–48, 150–63, 165, 167–87.

97. Shishkov, *Zapiski, mneniia,* 2:322, letter to Bardovskii, December 27, 1811. Khvostov found Shishkov's arguments "puerile" and wrote that "in some places the writing is strong and not bad, but in general this might have been suitable under Tsar Mikhail Romanov, not his descendants." He gives December 16, not 15, as the date the speech was given. Khvostov, 378, entry for December 16, 1811. On de Maistre, see "Aleksandr Shishkov i dve zapiski," 575.

98. Batiushkov, 2:205, St. Petersburg, February 27, 1812.

99. See Raeff, *Speransky,* 172–82.

100. Quoted in Shil'der, 3:367.

101. Maistre, 12:105, letter from de Maistre to Rossi, April 9/21, 1812. Vigel', 2:7–8. Shil'der, 3:45.

102. F. V. Rostopchin, "Tysiacha vosem'sot dvenadtsatyi god v Zapiskakh grafa F. V. Rostopchina," 646–49.

103. Shishkov, *Zapiski, mneniia,* 1:121–23. The dates of Shishkov's summoning to the palace and his appointment are in Shil'der, 3:64–66.

104. See the following chapter in this study.

CHAPTER 5:
THE 'WAR FOR THE FATHERLAND'

1. Maistre, 12:281–82, letter to King Victor Emmanuel, October 27/November 8, 1812. Vigel', 2:14–15. Adams, 426, diary entry for December 3, 1812 (NS). On militia-related unrest, see A. V. Predtechenskii, *Ocherki obshchestvenno-politicheskoi istorii Rossii v pervoi chetverti XIX veka,* 326–27. A. G. Tartakovskii, "Iz istorii odnoi zabytoi polemiki (Ob antikrepostnicheskikh 'diversiiakh' Napoleona v 1812 godu)."

2. T. Nipperdey, *Deutsche Geschichte 1800–1866: Bürgerwelt und starker Staat,* 15.

3. Doyle, 218, 418–19. Furet and Richet, 145–50, 183–85, 411.

4. See, e.g., H. W. Whelan, *Alexander III and the State Council: Bureaucracy and Counter-Reform in Late Imperial Russia,* 27–30.

5. "Perepiska Imperatora Aleksandra Pavlovicha s grafom F. V. Rostopchinym 1812–1814 gg.," 177, Moscow, June 11, 1812. See also his letters to Balashov from Moscow, July 23, 30, August 1, 10, 23, 29, 1812, in *Otechestvennaia Voina v pis'makh sovremennikov (1812–1815 gg.),* ed. N. F. Dubrovin, 60, 69, 76, 90, 109, 115; and "Pis'ma Rastopchina k Imperatoru," 433, 444–45, 522, 524, 545, 547, to Alexander I from Moscow, July 23, August 10, 14, 23, from Nara, September 21, 1812, and from Vladimir, October 1, 1812.

6. Rostopchin, "Tysiacha vosem'sot dvenadtsatyi god," 656, 684–85, 709.

7. Herzen thought these proclamations spoke in a "genuinely popular language," although Rostopchin himself was "frenchified"; Shishkov's influence on the populace, he asserted however, was "limited." Gertsen, 5:215.

8. I thank Slava Paperno for drawing my attention to this pun.

9. *Letuchie listki 1812 goda. Rostopchinskiia afishi,* ed. P. A. Kartavov, 13, 44. Another, less complete collection is *Rostopchinskiia afishi 1812 goda,* ed. A. S. Suvorin.

10. A. G. Tartakovskii, *Voennaia publitsistika 1812 goda,* 98. See also N. M. Mendel'son, "Rostopchinskiia afishi," in *Otechestvennaia voina i russkoe obshchestvo,* 4:83–91. Rostopchin, "Tysiacha vosem'sot dvenadtsatyi god," 666–67. *Arkhiv kniazia Vorontsova,* 8:314–15, Rostopchin to S. R. Vorontsov, Moscow, April 28 [1813]. Kartavov, *Rostopchinskiia afishi,* 58.

11. Dubrovin, *Voina v pis'makh,* 60–61, letter to Balashov, Moscow, July 23, 1812. "Pis'ma Rastopchina k Imperatoru," 540, Voronovo, September 19, 1812.

12. Quoted in Tartakovskii, *Voennaia publitsistika,* 60, from *Moskovskiia nebylitsy v litsakh* (published anonymously). K. Pokrovskii argues that Bulgakov was the author, in "Iz polemicheskoi literatury 1813 goda. (Moskovskie obyvateli i graf F. V. Rostopchin)." Bulgakov again argued that Rostopchin's great achievement was upholding order in "Razgovor Neapolitanskago Korolia Miu-

rata s Generalom Grafom M. A. Miloradovichem na avanpostakh armii 14 oktiabria 1812 goda (Otryvok iz Vospominanii 1812 goda)," 511. Rostopchin's friend Broker concurred in "Biografiia grafa Fedora Vasil'evicha Rostopchina, sostavlennaia A. F. Brokerom v 1826 godu," 164.

13. Dubrovin, *Voina v pis'makh,* 102, letter to Balashov, Moscow, August 18. "Moskva v 1812 godu. Graf Rostopchin-kniaziu Bagrationu," 650, letter from Moscow, August 6, 1812. On punishment of foreigners for pro-French utterances, see *Bumagi, otnosiashchiiasia do Otechestvennoi voiny 1812 goda,* ed. P. I. Shchukin, 1:113–16, letters from Rostopchin to Ivashkin, August 19, 26, 31, 1812. Kizevetter, *Otkliki,* 158–60. Mel'gunov, *Dela i liudi,* 140–44.

14. Kartavov, *Rostopchinskiia afishi,* 64. On peasant monarchism, see A. Gleason, *Young Russia: The Genesis of Russian Radicalism in the 1860s,* 6–12. Mel'gunov, *Dela i liudi,* 152, 159. O. V. Orlik, *"Groza dvenadtsatogo goda . . .,"* 29, 57. Rostopchin's letters to Bagration and to Moscow police chief Ivashkin suggest that he was quick to inflict exemplary punishment on foreigners, while his letters to the tsar and Balashov, and his reminiscences, dwell on efforts to protect them from the angry populace. See Kizevetter, *Otkliki,* 121–22. For the argument that the peasants' resistance to the French was by no means a sign of loyalty to the old regime (and that Rostopchin therefore was right), see Y. Tarasulo, "The Napoleonic Invasion of 1812."

15. Tartakovskii, *Voennaia publitsistika,* passim. Also, N. M. Druzhinin, *Izbrannye trudy: Vneshniaia politika Rossii, Istoriia Moskvy, Muzeinoe delo,* 91, 93. A collection of army bulletins was published by R. E. Al'tshuller and A. G. Tartakovskii: *Listovki Otechestvennoi voiny 1812 goda. Sbornik dokumentov.*

16. "Pis'ma Rastopchina k Imperatoru," 426, 442, 520, 541.

17. See, e.g., ibid., 520, Moscow, August 13, 1812.

18. Ibid., 429, Moscow, July 4, 1812. Kartavov, *Rostopchinskiia afishi,* 12.

19. "Pis'ma Rastopchina k Imperatoru," 426, 434, 442, 445, 548, Moscow, June 30, July 23, August 4 and 10, and Vladimir, October 1, 1812. Kizevetter, *Otkliki,* 161–69. For details on Vereshchagin's death, see Mel'gunov, *Dela i liudi,* 160–65. On Alexander I's reaction, see Shil'der, 3:377. On Kliucharev's and Vereshchagin's masonic connections, see Bakounine, 244–45, 584–85.

20. See Rostopchin, "Tysiacha vosem'sot dvenadtsatyi god," 650–54, 662–64. Kizevetter, *Otkliki,* 156–57. Mel'gunov and Sidorov, 2:184–95, 201.

21. P. de Ségur, *La campagne de Russie,* 112. A. de Caulaincourt, *With Napoleon in Russia: The Memoirs of General de Caulaincourt, Duke of Vicenza,* 126. See also Mme de Staël's reminiscences, in *Rossiia pervoi poloviny XIX veka glazami inostrantsev,* 36, and Dubrovin, *Voina v pis'makh,* 159, Robert Wilson to P., Borovsk, September 19/October 1, 1812. Rostopchin's message is reproduced in his *Sochineniia,* 197.

22. Kizevetter, *Otkliki,* 129–31.

23. Dubrovin, *Voina v pis'makh,* 108, Bagration to Rostopchin, near Semenovskaia [*sic*], August 22, 1812. Obolenskii, 140. *Pis'ma Karamzina k Dmitrievu,*

165–66, Moscow, August 20, and Nizhnii Novgorod, October 11, 1812. For his view of Rostopchin's leaflets, see Viazemskii, 7:194; on Zhukovskii, see 7:504. Viazemskii gives his own view on 7:194, 504–5. Vigel', 2:11–12. Dmitriev, *Melochi*, 243–44. *Arkhiv brat' ev Turgenevykh*, 3:200, N. I. Turgenev, diary entry, St. Petersburg, August 9 [1812]. *Ostaf' evskii arkhiv*, 1:328–29, A. I. Turgenev to P. A. Viazemskii, St. Petersburg, October 15, 1819. In 1812, though, A. I. Turgenev had seen Rostopchin more favorably. See *Pis'ma Aleksandra Turgeneva Bulgakovym*, eds. A. A. Saburov and I. K. Luppol, 134, [St. Petersburg], July 21 [1812].

24. Shishkov, *Zapiski, mneniia*, 1:125–26, 128–48. For an overview of his manifestoes (with a laudatory commentary), see N. A. Palitsyn, "Manifesty, pisannye Shishkovym v otechestvennuiu voinu, i patrioticheskoe ikh znachenie."

25. V., "Priezd Imperatora Aleksandra I v Moskvu. (11–18 iiulia 1812 goda)." See also A. S. Pushkin, *Sochineniia v trekh tomakh*, 3:119–21.

26. S. N. Glinka, *Zapiski o 1812 gode Sergeia Glinki, pervago ratnika Moskovskago Opolcheniia*, 2–9.

27. Ibid., 18–20.

28. Starobinski, 62–67.

29. Shishkov, *Zapiski, mneniia*, 1:151, 426–27. Ségur, 38, 89. Rostopchin, "Tysiacha vosem'sot dvenadtsatyi god," 674.

30. Rostopchin, "Tysiacha vosem'sot dvenadtsatyi god," 673–74.

31. Viazemskii, 2:341. Glinka, *Zapiski o 1812 gode*, 9–10, 27–28.

32. N. M. Druzhinin, *Izbrannye trudy*, 104. Soviet scholars usually treated Glinka as an incorrigible reactionary, but his patriotism appears to have briefly become "politically correct" during World War II. See S. Khrapkov, "Russkaia intelligentsiia v Otechestvennoi voine 1812 goda," 73.

33. Glinka, *Zapiski Glinki*, 227. Glinka seems to imply that this was actually a *higher* figure than what he accomplished in other years, but that makes little sense in light of the subscriber lists he published for 1811 and 1813.

34. Apparently he refused to spend the funds that the state allocated to him, which was characteristic of his selfless honesty. Viazemskii, 2:341. Dmitriev, *Melochi*, 104. Viazemskii's comment is quoted from 9:115, letter to D. G. Bibikov, Ostaf'evo, September 2, 1830.

35. S. N. Glinka, *Zapiski o Moskve i o zagranichnykh proisshestviiakh ot iskhoda 1812 do poloviny 1815 goda*, 40–44, *Zapiski*, 255, *Zapiski o 1812 gode*, 34, 42.

36. Tartakovskii, *Russkaia memuaristika*, 167. F. N. Glinka, *Pis'ma russkogo ofitsera*, 22, entry for September 2, 1812. The comment on wine is in Viazemskii, 8:365. The *Messenger* is quoted in I. I. Zamotik, "'Russkii Vestnik' Glinki," *Otechestvennaia voina i russkoe obshchestvo*, 5:134.

37. Glinka, *Zapiski o 1812 gode*, 14, 30, 60, 64, 78–82, 134–35, 140–41, 143–48; Glinka, *Zapiski o Moskve*, 85, 164–76, 200–24, 227–28, 249–50, 258, 276–77, 279, 297–300, 308–16, 335–36, 348–49. He was also fascinated by the

parallels between the events of 1812–14 and biblical prophesies. *Zapiski o Moskve*, 87–93.

38. Tartakovskii, *Voennaia publitsistika*, 67–69. Glinka, *Zapiski o 1812 gode*, 263.

39. *Arkhiv kniazia Vorontsova*, 8:315, letter to S. R. Vorontsov, Moscow, April 28 [1813]. Shil'der, 3:377, letter to Alexander I, Moscow, December 2/14, 1812.

40. Glinka, *Zapiski o 1812 gode*, 34.

41. Ibid., 91–92. See also Walker, "Reaction and Radicalism," for an interesting comparison of the views of Sergei and Fedor Glinka.

42. Shishkov, *Zapiski, mneniia*, 1:157–59.

43. Ibid., 1:438–42, 160. Ibid., 2:327, letter to Bardovskii, from Silesia, May 11, 1813.

44. Al'tshuller, *Predtechi*, 344–49. D. A. Zharinov, "Pervyia vpechatleniia voiny. Manifesty," *Otechestvennaia voina i russkoe obshchestvo*, 3:174–75.

45. AIRLI 13,947, l. 33. He was also flattered when foreigners admired them. See RNB, 862/3, ll. 81–81 ob.

46. Aksakov, 2:305–6. N. I. Grech, *Zapiski o moei zhizni*, 210. Rostopchin, "Tysiacha vosem'sot dvenadtsatyi god," 670. Viazemskii, 9:195–96, 10:257, diary entries for April 15, 1841, and [October 8, 1865]. Pushkin wrote: "This venerable old man is dear to us; he shines among the people / With the sacred memory of the year '12." Tartakovskii, *Voennaia publitsistika*, 48. Even writers who are usually critical of Shishkov acknowledge his impact. Khodasevich (236) and Shchebal'skii (201) point out that some of the phrases he coined were still heard one hundred years later. De Maistre (who knew no Russian) thought that Shishkov was "simple" and "pious" but that his style was inappropriate for official statements and did not "satisfy the European ear." Maistre, 13:207, to Vallaise, St. Petersburg, December 24, 1815/January 5, 1816. It should be noted that this remark was occasioned by the edict expelling de Maistre's Jesuit friends from St. Petersburg.

47. Shishkov, *Zapiski, mneniia*, 1:313, 319, 347, 349, letters from Philipsberg, January 16; Kalisz, February 12; Marienberg, August 12 and 14, 1813. Viazemskii, passing away sleepless nights reading, was amused at the "puerile simpleheartedness" of Shishkov's campaign memoirs and generally found "all his travel impressions and comments utterly childish" (Viazemskii, 10:60–61, entry for July 25, 1853).

48. Shishkov, *Zapiski, mneniia*, 1:165, 375, 384, 2:331–32, letters to Dar'ia Alekseevna, Frankfurt am Main, November 22 and December 19, 1813, and to Kikin, Vilna, December 1812. Ibid, 1:167–68, 381, letter to Dar'ia Alekseevna, Freiburg, December 15, 1813. RNB, 143/210, l. 1, Shishkov to Mariia Fedorovna, Liben [?], April 3, 1813. Stählin, 3:222. Kochubinskii, 59. For the argument that Kutuzov wanted to continue the war, see Druzhinin, 101, and Troitskii, 304–5. Some historians have asserted that Shishkov was the leader of the "antiwar"

faction: see *Osvoboditel' naia voina 1813 goda protiv napoleonovskogo gospod-stva,* ed. L. G. Beskrovnyi, 87.

49. Shishkov, *Zapiski, mneniia,* 1:238–43, 245.

50. ARAN, 100/1/354, l. 4, letter to Balashov, Karlsruhe, [no month] 15, 1814 (copy).

51. Shishkov, *Zapiski, mneniia,* 1:239, 252–57, 270, 272, 284. In his memoirs, Shishkov repeatedly dismissed Napoleon as a mere *prostoliudin,* a commoner; he also read Bible passages to the tsar, and "both of us shed quite a few tears." S. B. Okun', "Russkii narod i Otechestvennaia voina 1812 goda," 64–65. Mel'gunov, *Dela i liudi,* 235–36. Kartavov, *Rostopchinskiia afishi,* 75. Tartakovskii, *Voennaia publitsistika,* 67–69.

52. Shishkov, *Zapiski, mneniia,* 1:303–9. On the disappointment that this manifesto caused among the progressive intelligentsia, see Predtechenskii, *Ocherki,* 361.

53. S. de Choiseul-Gouffier, *Historical Memoirs of the Emperor Alexander I and the Court of Russia,* 140. For a Soviet view that the peasants were in fact motivated by a combination of religious fervor, patriotism, and hostility to serfdom, see Okun', "Russkii narod," 58.

54. "Pis'ma Rastopchina k Imperatoru," 550, 561, Vladimir, October 13, and Moscow, December 2, 1812. Druzhinin argues (101) that Rostopchin, like Shishkov, opposed continuing the war, and indeed, amidst his contemptuous portrayals of Alexander's ministers, he defended Rumiantsev, the foreign minister linked with the Tilsit alliance. Rostopchin, "Tysiacha vosem'sot dvenadtsatyi god," 653. J. L. Black also argues that he opposed continuing the war, in "Karamzin and the Notion of Defensive War," 38; Karamzin himself opposed the war all along (ibid.). For an overview of the conservatives' war aims—preserving the ancien régime and Russian expansion—see A. V. Predtechenskii, "Otrazhenie voin 1812–1814 gg. v soznanii sovremennikov," 240–41.

55. "Pis'ma Rastopchina k Imperatoru," 529, 538, Moscow, September 1, and Pakhra, September 13, 1812. Nikolai Mikhailovich, *Elisaveta,* 2:543–44, 549, Elisaveta Alekseevna to her mother, Kamennyi Ostrov, August 26/September 7, and St. Petersburg, September 24/October 6, 1812. Pypin, 300. See also Grech, 212.

56. Obolenskii, 156, Iu. A. Neledinskii-Meletskii to E. I. Nelidova, Vologda, October 10, 1812. Nikolai Mikhailovich, *Correspondance,* 83–84, Iaroslavl', September 3 and 6, 1812. "Pis'ma velikoi kniagini Ekateriny Pavlovny k inzhener-generalu F. P. Devolanu," 1970, Ekaterina to Devolant, Iaroslavl', September 6, 1812.

57. Pushkin, *Pis'ma,* 59, Iaroslavl', November 13, 1812. Vries, 54.

58. "Pis'ma Ekateriny Devolanu," 1995–96, letter to Devolant, Prague, November 1/October 20 [1813]. Bozherianov, 59–75. Bogoiavlenskii, 178–79. Vries, 59–62. Elenev, 11–56.

59. Pokrovskii, "Iz polemicheskoi literatury," 200. Mel'gunov, *Dela i liudi,*

227–31. El'nitskii, in *Russkii biograficheskii slovar'*, 288–90. As one resident observed, "Moscow is delighted at Rostopchin's dismissal." *Ferdinand Christin et la Princesse Tourkestanow. Lettres écrites de Pétersbourg et de Moscou. 1813–1819,* 146, Christin to Turkistanova, Moscow, September 3, 1814. Shil'der, 3:259–60.

60. See, for example, *Ferdinand Christin et Tourkestanow,* 444, 571–74, Christin to Turkistanova, Moscow, December 14, 1816; Turkistanova to Christin, Pavlovsk, May 19, 1817; Christin to Turkistanova, Moscow, May 28, 1817.

CHAPTER 6:
THE MENTAL WORLD OF THE HOLY ALLIANCE

1. L. Müller, *Russischer Geist und evangelisches Christentum: Die Kritik des Protestantismus in der russischen religiösen Philosophie und Dichtung im 19. und 20. Jahrhundert,* 9, and "Die Kritik des Protestantismus in der russischen Theologie und Philosophie," in *Die Ostkirche und die russische Christenheit,* ed. E. Benz, 27. For the argument that the Petrine reforms were "a kind of Reformation," see D. W. Treadgold, *The West in Russia and China: Religious and Secular Thought in Modern Times,* 1:105. The argument that the Church in fact retained great independence is made by Freeze in "Handmaiden of the State?"

2. N. F. Dubrovin, "Nashi mistiki-sektanty. Aleksandr Fedorovich Labzin i ego zhurnal 'Sionskii Vestnik,'" pt. 1, 180–86. G. Florovsky, *Ways of Russian Theology,* 1:162.

3. Mel'gunov and Sidorov, 1:133–35, 180. For an example, see Obolenskii, 91–92.

4. Z. V. David, "The Influence of Jacob Boehme on Russian Religious Thought." Treadgold, 122–27. S. I. Miropol'skii, "Fotii Spasskii, Iur'evskii arkhimandrit. Istoriko-biograficheskii ocherk," pt. 1, 15–18.

5. D. W. Treadgold, "Russian Orthodoxy and Society," in *Russian Orthodoxy under the Old Regime,* ed. R. L. Nichols and T. G. Stavrou, 21.

6. A quasi-ethnographic description of the sectarian milieu was given later in the nineteenth century by Pavel I. Mel'nikov (also known as Andrei Pecherskii) in his novels *V lesakh* and *Na gorakh.* I thank Marc Raeff for pointing this out to me.

7. P. Miliukov, *Outlines of Russian Culture,* 1:92–93, 102–3. See also the rest of his chapter on sectarianism in ibid. *Russkii biograficheskii slovar',* s.v. "Selivanov, Kondratii." N. F. Dubrovin, "Nashi mistiki-sektanty. Ekaterina Filippovna Tatarinova i Aleksandr Petrovich Dubovitskii," pt. 1, 33–39.

8. Chistovich, 54, 117. *Russkii biograficheskii slovar',* s.v. "Filaret." Miropol'skii, pt. 1, 20. Turkistanova was a maid of honor of Mariia Fedorovna. See *Ferdinand Christin et Tourkestanow,* 88, Turkistanova to Christin, St. Petersburg, January 18, 1814.

9. A. McConnell, *Tsar Alexander I: Paternalistic Reformer,* 190. Treadgold,

The West, 113, 117. On Labzin, see Dubrovin, "Labzin"; N. Derzhavin, "'Uchenik mudrosti' (A. F. Labzin i ego literaturnaia deiatel'nost')"; *Russkii biograficheskii slovar'*, s.v. "Labzin, Aleksandr Fedorovich"; his wife's memoirs, A. E. Labzina, *Vospominaniia Anny Evdokimovny Labzinoi 1758–1828*, ed. B. L. Modzalevskii; and Aksakov, 2:222–65. E. Benz, "Die russische Kirche und das abendländische Christentum," in *Die Ostkirche und die russische Christenheit*, 128–29. Chistovich, 50–53. Dubrovin, "Labzin," pt. 2, 117. On Saint-Martin's views, see the lengthy excerpt from his writings in Starobinski, 160–61.

10. Schlafly, "The Rostopchins and Roman Catholicism," 85–94 and passim; "Echoes of the French Revolution: Conservatism and the Catholic Church in Russia under Tsar Alexander I. The Jesuits," and "De Joseph de Maistre à la 'Bibliothèque rose': le Catholicisme chez les Rostopčin." M. Stepanov and F. Vermale, eds., "Zhozef de Mestr v Rossii," 606, passim. See also D. W. Edwards, "Count Joseph Marie de Maistre and Russian Educational Policy, 1803–1828"; C. Latreille, "Joseph de Maistre et le Tzar Alexandre Ier"; and P. Bliard, "L'Empereur Alexandre, les Jésuites et Joseph de Maistre, d'après des documents inédits." Bliard's essay defends the Jesuit position.

11. An interesting background study for this is Raeff, "Les Slaves."

12. W. W. Sawatsky, "Prince Alexander N. Golitsyn (1773–1844): Tsarist Minister of Piety," 45, 73. Goetze, 18, 25–29. Golovina, 209–10. Florovsky, 1:166. *Ferdinand Christin et Tourkestanow*, 70, letter to Christin, St. Petersburg, December 14, 1813. On his tenure at the Synod, see Sawatsky, "Minister of Piety," 57–68, and Chistovich, 17, 19–28. On his career until 1803, see Chistovich, 17–18. On Speranskii, see Chistovich, 39, and Dubrovin, "Labzin," pt. 1, 156, 160–61.

13. On Koshelev, see "Imperator Aleksandr I-i i Rodion Aleksandrovich Koshelev"; H. Schaeder, *Die dritte Koalition und die Heilige Allianz*, 52–53; and *Ferdinand Christin et Tourkestanow*, 778, Christin to Turkistanova, Moscow, March 31, 1819. On Mariia Fedorovna, see Chistovich, 222, and Mel'gunov and Sidorov, 2:148. On Alexander, see Florovsky, 1:164–66.

14. A. F. Rostopchin, *Matériaux*, 438, Golovin to Rostopchin, St. Petersburg, April 11, 1812. Shil'der, 3:92, 376. R. S. Edling, *Mémoires de la comtesse Edling (née Stourdza) demoiselle d'honneur de Sa Majesté l'Impératrice Elisabeth Alexéevna*, 79–80. Grech, 184.

15. Conversation between Alexander I and Prussian Bishop Eylert, Berlin, September 8/20, 1818, quoted in Shil'der, 3:378. Dubrovin, "Labzin," pt. 4, 108–12. Sawatsky, "Minister of Piety," 73, 500. W. W. Sawatsky, "Prince Alexander N. Golitsyn: Formidable or Forgettable?" 6. Edling, 77.

16. A. I. Turgenev, *Khronika russkogo. Dnevniki (1825–1826 gg.)*, ed. M. I. Gillel'son, 207, entry for Weimar, August 7/July 26, 1840. Nikolai Mikhailovich, *Elisaveta*, 2:486, reminiscences of Caroline von Freystedt. Markovich, "Zhozef de Mestr i Sent-Bëv v pis'makh k R. Sturdze-Edling," 383. For a more extensive discussion of the biographies of Roksandra and Aleksandr Sturdza, and an analy-

sis of their role in elaborating the Holy Alliance's ideology and shaping Russian foreign policy after 1815 (especially toward Germany), see my forthcoming article in *Forschungen zur osteuropäischen Geschichte* 54.

17. AIRLI, 288/1/2, "Ma Vie," ll. 18 ob–19 ob.

18. AIRLI, 288/1/2, "L'Histoire de mon enfance et de ma première jeunesse, écrite pour ma soeur. 1809," l. 3. E. von Paunel, "Das Geschwisterpaar Alexander und Roxandra Sturdza, verehelichte Gräfin Edling, in Deutschland und Rußland zur Zeit der Restauration," 83–85. Edling, 2.

19. Edling, 5–6. Lopukhin, 19–20.

20. Edling, 8–20. AIRLI, 288/1/2, "L'Histoire," ll. 7–9.

21. Ibid., ll. 9 ob–10, 12 ob–13. Sturdza, "Beseda," 6. Eidel'man, *Mgnoven'e,* 209, 212. The play is AIRLI, 288/1/13, "Rzhevskii. Tragediia v piati deistviiakh i v stikhakh. Petrograd 1807." This *delo* contains the manuscript for acts I–III of a tale of pre-Petrine heroism and chivalry that was just one of several plays he wrote at the time.

22. Sturdza, "Beseda," 6–9. Aksakov, 2:302.

23. Sturdza, "Beseda," 7–8, 11–22. The essay was later published as *Opyt uchebnago prednachertaniia dlia prepodavaniia Rossiiskomu Iunoshestvu Grecheskago iazyka.* Desnitskii, 127–28, entry for March 23, 1812. Sturdza's literary acquaintances included Pushkin, Griboedov, and Gogol.

24. Eidel'man, *Mgnoven'e,* 181.

25. I thank David M. McDonald for drawing my attention to the parallels between Sturdza and the Wisdom Lovers.

26. AIRLI, 288/1/2, "Ma Vie," ll. 16–17 ob. AIRLI, 288/1/2, l. 33, "Précis des années de service du Conseiller d'Etat actuel Stourdza. le, Mai 1823" (draft). Lotman, 130.

27. AIRLI, 288/1/2, "Ma Vie," ll. 20–21 ob. Edling, 39, 42–43. G. L. Arsh, "Ioann Kapodistriia v Rossii," 50–51. T. C. Prousis, "The Greeks of Russia and the Greek Awakening, 1774–1821." On Capodistrias's proposal to Roksandra Sturdza, see AIRLI, 288/1/125, ll. 79–81, 83 ob–84, 92 ob–93, Roksandra to Aleksandr Sturdza, [Karlsruhe] June 11, [Bruchsal] July 6, [Baden-Baden] August 1, 1814 (NS); UBB, nos. 7 and 8, Roksandra Sturdza to Jung-Stilling, Vienna, October 17 and November 8, 1814; AIRLI, 288/1/86, ll. 63–64, Aleksandr to Roksandra Sturdza, Vienna, June 24/12, 1814; A. de Falloux, *Lettres de Madame de Swetchine,* 1:120–21, 148, 178–79, Svechina to Roksandra Sturdza, St. Petersburg, March 30, June 1, and September 26, 1814. S. Th. Lascaris, *Capodistrias avant la révolution grecque. Sa carrière politique jusqu'en 1822. Etude d'histoire diplomatique et de droit international,* 29. A. S. Sturdza, "Vospominaniia o zhizni i deianiiakh grafa I. A. Kapodistrii, pravitelia Gretsii," 15–19.

28. *Mesiatsoslov s rospis'iu chinovnykh osob* (1807), chast' 1, 20.

29. Sturdza, "Vospominaniia," 18–24, 48–49. Markovich, 383–88.

30. Lotman, 83.

31. Edling, 29–32, 63–66, 134. F. Ley, *Alexandre Ier et sa Sainte-Alliance (1811–1825) avec des documents inédits*, 45–62. UBB, no. 23, Roksandra Sturdza to Jung-Stilling, September 5, 1815. AIRLI, 288/1/265, l. 3, Golitsyn to Roksandra Sturdza, n.pl., May 20, 1816. The chronology of her acquaintance with Koshelev remains unclear.

32. Edling, 106–17. On Roksandra's rivalry with Valueva, see Nikolai Mikhailovich, *Elisaveta*, 2:608, 3:151, 180, Elisaveta to her mother, Riga, November 25/December 7, 1815, Kamennyi Ostrov, August 31/September 12, 1820, and Tsarskoe Selo, May 27/June 8, 1821. On her quarrel with the empress (which she downplayed in her memoirs), see Falloux, *Lettres de Swetchine*, 108–9, 112–13, 126, 146–47, Svechina to Roksandra Sturdza, St. Petersburg, January 15 and February 2, n.pl., April 7, and St. Petersburg, June 1, 1814. The list of the empress's suite, and a diary of its travels, is in V. Ivanov, *Zapiski, vedennyia vo vremia puteshestviia imperatritsy Elisavety Alekseevny po Germanii v 1813, 1814 i 1815 godakh.*

33. *Russkii biograficheskii slovar'*, s.v. "Kridener, baronessa Varvara-Iuliia."

34. M. Geiger, *Aufklärung und Erweckung: Beiträge zur Erforschung Johann Heinrich Jung-Stillings und der Erweckungstheologie*, 13–16, 266–67.

35. *Arkhiv brat' ev Turgenevykh*, 3:210, N. I. Turgenev, diary entry, St. Petersburg, December 21, 1812. He met Jung-Stilling in 1813 or 1814; ibid., 447. Aksakov, 2:231. Lopukhin, 208. R. Kayser, "Zar Alexander I. und die deutsche Erweckung," 165–66. The actor A. S. Iakovlev liked Jung-Stilling's prophesies about Russia in *The Yearning*. Zhikharev, 2:376. About the "spirit world" of the mystics, Elisaveta remarked: "I shall know it some day, that's inevitable, and I don't want to spoil the pleasure of the surprise." Nikolai Mikhailovich, *Elisaveta*, 2:637, letter to her mother, St. Petersburg, December 16/28, 1816.

36. One result of this was a mass migration from southern Germany to the Caucasus in 1817, which Jung-Stilling thought premature. Geiger, *Aufklärung*, 196–97, 268–79, 286–94.

37. Edling, 132–33. See also F. Ley, *Madame de Krüdener et son temps 1764–1824*, 407, Juliette von Krüdener, diary entry, February 16, 1814. Dr. Ley, a descendant of the baroness, bases his books on the period on a large family archive from which he quotes extensively.

38. UBB, no. 24, Roksandra Sturdza to Jung-Stilling, September 24 [1815]. Shishkov disliked Jung-Stilling's "appearance" and "strange ideas." Krüdener's reputation also did not appeal to him, but he found a prayer meeting at her house inspiring. Shishkov, *Zapiski, mneniia*, 1:281–82. Krüdener's daughter believed that her mother had "converted" Ekaterina Pavlovna, but Ekaterina herself, a sober type, evidently thought Krüdener a dangerous person. Ley, *Krüdener*, 462, Juliette von Krüdener, diary entry, June 25, 1815. Vries, 87. Geiger, *Aufklärung*, 303–6.

39. AIRLI, 288/1/125, ll. 117 ob–118 ob, 100–100 ob, 106, letters to Svechina, (apparently) Bruchsal, May 22/10, 1814 [?], and Aleksandr, [Baden-

Baden] August 16, 1814 (NS) and [Baden-Baden, August 1814]. AIRLI, 288/1/86, Aleksandr to Roksandra Sturdza [apparently St. Petersburg, 1814]. It is not clear to which book he was referring. He had earlier written to her on Germany's "proselytizing spirit," "a religious Machiavellianism that builds political systems out of sacred materials," as Capodistrias had warned him. Ibid., l. 9, Bucharest, June 1812. AIRLI, 288/1/125, l. 82, Roksandra to Aleksandr Sturdza, [Karlsruhe] June 11, 1814 (NS).

40. AIRLI, 288/1/86, l. 98, 108–108 ob, 119–119 ob, Aleksandr to Roksandra Sturdza, Heidelberg, June 7/19, Paris, July 13/25 and September 12/24, 1815. Ley, *Krüdener,* 456–58, 491, 504–5, Juliette von Krüdener, diary entries, June 16, 19, 22, September 18, 30, October 9, 1815. Ley, *Alexandre,* 311–13.

41. UBB, nos. 31, 1 [St. Petersburg, spring 1816], Vienna, January 4, 1815 (the date mistakenly reads "1814"). On the convent, see Falloux, *Lettres de Swetchine,* 157–58, Svechina to Roksandra Sturdza, n.pl., June 29, 1814.

42. Ivanov, *Zapiski,* 1:90. Caroline von Freystedt observed that his "longest talks were with Miss Sturdza, whose intelligent conversation, into which she skillfully mixed subtle flattery, seemed to keep his interest the most." Quoted in Nikolai Mikhailovich, *Elisaveta,* 2:497. On her ties to the imperial couple, see also "Pis'ma imperatora Aleksandra Pavlovicha k R. S. Sturdze (grafine Edling)" and "Pis'ma imperatritsy Elisavety Alekseevny k R. S. Sturdze (grafine Edling)."

43. Edling, 140–51. Ley, *Alexandre,* 89. UBB, no. 9, Roksandra to Jung-Stilling, Vienna, December 15, 1814. On the meeting, see Ley, *Alexandre,* 313–15, Jung-Stilling to C. F. Spittler, Baden-Baden, July 20, 1814. Jung-Stilling was pleased to find that "[m]y views on the past, the present, and the future, and especially the coming Kingdom of God, are [Alexander's] exactly" (p. 314).

44. Copies of letters to Juliane von Krüdener, Karlsruhe, August 14, 1815, and October 16, 1814. Private collection of Dr. Francis Ley.

45. M. Geiger, "Roxandra Scarlatovna von Stourdza (1786–1844). Zur Erweckungsbewegung der Befreiungskriege," 399–400. Edling, 217–18.

46. UBB, no. 8, Vienna, November 8, 1814. Geiger, *Aufklärung,* 306–8.

47. AIRLI, 288/1/125, ll. 70 ob–71, Roksandra to Aleksandr Sturdza, n.pl., December 6 [1812]. P. V. Chichagov, *Mémoires de l'amiral Paul Tchitchagof, commandant en chef de l'armée du Danube, gouverneur des principautés de Moldavie et de Valachie en 1812,* 361. AIRLI, 288/1/86, ll. 27 ob–28 ob, Aleksandr to Roksandra Sturdza, Brest-Litovsk, October 8, 1812.

48. AIRLI, 288/1/86, ll. 67–68, 75, Aleksandr to Roksandra Sturdza, Vienna, July 8/20 and August 1/13, 1814. AIRLI, 288/1/125, ll. 92–92 ob, Roksandra to Aleksandr Sturdza, [Baden-Baden] August 1, 1814.

49. Edling, 145–46, 150. AIRLI, 288/1/86, l. 116, Aleksandr to Roksandra Sturdza, Paris, August 15/27, 1815. The memorandum is mentioned in Ley, *Krüdener,* 457, Juliette von Krüdener, diary entry, June 19, 1815. The original of the memorandum is in AVPRI, 133/468/7812, ll. 2–12 ob.

50. Ivanov, *Zapiski,* 2:49–71. Geiger, "Roxandra," 403–4, 408. L. Hein,

"Franz von Baader und seine Liebe zur Russischen Orthodoxen Kirche," 31–36.
E. Susini, *Lettres inédites de Franz von Baader,* 1:289–90, 2:485–99, Roksandra
Sturdza to Baader, n.pl., July 11, 1815 (letter and commentary).

51. AIRLI, 288/1/86, ll. 122, 31, Aleksandr to Roksandra Sturdza, Vienna,
[October] 13/25, and November 4, 1815. See also ll. 23 ob and 91 ob–92, Paris,
September 30, and Vienna, March 31/April 12, 1815. I. A. Kapodistrias,
Archeion Iōannou Kapodistria, vol. E, 108, Capodistrias to Stein, Vienna, De-
cember 16/28, 1815. AIRLI, 288/1/265, l. 2, Golitsyn to Roksandra Sturdza, St.
Petersburg, July 29, 1815.

52. Including the empress. Nikolai Mikhailovich, *Elisaveta,* 3:197, to her
mother, St. Petersburg, November 5/17, 1821. Hein, 53–59. D. Chizhevskii,
"Baader i Rossiia."

53. Golitsyn even had her report to him officially on religious matters, especially on Jung-Stilling, after she moved to Germany in 1816. AIRLI, 288/1/265,
ll. 9 ob–10 ob, 11–12, Golitsyn to Roksandra Sturdza, St. Petersburg, August 25
and December 16, 1816.

54. See the chapter "Samoderzhavie i krest'ianskii vopros" in S. V. Mironenko, *Samoderzhavie i reformy. Politicheskaia bor' ba v Rossii v nachale XIX v.*

55. Geiger, *Aufklärung,* 384–408, including the letter to her son-in-law, February 14, 1817. Metternich, for one, thought her a dangerous revolutionary (ibid).

56. Edling, 144, 112, 157, 13–14, 31, 24. Falloux, *Lettres de Swetchine,* 153,
letter of June 9, 1814.

57. UBB, no. 12, letter to Jung-Stilling, Munich, April 5, 1815. Edling, 203–5,
219. For her view on the general need for social and political reform in Russia after 1815, see ibid., 252–53.

58. F. B. Artz, *Reaction and Revolution 1814–1832,* 20. Hobsbawm, *Age of
Revolution,* 223.

59. S. R. Tompkins, "The Russian Bible Society—A Case of Religious Xenophobia," 251–58. J. Cohen Zacek, "The Russian Bible Society and the Russian
Orthodox Church," 411–17.

60. *Entsiklopedicheskii slovar',* s.v. "Bibleiskiia obshchestva v Rossii."

61. Sukhomlinov, *Istoriia,* 6:6, 14, 26–77.

62. Ibid., 6:123–59, 191–204, 221–31, 260, 280. I. I. Dmitriev, *Vzgliad na
moiu zhizn' (1823),* 116.

63. RNB, 656/21, l. 56 ob, Kozodavlev to Runich, St. Petersburg, April 6,
1815. On his support for religious tolerance, see Sukhomlinov, *Istoriia,* 6:204–5,
261–62. On his biography, see also *Russkii biograficheskii slovar',* s.v. "Kozodavlev, Osip Petrovich," and E. M. Garshin, "Odin iz russkikh Grakkhov proshlago stoletiia."

64. Sukhomlinov, *Istoriia,* 6:231–64.

65. AIRLI, 263/2/216, ll. 5–6 ob, Labzin to Runich, St. Petersburg, February
23/March 6, 1798.

66. AIRLI, 263/2/562, l. 1, Runich to Labzin, Moscow, July 24, 1805. AIRLI,

263/2/562, ll. 5–6 ob, Runich to Labzin, Moscow, February 15, 1806. *Russkii biograficheskii slovar'*, s.v. "Runich, Dmitrii Pavlovich" and "Kliucharev, Fedor Petrovich." See "Pis'ma Nikolaia Ivanovicha Novikova k D. P. Runichu," 1013–94, and "Pis'ma I. V. Lopukhina k D. P. Runichu," 1215–36. On Labzin's personality, see Aksakov, 2:245. Labzin tried to use Runich's connections in government to advance himself: AIRLI, 263/2/217, l. 5, Labzin to Runich, n.pl., n.d.

67. "Dmitrii Pavlovich Runich (Materialy dlia ego biografii)," 390. He complained to Labzin about "life here" in AIRLI, 263/2/562, l. 4 ob, Moscow, January 22, 1806. Kliucharev was no substitute for Labzin, at least initially (AIRLI, 263/2/562, l. 2, Runich to Labzin, Moscow, July 24, 1805), and he unsuccessfully sought a position in the Ministry of Police, arguing that his postal job offered no hopes for advancement (AIRLI, 263/2/599, ll. 14–15, Runich to Balashov, Moscow, February 16, 1811).

68. Runich, Kozodavlev, Labzin, Popov, and Lopukhin were all on the subscriber list for 1813.

69. Goetze, 97. *Russkii biograficheskii slovar'*, s.v. "Popov, Vasilii Mikhailovich." Sawatsky, "Minister of Piety," 248.

70. RNB, 656/21, l. 75 ob, Kozodavlev to Runich, St. Petersburg, December 7, 1815. On the monitoring of private correspondence, and Runich's apparent initial scruples and lack of zeal for it, see ibid., ll. 15–16, 64, 66–66 ob, 77, Kozodavlev to Runich, St. Petersburg, September 23, 1813, June 21, July 22, 1815, January 4, 1816. For Kozodavlev's desire for information on Moscow, see ibid., l. 43, letter to Runich, St. Petersburg, December 18, 1814. On manufacturers, see ibid., ll. 28, 31–31 ob, 35–36, 44, 53–53 ob, 65, 69, 71 ob, Kozodavlev to Runich, St. Petersburg, April 10, 22, October [no date], December 18, 1814, March 20, July 5, August 26, September 18, 1815. See also RNB, 656/37, ll. 108 ob–109, 137, Popov to Runich, St. Petersburg, September 2, December 8, 1814. See also AIRLI, 263/2/190, passim.

71. RNB, 656/37, ll. 21–21 ob, Popov to Runich, St. Petersburg, April 22, 1813. RNB, 656/21, ll. 11–11 ob, Kozodavlev to Runich, St. Petersburg, May 17, 1813. RNB, 656/37, l. 19, Popov to Runich, St. Petersburg, April 8, 1813. AIRLI, 263/2/577, l. 13 ob, Runich to Popov, Pokoevo, May 28, 1817.

72. RNB, 656/37, l. 29 ob, Popov to Runich, n.pl., July 4, 1813.

73. ARAN, 100/1/197-18, l. 225, Popov to Runich, St. Petersburg, July 21, 1815. On his views on the importance of the Bible, see his letter to Runich. RNB, 656/37, ll. 130–35 ob, St. Petersburg, November 30, 1814.

74. RNB, 656/37, ll. 30–30 ob, Popov to Runich, n.pl., July 4, 1813.

75. RNB, 656/37, l. 94, Popov to Runich, St. Petersburg, May 27, 1814. Ibid., ll. 35–35 ob, 58–60 ob, 129, Popov to Runich, St. Petersburg, August 15, 1813, February 10, 24, November 14, 1814. "Dmitrii Runich (Materialy)," 391, Runich to Popov, Moscow, March 29, 1815.

76. RNB, 656/37, l. 131 ob, 140, 71 ob, 78 ob, 42–42 ob, 128–29, Popov to Runich, St. Petersburg, November 30, December 18, April 1, 28, 1814, October

10, 1813, November 14, 1814.

77. *Allgemeine Deutsche Biographie,* s.v. "Arndt: Johann," "Arnold: Gottfried," "Weigel: Valentin." AIRLI, 263/1/178 and 181, library inventories of 1826.

78. Dmitrii P. Runich, "Iz zapisok Runicha," pt. 3, 611. "Dmitrii Runich (Materialy)," 392, Runich to Popov, Moscow, March 29, 1815; Popov shared this view (ARAN, 100/1/197-18, ll. 207–9, Popov to Runich, St. Petersburg, March 19 and 23, 1815).

79. AIRLI, 263/2/577, ll. 15–15 ob, Runich to Popov, Pokoevo, May 28, 1817. Runich, "Iz zapisok Runicha," pt. 3, 611–14. *Russkii biograficheskii slovar',* s.v. "Runich, Pavel Stepanovich."

80. Runich, "Iz zapisok Runicha," pt. 1, 52–53, 55–56, pt. 2, 349–55, pt. 3, 606–7, 626, pt. 4, 157–61, 165, and pt. 5, 383–84, 388–89. In a curious reversal of the conventional wisdom of the time, Runich argued (pt. 3, 606) that Moscow had to be destroyed in 1812 because the Francophile *nobility* might be seduced by Napoleon. Like Aleksandr Sturdza, Runich thought the ignorance and demoralization of the Orthodox clergy contributed to the spread of sectarianism and heresy (pt. 2, 337).

81. "Perepiska Imperatora s Rostopchinym," 207, to Alexander I, Moscow, June 22, 1814. Dubrovin, *Voina v pis'makh,* 498–99, Moscow, July 3, 1813. "Perepiska Imperatora s Rostopchinym," 198, Moscow, September 24, 1813. Rostopchin also disliked Roksandra Sturdza: "The two individuals who did the most to spoil the Emperor's original character are [his tutor] La Harpe and Miss Sturdza," he wrote. "She belonged to the mystical society of Germany, and it is she who first made Mrs. Krüdener fashionable and arranged a position in Russia for Mr. Stilling, the son of that famous mystic who was the apostle of the Martinists." *Arkhiv kniazia Vorontsova,* 8:409–10, to S. R. Vorontsov, Paris, October 4/16, 1820.

82. AIRLI, 263/2/599, l. 5, Runich to Pavel Mikhailovich, October 5, 1809. Runich, "Iz zapisok Runicha," pt. 1, 70–71.

83. Mel'gunov and Sidorov, 2:155–58, 202. ARAN, 100/1/197-17, ll. 16–21 ob: Runich to Golitsyn; Ivan Geim to Pavel I. Golenishchev-Kutuzov; Golenishchev-Kutuzov to "Siiatel'neishii graf" [A. K. Razumovskii]; Bishop Avgustin to "Siiatel'neishii Kniaz'" [Golitsyn]; Rostopchin to Viazmitinov (all of these letters are dated March 16, 1814). RNB, 656/21, l. 24 ob, Kozodavlev to Runich, St. Petersburg, March 30, 1814. See also "Pis'ma Lopukhina k Runichu," 1223, 1227–28, 1230, Voskresenskoe, April 26, May 10, June 21, November 26, 1814.

84. RNB, 656/37, ll. 63 ob–66, 71 ob, 78 ob, Popov to Runich, St. Petersburg, March 20, April 1, 28, 1814. ARAN, 100/1/197-17, ll. 22–22 ob, 26–26 ob, Golitsyn to Alexander, St. Petersburg, March 25, 1814, to Viazmitinov and Runich, March 30, 1814.

85. AIRLI, 263/2/599, ll. 71 ob–72, Runich to Pavel I. [Golenishchev-Kutuzov], Moscow, September 14, 1814. RNB, 656/37, l. 112, Popov to Runich, St.

Petersburg, September 25, 1814.

86. See, for example, R. Wortman, *The Development of a Russian Legal Consciousness*, 93. Shishkov expressed the traditional view when he admonished his nephew that "the only way that, together with your gentry status, you can also acquire your ancestors' honor and nobleness, is through loyal and diligent service." Service and simple Christian piety and virtue, he argued, were the keys to being a good officer and nobleman. A. S. Shishkov, *Put' chesti, ili Sovety molodomu ofitseru*, 18–19 and passim.

87. Florovsky, 1:164.

CHAPTER 7:

THE HOLY ALLIANCE EXPERIMENT

1. The index to Nikolai Mikhailovich's *Imperator Aleksandr I* lists Krüdener twenty-four times for the first volume (the second contains primary sources) but Roksandra Sturdza only once. V. O. Kliuchevskii similarly mentions the former's influence, not the latter's (*Sochineniia v deviati tomakh*, 4:415). This tendency also occurs in post-1917 scholarship. See, e.g., L. I. Strakhovsky, *Alexander I of Russia: The Man Who Defeated Napoleon*, 174–78; A. G. Mazour, *The First Russian Revolution, 1825: The Decembrist Movement, Its Origins, Development, and Significance*, 32; B. Pares, *A History of Russia*, 322; A. Kornilov, *Nineteenth Century Russia: From the Age of Napoleon to the Eve of Revolution*, 93–94, 115; N. V. Riasanovsky, *A History of Russia*, 349; and A. Walicki, *A History of Russian Thought: From the Enlightenment to Marxism*, 72. See also Mazour (31–37), who claims that "the servility of the literati to the state needs no better example than Admiral Shishkov"; here Mazour confuses attachment to tradition with subservience to a reformist and Westernizing, and later mystical, monarchy. A recent example of this misleading progressive/reactionary dichotomy (with Aleksandr Sturdza singled out as a particularly vile obscurantist) is G. E. Pavlova, *Organizatsiia nauki v Rossii v pervoi polovine XIX v.*, 63–77, 116, 120, passim.

2. See J. M. Hartley, "Is Russia Part of Europe? Russian Perceptions of Europe in the Reign of Alexander I."

3. Raeff, "Les Slaves," 546–48.

4. Grimsted, *Foreign Ministers*, 226.

5. Ibid., 236–38, 240–42.

6. AIRLI, 288/1/5, "Revue de l'année 1819," ll. 135 ob–136.

7. Ibid., l. 53 ob. A. S. Sturdza, *Œuvres posthumes religieuses, historiques, philosophiques et littéraires d'Alexandre de Stourdza* 3:287. (Since the volumes are not numbered, I am using the following system: "Etudes morales et religieuses . . ." is vol. 1; "Notions sur la Russie . . ." is vol. 2; "Souvenirs et portraits" is vol. 3; "La science des antiquités . . ." is vol. 4.) AIRLI, 288/1/4, "Souvenirs du règne de l'Empereur Alexandre," l. 90 ob. A. S. Sturdza, *Considérations sur la doctrine et l'esprit de l'Eglise orthodoxe*, 169–70, passim.

8. Schaeder, 47–48, 65.

9. Sturdza, *Considérations,* 169–70, 212–13. Sturdza, *Œuvres,* 1:33–34. AIRLI, 288/1/4, "Souvenirs du règne," ll. 82–83. Boffa, 104.

10. P. Ia. Chaadaev, *Polnoe sobranie sochinenii i izbrannye pis'ma,* 1: 88–96, passim.

11. Sturdza, *Œuvres,* 3:79–81; also 2:37–40, 70, 83–85, 91, 93–97, 108, 113–17, 148. RGADA, 3/1/78, ll. 106–27. AIRLI, 288/1/26b, ll. 289–300.

12. Sturdza, *Œuvres,* 4:162–209. A. S. Sturdza, *O vliianii zemledel'cheskikh zaniatii na umstvennoe i nravstvennoe sostoianie narodov,* 156, 168–70. AIRLI, 288/1/5, "Revue de l'année 1819," l. 24. AIRLI, 288/1/4, "Souvenirs du règne," l. 66. A. S. Sturdza, *Mémoire sur l'état actuel de l'Allemagne, par M. de S. . . . ., Conseiller d'Etat de S. M. I. de toutes les Russies,* 21.

13. Sturdza's arguments were fairly typical of the Continental Anglophobia described by A. D. Harvey in "European Attitudes to Britain During the French Revolution and Napoleonic Era," passim.

14. Sturdza, *Œuvres,* 4:83; also 3:220, 337, 383–84, 419, 466, 4:110, 206, 186, 197–98. A. S. Sturdza, *Mysli o liubvi k otechestvu* (n.pl., n.d.), 20. AVPRI, 133/468/7713, ll. 3–6 ob.

15. AIRLI, 288/1/4, "Souvenirs du règne," ll. 71–71 ob.

16. A. S. Sturdza, *Zapisnaia knizhka puteshestvennika protiv voli,* 38. Sturdza, *Œuvres,* 3:249, 228. AIRLI, 288/1/4, "Souvenirs du règne," l. 58 ob.

17. Sturdza, *Œuvres,* 2:174–82.

18. V. G. Sirotkin, "Velikaia frantsuzskaia burzhuaznaia revoliutsiia, Napoleon i samoderzhavnaia Rossiia," 47–51. For an example of Sturdza's work (apparently), see the unsigned article on the Holy Alliance in the government newspaper *Le Conservateur Impartial,* no. 36 (May 4, 1817), 188–90.

19. AIRLI, 288/1/2, "Précis," l. 33 ob–36.

20. For a summary of the background to this, see A. Martin, "A. S. Sturdza i 'Sviashchennyi soiuz' (1815–1823 gg.)," 147.

21. Two angry students even challenged Sturdza to a duel, but the authorities persuaded them to withdraw their challenge. AIRLI 288/1/58, ll. 135–135 ob, Konopack to Voigt, Jena, February 26, 1819.

22. C. Brinkmann, "Die Entstehung von Sturdzas 'Etat actuel de l'Allemagne.' Ein Beitrag zur Geschichte der deutsch-russischen Beziehungen," 99, Semler to Prussian Foreign Ministry, St. Petersburg, January 19/31, 1819. *Arkhiv brat'ev Turgenevykh,* 5:212–13, N. I. Turgenev, diary for October 9, 1819. *Pis'ma Turgeneva Bulgakovym,* 167, A. I. Turgenev to A. Bulgakov, n.pl., December 13, 1818. *Ostaf'evskii arkhiv,* 1:169–70, A. I. Turgenev to Viazemskii, December 11, 1818; 1:216, Viazemskii to A. I. Turgenev, Warsaw, April 12, 1819. RGADA, 3/1/78, ll. 106–27.

23. AIRLI 288/1/124, ll. 40–41 ob, Roksandra to Aleksandr Sturdza, [Weimar] April 21, 23, 1819. AVPRI 133/468/10083, ll. 26–26 ob, "extrait d'une lettre particulière," Dresden, April 15, 1819. AVPRI 133/468/7991, ll. 1–4, Stur-

dza to Nesselrode, Warsaw, April 11/23, 1819. AIRLI, 288/1/4, "Souvenirs du règne," l. 60 ob. AIRLI 288/1/58, ll. 143–46, Sturdza to Nesselrode, Warsaw, April 11/23, 1819. Petri, 433.

24. Viazemskii to Turgenev, April 12, 1819. AIRLI 288/1/124, ll. 53–54 ob, 56 ob–57, 58–58 ob, Roksandra to her mother and Aleksandr, Lucca, July 22, Livorno, August 6, 10, 1819. AIRLI 288/1/58, l. 218 ob, Brunnow to Sturdza, May 22, 1819.

25. Unfortunately for the historian, Alexander I mostly made his foreign policy decisions informally and orally, so he left no explicit written statements of his views on Sturdza's work in foreign policy.

26. AIRLI 288/1/186, ll. 15, 4–10, Capodistrias to Sturdza, November 11, 1819, and "Canevas approuvé par Sa Majesté l'Empereur à St. Pétersbourg, le 5 Novembre 1819."

27. AIRLI 288/1/27, ll. 110–11, Sturdza to Capodistrias, December 12, 1819.

28. AIRLI 288/1/186, l. 36, Capodistrias to Sturdza, January 11, 1820.

29. AIRLI, 288/1/5, "Revue de l'année 1819," ll. 10–12 ob, 29 ob–31 ob.

30. Ibid., ll. 66–69 ob, 72–73 ob, 77–93, 104–42 ob.

31. He had written that the goal of education was a society based on "the permanent and salutary harmony between *faith, learning* and *authority,* in other words between Christian piety, the enlightenment of minds and the civil order." A. S. Sturdza, *Nastavlenie dlia rukovodstva Uchenago komiteta, uchrezhdennago pri Glavnom Pravlenii uchilishch,* 2. He identified himself as its author, and described the foreign reaction to it, in AIRLI, 288/1/2, "Précis," l. 35 ob.

32. AIRLI 288/1/186, l. 129, Capodistrias to Sturdza, January 21, 1820. "Canevas approuvé par Sa Majesté," ll. 8–10.

33. AIRLI 288/1/186, ll. 93, 131, 151, Capodistrias to Sturdza, January 20, February 6, March 19, 1820. AIRLI 288/1/26v, ll. 416–16 ob, "Compte-rendu de la correspondance d'Oustié."

34. AIRLI 288/1/186, l. 165 ob, Capodistrias to Sturdza, April 6, 1820.

35. AIRLI 288/1/26, ll. 5–15, "Projet de rapport au Secrétaire d'Etat Comte Capodistrias. Oustié le 24 Avril 1820. No. 30." AIRLI 288/1/186, l. 209, Capodistrias to Sturdza, May 11, 1820.

36. AIRLI 288/1/26, ll. 18–27, "Projet . . . Oustié, le 1 Mai 1820. No. 31." All the "projets" ("de rapport au Secrétaire d'Etat Comte Capodistrias") cited below carry this same archival call number. "Compte-rendu," ll. 377 ob–378.

37. Ll. 265–66 ob, "Projet . . . Oustié, le 19 Septembre/1 Octobre 1820. No. 47." "Compte-rendu," l. 380.

38. Ll. 267–77 ob, "Projet . . . Oustié le 2/14 Octobre 1820. No. 48."

39. "Compte-rendu," ll. 381–82. AIRLI, 288/1/4, "Souvenirs du règne," ll. 38–39.

40. Ll. 289–300, "Projet . . . Sélichtché le 12/24 Octobre 1820. No. 49."

41. "Compte-rendu," ll. 383 ob–387 ob. RGADA 3/1/78, l. 55, Capodistrias to Sturdza, Troppau, November 21/October 2 [*sic*], 1820. AVPRI 133/468/10159,

ll. 52–52 ob, Capodistrias to Sturdza, Troppau, October 20/November 1, 1820.

42. AIRLI, 288/1/4, "Souvenirs du règne," ll. 66–68.

43. Ll. 348–52 ob, "Projet . . . Oustié le 7/19 Novembre 1820. No. 54." AIRLI, 288/1/84, Sturdza to Severin, November 6/18, 1820.

44. Ll. 425–32, "Projet . . . Oustié le 31 Décembre 1820/12 Janvier 1821. No. 59." "Compte-rendu," ll. 421 ob–422.

45. Brinkmann, 89–90.

46. AIRLI, 288/1/4, "Souvenirs du règne," l. 39. After this point, Sturdza's main concern in foreign policy was the Greek revolt against the Ottomans. See T. C. Prousis, "Aleksandr Sturdza: A Russian Conservative Response to the Greek Revolution."

47. RGADA, 3/1/78, Troppau, November 21/October 2 [sic], 1820.

48. Shil'der, 4:10–11. Sawatsky, "Minister of Piety," 209, 236–41, 249.

49. Mel'gunov, Dela i liudi, 246. AIRLI, 288/1/86, ll. 144–45 ob, Aleksandr to Roksandra Sturdza, St. Petersburg, January 24, 1817.

50. Sawatsky, "Minister of Piety," 296–310.

51. Sawatsky, "Golitsyn: Formidable or Forgettable?" 7.

52. Chistovich, 176–82. Sawatsky, "Minister of Piety," 242–47. Mel'gunov, Dela i liudi, 244. Goetze, 71–72. Ostaf'evskii arkhiv, 1:499.

53. C. H. Whittaker, The Origins of Modern Russian Education: An Intellectual Biography of Count Sergei Uvarov, 1786–1855, 1–55; "The Impact of the Oriental Renaissance in Russia: The Case of Sergej Uvarov"; and "The Ideology of Sergei Uvarov: An Interpretive Essay." L. M. Isabaeva, "Obshchestvenno-politicheskie vzgliady S. S. Uvarova v 1810–e gody." J. T. Flynn, "S. S. Uvarov's 'Liberal Years.'"

54. B. Hollingsworth, "Arzamas: Portrait of a Literary Society."

55. RNB, 656/21, ll. 76–77 ob., Kozodavlev to Runich, St. Petersburg, January 4, 1816. Russkii biograficheskii slovar', s.v. "Runich, Dmitrii Pavlovich." AIRLI, 263/2/577, ll. 13–15 ob, 21–21 ob., Runich to Popov, Pokoevo, May 28, 1817, May 20, 1818.

56. RNB, 656/38, ll. 85–85 ob, Popov to Runich, St. Petersburg, July 22, 1818.

57. Goetze, 128–29. RNB, 656/38, ll. 92–92 ob, Popov to Runich, St. Petersburg, March 11, 1819. Flynn, University Reform, 20, 81.

58. See Flynn, University Reform, 84–103, and "Magnitskii's Purge of Kazan University: A Case Study in the Uses of Reaction in Nineteenth-Century Russia"; A. Koyré, La philosophie et le problème national en Russie au début du XIXe siècle, 91–100, and "Un chapitre de l'histoire intellectuelle de la Russie: La persécution des philosophes sous Alexandre Ier." Kizevetter, Ocherki, 168–79. M. I. Sukhomlinov, Izsledovaniia i stat'i po russkoi literature i prosveshcheniiu, 1:216–33. E. Feoktistov, Materialy dlia istorii prosveshcheniia v Rossii. I: Magnitskii.

59. See, e.g., Viazemskii, 8:191.

60. See Sawatsky, "Minister of Piety," 274–75. Flynn, University Reform,

104–12. Sukhomlinov, *Izsledovaniia,* 1:239–397. Koyré, *La philosophie,* 102–12. Runich, "Iz zapisok Runicha," pt. 5, 380–81.

61. Epstein, 360–68.

62. Dubrovin, "Labzin," pt. 4, 117–18, passim. Zacek, "The Bible Society and the Orthodox Church," 420.

63. Dubrovin, "Tatarinova," passim.

64. See, e.g., Mark O'Connor, "Czartoryski, Józef Twardowski, and the Reform of Vilna University, 1822–1824."

65. See the articles by J. C. Zacek and B. Hollingsworth listed in the bibliography to this study. F. Walker argues that the "Pietist reaction" as a break with the past has been exaggerated: "Enlightenment and Religion in Russian Education in the Reign of Tsar Alexander I." The most thorough study of higher education in this era is Flynn, *University Reform.* See also K. Mayer, "Die Entstehung der 'Universitätsfrage' in Rußland. Zum Verhältnis von Universität, Staat und Gesellschaft zu Beginn des neunzehnten Jahrhunderts."

66. AIRLI, 288/1/86, ll. 144–45 ob, Aleksandr to Roksandra Sturdza, St. Petersburg, January 24, 1817. A. S. Sturdza, "O sud'be pravoslavnoi tserkvi russkoi v tsarstvovanie imperatora Aleksandra I-go. (Iz zapisok A. S. Sturdzy)," 273.

67. AIRLI, 288/1/2, "Précis," l. 35 ob, 36 ob. Flynn, *University Reform,* 82–83. RGIA, 732/1/17, 18, 19, 20, 21, 22, 23, volumes for 1818–1824.

68. Sturdza, *Nastavlenie dlia rukovodstva Uchenago komiteta.* Sturdza elaborated on this notion in his *Vera i vedenie ili Razsuzhdenie o neobkhodimom soglasii v prepodavanii religii i nauk pitomtsam uchebnykh zavedenii.*

69. Flynn, *University Reform,* 83–84. Sawatsky, "Minister of Piety," 259–62.

70. A. S. Sturdza, "Vospominaniia o Mikhaile Leont'eviche Magnitskom," 932. See also M. L. Magnitskii, "Duma na grobe grafini Roksandry Edling, urozhdennoi Sturdza."

71. Sturdza, "O sud'be," 280. Flynn, *University Reform,* 130–32. K. K. Walther, "Johann Baptist Schad in Rußland." AIRLI, 288/1/58, ll. 9–10 ob, 13, 17–19, Sturdza to Golitsyn, Weimar, December 8/20, 1818, Golitsyn to Sturdza, St. Petersburg, February 19, 24, 1819.

72. B. Hollingsworth, "A. P. Kunitsyn and the Social Movement in Russia under Alexander I." The thesis of the book (*Pravo estestvennoe,* 2 vols. [St. Petersburg, 1818–1820]) is discussed on pp. 126–28.

73. AIRLI 288/1/8, ll. 1–3 ob, 5–16 ob, "Proekt Otnosheniia k . . . Golitsynu. Selo Ust'e, Oktiabria 6. dnia, 1820 goda" and "Nachertanie metody dlia prepodavaniia estestvennago prava"; and RGIA, 732/1/20, ll. 18–36, February 10, 1821, and separate opinions (following the minutes of the meeting) by Magnitskii (February 13, 1821), Runich (February 16, 1821), and Uvarov (February 23, 1821).

74. RGIA, 732/1/20, l. 21 ob.

75. AIRLI, 288/1/8, ll. 1–3 ob, 5–16 ob.

76. RGIA, 732/1/20, ll. 19 ob, 21.

77. Ibid., ll. 28–28 ob. For Magnitskii's written opinion, see "Mnenie

deistvitel'nago statskago sovetnika Magnitskago, o Nauke Estestvennago Prava."
See also his "Rech' k Imperatorskomu Kazanskomu Universitetu, proiznesennaia
popechitelem onago Magnitskim, 15 Sentiabria, 1825 goda."

78. *Ostaf'evskii arkhiv,* 1:228, A. I. Turgenev to P. A. Viazemskii, St. Petersburg, May 7, 1819. AIRLI, 263/2/542, l. 11, December 4, 1820, Runich to Golitsyn.

79. AIRLI, 288/1/124, l. 117, Roksandra Sturdza to her mother, [Vienna] December 22, 1820 (NS). RGIA, 732/1/16, ll. 34–34 ob, January 2, 1817. Chistovich, 189–93, 224. Sturdza, "O sud'be," 274–76. Dubrovin, "Labzin," pt. 5,
64–91.

80. Sturdza, "O sud'be," 269–70, 272–73, 281–82, 286, and *Œuvres,* 3:155.

81. Sturdza, *Considérations.* He wrote the book in his free time, but the emperor had approved its outline. AIRLI, 288/1/2, "Précis," l. 35. AIRLI, 288/1/86,
ll. 126–126 ob, 134–134 ob, 136–37, 138 ob–39, Aleksandr to Roksandra Sturdza, Ust'e, August 29, and St. Petersburg, November 2/14, December 1/13,
16/28, 1816. The patriarchs of Constantinople and Jerusalem thanked him for the
book, which was translated into German, English, and Greek. A. S. Sturdza,
Pamiatnik trudov pravoslavnykh blagovestnikov russkikh s 1793 do 1853 goda,
ix. De Maistre promptly wrote a rebuttal, *Du Pape.* Maistre, 14:57–58, 82–83,
95–97, de Maistre to Severoli, St. Petersburg, February 11/23, 1817; to Vallaise,
St. Petersburg, April 1817; and to Rosaven, St. Petersburg, May 4/16, 1817. Sturdza later described *Considérations* as an immature work of his youth, most likely
because its ecumenical passages were a grudging concession to Holy Alliance
propaganda. Sturdza, *Œuvres,* 3:182. *Pis'ma A. S. Sturdzy k Innokentiiu,*
arkhiepiskopu khersonskomu i tavricheskomu, 6, Odessa, February 11, 1836.

82. AIRLI, 288/1/186, ll. 151–51 ob, Capodistrias to Sturdza, St. Petersburg,
March 19, 1820. Sturdza, *Œuvres,* 3:170–205 (on Joseph de Maistre), and "O
sud'be," 269. AIRLI, 288/1/9 ("de l'expulsion des Jésuites des deux Capitales").
See Schlafly, "Echoes of the French Revolution"; Edwards, "Joseph de Maistre";
and J. Flynn, "The Role of the Jesuits in the Politics of Russian Education,
1801–1820." Sawatsky ("Minister of Piety," 321–23) disagrees with Flynn over
the reasons for their expulsion. Capodistrias told Sturdza that it was "essential . . .
to avoid bringing up the Jesuit question in the abstract, as the Minister of Religion
does": AIRLI, 288/1/186, ll. 141–44 ob, St. Petersburg, February 28, 1820. *Sup-
plément, Le Conservateur Impartial,* no. 23 (March 19/31, 1820): 107–8.

83. Sturdza, "O sud'be," 287.

84. Ll. 92–94, "Projet . . . Oustié le 7 Avril 1820," and ll. 96–116, "Proekt
uchrezhdeniia Seminarii." He noted three years later that the idea "was destined
to be discussed and carried out by a Committee of Clergymen" (AIRLI, 288/1/2,
"Précis," l. 36 ob), but wrote in 1836 that it was only now being acted upon.
Pis'ma Sturdzy k Innokentiiu, 7, Odessa, February 11, 1836. Sturdza, *Œuvres,*
3:152–53.

85. *Pis'ma Sturdzy k Innokentiiu,* 49–51, Odessa, March 27, 1853.

86. See, e.g., Sturdza, *Œuvres,* 3:267–311.

87. See the recent study by T. Prousis, *Russian Society and the Greek Revolution.*

88. AIRLI, 288/1/25, "Projet . . . expédié le 2 Avril 1821." Sturdza made the same arguments in ll. 33–34 ob, "Projet . . . Oustié le, Avril 1821," and ll. 37–44 ob, "Projet . . . Oustié le 22 Mai 1821. No. 11." Capodistrias generally shared Sturdza's views on Greece. Grimsted, *Foreign Ministers,* 256–65. Most of Russian public opinion shared Sturdza's and Capodistrias's sympathy for the Greeks. Shil'der, 4:224–25.

89. AIRLI, 288/1/47, ll. 5 ob–6, St. Petersburg, November 30, 1821. Sturdza, "O sud'be," 280. His position on Greece is discussed in Prousis, "Sturdza."

90. AIRLI, 288/1/2, "Précis," l. 37. AIRLI, 288/1/312, l. 39, Sturdza to Alexander I, n.pl., n.d.

91. Sturdza, "Beseda," 13–14. On his literary acquaintances, see also A. S. Sturdza, "Dan' pamiati V. A. Zhukovskago i N. V. Gogolia;" *Perepiska V. A. Zhukovskago s A. S. Sturdzoiu,* ed. Diktiadis; A. F. Shidlovskii, ed., *Znakomstvo i perepiska N. V. Gogolia s A. S. Sturdzoiu.*

92. Shil'der, 4:468. *Pis'ma Karamzina k Dmitrievu,* 204, 218, 212, Karamzin to Dmitriev, St. Petersburg, January 18, Tsarskoe Selo, July 17, and St. Petersburg, April 23, 1817. On Karamzin's view of post-1815 international affairs, see Mitter, 276–77. Black, *Karamzin,* 90. *Pis'ma N. M. Karamzina k kniaziu P. A. Viazemskomu 1810–1826 (Iz Ostaf'evskago arkhiva),* 107, Karamzin to Viazemskii, St. Petersburg, December 8, 1820. *Pis'ma Karamzina k Dmitrievu,* 195–96, Karamzin to Dmitriev, Tsarskoe Selo, September 12, 1816.

93. Khodasevich, 258. *Pis'ma Karamzina k Viazemskomu,* 12, 39, 62, 92, Karamzin to Viazemskii, Tsarskoe Selo, June 8, 1816; St. Petersburg, November 5, 1817; Tsarskoe Selo, September 11, 1818; St. Petersburg, December 17, 1819. Bulich, 1:233. Al'tshuller, *Predtechi,* 357–59. Sukhomlinov, *Istoriia,* 7:228–35.

94. Shishkov, *Zapiski, mneniia,* 2:134.

95. Ibid., 2:109–34, 43–52. Mironenko, *Samoderzhavie,* 140.

96. Shishkov, *Zapiski, mneniia,* 2:141–46.

97. Ibid., 2:293–98. See his speeches, RGIA, 1673/1/30 (reproduced in "Aleksandr Semenovich Shishkov, 1824 g.") and 1673/1/40. Goetze, 288.

98. Shishkov, *Zapiski, mneniia,* 2:121, 153.

99. Shil'der, 4:185–86, Alexander I to Arakcheev, Troppau, November 5/17, 1820. Ibid., 4:232–36. V. V. Lapin, *Semenovskaia istoriia: 16–18 oktiabria 1820 g.* Chistovich, 223. Derzhavin, "'Uchenik mudrosti,'" 162–64. Zacek, "The Bible Society and the Orthodox Church," 424. Dubrovin, "Labzin," pt. 6, 38–45, and "Tatarinova," pt. 5, 225–33. Nikolai Mikhailovich, *Doneseniia avstriiskago poslannika pri russkom dvore Lebtselterna za 1816–1826 gody,* 83, Lebzeltern to Metternich, St. Petersburg, October 21, 1821.

100. Golitsyn thought himself a victim of the clergy: "This is a time of martyrs for the Holy Spirit, for throughout Europe the external Church seeks to portray

them as heretics and persecutes them." AIRLI, 288/1/265, ll. 24–24 ob, to Roksandra Sturdza, Tsarskoe Selo, August 23, 1824. Goetze, 201–9. Chistovich, 225–26, 244–45. Sawatsky, "Minister of Piety," 405–18. Kizevetter, *Ocherki,* 392–95. Mel'gunov, *Dela i liudi,* 287–89. P. Christoff, *The Third Heart: Some Intellectual-Ideological Currents and Cross Currents in Russia 1800–1830,* 73. Okun', *Istoriia,* 340.

101. Besides Miropol'skii, see "Iur'evskii arkhimandrit Fotii i ego tserkovno-obshchestvenaia deiatel'nost'"; J. L. Wieczynski, "Apostle of Obscurantism: The Archimandrite Photius of Russia (1792–1838)." Goetze hated Fotii (179–81).

102. See Flynn, *University Reform,* 161–77.

103. S. Monas, "Šiškov, Bulgarin, and the Russian Censorship," 131–34. Shishkov, *Zapiski, mneniia,* 2:163–290. AIRLI, 265/2/3112, l. 9, Shishkov to Serafim, n.pl., November 21, 1824. AIRLI, 154/60, ll. 5–7, recollections of I. N. Loboiko. V. A. Fedorov, *"Svoei sud'boi gordimsia my . . ." Sledstvie i sud nad dekabristami,* 245.

104. RGIA, 1673/1/44, l. 2, Shishkov to Nicholas I, n.d. [1828] (copy). Stoiunin, "Shishkov," pt. 4, 482–83. Kochubinskii, 248–57, 263, 288. Flynn, *University Reform,* 161–72.

105. AIRLI, 636/2/3, Shishkov to Nicholas I, n.d. [1828] (draft).

106. Goetze, 229–31. Dubrovin, "Tatarinova," pt. 5, 233–61. *Russkii biograficheskii slovar',* s.v. "Popov, Vasilii Mikhailovich." She was released in 1847 (after promising not to resume her religious activities) and the next year was allowed to move to Moscow, where she died in 1856. *Russkii biograficheskii slovar',* s.v. "Tatarinova, Ekaterina Filippovna."

107. Runich, "Iz zapisok Runicha," pt. 2, 353–57, pt. 5, 373–79. *Russkii biograficheskii slovar',* s.v."Runich, Dmitrii Pavlovich."

108. J. L. Wieczynski, ed., *The Modern Encyclopedia of Russian and Soviet History,* s.v. "Magnitskii, Mikhail Leont'evich," by J. T. Flynn.

109. Ibid., s.v. "Golitsyn, Alexander Nikolaevich," by D. L. Schlafly, Jr.

110. See A. F. Shidlovskii, ed., "Grafinia R. S. Edling v pis'makh k V. G. Tepliakovu." Sturdza, *Œuvres,* 3:50–59. Nikolai Mikhailovich, *Elisaveta,* 3:460, 481, 483–84, Elisaveta to her mother, Taganrog, October 12/24, December 17/29, 1825, December 21, 1825/January 2, 1826. Elisaveta survived her husband by only a few months.

111. Some of his works are listed in the Works Cited of this study. On his ties to *Moskvitianin,* where he often published, and its editor Pogodin, see N. Barsukov, *Zhizn' i trudy M. P. Pogodina,* 8:442, 9:25–27, 443, 451, 10:303–4, 359, 12:191–93. Prousis, "Sturdza," 328–31. *Pis'ma A. S. Sturdzy k ego dukhovniku, protoiereiu M. K. Pavlovskomu,* 36–37, M. A. Gagarina (née Sturdza) to Pavlovskii, Manzyr', June 18, 1854. Sturdza, *Pamiatnik,* gives the date of his death as June 15 (xxiii).

112. She apparently died on September 1, but sources differ on the precise date. AIRLI, Kartoteka B. L. Modzalevskago, card 1827. Her illness is mentioned

in Nikolai Mikhailovich, *Elisaveta,* 3:436, Elisaveta Alekseevna to her mother, Tsarskoe Selo, July 18/30, 1825.

113. Przecławski, 383. *Arkhiv brat'ev Turgenevykh,* 6:48, Viazemskii to A. I. Turgenev and Zhukovskii, Moscow, November 20, 1826. Goetze liked Iuliia Osipovna Shishkova and recalled that it was a happy marriage. Goetze, 284–85, 287. Kochubinskii, 288–89. Aksakov was appalled at Shishkov's new Polish "friends," who, he felt, were not worthy of the old man. Aksakov, 2:308–9.

114. Aksakov, 2:311.

115. According to Mikhail Sh. Fainshtein (oral communication), the admiral was one of only two officials whose funerals Nicholas found worth attending. Benckendorff, the chief of the secret police, was the other. AIRLI, 636/2/15, "Priglasitel'nyi bilet na pokhorony Shishkova A. S." Goetze, 319.

CONCLUSION

1. W. B. Lincoln, *In the Vanguard of Reform: Russia's Enlightened Bureaucrats 1825–1861,* 134–35. M. Malia, *Alexander Herzen and the Birth of Russian Socialism,* 58. M. A. Polievktov, *Nikolai I: Biografiia i obzor tsarstvovaniia,* 71, 294. Raeff, *Comprendre,* 118–20, 167–69. Kizevetter, *Ocherki,* 193–94.

2. On noble hostility to university education as a prerequisite for service, especially if the universities were open to nonnobles, see J. T. Flynn, "The Universities, the Gentry, and the Russian Imperial Services, 1815–1825." (The title of the article is misleading: it actually covers the first half of Alexander I's reign.)

3. On the ambivalent stance of Russian romantic nationalists (such as M. P. Pogodin and S. P. Shvevyrev) toward Shishkov's legacy, see E. C. Thaden, *Conservative Nationalism in Nineteenth-Century Russia,* 25.

4. See Prousis, "Sturdza," 331.

5. See Whittaker, *Uvarov,* 94–119.

6. See, for example: Mayer, *Persistence,* 5–15; H.-U. Wehler, *Das Deutsche Kaiserreich 1871–1918,* 76; and "Conflict and Cohesion Among German Elites in the Nineteenth Century," in *Imperial Germany,* ed. J. Sheehan, 82.

7. Shishkov's interest in folk culture appealed to many younger literati (including some of the Decembrists) after 1815. However, they often gave it a distinctly non-Shishkovian romantic twist and used it to formulate a socially and politically liberal nationalism. Christoff, 31–33. Bonamour, 79, 87–88.

8. See Hartley, passim.

9. Nicholas I and his associates felt ambivalent and distrustful toward nationalism. See N. V. Riasanovsky, *Nicholas I and Official Nationality in Russia, 1825–1855,* 227–31, 237–38.

10. See K. P. Pobedonostsev, *Reflections of a Russian Statesman.* By his time, the domestic challenge to the ancien régime was far more severe than eighty years earlier under Alexander I, and his book accordingly is a shrill and, it seems, pessimistic echo of the obscurantist sides of Shishkov's and Sturdza's thought.

11. Sturdza's role as an intellectual link between the Orthodox conservatives of the 1820s and the Slavophiles is pointed out by Müller, 27.

12. See, e.g., Solzhenitsyn's 1990 essay *Kak nam obustroit' Rossiiu,* 26, 29, passim, and his "What Kind of 'Democracy' Is This?" *New York Times,* January 4, 1997. I thank Jacob and Norah Kaltenbach for drawing my and other historians' attention to this opinion column by Solzhenitsyn.

Works Cited

MANUSCRIPT SOURCES

Documents from Russian archives are cited thus: *fond / opis' / delo, l[ist]*. The backside of a *list,* following Russian custom, is cited as "ob." Dates are given according to the calendar in force in Russia. Dates given according to the Western calendar are identified as "NS" (New Style).

Arkhiv Instituta Russkoi literatury Rossiiskoi Akademii Nauk (AIRLI), St. Petersburg:

> *fond*   154 Arkhiv I. N. Loboiki
> 263 Arkhiv D. P. Runicha
> 265 Arkhiv zhurnala "Russkaia Starina"
> 288 Arkhiv A. S. Sturdzy
> 322 Arkhiv D. I. Khvostova
> 358 Arkhiv kn. M. I. Kutuzova-Smolenskogo
> 636 Arkhiv A. S. Shishkova
> Kartoteka B. L. Modzalevskago

Arkhiv vneshnei politiki Rossiiskoi Imperii (AVPRI), Moscow:

> *fond*   133 Kantseliariia ministra inostrannykh del Rossii

Works Cited

Rossiiskaia Natsional'naia Biblioteka (RNB), St. Petersburg:
  fond 143 G. I. Villamov
       656 D. P. Runich
       862 A. S. Shishkov
Rossiiskii Gosudarstvennyi arkhiv drevnykh aktov (RGADA), Moscow:
  fond 3 Dela, otnosiashchiesia do vnutrennei i vneshnei politiki
       Rossii
Rossiiskii Gosudarstvennyi arkhiv Voenno-Morskogo Flota (RGAVMF), St. Petersburg:
  fond 166 Departament Morskogo Ministra, po chasti Admiral-
       teiskogo Departamenta
       406
Rossiiskii Gosudarstvennyi istoricheskii arkhiv (RGIA), St. Petersburg:
  fond 732 Glavnoe pravlenie uchilishch
       733 Departament narodnogo prosveshcheniia
       734 Uchenyi komitet
       777 Petrogradskii komitet po delam pechati (Peterburgskii
       tsenzurnyi komitet)
       1163 Komitet okhraneniia obshchei bezopasnosti
       1673 A. S. Shishkov
Rossiiskii Gosudarstvennyi voenno-istoricheskii arkhiv (RGVIA), Moscow:
  fond 474 Kollektsiia Voenno-Uchenogo Arkhiva
Sankt-Peterburgskoe Otdelenie Arkhiva Rossiiskoi Akademii Nauk (ARAN), St. Petersburg:
  fond 100 Dubrovin, Nikolai Fedorovich (documents in this collec-
       tion are usually copies, not originals)
Universitätsbibliothek Basel (UBB):
       Handschriftlicher Nachlaß Schwarz, Abt. X, letters from
       Roksandra Sturdza to Johann-Heinrich Jung-Stilling
Private collection of Dr. Francis Ley, Paris, France

PRINTED COLLECTIONS OF LETTERS

Dubrovin, Nikolai F., ed. *Otechestvennaia Voina v pis'makh sovremennikov (1812–1815 gg.).* Supplement to *Zapiski Imperatorskoi Akademii Nauk,* vol. 43, no. 1. St. Petersburg, 1882.
Falloux, Alfred Pierre Frédéric de, ed. *Lettres de Madame de Swetchine.* 6th ed., vol. 1. Paris, 1901.
Ferdinand Christin et la Princesse Tourkestanow, lettres écrites de Pétersbourg et de Moscou, 1813–1819. "Archives Russes." Moscow, 1882.
Modzalevskii, B. L., ed. "K biografii Novikova. Pis'ma ego k Labzinu, Chebotarevu i dr. 1797–1815." *Russkii Bibliofil* bk. 3 (1913): 5–39 (pt. 1); 4 (1913): 14–42 (pt. 2).

————, ed. "Pis'ma grafa F. V. Rostopchina k A. F. Labzinu." *Russkaia Starina* 153 (February 1913): 419–30.

"Moskva v 1812 godu. Graf Rostopchin-kniaziu Bagrationu." *Russkaia Starina* 40 (December 1883): 649–51.

Nikolai Mikhailovich, Grand Duke. *Correspondance de l'Empereur Alexandre Ier avec sa soeur la Grande-Duchesse Catherine, Princesse d'Oldenbourg, puis Reine de Wurtemberg 1805–1818.* St. Petersburg, 1910.

————. *Doneseniia avstriiskago poslannika pri russkom dvore Lebtselterna za 1816–1826 gody.* St. Petersburg, 1913.

————. *Imperatritsa Elisaveta Alekseevna, supruga Imperatora Aleksandra I.* 3 vols. St. Petersburg, 1908–1909.

"Perepiska Imperatora Aleksandra Pavlovicha s grafom F. V. Rostopchinym 1812–1814 gg." *Russkaia Starina* 77 (January 1893): 173–208.

Perepiska V. A. Zhukovskago s A. S. Sturdzoiu. Ed. Diktiadis. Odessa, 1855.

Petri, Hans. "R. de Stourdza und der Reichsfreiherr vom Stein." *Südost-Forschungen* 28 (1969): 280–83.

Pis'ma Aleksandra Turgeneva Bulgakovym. Ed. A. A. Saburov and I. K. Luppol. Moscow, 1939.

"Pis'ma A. S. Shishkova grafu Dmitriiu Ivanovichu Khvostovu." *Russkaia Starina* 86 (April 1896): 33–38.

Pis'ma A. S. Sturdzy k Innokentiiu, arkhiepiskopu khersonskomu i tavricheskomu. Odessa, 1894.

Pis'ma A. S. Sturdzy k ego dukhovniku, protoiereiu M. K. Pavlovskomu. Odessa, 1895.

"Pis'ma grafa F. V. Rastopchina k Imperatoru Aleksandru Pavlovichu." *Russkii Arkhiv* no. 8 (1892): 419–46, 519–65.

"Pis'ma imperatora Aleksandra Pavlovicha k R. S. Sturdze (grafine Edling)." *Russkii Arkhiv* no. 11 (1888): 373–77.

"Pis'ma imperatritsy Elisavety Alekseevny k R. S. Sturdze (grafine Edling)." *Russkii Arkhiv* no. 11 (1888): 378–84.

"Pis'ma I. V. Lopukhina k D. P. Runichu." *Russkii Arkhiv* (1870): 1215–36.

"Pis'ma Nikolaia Ivanovicha Novikova k D. P. Runichu." *Russkii Arkhiv* (1871): 1013–94.

Pis'ma N. M. Karamzina k I. I. Dmitrievu. Ed. Ia. Grot and P. Pekarskii. St. Petersburg, 1866.

Pis'ma N. M. Karamzina k kniaziu P. A. Viazemskomu 1810–1826 (Iz Ostaf'evskago arkhiva). Ed. Nikolai Barsukov. St. Petersburg, 1897.

"Pis'ma velikoi kniagini Ekateriny Pavlovny k inzhener-generalu F. P. Devolanu." *Russkii Arkhiv* (1870): 1967–2014.

"Pis'mo grafa F. V. Rostopchina k velikoi kniagine Ekaterine Pavlovne." *Russkii Arkhiv* (1876): 374–75.

"Pis'mo grafa Rostopchina k imperatoru Aleksandru I-mu s donosom na Speranskago." *Russkaia Starina* 122 (May 1905): 412–16.

Works Cited

"Pis'mo grafini Edling k grafu Kapodistrii." *Russkii Arkhiv* no. 11 (1891): 419–23.

"Politicheskaia perepiska generala Savari vo vremia prebyvaniia ego v S.-Peterburge v 1807 g." *Sbornik Imperatorskago Russkago Istoricheskago Obshchestva* 83 (1892) (entire volume).

Pushkin, E. A., ed. *Pis'ma velikoi kniagini Ekateriny Pavlovny*. Tver', 1888.

"Reskript Aleksandra I grafu Rostopchinu po povodu pis'ma ego o slukhakh i bezporiadkakh v provintsii." *Russkaia Starina* 111 (September 1902): 634.

"Russkii puteshestvennik proshlago veka za granitseiu (Sobstvennoruchnyia pis'ma A. S. Shishkova 1776 i 1777 g.)." *Russkaia Starina* 90 (May 1897): 409–23 (pt. 1); (June 1897): 619–32 (pt. 2); 91 (July 1897): 197–224 (pt. 3).

Shidlovskii, A. F., ed. "Grafinia R. S. Edling v pis'makh k V. G. Tepliakovu." *Russkaia Starina* 87 (August 1896): 405–22.

————, ed. *Znakomstvo i perepiska N. V. Gogolia s A. S. Sturdzoiu*. N.pl., n.d. Originally published in *Vestnik vsemirnoi istorii* no. 1 (1899).

Susini, Eugène, ed. *Lettres inédites de Franz von Baader*. 4 vols. Paris, 1942; Vienna, 1951; Paris, 1967.

"Tri pis'ma grafa F. V. Rostopchina k Velikoi Kniagine Ekaterine Pavlovne." *Russkii Arkhiv* (1869): 759–62.

Wilmot, Martha and Catherine. *The Russian Journals of Martha and Catherine Wilmot: Being an Account by two Irish Ladies of their Adventures in Russia as Guests of the celebrated Princess Daschkaw, containing vivid Descriptions of contemporary Court Life and Society, and lively Anecdotes of many interesting historical Characters, 1803–1808*. Ed. Marchioness of Londonderry and H. M. Hyde. London, 1934.

PRINTED PRIMARY SOURCES

Anon. "1811. Vozrazhenie neizvestnago na knigu, sochinennuiu grafom Stroinovskim, *O usloviiakh s krest'ianami*." *Chteniia v Imperatorskom Obshchestve istorii i drevnostei rossiiskikh* bk. 2 (April–June 1860): 195–202. Another version of this text was published as "Vozrazhenie kniazia Volodimira Mikhailovicha Volkonskago na knigu: 'O usloviiakh pomeshchikov s ikh krest'ianami, soch. grafa Stroinovskago, 1811 goda.'" Ibid., bk. 4, "smes'" (1872): 180–85.

Adams, Charles Francis, ed. *John Quincy Adams in Russia, comprising portions of The Diary of John Quincy Adams from 1809 to 1814*. New York, Washington, D.C., and London, 1970.

Aksakov, Sergei T. *Sobranie sochinenii v chetyrekh tomakh*. Ed. S. Mashinskii. 4 vols. Moscow, 1955–1956.

"Aleksandr Semenovich Shishkov, 1824 g." *Russkaia Starina* 62 (May 1889): 466–67.

"Aleksandr Semenovich Shishkov i dve vsepoddanneishiia ego zapiski." *Russkaia Starina* 87 (September 1896): 573–89.

Al'tshuller, R. E., and Andrei G. Tartakovskii. *Listovki Otechestvennoi voiny 1812 goda. Sbornik dokumentov.* Moscow, 1962.

Arkhiv brat'ev Turgenevykh. Ed. E. I. Tarasov. 6 vols. St. Petersburg-Petrograd, 1911–1921.

Arkhiv kniazia Vorontsova. 40 vols. Moscow, 1870–1895.

Batiushkov, Konstantin N. *Sochineniia v dvukh tomakh.* 2 vols. Moscow, 1989.

Broker, Aleksandr F. "Biografiia grafa Fedora Vasil'evicha Rostopchina, sostavlennaia A. F. Brokerom v 1826 godu." *Russkaia Starina* 77 (January 1893): 161–72.

Bulgakov, Aleksandr Ia. "Razgovor Neapolitanskago Korolia Miurata s Generalom Grafom M. A. Miloradovichem na avanpostakh armii 14 oktiabria 1812 goda (Otryvok iz Vospominanii 1812 goda)." *Moskvitianin* bk. 2 (1843): 499–520.

Caulaincourt, Armand de. *With Napoleon in Russia: The Memoirs of General de Caulaincourt, Duke of Vicenza.* New York, 1935.

Chaadaev, Petr Ia. *Polnoe sobranie sochinenii i izbrannye pis'ma.* 2 vols. Moscow, 1991.

Chichagov, Pavel V. *Mémoires de l'amiral Paul Tchitchagof, commandant en chef de l'armée du Danube, gouverneur des principautés de Moldavie et de Valachie en 1812.* Ed. Charles Gr. Lahovary. Paris and Bucharest, 1909.

Choiseul-Gouffier, Sophie de. *Historical Memoirs of the Emperor Alexander I and the Court of Russia.* Trans. Mary Berenice Patterson. Chicago, 1900.

Le Conservateur Impartial.

Derzhavin, Gavriil R. *Zapiski Derzhavina (1743–1812).* In *Sochineniia Derzhavina s ob"iasnitel'nymi primechaniiami Ia. Grota,* vol. 6: *Perepiska i "Zapiski."* St. Petersburg, 1871; repr., n.pl., 1973.

Dmitriev, Ivan I. *Vzgliad na moiu zhizn' (1823).* Repr. ed. of *Sochineniia Ivana Ivanovicha Dmitrieva.* Ed. A. A. Floridov. St. Petersburg, 1895; repr. Cambridge, England, 1974.

Dmitriev, Mikhail A. *Melochi iz zapasa moei pamiati.* Moscow, 1869.

"Dmitrii Pavlovich Runich (Materialy dlia ego biografii)." *Russkaia Starina* 95 (August 1898): 389–94.

Dolgorukov, Petr. *Rossiiskaia rodoslovnaia kniga.* 4 vols. St. Petersburg, 1854–1857.

Edling, Roksandra S. *Mémoires de la comtesse Edling (née Stourdza) demoiselle d'honneur de Sa Majesté l'Impératrice Elisabeth Alexéevna.* Moscow, 1888.

Works Cited

G. I. S. "Naselenie S.-Peterburga v 1808 g." *Russkaia Starina* 45 (March 1890): 870–72.

Gertsen, Aleksandr I. *Sobranie sochinenii v vos'mi tomakh.* 8 vols. Moscow, 1975.

Glinka, Fedor N. *Pis'ma russkogo ofitsera.* Moscow, 1987.

Glinka, Sergei N. *Zapiski o 1812 gode Sergeia Glinki, pervago ratnika Moskovskago Opolcheniia.* St. Petersburg, 1836.

———. *Zapiski o Moskve i o zagranichnykh proisshestviiakh ot iskhoda 1812 do poloviny 1815 goda, s prisovokupleniem statei: I) Aleksandr Pervyi i Napoleon. II) Napoleon i Moskva.* St. Petersburg, 1837.

———. *Zapiski Sergeia Nikolaevicha Glinki.* St. Petersburg, 1895.

———. *Zerkalo novago Parizha, ot 1789 do 1809 goda.* 2 vols. in 1. Moscow, 1809.

Goetze, Peter von. *Fürst Alexander Nikolajewitsch Galitzin und seine Zeit. Aus den Erlebnissen des Geheimraths Peter von Goetze.* Leipzig, 1882.

Golovina, Varvara N. *Souvenirs de la Comtesse Golovine née Princesse Galitsine 1766–1821.* Ed. and intro. K. Waliszewski. Paris, 1910.

Grech, Nikolai I. *Zapiski o moei zhizni.* Ed. E. G. Kapustina. Moscow, 1990.

Ivanov, V. *Zapiski, vedennyia vo vremia puteshestviia imperatritsy Elisavety Alekseevny po Germanii v 1813, 1814 i 1815 godakh.* 2 vols. St. Petersburg, 1833.

Kapodistrias, Iōannēs Antōniou. "Aperçu de ma carrière publique, depuis 1798 jusqu'à 1822." *Sbornik russkago istoricheskago obshchestva* 3 (1868): 163–296.

———. *Archeion Iōannou Kapodistria.* Ed. Kōstas Daphnēs. Trans. Geōrg. Ploumidēs and Aristeidēs Stergellēs. 10 vols. Kerkyra, 1976–1983.

Karamzin, Nikolai M. *Neizdannyia sochineniia i perepiska Nikolaia Mikhailovicha Karamzina.* Vol. 1. St. Petersburg, 1862.

———. *Izbrannye stat'i i pis'ma.* Moscow, 1982.

Kartavov, P. A., ed. *Letuchie listki 1812 goda. Rostopchinskiia afishi.* St. Petersburg, 1904.

Khvostov, Dmitrii I. "Iz arkhiva Khvostova." Ed. A. V. Zapadov. Akademiia Nauk SSSR, Institut literatury (Pushkinskii Dom). *Literaturnyi Arkhiv: Materialy po istorii literatury i obshchestvennogo dvizheniia.* Vol. 1. Ed. S. D. Balukhatyi, N. K. Piksanov, and O. V. Tsekhnovitser. Moscow and Leningrad, 1938.

Labzina, Anna E. *Vospominaniia Anny Evdokimovny Labzinoi 1758–1828.* Ed. B. L. Modzalevskii. St. Petersburg, 1914; repr. Cambridge, England, 1974.

Lopukhin, Ivan V. *Zapiski Senatora I. V. Lopukhina.* Moscow, 1990; repr. of 1859 ed.

Lubianovskii, Fedor P. "Vospominaniia Fedora Petrovicha Lubianovskago." *Russkii Arkhiv* (1872): 449–533.

Magnitskii, Mikhail L. "Mnenie deistvitel'nago statskago sovetnika Magnitskago, o Nauke Estestvennago Prava; Rech' k Imperatorskomu Kazanskomu Universitetu, proiznesennaia popechitelem onago Magnitskim, 15 Sentiabria, 1825 goda; Otnoshenie popechitelia Kazanskago uchebnago okruga k Mitropolitu Novgorodskomu, S.-Peterburgskomu, Estliandskomu i Finliandskomu, ot 24 Maia, 1824 goda." *Chteniia v Imperatorskom Obshchestve istorii i drevnostei rossiiskikh* bk. 4, "smes'" (October–December 1861): 157–63.

———. "Duma na grobe grafini Roksandry Edling, urozhdennoi Sturdza." *Moskvitianin* pt. 2, no. 3 (1844): 87–91.

Maistre, Joseph de. *Œuvres complètes de J. de Maistre.* New ed. 14 vols. Lyon, 1884–1886; repr. Geneva, 1979.

Markovich, A. "Zhozef de Mestr i Sent-Bëv v pis'makh k R. Sturdze-Edling." *Literaturnoe nasledstvo* 33–34 (1939): 379–456.

Mesiatsoslov s rospis'iu chinovnykh osob, ili obshchii shtat Rossiiskoi Imperii, na leto ot Rozhdestva Khristova 1807. St. Petersburg, 1807.

Obolenskii, Dmitrii, ed. *Khronika nedavnei stariny. Iz arkhiva kniazia Obolenskago-Neledinskago-Meletskago.* St. Petersburg, 1876.

"O grafe F. V. Rostopchine i o sobytiiakh 1812 goda v Moskve." *Chteniia v Imperatorskom Obshchestve istorii i drevnostei rossiiskikh* bk. 4, "smes'" (October–December 1861): 167–82.

Ostaf'evskii Arkhiv kniazei Viazemskikh, ed. S. D. Sheremetev. St. Petersburg, 1899–1913.

Pobedonostsev, Konstantin P. *Reflections of a Russian Statesman.* Ann Arbor, Mich., 1965.

Przecławski, O. "Aleksandr Semenovich Shishkov, r. 1754 ϯ1841 g. Vospominaniia O. A. Przhetslavskago." *Russkaia Starina* 13 (July 1875): 383–402.

Pushkin, Aleksandr S. *Sochineniia v trekh tomakh.* 3 vols. Moscow, 1985–1986.

Rossiia pervoi poloviny XIX v. glazami inostrantsev. Ed. Iurii A. Limonov. Leningrad, 1991.

Rostopchin, Andrei F., ed. *Matériaux en grande partie inédits pour la biographie future du Comte Théodore Rastaptchine, rassemblés par son fils.* Brussels, 1864.

Rostopchin, Fedor V. *Okh, frantsuzy!* Ed. G. D. Ovchinnikov. Moscow, 1992.

———. *Sochineniia Rastopchina (grafa Feodora Vasil'evicha).* Ed. Aleksandr Smirdin. St. Petersburg, 1853.

———. "Tysiacha vosem'sot dvenadtsatyi god v Zapiskakh grafa F. V. Rostopchina." Trans. I. I. Oreus. *Russkaia Starina* 64 (December 1889): 643–725.

———. "Zamechanie grafa F. V. Rastopchina na knigu g-na Stroinovskago." *Chteniia v Imperatorskom Obshchestve istorii i drevnostei rossiiskikh* bk. 2 (April–June 1860): 203–17.

———. "Zapiska o Martinistakh, predstavlennaia v 1811 godu grafom

Rostopchinym velikoi kniagine Ekaterine Pavlovne." *Russkii Arkhiv* bk. 3 (1875): 75–81.

Rostoptchine, Lydie. *Les Rostoptchine.* N.pl., 1984.

———, ed. *Œuvres inédites du Comte Rostoptchine, avec une "Etude sur le Gouverneur de Moscou."* Paris, 1894.

Runich, Dmitrii P. "Iz zapisok Runicha." Trans. V. V. Timoshchuk. *Russkaia Starina* 105 (January 1901): 47–77 (pt. 1); (February 1901): 325–57 (pt. 2); (March 1901): 596–633 (pt. 3); 106 (April 1901): 153–68 (pt. 4); (May 1901): 373–94 (pt. 5).

Ruskoi Vestnik.

Savary, René. "La cour de Russie en 1807–1808. Notes sur la cour de Russie et Saint-Pétersbourg, écrites en décembre 1807 par le général Savary." Ed. Albert Vandal. *Revue d'histoire diplomatique* (1890): 399–419.

———. *Memoirs of the Duke of Rovigo, (M. Savary,) Written by Himself: Illustrative of the History of the Emperor Napoleon.* 4 vols. London, 1828.

Schlözer, August Ludwig von. *Obshchestvennaia i chastnaia zhizn' Avgusta Liudviga Shletsera, im samym opisannaia. Prebyvanie i sluzhba v Rossii, ot 1761 do 1765 g. Izvestiia o togdashnei russkoi literature.* Trans. and ed. V. Kenevich. *Sbornik Otdeleniia russkago iazyka i slovesnosti Imperatorskoi Akademii nauk* vol. 13. St. Petersburg, 1875.

Schubert, Friedrich von. *Unter dem Doppeladler: Erinnerungen eines Deutschen in russischem Offiziersdienst, 1789–1814.* Ed. Erik Amburger. Stuttgart, 1962.

Ségur, Philippe Paul Comte de. *La campagne de Russie.* Geneva, 1972.

Shchukin, Petr I., ed. *Bumagi, otnosiashchiiasia do Otechestvennoi voiny 1812 goda.* 10 vols. Moscow, 1897–1908.

Shishkov, Aleksandr S. *Put' chesti, ili Sovety molodomu ofitseru.* Moscow, 1837.

———. *Sobranie Sochinenii i Perevodov Admirala Shishkova.* 16 vols. St. Petersburg, 1818–1834.

———. *Zapiski admirala A. S. Shishkova, vedennyia im vo vremia puteplavaniia ego iz Kronshtada v Konstantinopol'.* St. Petersburg, 1834.

———. *Zapiski, mneniia i perepiska admirala A. S. Shishkova.* 2 vols. Ed. N. Kiselev and Iu. Samarin. Berlin, 1870.

Solzhenitsyn, Aleksandr I. *Kak nam obustroit' Rossiiu: Posil'nye soobrazheniia.* Leningrad, 1990.

Stedingk, Curt von. *Mémoires posthumes du feld-maréchal Comte de Stedingk, rédigés sur des lettres, dépêches et autres pièces authentiques laissées à sa famille.* Ed. Général Comte de Björnstjerna. 3 vols. Paris, 1844–1847.

Stepanov, M., and F. Vermale, eds. "Zhozef de Mestr v Rossii." *Literaturnoe nasledstvo* 29–30 (1937): 577–726.

Sturdza, Aleksandr S. "Beseda liubitelei russkago slova i *Arzamas,* v tsarstvovanie Aleksandra I-go i moi vospominaniia." *Moskvitianin* no. 21, bk. 1 (November 1851): 3–22.

————. *Considérations sur la doctrine et l'esprit de l'Eglise orthodoxe.* Weimar, 1816.

————. "Dan' pamiati V. A. Zhukovskago i N. V. Gogolia." *Moskvitianin* no. 20, bk. 2 (1852): 213–28.

————. *Ideal i podrazhanie v iziashchnykh iskusstvakh.* Moscow, 1842.

————. *Khristianskiia besedy istoricheskiia i nravstvennyia.* Odessa, 1848. Originally published in French as *Etudes religieuses, historiques et morales.*

————. *Mémoire sur l'état actuel de l'Allemagne, par M. de S. . . . . . ., Conseiller d'Etat de S. M. I. de toutes les Russies.* Paris, November 1818.

————. *Mysli o liubvi k otechestvu.* N.pl., n.d.

————. *Nadgrobnoe slovo kniaziu Aleksandru Nikolaevichu Golitsynu.* St. Petersburg, 1859.

————. *Nastavlenie dlia rukovodstva Uchenago komiteta, uchrezhdennago pri Glavnom Pravlenii uchilishch.* N.pl., n.d.

————. *Nechto o etimologii i estetike po otnosheniiu k istorii i k nauke drevnostei.* Moscow, 1842.

————. *Nechto o filosofii khristianskoi.* Moscow, 1844.

————. "Ob Ivane Nikitiche Inzove." *Moskvitianin* bk. 1 (1847): 217–28.

————. "O Blagotvoritel'nosti Obshchestvennoi." *Zhurnal Imperatorskago Chelovekoliubivago Obshchestva, izdavaemyi Komitetom Onago po uchenoi chasti* pt. 2 (December 1817): 364–84.

————. "O chastnoi blagotvoritel'nosti." *Ibid.* (November 1817): 218–31.

————. *Œuvres posthumes religieuses, historiques, philosophiques et littéraires.* 5 vols. Paris, 1858–1861.

————. *Opyt uchebnago prednachertaniia dlia prepodavaniia Rossiiskomu Iunoshestvu Grecheskago iazyka, sochinenie Aleksandra Sturdzy, chitannoe v Besede liubitelei ruskago slova v 1812 godu.* St. Petersburg, 1817.

————. "O sud'be pravoslavnoi tserkvi russkoi v tsarstvovanie imperatora Aleksandra I-go. (Iz zapisok A. S. Sturdzy)." *Russkaia Starina* 15 (February 1876): 266–88.

————. *O vliianii zemledel'cheskikh zaniatii na umstvennoe i nravstvennoe sostoianie narodov.* Odessa, 1834.

————. *O vsenarodnom rasprostranenii gramotnosti. Donesenie Imperatorskomu Moskovskomu Obshchestvu Sel'skago Khoziaistva.* Moscow, 1848.

————. *Pamiatnik trudov pravoslavnykh blagovestnikov russkikh s 1793 do 1853 goda.* Moscow, 1857.

————. *Pis'ma o dolzhnostiakh sviashchennago sana.* 3d ed. Odessa, 1843.

————. *Ruchnaia kniga pravoslavnago khristianina.* St. Petersburg, 1830.

————. *Vera i vedenie ili Razsuzhdenie o neobkhodimom soglasii v prepodavanii religii i nauk pitomtsam uchebnykh zavedenii.* Odessa, 1833.

Works Cited

———. "Vospominaniia o Mikhaile Leont'eviche Magnitskom." *Russkii Arkhiv* (1868): 926–38.

———. "Vospominaniia o Nikolae Mikhailoviche Karamzine." *Moskvitianin* bk. 9 (1846): 145–54.

———. "Vospominaniia o zhizni i deianiiakh grafa I. A. Kapodistrii, pravitelia Gretsii." *Chteniia v Imperatorskom Obshchestve istorii i drevnostei rossiiskikh* bk. 2, "Materialy otechestvennye" (April–June 1864): 1–192.

———. *Zapisnaia knizhka puteshestvennika protiv voli.* Moscow, 1847.

Suvorin, A. S., ed. *Rostopchinskiia afishi 1812 goda.* St. Petersburg, 1889.

Turgenev, Aleksandr I. *Khronika russkogo. Dnevniki (1825–1826 gg.).* Ed. M. I. Gillel'son. Moscow and Leningrad, 1964.

Varnhagen von Ense, Karl August. *Werke in fünf Bänden.* Ed. Konrad Feilchenfeldt. Frankfurt am Main, 1987–1990.

Viazemskii, Petr A. *Polnoe sobranie sochinenii kniazia P. A. Viazemskago.* Ed. S. D. Sheremetev. 12 vols. St. Petersburg, 1878–1896.

Vigel', Filip F. *Zapiski.* Ed. S. Ia. Shtraikh. 2 vols. Moscow, 1928; repr. Cambridge, England, 1974.

Zhikharev, Stepan P. *Zapiski sovremennika.* 2 vols. Leningrad, 1989.

Zhukovskii, Vasilii A. *Sobranie sochinenii v 4–kh tomakh.* Moscow and Leningrad, 1960.

SECONDARY SOURCES

A. N. Radishchev: Materialy i Issledovaniia. Literaturnyi arkhiv. Moscow and Leningrad, 1936.

Akademiia Nauk SSSR, Institut russkoi literatury (Pushkinskii Dom). *Slovar' russkikh pisatelei XVIII veka.* Vol. 1. Leningrad, 1988.

Allgemeine Deutsche Biographie. 56 vols. 1875–1912; repr. ed. Berlin, 1967–1971.

Al'tshuller, Mark. "A. S. Shishkov o frantsuzskoi revoliutsii." *Russkaia literatura* no. 1 (1991): 144–49.

———. *Predtechi slavianofil'stva v russkoi literature (Obshchestvo "Beseda liubitelei russkogo slova").* Ann Arbor, Mich., 1984.

———. "*Rassuzhdenie o starom i novom sloge rossiiskogo iazyka* kak politicheskii dokument (A. S. Shishkov i N. M. Karamzin)." In *Russia and the West in the Eighteenth Century: Proceedings of the Second International Conference organized by the study group on Eighteenth-Century Russia and held at the University of East Anglia, Norwich, England, 17–22 July, 1981.* Ed. Anthony Glenn Cross. Newtonville, Mass., 1983.

———. "An Unknown Poem by A. S. Shishkov." *Oxford Slavonic Papers* n.s. 15 (1982): 95–102.

Amburger, Erik. *Geschichte der Behördenorganisation Rußlands von Peter dem Großen bis 1917.* Leiden, 1966.

Anderson, Benedict. *Imagined Communities: Reflections on the Origin and Spread of Nationalism.* Rev. ed. London and New York, 1991.

Anisimov, Evgenii V. *Vremia petrovskikh reform.* Leningrad, 1989.

Arsh, G. L. "Ioann Kapodistriia v Rossii." *Voprosy Istorii* no. 5 (1976): 49–65.

Artz, Frederick B. *Reaction and Revolution 1814–1832.* New York and London, 1950.

Augustine, Wilson R. "Notes Toward a Portrait of the Eighteenth-Century Russian Nobility." *Canadian Slavic Studies* 4, no. 3 (fall 1970): 373–425.

Aurova, N. N. "Idei prosveshcheniia v 1-m kadetskom korpuse (konets XVIII-pervaia chetvert' XIX v.)." *Vestnik Moskovskogo Universiteta,* seriia 8, *istoriia* no. 1 (1996): 34–42.

Baehr, Stephen L. "Regaining Paradise: The 'Political Icon' in Seventeenth-and Eighteenth-Century Russia." *Russian History* 11, nos. 2–3 (summer–fall 1984): 148–67.

Bakounine [Bakunina], Tatiana A. *Répertoire biographique des franc-maçons russes (XVIIIᵉ et XIXᵉ siècles).* Paris, 1967.

Bantysh-Kamenskii, Dmitrii N. *Slovar' dostopamiatnykh liudei russkoi zemli, soderzhashchii v sebe zhizn' i deianiia znamenitykh polkovodtsev, ministrov i muzhei gosudarstvennykh, velikikh ierarkhov pravoslavnoi tserkvi, otlichnykh literatorov i uchenykh, izvestnykh po uchastiiu v sobytiiakh otechestvennoi istorii.* 5 vols. Moscow, 1836. *Dopolnenie.* 3 vols. St. Petersburg, 1847.

Barsukov, Nikolai. *Zhizn' i trudy M. P. Pogodina.* 22 vols. St. Petersburg, 1888–1910.

Becker, Seymour. "Contributions to a Nationalist Ideology: Histories of Russia in the First Half of the Nineteenth Century." *Russian History* 13, no. 4 (winter 1986): 331–53.

Benz, Ernst, ed. *Die Ostkirche und die russische Christenheit.* Tübingen, 1949.

Beskrovnyi, L. G., ed. *Osvoboditel'naia voina 1813 goda protiv napoleonovskogo gospodstva.* Moscow, 1965.

Bittner, Konrad. "Herdersche Gedanken in Karamzins Geschichtsschau." *Jahrbücher für Geschichte Osteuropas* n.s. 7, no. 3 (1959): 237–69.

Black, J. Laurence. *Citizens for the Fatherland: Education, Educators, and Pedagogical Ideals in Eighteenth-Century Russia.* Boulder, Colo., and New York, 1979.

———, ed. *Essays on Karamzin: Russian Man-of-Letters, Political Thinker, Historian, 1766–1826.* The Hague and Paris, 1975.

———. "History in Politics: Karamzin's *Istoriia* as an Ideological Catalyst in Russian Society." *Laurentian University Review* 1, no. 2 (1968): 106–13.

———. *Nicholas Karamzin and Russian Society in the Nineteenth Century: A Study in Russian Political and Historical Thought.* Toronto and Buffalo, 1975.

———. "N. M. Karamzin, Napoleon, and the Notion of Defensive War in Russian

Works Cited

History." *Canadian Slavonic Papers* 12, no. 1 (spring 1970): 30–46.

Bliard, P. "L'Empereur Alexandre, les Jésuites et Joseph de Maistre, d'après des documents inédits." *Etudes* 130 (1912): 234–44.

Blum, Jerome. *Lord and Peasant in Russia from the Ninth to the Nineteenth Century*. Princeton, N.J., 1961.

Boffa, Massimo. "La Révolution française et la contre-Révolution." In *L'Héritage de la Révolution française*, ed. François Furet. [Paris] 1989.

Bolenko, K. G. "'Kleine Kinderbibliothek' I. G. Kampe v perevode A. S. Shishkova." *Vestnik Moskovskogo Universiteta, seriia 8, istoriia* no. 3 (1996): 57–68.

Bonamour, Jean. *A. S. Griboedov et la vie littéraire de son temps*. Paris, 1965.

Bozherianov, Ivan N. *Velikaia kniaginia Ekaterina Pavlovna, chetvertaia doch' Imperatora Pavla I, gertsoginia ol'denburgskaia, koroleva virtembergskaia, 1788 †1818. Biograficheskii ocherk s prilozheniem portreta i avtografa*. St. Petersburg, 1888.

Brinkmann, Carl. "Die Enstehung von Sturdzas 'Etat actuel de l'Allemagne.' Ein Beitrag zur Geschichte der deutsch-russischen Beziehungen." *Historische Zeitschrift* 120 (1919): 80–102.

Bulich, Nikolai N. *Ocherki po istorii Russkoi literatury i prosveshcheniia s nachala XIX veka*. 2 vols. St. Petersburg, 1902–1905.

Cherdakov, D. N. "Semantika slova i razvitie russkogo iazyka v kontseptsii A. S. Shishkova." *Vestnik Sankt-Peterburgskogo Gosudarstvennogo Universiteta, seriia 2, vypusk 1*, no. 2 (1996): 37–44.

Chistovich, I. A. *Rukovodiashchiie deiateli dukhovnago prosveshcheniia v Rossii v pervoi polovine tekushchago stoletiia*. St. Petersburg, 1894.

Chizhevskii, Dm. "Baader i Rossiia." *Novyi Zhurnal/The New Review* bk. 35 (1953): 301–10.

Christian, David. "The Political Ideals of Michael Speransky." *Slavonic and East European Review* 54, no. 2 (April 1976): 192–213.

———. "The Political Views of the Unofficial Committee in 1801: Some New Evidence." *Canadian-American Slavic Studies* 12, no. 2 (summer 1978): 247–65.

———. "The 'Senatorial Party' and the Theory of Collegial Government, 1801–1803." *Russian Review* 38, no. 3 (July 1979): 298–322.

Christoff, Peter K. *The Third Heart: Some Intellectual-Ideological Currents and Cross Currents in Russia 1800–1830*. The Hague and Paris, 1970.

Confino, Michael. "A propos de la notion de service dans la noblesse russe aux XVIIIe et XIXe siècles." *Cahiers du Monde russe et soviétique* 34, nos. 1–2 (January–June 1993): 47–58.

———. "Le paysan russe jugé par la noblesse au XVIIIe siècle." *Revue des Etudes slaves* 38 (1961): 51–63.

Cross, Anthony Glenn. "Karamzin and England." *Slavonic and East European Review* 43, no. 100 (December 1964): 91–114.

———. "Karamzin's *Moskovskii Zhurnal:* Voice of a Writer, Broadsheet of a Movement." *Cahiers du Monde russe et soviétique* 28, no. 2 (April–June 1987): 121–26.

———. "Karamzin Studies: For the Bicentenary of the Birth of N. M. Karamzin (1766–1966)." *Slavonic and East European Review* 45, no. 104 (January 1967): 1–11.

———. "N. M. Karamzin's 'Messenger of Europe' *(Vestnik Yevropy),* 1802–1803." *Forum for Modern Language Studies* 5, no. 1 (January 1969): 1–25.

———. *N. M. Karamzin: A Study of His Literary Career (1783–1803).* Carbondale, Ill., 1971.

———. "Russian Perceptions of England, and Russian National Awareness at the End of the Eighteenth and the Beginning of the Nineteenth Centuries." *Slavonic and East European Review* 61, no. 1 (January 1983): 89–106.

Darnton, Robert, and Daniel Roche, eds. *Revolution in Print: The Press in France 1775–1800.* Berkeley and London, 1989.

David, Zdenek V. "The Influence of Jacob Boehme on Russian Religious Thought." *Slavic Review* 21, no. 1 (March 1962): 43–64.

Derzhavin, N. "'Uchenik mudrosti' (A. F. Labzin i ego literaturnaia deiatel'nost')." *Istoricheskii Vestnik* 129 (July 1912): 137–75.

Desnitskii, Vasilii A. *Izbrannye stat'i po russkoi literature XVIII–XIX vv.* Moscow and Leningrad, 1958.

Dickinson, H. T., ed. *Britain and the French Revolution, 1789–1815.* New York, 1990.

Diktiadis. "Kratkoe svedenie ob A. S. Sturdze." *Chteniia v Imperatorskom Obshchestve istorii i drevnostei rossiiskikh* bk. 2, "Materialy otechestvennye" (April–June 1864): 193–205.

Dodelev, M. A. "Rossiia i voina ispanskogo naroda za nezavisimost' (1808–1814)." *Voprosy Istorii* no. 11 (1972): 33–44.

Doyle, William. *The Oxford History of the French Revolution.* Oxford and New York, 1989.

Druzhinin, Nikolai M. *Izbrannye trudy: Vneshniaia politika Rossii, Istoriia Moskvy, Muzeinoe delo.* Moscow, 1988.

Dubrovin, Nikolai F. "Nashi mistiki-sektanty. Aleksandr Fedorovich Labzin i ego zhurnal 'Sionskii Vestnik.'" *Russkaia Starina* 81 (September 1894): 145–203 (pt. 1); 82 (October 1894): 101–26 (pt. 2); (November 1894): 58–91 (pt. 3); (December 1894): 98–132 (pt. 4); 83 (January 1895): 56–91 (pt. 5); (February 1895): 35–52 (pt. 6).

———. "Nashi mistiki-sektanty. Ekaterina Filippovna Tatarinova i Aleksandr Petrovich Dubovitskii." *Russkaia Starina* 84 (October 1895): 33–64 (pt. 1); (November 1895): 3–43 (pt. 2); (December 1895): 51–93 (pt. 3); 85 (January 1896): 5–51 (pt. 4); (February 1896): 225–63 (pt. 5).

Works Cited

————. "Posle otechestvennoi voiny (Iz russkoi zhizni v nachale XIX veka)." *Russkaia Starina* 116 (November 1903): 241–71 (pt. 1); (December 1903): 481–514 (pt. 2); 117 (January 1904): 5–28 (pt. 3); (February 1904): 241–74 (pt. 4); (March 1904): 481–515 (pt. 5); 118 (April 1904): 5–34 (pt. 6); (May 1904): 241–64 (pt. 7).

————. "Russkaia zhizn' v nachale XIX veka." *Russkaia Starina* 96 (December 1898): 481–516 (pt. 1); 97 (January 1899): 3–38 (pt. 2); (February 1899): 241–64 (pt. 3); (March 1899): 539–69 (pt. 4); 98 (April 1899): 53–75 (pt. 5); (June 1899): 481–508 (pt. 6); 99 (August 1899): 241–70 (pt. 7); 103 (September 1900): 457–83 (pt. 8); 104 (October 1900): 53–81 (pt. 9); (November 1900): 257–75 (pt. 10); 107 (September 1901): 449–63 (pt. 11); 108 (October 1901): 5–41 (pt. 12); (November 1901): 241–64 (pt. 13); (December 1901): 465–94 (pt. 14); 109 (January 1902): 5–33 (pt. 15); (February 1902): 228–55 (pt. 16); 111 (July 1902): 5–30 (pt. 17); (August 1902): 225–47 (pt. 18); (September 1902): 449–71 (pt. 19); 112 (October 1902): 5–33 (pt. 20); (November 1902): 209–41 (pt. 21); (December 1902): 417–50 (pt. 22); 113 (January 1903): 37–65 (pt. 23).

Dudek, G. "Die Französische Revolution im Urteil N. M. Karamzins." *Zeitschrift für Slawistik* 34, no. 3 (1989): 345–51.

Edwards, David W. "Count Joseph Marie de Maistre and Russian Educational Policy, 1803–1828." *Slavic Review* 36, no. 1 (March 1977): 54–75.

Eidel'man, Natan Ia. *Gran' vekov: Politicheskaia bor'ba v Rossii. Konets XVIII–nachalo XIX stoletiia.* Moscow, 1982.

————. *Mgnoven'e slavy nastaet . . .: God 1789–i.* Leningrad, 1989.

Elenev, Nikolai A. *Puteshestvie vel. kn. Ekateriny Pavlovny v Bogemiiu v 1813 godu.* Prague, 1936.

Elorza, Antonio. "Hacia una tipología del pensamiento reaccionario en los orígenes de la España contemporánea." *Cuadernos hispanoamericanos* 203 (November 1966): 370–85.

Entsiklopedicheskii slovar'. Ed. F. A. Brokgauz and I. A. Efron. 41 vols. St. Petersburg, 1890–1905.

Epstein, Klaus. *The Genesis of German Conservatism.* Princeton, N.J., 1966.

Eroshkina, Alla N. "Deiatel' epokhi prosveshchennogo absoliutizma I. I. Betskoi." *Voprosy Istorii* no. 9 (1993): 165–70.

Eynard, Charles. *Vie de Madame de Krüdener.* 2 vols. Paris, Lausanne, and Geneva, 1849.

Fainshtein, Mikhail Sh., and Viacheslav V. Kolominov. *Khram muz slovesnykh (Iz istorii Rossiiskoi Akademii).* Leningrad, 1986.

Fainshtein, Mikhail Sh., and L. L. Kutina. "Aleksandr Semenovich Shishkov (1754–1841)." *Russkaia Rech'* (July–August 1984): 117–22.

Fedorov, Vladimir A. *"Svoei sud'boi gordimsia my . . ." Sledstvie i sud nad dekabristami.* Moscow, 1988.

Works Cited

Feoktistov, E. *Materialy dlia istorii prosveshcheniia v Rossii. I: Magnitskii.* St. Petersburg, 1865.

Florovsky, Georges. *Ways of Russian Theology.* General ed. Richard S. Haugh. Trans. Robert L. Nichols. 2 vols. Vaduz and Belmont, Mass., 1979–1987.

Flynn, James T. "Magnitskii's Purge of Kazan University: A Case Study in the Uses of Reaction in Nineteenth-Century Russia." *Journal of Modern History* 43 (1971): 598–614.

———. "The Role of the Jesuits in the Politics of Russian Education, 1801–1820." *Catholic Historical Review* 56, no. 2 (July 1970): 249–65.

———. "S. S. Uvarov's 'Liberal Years.'" *Jahrbücher für Geschichte Osteuropas* 20, no. 4 (December 1972): 481–91.

———. "The Universities, the Gentry, and the Russian Imperial Services, 1815–1825." *Canadian Slavic Studies* 2, no. 4 (winter 1968): 486–503.

———. *The University Reform of Tsar Alexander I 1802–1835.* Washington, D.C., 1988.

Freeze, Gregory L. "A Case of Stunted Anticlericalism: Clergy and Society in Imperial Russia." *European Studies Review* 13 (1983): 177–200.

———. "Handmaiden of the State? The Church in Imperial Russia Reconsidered." *Journal of Ecclesiastical History* 36, no. 1 (January 1985): 82–102.

Fridlender, G. M., ed. *Velikaia frantsuzskaia revoliutsiia i russkaia kul'tura.* Leningrad, 1990.

Furet, François. *La Révolution française de Turgot à Napoléon.* Vol. 1. Paris, 1988.

Furet, François, and Denis Richet. *La Révolution française.* Paris, 1965, 1973.

Fuye, Maurice de la. "Rostoptchine, Chancelier du Tzar Paul Ier." *Revue d'histoire diplomatique* no. 1 (January–March 1936): 1–26.

———. *Rostoptchine: Européen ou slave?* Paris, 1937.

Garde, Paul. "Šiškov et Karamzin: deux ennemis?" *Studia Slavica Mediaevalia et Humanistica.* Istituto Universitario Orientale, Napoli, Dipartimento di Studi dell'Europa Orientale. Rome, 1986.

Garshin, Evgenii M. "Odin iz russkikh Grakkhov proshlago stoletiia." *Istoricheskii Vestnik* 41 (September 1890): 621–28.

Geiger, Max. *Aufklärung und Erweckung: Beiträge zur Erforschung Johann Heinrich Jung-Stillings und der Erweckungstheologie.* Basler Studien zur historischen und systematischen Theologie, ed. Max Geiger. Vol. 1. Zürich, 1963.

———. "Roxandra Scarlatovna von Stourdza (1786–1844). Zur Erweckungsbewegung der Befreiungskriege." *Theologische Zeitschrift Basel* pt. 2, no. 3 (1956): 393–408.

Gleason, Abbott. *Young Russia: The Genesis of Russian Radicalism in the 1860s.* New York, 1980.

Works Cited

Gooding, John. "The Liberalism of Michael Speransky." *Slavonic and East European Review* 64, no. 3 (July 1986): 401–24.

———. "Speransky and Baten'kov." *Slavonic and East European Review* 66, no. 3 (July 1988): 400–25.

Gordin, Arkadii M. *Pushkinskii Peterburg.* 2d ed. Leningrad, 1991.

Grasshoff, Helmut, ed. *Literaturbeziehungen im 18. Jahrhundert: Studien und Quellen zur deutsch-russischen und russisch-westeuropäischen Kommunikation.* East Berlin, 1986.

Grimsted, Patricia Kennedy. "Capodistrias and a 'New Order' for Restoration Europe: The 'Liberal Ideas' of a Russian Foreign Minister, 1814–1822." *Journal of Modern History* 40, no. 2 (June 1968): 166–92.

———. *The Foreign Ministers of Alexander I: Political Attitudes and the Conduct of Russian Diplomacy, 1801–1825.* Berkeley and Los Angeles, 1969.

Hartley, Janet M. "Is Russia Part of Europe? Russian Perceptions of Europe in the Reign of Alexander I." *Cahiers du Monde russe et soviétique* 33, no. 4 (1992): 369–86.

Harvey, Arnold David. "European Attitudes to Britain During the French Revolution and Napoleonic Era." *History* 63 (1978): 356–65. Repr. as "The Continental Images of Britain." In *Napoleon and His Times: Selected Interpretations.* Ed. Frank A. Kafker and James M. Laux. Malabar, Fla., 1991.

Haumant, Emile. *La culture française en Russie (1700–1900).* Paris, 1910.

Hein, Lorenz. "Franz von Baader und seine Liebe zur Russischen Orthodoxen Kirche." *Kyrios* n.s. 12, nos. 1–2 (1972): 31–59.

Herrero, Javier. *Los orígenes del pensamiento reaccionario español.* Madrid, 1988.

Hobsbawm, Eric J. *The Age of Revolution 1789–1848.* Cleveland and New York, 1962.

Hobsbawm, Eric J., and Terence Ranger, eds. *The Invention of Tradition.* Cambridge, England, 1983.

Hollingsworth, Barry. "A. P. Kunitsyn and the Social Movement in Russia under Alexander I." *Slavonic Review* 43, no. 100 (December 1964): 115–29.

———. "Arzamas: Portrait of a Literary Society." *Slavonic and East European Review* 44, no. 103 (1966): 306–26.

———. "John Venning and Prison Reform in Russia, 1819–1830." *Slavonic and East European Review* 48, no. 113 (October 1970): 537–56.

———. "Lancasterian Schools in Russia." *Durham Research Review* 5, no. 17 (September 1966): 59–74.

Holtman, Robert B. *The Napoleonic Revolution.* Philadelphia, New York, and Toronto, 1967.

Hunt, Lynn. *The Family Romance of the French Revolution.* Berkeley and Los Angeles, 1992.

Iakimovich, Iuliia K. *Deiateli russkoi kul'tury i slovarnoe delo*. Moscow, 1985.

Ignatieff, Leonid. "French Emigrés in Russia after the French Revolution. French Tutors." *Canadian Slavonic Papers* 8 (1966): 125–31.

Ignatovich, I. "Krest'ianskie volneniia pervoi chetverti XIX veka." *Voprosy Istorii* no. 9 (1950): 48–70.

"Imperator Aleksandr I-i i Rodion Aleksandrovich Koshelev." *Russkaia Starina* 162 (May 1915): 326–37.

Isabaeva, L. M. "Obshchestvenno-politicheskie vzgliady S. S. Uvarova v 1810–e gody." *Vestnik Moskovskogo universiteta, seriia 8, istoriia* no. 6 (November–December 1990): 24–35.

"Iur'evskii arkhimandrit Fotii i ego tserkovno-obshchestvenaia deiatel'nost'." *Trudy Kievskoi dukhovnoi Akademii* 1 (February 1875): 372–84, 2 (June 1875): 696–717.

James, Edward. *The Franks*. Oxford, England, and Cambridge, Mass., 1988.

Jenkins, Michael. *Arakcheev, Grand Vizier of the Russian Empire*. London, 1969.

Jones, Colin, ed. *Britain and Revolutionary France: Conflict, Subversion and Propaganda*. Exeter, England, 1983.

Bogoiavlenskii S., "Imperator Aleksandr I i velikaia kniaginia Ekaterina Pavlovna." In *Tri veka. Rossiia ot smuty do nashego vremeni*. Ed. V. V. Kallash. 6 vols. Moscow, 1912–1913.

Karnovich, Evgenii P. *Zamechatel'nyia i zagadochnyia lichnosti XVIII i XIX stoletii*. St. Petersburg, 1884; repr. Leningrad, n.d.

Karpets, Vladimir I. *Muzh otechestvoliubivyi: Istoriko-literaturnyi ocherk*. Moscow, 1987.

Kayser, Rudolf. "Zar Alexander I. und die deutsche Erweckung." *Theologische Studien und Kritiken* no. 2 (1932): 160–85.

Kazakov, N. I. "Napoleon glazami ego russkikh sovremennikov." *Novaia i noveishaia istoriia* no. 3 (May–June 1970): 31–47, and no. 4 (July–August 1970): 42–55.

Khodasevich, Vladislav F. *Derzhavin*. Moscow, 1988.

Khrapkov, S. "Russkaia intelligentsiia v Otechestvennoi voine 1812 goda." *Istoricheskii zhurnal* bk. 2/114 (1943): 72–76.

Kizevetter, Aleksandr A. *Istoricheskie ocherki*. Moscow, 1912; repr. The Hague, 1967.

———. *Istoricheskie otkliki*. Moscow, 1915.

———. "N. M. Karamzin." *Russkii Istoricheskii Zhurnal* nos. 1–2 (1917): 9–26.

Kliuchevskii, Vasilii O. *Sochineniia v deviati tomakh*. 9 vols. Moscow, 1987–1990.

Kochubinskii, A. A. *Nachal'nye gody russkago slavianovedeniia. Admiral Shishkov i kantsler gr. Rumiantsov*. Odessa, 1887–1888.

Kolchin, Peter. *Unfree Labor: American Slavery and Russian Serfdom*. Cambridge, Mass., and London, 1987.

Kornilov, Alexander. *Nineteenth Century Russia: From the Age of Napoleon to the Eve of Revolution*. Trans. Alexander S. Kaun. Ed. Robert Bass. New York, 1966.

Koyré, Alexandre. *La philosophie et le problème national en Russie au début du XIXᵉ siècle*. Paris, 1929; repr. n.pl., 1976.

———. "Un chapitre de l'histoire intellectuelle de la Russie: La persécution des philosophes sous Alexandre Iᵉʳ." *Le Monde Slave* (1926): 90–117.

Kriuchkova, M. A. "Russkaia memuaristika vtoroi poloviny XVIII v. kak sotsiokul'turnoe iavlenie." *Vestnik Moskovskogo Universiteta* seriia 8, *istoriia* no. 1 (1994): 17–28.

Kukiel, Marian. *Czartoryski and European Unity 1770–1861*. Princeton, N.J., 1955.

Kupreianova, E. N. "Frantsuzskaia revoliutsiia 1789–1794 godov i bor'ba napravlenii v russkoi literature pervoi chetverti XIX veka." *Russkaia literatura* no. 2 (1978): 87–107.

Lapin, Vladimir V. *Semenovskaia istoriia: 16–18 oktiabria 1820 goda*. Leningrad, 1991.

Lascaris, Stamati Th. *Capodistrias avant la révolution grecque. Sa carrière politique jusqu'en 1822. Etude d'histoire diplomatique et de droit international*. Lausanne, 1918.

Latreille, Camille. "Joseph de Maistre et le Tzar Alexandre Iᵉʳ." *La Revue hebdomadaire* August 17, 1918: 302–47.

La Vopa, Anthony J. "Conceiving a Public: Ideas and Society in Eighteenth-Century Europe." *Journal of Modern History* 64 (March 1992): 79–116.

LeDonne, John P. *Absolutism and Ruling Class: The Formation of the Russian Political Order 1700–1825*. New York and Oxford, 1991.

———. "The Eighteenth-Century Russian Nobility: Bureaucracy or Ruling Class?" *Cahiers du Monde russe et soviétique* 34, nos. 1–2 (January–June 1993): 139–48.

Leningradskii Gosudarsvennyi universitet imeni A. A. Zhdanova, Filologicheskii institut, *Ocherki po istorii russkoi zhurnalistiki i kritiki*. Vol. 1, *XVIII vek i pervaia polovina XIX veka*. Leningrad, 1950.

Ley, Francis. *Alexandre Iᵉʳ et sa Sainte-Alliance (1811–1825) avec des documents inédits*. Paris, 1975.

———. *Madame de Krüdener et son temps 1764–1824*. Paris, 1961.

Lincoln, W. Bruce. *In the Vanguard of Reform: Russia's Enlightened Bureaucrats 1825–1861*. DeKalb, Ill., 1982.

Lipski, Alexander. "A Russian Mystic Faces the Age of Rationalism and Revolution: Thought and Activity of Ivan Vladimirovich Lopukhin." *Church History* 36, no. 2 (June 1967): 170–88.

Lotman, Iurii M. *Besedy o russkoi kul'ture: Byt i traditsii russkogo dvorianstva (XVIII-nachalo XIX veka)*. St. Petersburg, 1994.

Lotman, Iu. M., and B. Uspenskii. "Spory o iazyke v nachale XIX v. kak fakt russkoi kul'tury ('Proisshestvie v tsarstve tenei, ili sud'bina rossiiskogo iazyka'—neizvestnoe sochinenie Semena Bobrova)." *Uchenye zapiski tartuskogo gosudarstvennogo universiteta,* vol. 358, *Trudy po russkoi i slavianskoi filologii,* vol. 24, *literaturovedenie.* (1975): 168–254.

Madariaga, Isabel de. *Russia in the Age of Catherine the Great.* New Haven, Conn., and London, 1981.

Malia, Martin. *Alexander Herzen and the Birth of Russian Socialism.* New York, 1965.

Marasinova, E. N. "Russkii dvorianin vtoroi poloviny XVIII v. (sotsio-psikhologiia lichnosti)." *Vestnik Moskovskogo universiteta,* seriia 8, *istoriia* no. 1 (1991): 17–28.

Marker, Gary. *Publishing, Printing, and the Origins of Intellectual Life in Russia, 1700–1800.* Princeton, N.J., 1985.

Martin, Alexander M. "A. S. Sturdza i 'Sviashchennyi soiuz' (1815–1823 gg.)." *Voprosy Istorii* no. 11 (1994): 145–51.

Mayer, Arno J. *The Persistence of the Old Regime: Europe to the Great War.* New York, 1981.

Mayer, Klaus. "Die Entstehung der 'Universitätsfrage' in Rußland. Zum Verhältnis von Universität, Staat und Gesellschaft zu Beginn des neunzehnten Jahrhunderts." *Forschungen zur osteuropäischen Geschichte* 25 (1978): 229–38.

Mazour, Anatole G. *The First Russian Revolution, 1825: The Decembrist Movement, Its Origins, Development, and Significance.* Stanford, 1937, reissued 1961.

McConnell, Allen. *Tsar Alexander I: Paternalistic Reformer.* New York, 1970.

McGrew, Roderick E. *Paul I of Russia 1754–1801.* Oxford, 1992.

Mel'gunov, Sergei P. *Dela i liudi aleksandrovskogo vremeni.* Vol. 1. Berlin, 1923.

———. "Eshche o Rostopchine." *Golos Minuvshago* no. 7 (July 1913): 239–40.

———. "Kritika i bibliografiia. A. Kizevetter. Istoricheskie ocherki." *Golos Minuvshago* nos. 5–6 (May–June 1916): 409–12.

Mel'gunov, Sergei P., and P. I. Sidorov, eds. *Masonstvo v ego proshlom i nastoiashchem,* 2 vols. N.pl. [1914–1915]; repr. Moscow, 1991.

Miliukov, Paul. *Outlines of Russian Culture.* 3 vols. Vol. 1: *Religion and the Church.* Ed. Michael Karpovich, trans. Valentine Ughet and Eleanor Davis. South Brunswick, N.J., and New York, 1972.

Mironenko, Sergei V. *Samoderzhavie i reformy: Politicheskaia bor'ba v Rossii v nachale XIX v.* Moscow, 1989.

Mironenko, Sergei V., and M. V. Nechkina, eds. *Dekabristy. Biograficheskii spravochnik.* Moscow, 1988.

Miropol'skii, S. I. "Fotii Spasskii, Iur'evskii arkhimandrit. Istoriko-biograficheskii ocherk." *Vestnik Evropy* 6 (November 1878): 8–59 (pt. 1); (December 1878): 587–636 (pt. 2).

Mitter, Wolfgang. "Die Entstehung der politischen Anschauungen Karamzins."

Works Cited

Forschungen zur osteuropäischen Geschichte 2 (1955): 165–285.

Monas, Sidney. "Šiškov, Bulgarin, and the Russian Censorship." In *Russian Thought and Politics*. Ed. Hugh McLean, Martin Malia, and George Fischer. Harvard Slavic Studies, vol. 4. Cambridge, Mass., 1957.

Monnier, André. "La naissance d'une idéologie nationaliste en Russie au siècle des lumières." *Revue des Etudes slaves* 52, no. 3 (1979): 265–72.

Müller, Ludolf. *Russischer Geist und evangelisches Christentum: Die Kritik des Protestantismus in der russischen religiösen Philosophie und Dichtung im 19. und 20. Jahrhundert*. Witten an der Ruhr, 1951.

Narkiewicz, Olga A. "Alexander I and the Senate Reform." *Slavonic and East European Review* 47, no. 108 (January 1969): 115–36.

Neuschäffer, Hubertus. *Katharina II. und die baltischen Provinzen*. Beiträge zur baltischen Geschichte, vol. 2. Hannover-Döhren [1975].

Nichols, Robert L., and Theofanis George Stavrou, eds. *Russian Orthodoxy under the Old Regime*. Minneapolis, 1978.

Nikolai Mikhailovich. *Imperator Aleksandr I. Opyt istoricheskago izsledovaniia*. 2 vols. St. Petersburg, 1912.

Nipperdey, Thomas. *Deutsche Geschichte 1800–1866: Bürgerwelt und starker Staat*. Munich, 1983.

———. *Nachdenken über die deutsche Geschichte*. Munich, 1986.

O'Connor, Mark. "Czartoryski, Józef Twardowski, and the Reform of Vilna University, 1822–1824." *Slavonic and East European Review* 65, no. 2 (April 1987): 183–200.

"O grafe F. V. Rostopchine i o sobytiiakh 1812 goda v Moskve." *Chteniia v Imperatorskom Obshchestve istorii i drevnostei rossiiskikh* bk. 4, "smes'" (October–December 1861): 167–82.

Okun', Semen B. *Istoriia SSSR 1796–1825. Kurs lektsii*. Leningrad, 1948. Reissued as *Istoriia SSSR: Lektsii*. 2 vols. Leningrad, 1974–1978.

———. "Russkii narod i Otechestvennaia voina 1812 goda." *Istoriia SSSR* no. 4 (July–August 1962): 52–65.

Orlik, Ol'ga V. *"Groza dvenadtsatogo goda . . ."* Moscow, 1987.

Otechestvennaia voina i russkoe obshchestvo, 1812–1912. Ed. A. K. Dzhivelegov, S. P. Mel'gunov and V. I. Picheta. 7 vols. Moscow, 1911–1912.

Ovchinnikov, G. D. "'I dyshit umom i iumorom togo vremeni . . .' (O literaturnoi reputatsiei F. V. Rostopchina)." *Russkaia literatura* 1 (1991): 149–55.

Palitsyn, N. A. "Manifesty, pisannye Shishkovym v otechestvennuiu voinu, i patrioticheskoe ikh znachenie." *Russkaia Starina* 150 (June 1912): 477–91.

Pares, Bernard. *A History of Russia*. New York, 1965.

Paunel, Eugen von. "Das Geschwisterpaar Alexander und Roxandra Sturdza, verehelichte Gräfin Edling, in Deutschland und Rußland zur Zeit der

Restauration." *Südost-Forschungen* 9 (1944): 81–125.

Pavlova, Galina E. *Organizatsiia nauki v Rossii v pervoi polovine XIX v.* Moscow, 1990.

Petri, Hans. "Alexander und Ruxandra [*sic*] Stourdza: Zwei Randfiguren europäischer Geschichte." *Südost-Forschungen* 22 (1963): 401–36.

Pingaud, Léonce. "L'Empereur Alexandre Ier et la Grande-Duchesse Catherine Paulovna d'après leur correspondance." *Revue d'histoire diplomatique* (1911): 379–95.

———. "L'Impératrice Elisabeth Alexiéivna, d'après des documents nouveaux." *Revue d'histoire diplomatique* (1910): 533–63.

Pipes, Richard. "Karamzin's Conception of the Monarchy." In *Russian Thought and Politics.* Ed. Hugh McLean, Martin Malia, and George Fischer. Harvard Slavic Studies, vol. 4. Cambridge, Mass., 1957.

———. *Karamzin's Memoir on Ancient and Modern Russia: A Translation and Analysis.* New York, 1966.

Pokrovskii, K. "Graf F. V. Rastopchin i ego komediia 'Vesti ili Ubityi zhivoi.'" *Chteniia v Imperatorskom Obshchestve istorii i drevnostei rossiiskikh* bk. 1, section 2 (1912): 1–26.

———. "Iz polemicheskoi literatury 1813 goda. (Moskovskie obyvateli i graf F. V. Rostopchin)." *Golos Minuvshago* no. 8 (August 1914): 196–202.

Polievktov, Mikhail A. *Nikolai I: Biografiia i obzor tsarstvovaniia.* Moscow, 1918.

Popov, Ivan V., ed. *Pisatel' i kritika. XIX vek: Mezhvuzovskii sbornik nauchnykh trudov.* Kuibyshev, 1987.

Predtechenskii, Anatolii V. *Ocherki obshchestvenno-politicheskoi istorii Rossii v pervoi chetverti XIX veka.* Moscow and Leningrad, 1957.

———. "Otrazhenie voin 1812–1814 gg. v soznanii sovremennikov." *Istoricheskie zapiski* 31 (1950): 222–44.

Prousis, Theophilus C. "Aleksandr Sturdza: A Russian Conservative Response to the Greek Revolution." *East European Quarterly* 26, no. 3 (September 1992): 309–44.

———. "The Greeks of Russia and the Greek Awakening, 1774–1821." *Balkan Studies* 28, no. 2 (1987): 259–80.

———. *Russian Society and the Greek Revolution.* DeKalb, Ill., 1994.

Pypin, A. N. *Izsledovaniia i stat'i po epokhe Aleksandra I.* Vol. 3. *Obshchestvennoe dvizhenie v Rossii pri Aleksandre I.* Petrograd, 1918.

Raeff, Marc. *Comprendre l'ancien régime russe: Etat et société en Russie impériale. Essai d'interprétation.* Paris, 1982.

———. *Michael Speransky: Statesman of Imperial Russia, 1772–1839.* 2d ed. The Hague, 1969.

———. *Origins of the Russian Intelligentsia: The Eighteenth-Century Nobility.* New York, 1966.

Works Cited

———. "Seventeenth-Century Europe in Eighteenth-Century Russia? (Pour prendre congé du dix-huitième siècle russe)." *Slavic Review* 41, no. 4 (winter 1982): 611–19.

———. "Les Slaves, les Allemands et les 'Lumières.'" *Canadian Slavic Studies* 1, no. 4 (winter 1967): 521–51.

———. *The Well-Ordered Police State: Social and Institutional Change through Law in the Germanies and Russia, 1600–1800.* New Haven, Conn., and London, 1983.

Ragsdale, Hugh. *Détente in the Napoleonic Era: Bonaparte and the Russians.* Lawrence, Kans., 1980.

Ransel, David L. *The Politics of Catherinian Russia: The Panin Party.* New Haven, Conn., and London, 1975.

Regemorter, Jean-Louis van. "Deux images idéales de la paysannerie russe à la fin du XVIIIe siècle." *Cahiers du Monde russe et soviétique* 9, no. 1 (January–March 1968): 5–19.

Riabinin, D. "Aleksandr Ardalionovich Shishkov 2-i, 1799–1833." *Istoricheskii Vestnik* 38 (October 1889): 42–69.

Riall, Lucy. *The Italian Risorgimento: State, Society and National Unification.* London and New York, 1994.

Riasanovsky, Nicholas V. *A History of Russia.* 3d ed. New York, 1977.

———. *Nicholas I and Official Nationality in Russia, 1825–1855.* Berkeley, Los Angeles, and London, 1959.

———. *A Parting of Ways: Government and the Educated Public in Russia 1801–1855.* Oxford, 1976.

Rogger, Hans. "The Russian National Character: Some Eighteenth-Century Views." In *Russian Thought and Politics.* Ed. Hugh McLean, Martin E. Malia, and George Fisher. Harvard Slavic Studies, vol. 4. Cambridge, Mass., 1957.

Russkii biograficheskii slovar'. Ed. A. A. Polovtsov. 25 vols. St. Petersburg, 1896–1911; repr. New York, 1962.

Safonov, Mikhail M. *Problema reform v pravitel'stvennoi politike Rossii na rubezhe XVIII i XIX vv.* Leningrad, 1988.

Safonov, Mikhail M., and Eleonora N. Filippova. "Neizvestnyi dokument po istorii obshchestvenno-politicheskoi mysli Rossii nachala XIX v." *Vspomogatel'nye Istoricheskie Distsipliny* 16 (1985): 179–89.

Saunders, David B. "Historians and Concepts of Nationality in Early Nineteenth-Century Russia." *Slavonic and East European Review* 60, no. 1 (January 1982): 44–62.

Sawatsky, Walter W. "Prince Alexander N. Golitsyn: Formidable or Forgettable?" American Association for the Advancement of Slavic Studies paper, Phoenix, Ariz., November 1992.

———. "Prince Alexander N. Golitsyn (1773–1844): Tsarist Minister of Piety." Ph.D. diss., University of Minnesota, 1976.

Schaeder, Hildegard. *Die dritte Koalition und die Heilige Allianz. Nach neuen*

Quellen. Königsberg and Berlin, 1934.

Schama, Simon. *Citizens: A Chronicle of the French Revolution*. New York, 1989.

Schlafly, Daniel L. "De Joseph de Maistre à la 'Bibliothèque rose': le Catholicisme chez les Rostopčin." *Cahiers du Monde russe et soviétique* 11 (January–March 1970): 93–109.

———. "Echoes of the French Revolution: Conservatism and the Catholic Church in Russia under Tsar Alexander I. The Jesuits." American Historical Association paper, San Francisco, December 1989.

———. "The Rostopchins and Roman Catholicism in Early Nineteenth Century Russia." Ph.D. diss., Columbia, 1972.

Schmidt, Christoph. "Aufstieg und Fall der Fortschrittsidee in Rußland." *Historische Zeitschrift* 263, no. 1 (August 1996): 1–30.

Schnabel, Franz. *Deutsche Geschichte im neunzehnten Jahrhundert*. Vol. 1: *Die Grundlagen*. 4th ed. Freiburg, 1948.

Shchebal'skii, P. "A. S. Shishkov, ego soiuzniki i protivniki." *Russkii Vestnik* 90 (November 1870): 192–254.

Sheehan, James J., ed. *Imperial Germany*. New York and London, 1976.

Shil'der, Nikolai K. *Imperator Aleksandr Pervyi: Ego zhizn' i tsarstvovanie*. 4 vols. St. Petersburg, 1897.

Shmidt, Sigurd O. "Obshchestvennoe samosoznanie noblesse russe v XVI–pervoi treti XIX v." *Cahiers du Monde russe et soviétique* 34, nos. 1–2 (January–June 1993): 11–32.

Sidorova, L. P. "Rukopisnye zamechaniia sovremennika na pervom izdanii tragedii V. A. Ozerova 'Dmitrii Donskoi.'" *Zapiski otdela rukopisei Gosudarstvennoi biblioteki SSSR im. V. I. Lenina* no. 18 (1956): 142–79.

Sirotkin, Vladlen G. "Napoleonovskaia 'voina per'ev' protiv Rossii." *Novaia i noveishaia istoriia* no. 1 (1981): 137–52.

———. "Russkaia pressa pervoi chetverti XIX veka na inostrannykh iazykakh kak istoricheskii istochnik." *Istoriia SSSR* no. 4 (1976): 77–97.

———. "Velikaia frantsuzskaia burzhuaznaia revoliutsiia, Napoleon i samoderzhavnaia Rossiia." *Istoriia SSSR* no. 5 (1981): 39–56.

Smith, Douglas. "Freemasonry and the Public in Eighteenth-Century Russia." *Eighteenth-Century Studies* 29, no. 1 (1995): 25–44.

Sorokin, Iurii A. "Pavel I." *Voprosy Istorii* no. 11 (November 1989): 46–69.

Springer, Arnold. "Gavriil Derzhavin's Jewish Reform Project of 1800." *Canadian-American Slavic Studies* 10, no. 1 (spring 1976): 1–23.

Stählin, Karl. *Geschichte Rußlands von den Anfängen bis zur Gegenwart*. 4 vols. in 5. Königsberg and Berlin, 1929–1939; repr. Graz, 1961.

Starobinski, Jean. *1789, Les Emblèmes de la raison*. Paris, 1979.

Stoiunin, V. Ia. "Aleksandr Semenovich Shishkov: Biografiia." *Vestnik Evropy* 67, pt. 5, no. 9 (September 1877): 236–71 (pt. 1); no. 10 (October 1877): 502–47 (pt. 2); vol. 68, pt. 6, no. 11 (November 1877): 47–118 (pt. 3);

no. 12 (December 1877): 465–522 (pt. 4).

Strakhovsky, Leonid I. *Alexander I of Russia: The Man Who Defeated Napoleon.* New York, 1947.

Sturdza, Alexandre A. C. *De l'histoire diplomatique des Roumains 1821–1859: Règne de Michel Sturdza, Prince régnant de Moldavie 1834–1849.* Paris, 1907.

Sukhomlinov, Mikhail I. *Istoriia Rossiiskoi akademii.* 8 vols. *Sbornik Otdeleniia russkago iazyka i slovesnosti Imperatorskoi Akademii nauk.* St. Petersburg, 1874–1888.

———. *Izsledovaniia i stat'i po russkoi literature i prosveshcheniiu.* 2 vols. St. Petersburg, 1889; repr. The Hague and Paris, 1970.

Tarasulo, Yitzhak Y. "The Napoleonic Invasion of 1812 and the Political and Social Crisis in Russia." Ph.D. diss., Yale, 1983.

Tartakovskii, Andrei G. "Iz istorii odnoi zabytoi polemiki (Ob antikrepostnicheskikh 'diversiiakh' Napoleona v 1812 godu)." *Istoriia SSSR* no. 2 (1968): 25–43.

———. *Russkaia memuaristika XVIII-pervoi poloviny XIX v. Ot rukopisi k knige.* Moscow, 1991.

———. *Voennaia publitsistika 1812 goda.* Moscow, 1967.

Thaden, Edward C. *Conservative Nationalism in Nineteenth-Century Russia.* Seattle, 1964.

Tikhonravov, N. S. *Sochineniia N. S. Tikhonravova.* 3 vols. in 4. Moscow, 1898.

Tompkins, Stuart R. "The Russian Bible Society—A Case of Religious Xenophobia." *American Slavic and East European Review* 7 (1948): 251–68.

Torke, Hans J. "Continuity and Change in the Relations between Bureaucracy and Society in Russia, 1613–1861." *Canadian Slavic Studies* 5, no. 4 (winter 1971): 457–76.

Treadgold, Donald W. *The West in Russia and China: Religious and Secular Thought in Modern Times.* 2 vols. Vol. 1: *Russia 1472–1917.* Cambridge, England, 1973.

Troitskii, Nikolai A. *1812: Velikii god Rossii.* Moscow, 1988.

V. "Priezd Imperatora Aleksandra I v Moskvu. (11–18 iiulia 1812 goda)." *Russkaia Starina* 151 (July 1912): 71–85.

Vasil'ev, A. "Progressivnyi podokhodnyi nalog 1812 g. i padenie Speranskago." *Golos minuvshago* nos. 7–8 (July–August 1916): 332–40.

Vernadskij, G. "Le césarévitch Paul et les franc-maçons de Moscou." *Revue des Etudes slaves* 3, nos. 3–4 (1923): 268–85.

———. "Reforms under Czar Alexander I: French and American Influences." *Review of Politics* 9, no. 1 (January 1947): 47–64.

Voprosy istorii Rossii XIX–nachala XX veka. Mezhvuzovskii sbornik. Leningrad, 1983.

Vries de Gunzburg, Irène de. *Catherine Pavlovna, Grande-Duchesse de Russie, 1788–1819*. Amsterdam, 1941.

Walicki, Andrzej. *A History of Russian Thought: From the Enlightenment to Marxism*. Trans. Hilda Andrews-Rusiecka. Stanford, 1979.

———. *The Slavophile Controversy: History of a Conservative Utopia in Nineteenth-Century Russian Thought*. Oxford, 1975.

Walker, Franklin A. "Enlightenment and Religion in Russian Education in the Reign of Tsar Alexander I." *History of Education Quarterly* 32, no. 3 (fall 1992): 343–60.

———. "Reaction and Radicalism in the Russia of Tsar Alexander I: The Case of the Brothers Glinka." *Canadian Slavonic Papers* 21, no. 4 (December 1979): 489–502.

Walther, Karl Klaus. "Johann Baptist Schad in Rußland." *Jahrbücher für Geschichte Osteuropas* 40, no. 3 (1992): 340–65.

Wehler, Hans-Ulrich. *Das Deutsche Kaiserreich 1871–1918*. Göttingen, 1983.

Whelan, Heide W. *Alexander III and the State Council: Bureaucracy and Counter-Reform in Late Imperial Russia*. New Brunswick, N.J., 1982.

Whiting, Kenneth R. "Aleksei Andreevich Arakcheev." Ph.D. diss., Harvard, 1951.

Whittaker, Cynthia Hyla. "The Idea of Autocracy among Eighteenth-Century Russian Historians." *Russian Review* 55 (April 1996): 149–71.

———. "The Ideology of Sergei Uvarov: An Interpretive Essay." *Russian Review* 37, no. 2 (April 1978): 158–76.

———. "The Impact of the Oriental Renaissance in Russia: The Case of Sergej Uvarov." *Jahrbücher für Geschichte Osteuropas* 26, no. 4 (1978): 503–24.

———. *The Origins of Modern Russian Education: An Intellectual Biography of Count Sergei Uvarov, 1786–1855*. DeKalb, Ill., 1984.

———. "The Reforming Tsar: The Redefinition of Autocratic Duty in Eighteenth-Century Russia." *Slavic Review* 51, no. 1 (spring 1992): 77–98.

Wieczynski, Joseph L. "Apostle of Obscurantism: The Archimandrite Photius of Russia (1792–1838)." *Journal of Ecclesiastical History* 22, no. 4 (October 1971): 319–31.

———. "The Mutiny of the Semenovsky Regiment in 1820." *Russian Review* 29, no. 1 (1970): 167–80.

———, ed. *The Modern Encyclopedia of Russian and Soviet History*. 54 vols. Gulf Breeze, Fla., 1976–1990.

Wortman, Richard. *The Development of a Russian Legal Consciousness*. Chicago and London, 1976.

Zacek, Judith Cohen. "A Case Study in Russian Philanthropy: The Prison Reform Movement in the Reign of Alexander I." *Canadian Slavic Studies* 1, no. 2 (summer 1967): 196–211.

———. "The Imperial Philanthropic Society in the Reign of Alexander I." *Canadian-American Slavic Studies* 9, no. 4 (winter 1975): 427–36.

———. "The Lancastrian School Movement in Russia." *Slavonic and East European Review* 45, no. 105 (July 1967): 343–67.

———. "The Russian Bible Society and the Catholic Church." *Canadian Slavic Studies* 5, no. 1 (spring 1971): 35–50.

———. "The Russian Bible Society and the Russian Orthodox Church." *Church History* 35, no. 4 (December 1966): 411–37.

Zapadov, A. V., ed. *Istoriia russkoi zhurnalistiki XVIII–XIX vekov.* Moscow, 1973.

Index

Index